The World Turned Inside Out

Cover image: Walter Withers, 'The Drover', Oil on Canvas (1912). Image above: Thomas Benjamin Kennington, 'Homeless', Oil on Canvas (1890).

Both reproduced with permission of the Bendigo Art Gallery, where the two paintings are on display. Together, like panels in a comic book sequence, they tell a story: the child moves away from dysfunction, hunger, and the 'satanic mills'. His sickly pale face turns into a vigorous red neck, rain turns into sunshine, lack of nourishment turns into an enormous amount of meat, and a precarious childhood in the Old World is followed by secure manhood in the new one. This book tells the global history of this fantasy.

The World Turned Inside Out

Settler Colonialism as a Political Idea

Lorenzo Veracini

London • New York

First published by Verso 2021

1 3 5 7 9 10 8 6 4 2

Verso
UK: 6 Meard Street, London W1F 0EG
US: 20 Jay Street, Suite 1010, Brooklyn, NY 11201
versobooks.com

Verso is the imprint of New Left Books

ISBN-13: 978-1-83976-382-3
ISBN-13: 978-1-83976-383-3 (UK EBK)
ISBN-13: 978-1-83976-384-1 (US EBK)

British Library Cataloguing in Publication Data
A catalogue record for this book is available from the British Library

Library of Congress Cataloging-in-Publication Data
A catalog record for this book is available from the Library of Congress

Typeset in Minion by Hewer Text UK Ltd, Edinburgh
Printed and bound by CPI Group (UK) Ltd, Croydon CR0 4YY

This one is for Clare. She was there when I wasn't.

Contents

Introduction

The World Turned Inside Out rather than Upside Down

William Lane and his comrades removed to 'New Australia', Paraguay, after the Queensland shearers' strike of 1891 had been ruthlessly repressed. Lane was a well-travelled 'socialist' and a prolific journalist: originally from England, he had been in Montreal and in Michigan before moving to Australia.[1] For him, and for the utopian socialists who followed him, New Australia was a response to defeat. The plan was that wonderful news about the 'colony' in Paraguay would have convinced the Australian authorities to reimport its cooperative organising principles. The colony did not prosper and Lane eventually made his way to Auckland, New Zealand, where he became a conservative imperialist and right-wing commentator. He had consistently been a racist advocate of the 'brotherhood' of English-speaking white men. Lane espoused the concept of 'common-hold' as opposed to 'common-wealth', arguing that a member of society

1 Vast areas of Paraguay had been depopulated during the war of 1864–70, and the government had allocated vast tracts to various colonial endeavours on favourable terms, including free land and tax exemptions. In Michigan, Lane had discovered the works of William Morris, Edward Bellamy, Laurence Gronlund, and Henry George – all of whom are discussed in this book. On Lane, see Gavin Souter, *A Peculiar People: The Australians in Paraguay* (Sydney: Angus & Robertson, 1968); Michael Wilding, *The Paraguayan Experiment* (Melbourne: Penguin, 1984); Anne Whitehead, *Paradise Mislaid: In Search of the Australian Tribe of Paraguay* (St Lucia: University of Queensland Press, 1997); John Kellett, 'William Lane and "New Australia": A Reassessment', *Labour History* 72 (1997), pp. 1–18.

should be able to withdraw their own share of their society's wealth if they decided to leave. They should be able to travel with an endowment; their wealth should travel with them. The concept was ideal for sovereign people on the move. But the *Colonia Nueva Australia* was not only about responding to defeat; it was also a way to advocate coherently for political change given the recession, the repression, and the general circumstances of 1890s Australia. If a new world could not be built in one location, it might be built elsewhere (another response to defeat was the establishment of the Australian labour movement; those who decided to persevere aimed to change society where they were). As we will see, Lane is certainly not an isolated example of this sensitivity when facing defeat and crisis. This book appraises the global history of the exchange between emplaced and displaced transformation.

Voluntary displacement can be a political stand, which is ironic, considering that 'making a stand' usually implies a determination to remain still. As this book will relate, settling communities in 'empty lands' somewhere else has often been proposed throughout modernity as a way to head off revolutionary tensions. Building on a growing body of research on settler colonialism as a specific mode of domination and on its political imaginaries, the book uncovers an autonomous, influential and coherent transnational political tradition. It appraises a recurring and yet under-analysed stance: facing the prospect of revolutionary upheaval, many highlighted the need to 'remove' to separate locations while celebrating the 'regenerative' possibilities of such a move. 'Tradition' literally means carrying something forward; it derives from the Latin term for 'carry across'. In the case of the politics of volitional displacement, 'tradition' was both a literal and a metaphorical process. It was by displacement to somewhere else that those who embraced the 'new' locales constituted a political tradition.[2]

'Modernity' is often linked to the anxious perception of upheaval.[3] Reinhart Koselleck, for example, authoritatively concluded that

2 For Paul Gilroy, a tradition is the 'living memory of the changing same'. Paul Gilroy, *The Black Atlantic: Modernity and Double Consciousness* (Cambridge, MA: Harvard University Press, 1993), p. 198.

3 See Roger Griffin, *Modernism and Fascism: The Sense of a Beginning under Mussolini and Hitler* (Houndmills: Palgrave Macmillan, 2007).

modernity is defined by a 'state of permanent crisis', while Raymond Williams summed up modernity as the 'long revolution'.[4] Talking about 'dual revolutions', Eric Hobsbawm also emphasised the modernity–crisis–revolution nexus.[5] Those who decided to relocate as they perceived the impending upheaval that modernity brought contributed to a developing global imagination of settlement. They were opting out of both revolution and reaction and, in a sense, out of modernity – or at least what they perceived to be its most intractable contradictions. Their recurring insistence on 'quiet possession' underscores the perception of turbulent times defined by loss, the very opposite of possession. They felt they had to go.

There are many displacements. While volitional and forced displacements are often difficult to disentangle from each other, the two may be considered as opposite ends of a spectrum of possibility. This book focuses on the volitional end of this spectrum, even if those who advocated voluntary displacement would typically have argued that it was an absolute necessity: that there was ultimately no choice. Thus, the book's focus does not deny other dislocations – there were many – or that nonvoluntary displacements did not interact with voluntary ones. Either way, opting out demanded an elsewhere. The places had always been there and were not empty, many indigenous sovereign polities populated these lands, but settler colonialism as a globally expanding mode of domination and new modes of transport provided control and access to many elsewheres.

If you decide to go, it must sound like a viable proposition. You must think you will be empowered in the colony. In the last twenty years or so, settler colonial studies has emerged as an autonomous scholarly

4 Reinhart Koselleck, *Kritik und Krise. Eine Studie zur Pathogenese der bürgerlichen Welt* (Frankfurt am Main: Suhrkamp, 1973), p. 1; Raymond Williams, *The Long Revolution* (New York: Harper & Row, 1966), p. x. See also Perry Anderson, 'Modernity and Revolution', *New Left Review* I/144 (March–April 1984), pp. 96–113.

5 Eric J. Hobsbawm, *The Age of Revolution, 1789–1846* (New York: New American Library, 1962). The very notion of 'modernity' is fraught, and the question of whether it even exists is a legitimate one; but the widespread *perception* of modernity is undeniable. See Björn Wittrock, 'History and Sociology: Transmutations of Historical Reasoning in the Social Sciences', in Peter Hedström, Björn Wittrock, eds, *Frontiers of Sociology* (Leiden: Brill, 2009), pp. 77–111. Wittrock concludes (p. 79) that modernity is associated with the 'notion of a conceptual and epistemic revolution'.

subfield.[6] Following a growing debate, *Settler Colonial Studies*, a scholarly journal dedicated to the comparative study of settler colonialism as a specific mode of domination, was eventually established in 2010. A considerable body of comparative literature has focused on a variety of themes, including the current relationships between indigenous peoples and settlers; the historical acquisition by settlers of indigenous lands; the evolution of the economies of the 'new' lands; the 'networked' transcolonial circulation of ideas between settler colonies and, later, between settler polities; and the cultural processes of settler 'indigenisation'.[7] But

6 See Patrick Wolfe, *Settler Colonialism and the Transformation of Anthropology* (London: Cassell, 1999); David Pearson, *The Politics of Ethnicity in Settler Societies* (Houndmills: Palgrave Macmillan, 2001); Lynette Russell, ed., *Colonial Frontiers: Indigenous–European Encounters in Settler Societies* (Manchester: Manchester University Press, 2001); Caroline Elkins and Susan Pedersen, eds, *Settler Colonialism in the Twentieth Century: Projects, Practices, Legacies* (London: Routledge, 2005); Carole Pateman, 'The Settler Contract', in Carole Pateman, Charles W. Mills, *Contract and Domination* (Cambridge: Polity, 2007), pp. 35–78; James Belich, *Replenishing the Earth: The Settler Revolution and the Rise of the Anglo-World, 1783–1939* (Oxford: Oxford University Press, 2009); Tracey Banivanua Mar and Penelope Edmonds, eds, *Making Settler Colonial Space* (Houndmills: Palgrave Macmillan, 2010); Penelope Edmonds, *Urbanizing Frontiers* (Vancouver: University of British Columbia Press, 2010); Lisa Ford, *Settler Sovereignty* (Cambridge, MA: Harvard University Press, 2010); Lorenzo Veracini, *Settler Colonialism: A Theoretical Overview* (Houndmills: Palgrave Macmillan, 2010); Fiona Bateman and Lionel Pilkington, eds, *Studies in Settler Colonialism: Politics, Identity and Culture* (Houndmills: Palgrave Macmillan, 2011). For an entry point into critiques of settler colonial studies, see, for example, Cynthia G. Franklin, Njoroge Njoroge and Suzanna Reiss, 'Tracing the Settler's Tools: A Forum on Patrick Wolfe's Life and Legacy', *American Quarterly* 69: 2 (2017), pp. 235–90.

7 Paul Havemann, ed., *Indigenous Peoples' Rights in Australia, Canada and New Zealand* (Auckland: Oxford University Press, 1999); Duncan Ivison, Paul Patton, Will Sanders, eds, *Political Theory and the Rights of Indigenous Peoples* (Cambridge: Cambridge University Press, 2000); Peter H. Russell, *Recognizing Aboriginal Title: The Mabo Case and Indigenous Resistance to English Settler Colonialism* (Toronto: University of Toronto Press, 2005); John C. Weaver, *The Great Land Rush and the Making of the Modern World, 1650–1900* (Montreal: McGill-Queen's University Press, 2003); Stuart Banner, *How the Indians Lost Their Land* (Cambridge, MA: Harvard University Press, 2007); Stuart Banner, *Possessing the Pacific* (Cambridge, MA: Harvard University Press, 2007); Donald Denoon, *Settler Capitalism: The Dynamics of Dependent Development in the Southern Hemisphere* (Oxford: Clarendon Press, 1983); Belich, *Replenishing the Earth*; Christopher Lloyd, Jacob Metzer and Richard Sutch, eds, *Settler Economies in World History* (Leiden: Brill, 2013); Alan Lester, 'British Settler Discourse and the Circuits of Empire', *History Workshop Journal* 54 (2002), pp. 25–48; Marilyn Lake and Henry Reynolds, *Drawing the Global Colour Line: White Men's Countries and the Question of Racial Equality* (Melbourne: Melbourne University Press, 2008); Gérard

the political sensibility and the rhetorical traditions that accompanied the global history of settler-colonial expansion, remain under-researched.[8] Political history remains a nationally framed discipline.

This is problematic because the political projects that advocated displacement escape nationality by definition. They disappear from the frame as they depart, and when they reappear in distant locations they are seen as contributing to the history of the new setting. The *political geometry* that underpins their politics, the ways in which relocating is politics, is overlooked.[9] Besides, settler colonialism as a global phenomenon is underpinned by an eminently transnational 'archive' of images and ideas.[10] This book rescues the histories of multiple displacements from being stranded within nationally defined historiographies. There are already excellent exceptions to this pattern. Marilyn Lake and Henry Reynolds, for example, have focused on transnational debates pertaining to racial ideologies, as has Patrick Wolfe.[11] Barbara Arneil's work on 'domestic colonies' as segregated spaces where improvements for land and people

---

Bouchard, *The Making of the Nations and Cultures of the New World* (Montreal: McGill-Queen's University Press, 2008); Robert J. C. Young, *The Idea of English Ethnicity* (Malden, MA: Blackwell, 2008).

8 For exceptions to this neglect, see John L. Thomas, *Alternative America: Edward Bellamy, Henry George, Henry Demarest Lloyd and the Adversary Tradition* (Cambridge, MA: Harvard University Press, 1987); Marilyn Lake, *Progressive New World: How Settler Colonialism and Transpacific Exchange Shaped American Reform* (Cambridge, MA: Harvard University Press, 2018). Thomas emphasises the 'adversary' tradition – a rejection of large-scale capitalism and bureaucratic socialism born out of crisis and class conflict. See also Andrekos Varnava, ed., *Imperial Expectations and Realities: El Dorados, Utopias and Dystopias* (Manchester: Manchester University Press, 2015).

9 Political 'geometry' and political arithmetic, a founding category of modern economics, are related. William Petty, who coined the notion of 'political arithmetick' in 1690, was operating in the context of a very specific political geometry: he famously conducted the 'Down Survey' in Ireland, a process that involved and accompanied, as Allan Greer has noted, 'dispossession and reallocation on a grand scale' – the dispossession of indigenous peasants and the land's reallocation to exogenous settlers. See Allan Greer, *Property and Dispossession: Natives, Empires and Land in Early Modern America* (New York: Cambridge University Press, 2018), p. 282; Brenna Bhandar, *Colonial Lives of Property: Law, Land, and Racial Regimes of Ownership* (Durham, NC: Duke University Press, 2018).

10 Lorenzo Veracini, 'Colonialism and Genocides: Notes for the Analysis of a Settler Archive', in A. Dirk Moses, ed., *Empire, Colony, Genocide: Conquest, Occupation, and Subaltern Resistance in World History* (New York: Berghahn, 2008), pp. 148–61.

11 See Lake and Reynolds, *Drawing the Global Colour Line*; Patrick Wolfe, *Traces of History: Elementary Structures of Race* (London: Verso, 2016).

would arise from agricultural labour – a veritable 'transnational colonial network' of domestic colonialism – has similarly outlined the global circulation of colonial practices and political ideas.[12] For Arneil, the domestic colonies were nodes in this network, while the network had conceptual and material dimensions: ideas as well as bodies travelled, and promoters looked attentively at each other's efforts. The 'archive of settlement' uncovered in this book was propagated in very similar ways.[13]

Arneil focused on the Dutch founder of early-nineteenth-century domestic colonialism, Johannes Van den Bosch, who saw the farm colonies he was establishing, the 'Colonies of Benevolence', as supporting an emerging capitalist regime because productive labourers ready to enter the labour market would be moulded in these secluded spaces (a worthwhile investment, even though the colonies would detract from labour markets in the short term). The colonies became a veritable template in an international network of domestic colonial activity – an activity prompted by pan-European social and economic crisis following the end of the Napoleonic Wars.[14]

12 Barbara Arneil, *Domestic Colonies* (Oxford: Oxford University Press, 2017), pp. 20, 60, 240. Robert Hind's seminal overview of internal colonialism, however, had already mentioned an early-nineteenth-century transnational European network and the 'proliferation of small-scale, philanthropic, and carefully directed ventures'. Hind noted that the 'Reverend Joseph Townsend regarded eighteenth-century county workhouses in England as colonies "to which a few of the superabundant members of the community have been transported to make room for others"'; that the 'More sisters considered that their late-eighteenth-century schemes of social and religious engineering were creating colonies, a "Botany Bay" and a "Sierra Leone", in the Mendips'; that '"Colonies for the poor" were successfully established at Frederick's Oord in northern Holland from 1818'; that 'Alexander D'Junkovsky translated William Allen's *Colonies at Home: or, The Means for Rendering the Industrious Labourer Independent of Parish Relief* (1826) into the Russian language'; that the Russian minister of the interior 'ordered it to be translated into German for the use of German colonists in Russia'; and that 'Maria Edgeworth had no doubt that "colonization at home would be preferable to colonization abroad, if it can be carried into effect, because it would, in the first place, save all the risk, expense, and suffering of emigration, and would, in the next place, secure the home country the benefits of increased and improved cultivation and civilization"'. Robert J. Hind, 'The Internal Colonial Concept', *Comparative Studies in Society and History* 26: 3 (1984), pp. 562–3.

13 Cecilia Morgan also refers to the transnational circulation of an ideology of improvement through displacement. This ideology, however, exceeded the boundary of the British world. See Cecilia Morgan, *Building Better Britains? Settler Societies in the British World* (Toronto: University of Toronto Press, 2017).

14 The colonies would transform the idle poor 'from the inside out', and turn them into industrious citizens. They were located away from urban centres, would focus on subsistence production, and would not be a burden to the state. Arneil, *Domestic Colonies*, p. 40.

This network operated through the diffusion and circulation of exemplary models. It is significant that Van den Bosch was interested in poverty relief in the Netherlands but also had extensive colonial experience in Java, where he had developed a new system of forced crop delivery underpinned by a form of indirect rule. His 'Cultivation System' was a response to a spate of anticolonial insurrections; the Colonies of Benevolence in the metropole were a response to the perception of increasing social unrest.[15]

Revolution and colonialism were linked. Indeed, poverty concerned Van den Bosch greatly, but he was more concerned by the possible outcomes of poverty in terms of social instability, against a background of economic depression, rapid industrialisation and urbanisation. His *Discourse on the opportunity, the best way of introduction and the important benefits of a General Institution for the Poor in the Kingdom of the Netherlands* (1818) argued that, since

> the poverty of our times is a consequence of our present social institutions, and must therefore be considered susceptible to a considerable increase, as the most recent circumstances of England, and part of Germany and Switzerland, seem to prove – then it is undeniably also true that this must finally have consequences, dangerous as much for the security of society in general, as for the special interest of the more affluent classes; and that the State, by extension, could be subjected to disturbances by others, the more harrowing as the number of its needy members would have grown, and the tendency, the urge, to provide themselves by force with what they have been denied by the course of circumstances, would find stronger encouragement in the greatness of their misery.[16]

Albert Schrauwers concluded that the Colonies of Benevolence 'were designed to create work for, govern, and reform potentially revolutionary paupers'.[17] But Van den Bosch did not intend to resist the

15 See Albert Schrauwers, 'The "Benevolent" Colonies of Johannes van den Bosch: Continuities in the Administration of Poverty in the Netherlands and Indonesia', *Comparative Studies in Society and History* 43: 2 (2001), pp. 298–328, esp. p. 314; Albert Schrauwers, 'Colonies of Benevolence: A Carceral Archipelago of Empire in the Greater Netherlands', *History and Anthropology* 31: 3 (2020), pp. 352–70.

16 Johannes Van den Bosch, *Discourse* (1818), p. 5, available at dbnl.org.

17 Schrauwers, '"Benevolent" Colonies of Johannes van den Bosch', p. 323.

newly developing system of capitalist relations; he only aimed to protect the state from the consequences of its development. His project thus focused on moors and peatlands that could be understood as 'empty' (even though they were not, of course – they were commons): locations where his colonists were to be temporarily segregated from society, and perform 'spade husbandry', a labour-intensive agricultural technique that is mentioned frequently in the projects appraised in this book.

Like Edward Gibbon Wakefield would (more on him later), Van Den Bosch criticised the liberal political economists; he recognised that poverty was an inevitable result of economic development, and that a program of amelioration in a 'colonial' setting was needed to counter its destabilising effects. Indeed, while the imagination of settlement is long-lasting and widespread, one of its crucial features – a trope that scholars have neglected so far but that will emerge strongly in this book – is that the sources that constitute it routinely and explicitly frame the prospected dislocation as an *alternative* to revolution. This trope, which unites those who find revolution likely and yet abhorrent with those who find it desirable but impossible, invites further inquiry.

Despite obvious ideological cleavages, the idea of establishing regenerative sociopolitical bodies elsewhere as an alternative to growing revolutionary tensions (or as a result of their repression – repression is, after all, the ultimate alternative) is long-lasting and recurrent. The very idea of moving collectively as a political act is ubiquitous in the political traditions of Western modernity.[18] John Milton had concluded in the seventeenth century: 'One's Country is wherever it is well with one' (while God was 'the Sovereign Planter').[19] He was quoting Cicero.[20]

18 See, for example, Michael Walzer, *Exodus and Revolution* (New York: Basic, 1985).

19 Indeed, *Paradise Lost* can be seen as an allegory distinguishing starkly between 'Satanic' colonialism and the imperial ruthlessness of Spain on the one hand (to be abhorred), and Adam and Eve's 'planting' of Eden and the Puritan settlement of New England on the other (to be upheld). Adam and Eve peacefully settle Eden and enjoy its abundance before Satan finds and ruins them. Eden looks and feels like the New World; moving there, as the Puritans had done, could be seen as a return. See Sebastian Peraic, 'Milton and Empire: Satanic and Edenic Colonization in *Paradise Lost*', unpublished dissertation, University of California, Los Angeles, 2020.

20 Cicero, quoting Pacuvius: '*Patria est, ubicunque est bene*' ('Wherever I am comfortable, there is my country', or 'My country is wherever I find happiness'). This is a crucial passage: belonging is no longer prescriptive, deriving from where one is born, but becomes ascriptive, depending on where one *opts* to belong. M. Tulli Ciceronis, *Tusculanarum Disputationum* (Cambridge: Cambridge University Press, 1934), vol. 2, V, 37.

Many would refer to both Milton and Cicero to explain what they planned to do: irrespective of birth, one's country could now really be somewhere else.[21]

The title of this book, *The World Turned Inside Out*, refers to the political traditions that envisaged displacement as a solution to rising contradictions, and underscores their difference from the revolutionary traditions that Christopher Hill seminally encapsulated in the phrase 'the world turned upside down'.[22] The aim is to emphasise the spatial separation that is implicit in the distinction between an inside and an outside, and between metropole and settler colony. Conservatism, liberalism and radicalism debated the advisability of change and the most appropriate speed of its course, but generally neglected to discuss its location.[23] These ideologies focused primarily on time rather than space (even though, as this book will show, they also experimented with the possibility of displaced change). Conversely, the political tradition invoked in 'the world turned inside out' seeks to change the world by changing worlds; its supporters aim to establish political orders elsewhere rather than replace existing ones.[24] Thus if 'the world turned upside down' can be used as a synonym for revolution, 'the world turned inside out' as it is used in this book should be seen as its antonym.

21 Benjamin Franklin's famous rendition of this trope was: 'Where liberty dwells there is my country'. It has been interpreted parochially to refer to the United States, but Franklin was here describing a volitional polity: it could be anywhere.

22 Christopher Hill, *The World Turned Upside-Down: Radical Ideas During the English Revolution* (London: Penguin, 1972).

23 On the evolution of these debates following the French revolutionary transformations, for example, see Immanuel Wallerstein, *World-System Analysis: An Introduction* (Durham, NC: Duke University Press, 2004), pp. 60–75.

24 See Lorenzo Veracini, 'Suburbia, Settler Colonialism and the World Turned Inside Out', *Housing, Theory and Society* 29: 4 (2012), pp. 339–57; Lorenzo Veracini, 'Ian Turner's *The Australian Dream* and Australia's "Settler Transition"', *Journal of Australian Studies* 40: 3 (2016), pp. 302–18. James Livingston has already defined the 'world turned inside out' that follows a revolutionary crisis. In the instances he analysed, following the evolution of public culture in the United States during the 1970s, 1980s and 1990s, it was the sense of a coming apocalypse (when 'everything – law and order, manhood, fatherhood, womanhood, family, heterosexuality, even national honor – is ending, the apocalypse is now') that promoted the triumph of the conservative revolution. James Livingston, *The World Turned Inside Out: American Thought and Culture at the End of the 20th Century* (New York: Rowman & Littlefield, 2010), p. 63.

This distinction is predicated on a flexible definition of 'revolution', not merely as regime change, but as a transformative process that radically, even if gradually, reconstitutes all social relationships (the advocates of displacement, as this book will show, often perceived all changes to the 'natural' order of society as revolutionary upheaval). Nonetheless, an emphasis on the ability to relocate in order to establish new political orders is crucial in understanding settler societies as sites of unprecedented political experimentation.[25] In these societies, during the age of what historian James Belich has called the global 'settler revolution', the process that saw several settler 'neo-Europes' become firmly established in several continents (a momentous global process that did not escape the attention of many contemporary observers), the world turned inside out was practised as well as imagined.[26] This book relies on Belich's conceptualisation, especially in how its chapters are organised, but expands the notion of a global settler revolution, arguing that it was a process with specific political and ideological dimensions beyond economic and demographic ones.

Beside this introduction and a conclusion, *The World Turned Inside Out* comprises four main chapters that narrate the evolution of a global

---

25 Eminent historian Marc Ferro noted that 'emigration and revolution' are 'mutually connected' phenomena, and thought that emigration could be seen as an individual counterpoint to collective rebellion. He did not pursue this insight, and yet collective emigration and settler colonialism could also be seen as a counterpoint to individual rebellion. Marc Ferro, *Colonization: A Global History* (London: Routledge, 1997), p. 352.

26 Belich, *Replenishing the Earth*. See also Alfred Crosby, *Ecological Imperialism: The Biological Expansion of Europe, 900–1900* (Cambridge: Cambridge University Press, 2004). Future US President Theodore Roosevelt famously noted in *The Winning of the West* (1889): 'It is of incalculable importance that America, Australia, and Siberia should pass out of the hands of their red, black, and yellow aboriginal owners, and become the heritage of the dominant world races'. He added: 'Never before have there been so many opportunities for commonwealth builders; new States have been pitched on the banks of the Saskatchewan, the Columbia, the Missouri, and the Colorado, on the seacoast of Australia and in the interior of Central Africa'. Roosevelt knew the difference between settler-colonial and other types of conquest. The former was the 'kind of colonizing conquest, whereby the people of the United States have extended their borders', a development that 'has much in common with similar movements in Canada and Australia, all of them standing in sharp contrast to what has gone on in Spanish-American lands'. He saw a global process defined by state-building and racial exclusion. Roosevelt's 'West' was also north, east and south. Cited in Lake and Reynolds, *Drawing the Global Colour Line*, p. 101.

political tradition. Chapter 1 outlines its development up to the beginning of the global settler revolution – the moment in which the settlers began to assert their own political sovereignty, not merely by removing to places where they could not be reached, but also by formally severing political connection. Chapter 2 follows the evolution of this process up to the peak of the global settler revolution, when a global network of autonomous settler-colonial 'neo-Europes' became fully entrenched in a developing global international landscape.[27] Chapter 3 delineates the evolution of the settler colonial political tradition up to the end of the global settler revolution. The settler revolution eventually ended, even if its legacies remained. Spatial separation was undone by new technologies (such as electricity); and, while new technologies were applied to offset this reversal (irrigation, refrigeration, and so on), the prospect of removing to some distant location and settling on the land ultimately lost the appeal it had once had. But the political traditions of this historically specific migratory culture survived the end of the settler revolution. In Chapter 4, I explore the resilience of these traditions, which continue to shape the global present.

For a long time, displacement was understood as a genuine and viable alternative to both revolution and reaction: as sovereignty became emplaced or territorialised throughout modernity, displacement enabled the vision of political regimes separating spatially from others without conflict.[28] The notions of revolution and reaction focus on vertical relationships and specific geographies that are either sustained or reconfigured; settler colonialism focuses on horizontality. Radically distinct conceptions of political geometry are at stake here, which this book seeks to examine closely.[29] In doing so, it follows David Armitage's

27 See Alison Bashford, 'Immigration Restriction: Rethinking Period and Place from Settler Colonies to Postcolonial Nations', *Journal of Global History* 9: 1 (2014).

28 See Perry Anderson, *Lineages of the Absolutist State* (London: Verso, 1979); Ford, *Settler Sovereignty*.

29 Yet again, moving to different locations and setting up new polities is predicated on the ability to replace indigenous sovereignties and populations. As Kate Fullagar and Michael McDonnell have suggested, the expanding settler-colonial world of the revolutionary age turned indigenous worlds upside down at a fierce rate. The title of Colin Calloway's book assembling indigenous sources facing the settler-colonial onslaught also articulates this nexus. As replacement and displacement remain intertwined, the settler-colonial world presupposes a double displacement that empties the 'Old World' as well as the indigenous 'new' ones. See Kate Fullagar and Michael A.

call for a new mode of intellectual history, and for a scholarship that finally appraises 'the spatial dimensions of context'. 'Space', Armitage concluded, 'is the final frontier for intellectual history'.[30] Settler colonialism is indeed a privileged site for an intellectual history that considers actual rather than abstract space.

The pages that follow outline many imagined and practical efforts to reconstitute 'worlds' elsewhere as an alternative to the perception of social upheaval. Despite numerous references to moments of social imperialism as systematic attempts to divert growing class tensions (arch-imperialist Cecil Rhodes had argued that, in order 'to save the 40,000,000 inhabitants of the United Kingdom from a bloody civil war, we colonial statesmen must acquire new lands to settle the surplus population', and that if 'you want to avoid civil war, you must become imperialists'), such a political sensibility, the idea that settler migration is an effective means of heading off social unrest, and its relationship with settler colonialism as a specific mode of domination remain unexplored.[31] The nexus involving growing contradictions, revolution and the imagination of settlement also remains underanalysed.[32] These themes have been the subject of significant debate, of course. We are familiar, for example, with Turnerian arguments about frontiers as 'safety valves' (and their critiques), and with

---

McDonnell, eds, *Facing Empire: Indigenous Experiences in a Revolutionary Age* (Baltimore: Johns Hopkins University Press, 2018); Colin G. Calloway, ed., *The World Turned Upside Down: Indian Voices from Early America* (Boston: St Martin's, 1994).

30 David Armitage, 'The International Turn in Intellectual History', in Darrin M. McMahon and Samuel Moyn, eds, *Rethinking Modern European Intellectual History* (New York: Oxford University Press, 2014), pp. 5, 13.

31 Cited in Bernard Porter, *The Lion's Share: A Short History of British Imperialism, 1850–2004* (London: Pearson, 2004), p. 135. See also John MacKenzie's ground-breaking work on imperial propaganda, which concluded that colonialism created 'a national purpose with a high moral content' and 'class conciliation'. John M. MacKenzie, *Propaganda and Empire: The Manipulation of British Public Opinion, 1880–1960* (Manchester: Manchester University Press, 1984), p. 2. Yet again, Joseph Schumpeter had already famously noted that imperialism *follows* crisis (or the perception of a coming crisis). See Joseph Schumpeter, *Imperialism and Social Classes* (Oxford: Basil Blackwell, 1951 [1919]), esp. pp. 83–5.

32 However, as Dean Itsuji Saranillio has insightfully noted, 'Political thinkers in the early nineteenth century imagined that the establishment of white settler colonies, particularly in North America, would resolve the poverty capitalism produced in Europe'. Dean Itsuji Saranillio, *Unsustainable Empire: Alternative Histories of Hawai'i Statehood* (Durham, NC: Duke University Press, 2018), p. 10.

Werner Sombart's question about an alleged lack of socialism in the United States.[33] But displacement is absent from these debates; and if it is added to the analytical mix, an autonomous political tradition comes to light. Indeed, each of the movements and projects described in this book has been the subject of detailed historical analysis. But attention has focused on the contextual circumstances of such movements and on the social systems they set out to build, not on the specific project of establishing their social experiments *somewhere else*. Neglect of actual movement (political movements normally are 'movements' only in a metaphorical sense), whether real or merely projected, is in this context especially inappropriate, because displacement is not a by-product of these movements' activity, but its fundamental method.

Accounts of the various 'cities on the hill', and of the metaphorical structures that sustain them, have focused on the specific characteristics of the imagined social orders concerned.[34] US presidents Kennedy and Reagan revived this image to great effect, albeit for very different purposes; but similarly influential variations of this trope have emerged elsewhere in the settler-colonial world. In Zionist traditions it takes the form of the 'light unto the nations'; in Australia it appears as Ben Chifley's 'light on the hill'. That these imaginings are necessarily predicated on displacement (one has first to get to a hill somewhere else to build a city, and then someone has to turn on the light), and that many must remain where they are to see it from a distance, has not received less attention.[35]

Because of its diffuse characteristics, recovering the settler-colonial world may require what historian Carlo Ginzburg called a method 'more morphologic than historical' (after all, geometry, even when 'political', deals primarily with shapes). Introducing an edited collection of his essays, Ginzburg retrospectively recognised a crucial feature of his methodology:

33 Werner Sombart, *Why Is There No Socialism in the United States?* (London: Macmillan, 1976 [1906]). See also Eric Foner, 'Why Is There No Socialism in the United States?' *History Workshop Journal* 17: 1 (1984).

34 See Frances FitzGerald, *Cities Upon a Hill* (New York: Simon & Schuster, 1981).

35 An auditory variant of this positional geometry refers to the 'shot' that proclaims settler independence in North America and must be heard 'around the world'.

> I suddenly realised that in the research that I was conducting for years on the Sabbath I was using a method more morphologic than historical. My gathering of myths and beliefs from different cultural backgrounds was based on formal affinities . . . I used morphology as a probe to reach a layer unattainable to the usual tools of historical knowledge.[36]

This book likewise takes as its point of departure a collection of fragments arising from very diverse cultural settings, thus also adopting a morphologic approach. Its aim is to explore the nexus linking a recurrent emphasis on the possibility of displacement to 'empty' lands elsewhere with the search for an alternative to revolution.

On Sunday, 1 April 1649, a small group of poor men collected on St George's Hill, outside London. They started digging the land as a 'symbolic assumption of ownership of the common lands.'[37] In a few days, this Occupy movement *ante litteram* counted four or five thousand adherents. One year later, 'the colony had been forcibly dispersed, huts and furniture burnt', and the Diggers had been 'chased away from the area.'[38] The crucial etymological association of 'colony', via Latin, with the idea of cultivation, which is what the Diggers were ostensibly performing, should be noted here. The Diggers, however, were also performing a collective revolutionary act, and those who determined that the Diggers should be dispersed were well aware of its significance. One side pursued the restoration of the commons, which had only recently been expropriated; the other side strove to defend that originary appropriation. The two sides were struggling over the same geography.

But there was a third option. Many others had understood the word 'colony' in the context of its other acquired meaning – that of overseas possession. They had other plans, and realised that a similar act could

---

36 'Improvvisamente mi accorsi che nella ricerca in corso da anni sul sabba stavo adoperando un metodo molto piú morfologico che storico. Raccoglievo miti e credenze provenienti da ambiti culturali diversi, sulla base di affinità formali . . . Usavo la morfologia come una sonda, per scandagliare uno strato inattingibile agli strumenti consueti della conoscenza storica.' Carlo Ginzburg, *Miti emblemi spie: Morfologia e storia* (Torino: Einaudi, 1986), pp. xiv–xv (my translation).

37 Hill, *World Turned Upside-Down*, p. 110.

38 Ibid., p. 113.

have a completely different meaning if it occurred in another place. While Hill's seminal work focused on England, there was already a non-revolutionary alternative. This alternative already had, by then, a significant history in Ireland and in North America, and it is perhaps telling that the settlement of Ireland – a foundational moment in the consolidation of this political tradition – became royal policy after the Munster rebellion, a gory event that profoundly shocked all those who knew about it.[39] This book explores the transnational coherence of this alternative by focusing on the political imagination that sustained it. It focuses on a number of key moments, and it is inclusive but far from exhaustive; further research would have uncovered many more instances of voluntary displacement as a political approach.

What unites those who advocated displacement, despite profound ideological differences and beyond generic and contextual specificities, is that they all envisaged a foundational displacement to locales they understood as empty, and that they all presupposed what would become known as the legal doctrine of *terra nullius*.[40] They also all conceived displacement as a response to growing revolutionary tensions (as we have seen, they understood revolution as 'upheaval'), and all envisaged displacement as a way to establish demonstrative exemplars of regenerative life and polities.

This book thus outlines the evolution of the long-lasting expectation that settler-colonial locales would produce non-revolutionary circumstances where actual or potential revolutionaries could be turned into 'sturdy yeomen' and independent farmers, and where examples of reconstituted hierarchical, or egalitarian but equally conflictless societies could be reproduced.[41] This, as will emerge, is a long-lasting idea: Alexis de

39 A 1572 pamphlet by Sir Thomas Smith promoting the colonisation of the Ards in eastern Ulster had argued for the English reinvasion of Ireland by a new method: private funds were to be raised through a stock company, while boosterist propaganda was used to advertise the colonising enterprise. Smith's pamphlet argued that it was the prospect of social unrest that made colonisation absolutely necessary. See Hiram Morgan, 'The Colonial Venture of Sir Thomas Smith in Ulster, 1571–1575', *Historical Journal* 28: 2 (1985).

40 On the notion of *terra nullius* as foundational to the 'settler contract', see Pateman, 'Settler Contract', pp. 35–78.

41 Or at least act as 'drains' swallowing up potential revolutionaries. In *Commonplace Book for the Years 1635–1636*, Thomas Bowdler remarked that the Caribbean and Chesapeake colonies (all characterised by high colonist morbidity) 'serve

Tocqueville, Frederick Jackson Turner, Israeli kibbutzim, and many other advocates of what could be referred to as settler colonialism's 'anthropological' rather than actual revolution partook of it.[42] English novelist Anthony Trollope visited Australia at the peak of the global settler revolution in 1871 (a revolutionary year), and his *Australia and New Zealand* (1873) summed up this widespread notion: 'I have no doubt whatever', he said, 'that the born colonist is superior to the emigrant colonist – any more than I have that the emigrant is superior to his weaker brother whom he leaves behind him. The best of our workmen go from us, and produce a race superior to themselves'.[43] Displacement had turned class into race; class was left behind, the world was turned inside out rather than upside down, and an exemplary polity to come was being established. In turn, the new polity could feed back to the Old World, undoing revolution there as well. As this book will show, this is also a recurrent proposition: the polities established in the context of this tradition would thus embody a series of pre-emptive counterrevolutions.

Finally, those who aimed to turn the world inside out also embraced in one way or another autonomous rural self-sufficiency, and thought that this self-sufficiency, often referred to as 'independence', could enable them to opt out of growing contradictions. Faced with the prospect of increasing poverty, struggle and civil war, they opted to relocate to where they hoped that contradictions could not follow them. Canadian historical geographer Cole Harris aptly describes this endeavour:

---

for drains to unload their populous state which else would overflow its own banks by continuance of peace and turn head upon itself or make a body fit for any rebellion'. Cited in Nicholas Canny, 'The Origins of Empire: An Introduction', in Nicholas Canny, ed., *The Origins of Empire: British Overseas Enterprise to the Close of the Seventeenth Century* (Oxford: Oxford University Press, 1998), pp. 19–20.

42 The actual performance of these societies was less exciting. Miles Fairburn's work on nineteenth-century New Zealand, for example, highlighted isolation, alcoholism, and desperation. Miles Fairburn, *The Ideal Society and Its Enemies: The Foundations of Modern New Zealand Society, 1850–1900* (Auckland: Auckland University Press, 1989).

43 Anthony Trollope, *Australia and New Zealand* (Leipzig: Bernhard Tauchnitz, 1873), p. 129; also cited in Ken Gelder and Rachel Weaver, *Colonial Australian Fiction: Character Types, Social Formations and the Colonial Economy* (Sydney: Sydney University Press, 2017), p. 21. See also Jonathon Hyslop, 'The Imperial Working Class Makes Itself White', *Journal of Historical Sociology* 12: 4 (1999). Bound together 'by flows of population which traversed the world', this class escapes the wage relation laterally through an embrace of racial exclusion.

> Many settlers became property owners, holders of land in fee simple, beneficiaries of a landed opportunity that, previously, had been unobtainable. But use values had not given way entirely to exchange values, nor was labour entirely detached from land. Indeed, for all the work associated with it, the pioneer farm offered a temporary haven from capital. The family would be relatively autonomous (it would exploit itself). There would be no outside boss. Cultural assumptions about land as a source of security and family-centered independence; assumptions rooted in centuries of lives lived elsewhere seemed to have found a place of fulfilment. Often this was an illusion – the valleys of British Columbia are strewn with failed pioneer farms – but even illusions drew immigrants and occupied them with the land.[44]

It was a temporary solution, and it was illusory – contradictions catch up; but it had tremendous power.[45] And it sounded like a good proposition, even though, as Harris notes perhaps unintentionally, the settlers were occupied by land as much as they occupied it.

On the basis of these shared characteristics, *The World Turned Inside Out* traces the evolution of a political tradition through the analysis of the texts and social contexts that expressed it. These texts are read against the perception of forthcoming upheaval, as it is this awareness that prompted a decision to relocate. Methodologically, this approach requires a paradigm shift (considering the book's emphasis on displacement, 'shift' may indeed be apt). This book does not rely on newly unearthed evidence, it does not address previously overlooked sources, and it does not reveal previously unknown events; rather, it offers a reconceptualisation. The shift is away from a focus on the contradiction between revolution and reaction in specific locations, and towards an appraisal of what emerges as revolution's second significant 'other': the world turned inside out.

---

44 Cole Harris, 'How Did Colonialism Dispossess? Comments from an Edge of Empire', *Annals of the Association of American Geographers* 94: 1 (2004), p. 173.

45 Karl Marx had already argued that the escape can only be temporary: 'Notwithstanding California and Australia, notwithstanding the immense and unprecedented migration, there must even, without any particular accident, in due time arrive a moment when the extension of the markets is unable to keep pace with the extension of British manufactures, and this disproportion must bring about a new crisis, as it has done in the past'. Karl Marx, 'Revolution in China and in Europe' (1853), available at marxists.org.

The opposition pitting revolution against counterrevolution – a struggle that has understandably been the topic of sustained historical research – is largely devoid of any spatial dimension. The bloody clashes between them have concerned the power to shape the same geography and the same society. Temporally, there can be no simultaneity: revolution, even if it is brief and abortive (as, for example, in 1848, 1871 and 1919), must occur first. Alternatively, it is pre-emptive counterrevolution that takes chronological precedence. While in these cases simultaneity is denied by cospatiality, it is significant that the three general options identified in this book's framing correspond to three basic responses to crisis: fight, fright, and flight; or, as Albert Hirschman famously suggested in a seminal 1970 intervention, 'voice', 'loyalty', and 'exit'.[46]

As the following chapters will illustrate, the perception of impending 'upheaval' is what most concerned the advocates of displacement (the term 'upheaval', of course, itself implies a vertical dislocation). Indeed, this book adopts a flexible definition of revolution that I believe the promoters of the world turned inside out would have recognised. Besides, only in the twentieth century did 'revolution' acquire the apocalyptic associations we are now familiar with. In the nineteenth century, and especially in the Anglosphere, the term was easily associated with the rhetoric of the 'Glorious' Revolution, with revered Founding Fathers, and with honourable constitutionalisms – 'revolution' once evoked the prospect of restored social peace, as well as its dissolution.[47] Facing upheaval, many advocated displacement – though many others embraced revolution after considering displacement.[48]

46 Albert O. Hirschman, *Exit, Voice, and Loyalty: Responses to Decline in Firms, Organizations, and States* (Cambridge, MA: Harvard University Press, 1970). Recognising that America was founded on 'exit' (rather than 'voice' or 'loyalty') through its Puritan founding and its later 'frontier' reconstitution, Hirschman suggested that the 'present-day "cop-out" movement of groups like the hippies is very much in the American tradition' (p. 108).

47 David Armitage, 'Every Great Revolution Is a Civil War', in Keith Michael Baker, Dan Edelstein, eds, *Scripting Revolution* (Stanford, CA: Stanford University Press, 2013), pp. 57–68, 269–71.

48 Italian nationalist hero Giuseppe Garibaldi and Indian nationalist hero Mahatma Gandhi, for example. On the former's displacements, see Lorenzo Veracini, 'Postcolonial Garibaldi?' *Modern Italy* 24: 1 (2019). The latter resented the materialism he saw embodied in the British Raj and in urban modernity (a type of revolution), and believed that *satyagraha*, civil resistance, would be a means for returning humanity to its natural condition. For several years Gandhi was involved in intentional communities in South

These displacements, however, were not utopian. Ruth Levitas defines the utopian method as a reconstitution of society that is 'imaginary'; but the world turned inside out is about really existing places, and typically builds heterotopias or 'grounded utopias' instead.[49] These two traditions, however, interacted and overlapped significantly. Assessing this overlap,

---

Africa, and it was in these 'colonies' that he experimented with self-renunciation and nonviolence, as he engaged with Theosophist ideas and with the philosophies of John Ruskin and Leo Tolstoy, Ralph Waldo Emerson and Henry David Thoreau. The Phoenix cooperative settlement, near Durban, was an experiment in communal living, self-sufficiency through vegetable gardening, and education (Gandhi believed that vegetarianism would decentralise society because more people would need to move back to the land) – even if the settlement was primarily meant to support the production of the *Indian Opinion* newspaper, which would then be independent of any other funding (the Phoenix 'settlers' were to dedicate themselves to its publication). *Indian Opinion* was intended to link the colony back to the wider world and the political struggle for emancipation. Tolstoy Farm, near Johannesburg, was linked to the second *satyagraha* campaign, and it would become a haven for the families of the militants who had been incarcerated. The communal character of this colony was even more pronounced, and the settlers were entirely self-sufficient. These colonies were multiethnic, multiracial and religiously inclusive. Gandhi, however, eventually moved back to India and embraced the nationalist and revolutionary struggle there (even though, as Nehru noted, he always 'suspected socialism and more particularly Marxism'). After 1914, return and anticolonial revolution undid displacement. The *ashrams* Gandhi established there were located at the heart of the struggle, not away from it. Cited in Bimanbehari Majumdar, 'Gandhi and Socialism', *Indian Literature* 12: 3 (1969), pp. 5–13. See also James D. Hunt, Surendra Bhana, 'Spiritual Rope-Walkers: Gandhi, Kallenbach, and the Tolstoy Farm, 1910–13', *South African Historical Journal* 58: 1 (2007).

49 See Ruth Levitas, 'Educated Hope: Ernst Bloch on Abstract and Concrete Utopia', *Utopian Studies* 1: 2 (1990). Michel Foucault remarked that colonies can be heterotopian places. Heterotopias 'have a function in relation to all the space that remains', he noted, adding: 'their role is to create a space that is other, another real space, as perfect, as meticulous, as well arranged as ours is messy, ill constructed, and jumbled. This latter type would be the heterotopia . . . of compensation, and I wonder if certain colonies have not functioned somewhat in this manner. In certain cases, they have played, on the level of the general organization of terrestrial space, the role of heterotopias. I am thinking, for example, of the first wave of colonization in the seventeenth century, of the Puritan societies that the English had founded in America and that were absolutely perfect other places. I am also thinking of those extraordinary Jesuit colonies that were founded in South America: marvellous, absolutely regulated colonies in which human perfection was effectively achieved'. For Foucault, the need for 'compensation' follows the perception of crisis: heterotopias and crisis are 'connected'. Michel Foucault, 'Of Other Spaces', in Michel Foucault, *Heterotopia and the City: Public Space in a Postcivil Society* (London: Routledge, 2008), p. 27. On 'grounded utopias', see Charles Price, Donald Nonini and Erich Fox Tree, 'Grounded Utopian Movements: Subjects of Neglect', *Anthropological Quarterly* 81: 1 (2008).

Belich invoked 'secular utopianism', noting that 'utopianisms looked up to heaven, forward to the future, or back to an idealized past', whereas settler utopianism 'looked out – to the newlands'.[50] In any case, there is a crucial difference between utopian traditions and those associated with a world turned inside out: the former generally imagine places that are 'other' in order to sustain a demand for emplaced transformation, while the latter envisage other places in an attempt to sustain displaced transformation.

Like reaction, but unlike utopianisms, displacement as a political tradition constitutes a type of political consciousness that abhors revolution. Rather than countering it once it has occurred, however, displacement pre-empts revolution. In these cases, simultaneity is predicated on physical distanciation, and all attempts to project 'fragments' of a mother country onto locales that are understood as *terra nullius* must follow a foundational dislocation. These projections, while profoundly diverse in their manifestations, as Louis Hartz was already arguing in the 1960s, shared an underlying determination to prevent the exportation and subsequent emergence in the new lands of the social tensions that had made revolution in the mother country a possibility in the first place ('in the first place' seems an especially apt expression here).[51] Hartz's definition of 'fragment extrication' – the creation of the 'new' settler countries – emphasised the novelty of a situation that was 'unknown to either the "traditionalist" or "revolutionary" experiences of Europe'.[52]

Sacvan Bercovitch had detected a similar dynamic:

> In [American culture], I concluded, the true conservatives were on the left; their characteristic strategy was to displace radical alternatives

50 James Belich, 'The Rise of the Angloworld: Settlement in North America and Australasia, 1784–1918', in Phillip Buckner and R. Douglas Francis, eds, *Rediscovering the British World* (Calgary: University of Calgary Press, 2005), p. 51.

51 Louis Hartz, *The Founding of New Societies* (San Diego: Harvest/HBJ, 1964). Hartz's seminal work mentioned this aspect of 'fragmentation' only in passing. Similarly, in a note dealing specifically with the 'American' and 'liberal' traditions, and recognising the foundational nexus linking displacement and crisis, Hartz concluded: 'In a real sense physical flight is the American substitute for the European experience of social revolution'. Louis Hartz, *The Liberal Tradition in America* (New York: Harcourt, Brace & World, 1955), p. 65. See also Kevin Bruyneel, 'The American Liberal Tradition', *Settler Colonial Studies* 3: 33–4 (2013).

52 Hartz, *Founding of New Societies*, p. 28.

> with an indigenous tradition of reform. Thus the alternative implicit in Nat Turner's revolt had been absorbed into the exemplary American protest embodied in *The Narrative of Frederick Douglass*; so, too, in the long run, were the alternatives offered by Paul Robeson and Malcolm X. The quintessentially liberal programs for change that linked Elizabeth Cady Stanton to Gloria Steinem encompassed, blurred, and eventually eliminated other feminist alternatives (those which did not focus on America), from the Grimké sisters to Angela Davis. It was the cultural work of Emerson and the Emersonians, from (say) William James through Paul Goodman, to obviate socialist or communist alternatives to capitalism. This form of cultural work joined Jefferson to Thoreau and both to Martin Luther King Jr, in an omnivorous oppositionalism that ingested all competing modes of radicalism – from the Fourierists to Herbert Marcuse and Noam Chomsky – in the course of redefining injustice as un-American, revolution as the legacy of '76, and inequalities of class, race, and gender as disparities between the theory and the practice of American-ness.[53]

Metaphorically displacing radical alternatives, as well as contradictions, was important; this was the role of the 'pastoral ideal' in America, even though the pastoral ideal exceeded America. And yet there were many instances in which this displacement was literal.[54] Bercovitch knew that the 'rituals of consensus' were designed to displace revolution: according to him, the 'leaders of Puritan New England had devised the errand to bring a group of potential revolutionaries under control', and the 'patriot Whigs took control of the republic by translating the errand into the rhetoric of continuing revolution'.[55] It was a revolutionary project aimed at displacing radical alternatives: Bercovitch had detected the world turned inside out (even if he did not use the expression).

53 Sacvan Bercovitch, *The Rites of Assent: Transformations in the Symbolic Construction of America* (New York: Routledge, 1993), p. 19.

54 See Leo Marx, *The Machine in the Garden: Technology and the Pastoral in America* (Oxford: Oxford University Press, 1964). Marx focuses on the 'ruling motive of the good shepherd, leading figure of the classic, Virgilian mode, [which] was to withdraw from the great world and begin a new life in a fresh, green landscape' (p. 3).

55 Bercovitch, *Rites of Assent*, p. 42.

And so did Edmund S. Morgan, for whom the Puritans

> carried out a revolution, rendered bloodless only by the three thousand miles of ocean that separated them from the government they would otherwise have had to overthrow in order to do what they did. In Massachusetts they created what amounted to a republic, substituting annually elected rulers for a hereditary monarchy and independent self-starting churches for the whole hierarchical structure of the Church of England.[56]

Separation is sovereignty without a fight – that is, without a fight with the sovereign one is escaping, even if one has to contend with the indigenous sovereign one is encountering.[57]

Demonstrating that each individual emigrant-settler in the long history of global modern settler colonialism embraced this tradition would be impossible, even though those who embraced displacement as a political approach would have engaged with widely circulating and readily available ideas surrounding the possibility of settling elsewhere. Millions were on the move in any case – the vast majority out of necessity rather than political deliberation. But advocates of settlement often saw emigrants as potential assets, while those emigrants routinely used the resources mobilised by collective settlements to pursue their own personal projects.[58] *The World Turned Inside*

---

56 Edmund S. Morgan, *The Genuine Article: A Historian Looks at Early America* (New York: Norton, 2005), p. 9. Morgan later calls it a 'truly revolutionary reform' (p. 14) – that is, not a revolution.

57 Greg Grandin's genealogy of the idea of a 'border wall' in the United States also foregrounds an ongoing ability to displace contradictions spatially rather than confronting them directly. Grandin also analyses the notion of a 'safety valve' – a metaphor that enjoyed immense circulation and became useful for a political tradition that aimed to evade contradictions rather than contain or address them. See Greg Grandin, *The End of the Myth: From Frontier to the Border Wall in the Mind of America* (New York: Henry Holt, 2019), esp. p. 68–82.

58 Joanna Brooks insightfully focused on the emigrants' feelings: they were unfree, dispossessed; they felt 'ruefulness, desolation, and betrayal'. Brooks refers to the 'impossible or catastrophic situations that made England uninhabitable to [her] ancestors and thousands upon thousands of other English labouring-class migrants who colonized America', and concludes that England 'colonized its own lands and dislocated its own indigenous peoples before colonizing abroad'. Brooks emphasises deforestation, economic modernisation, the collapse of traditional family bonds and social ties, loss of connection to ancestral homes and traditional ways, and social disruption. The destruction of peasant worlds produced a settler-colonial impulse: we 'came here as the rejected ones, pushed

Out does not assume that such a sensitivity can be documented, that the targeted authors were directly connected, or that the promoters of settlement as an alternative to revolution believed they were contributing to a coherent tradition (they did not see themselves as 'world turned inside out-ists', even if I suspect they would have understood each other; while this book names a political tradition that has generally gone without a name, naming it enables its reconstruction).[59] Wakefield, one of this tradition's most articulate early advocates, summed it up as the 'art of colonisation'.[60] Wakefield's highbrow approach was restated in a more demotic rendition in Mark Twain's narration of Huckleberry Finn lighting 'out for the Territory ahead of the rest'.[61] The former aimed to restore and retain control; the latter expressed a liberatory reflex. Both embraced displacement.

The following chapters focus on the theoreticians and planners of 'colonies' large and small, those who succeeded and those who failed, on their reasoning, and on the transnational networks of information that linked them together. The advocates of displacement produced a plethora of declarative documents: sermons, associative covenants, pamphlets, emigrants' manuals, travelogues, novels, articles, political

---

into the water or across the sea'. And yet: 'Whatever form of dispossession and betrayal had been meted out to us we meted out to the other peasant peoples – indigenous and African – of the Atlantic world'; the emigrants were thus 'tools of empire'. Joanna Brooks, *Why We Left: Untold Stories and Songs of America's First Immigrants* (Minneapolis: University of Minnesota Press, 2013), pp. 15, 19, 101, 167.

59 It is telling that many of its practitioners were a 'people with no name'. See Patrick Griffin, *The People with No Name: Ireland's Ulster Scots, America's Scots Irish, and the Creation of a British Atlantic World, 1689–1764* (Princeton, NJ: Princeton University Press, 2001). Then again, retrospective naming is inevitable. John Locke, for example, as Duncan Bell has noted, is routinely 'conscripted' as a paradigmatic 'liberal', even if he would not have understood the term. Indeed, Locke could be seen as a theorist of the world turned inside out, too: a theorist both of primitive accumulation in England and of an escape from it in America. It may seem like a contradiction, but he was referring to different geographies – consistency through displacement. Duncan Bell, *Reordering the World: Essays on Liberalism and Empire* (Princeton, NJ: Princeton University Press, 2016), p. 9.

60 See Edward Gibbon Wakefield, 'A View of the Art of Colonization' (1849), in M. F. Lloyd Pritchard, ed., *The Collected Works of Edward Gibbon Wakefield* (Glasgow: Collins, 1968).

61 Here is the full passage: 'But I reckon I got to light out for the territory ahead of the rest, because Aunt Sally she's going to adopt me and sivilize me, and I can't stand it. I been there before'. Mark Twain, *The Adventures of Huckleberry Finn*, 1884, available at gutenberg.org.

tracts, 'boosterist' propaganda, utopian and non-utopian novels, legislative acts, settlement schemes, and official reports.[62] Their work represents a substantial corpus of texts that was often widely circulated and reproduced (documents prepared for public circulation are excellent guides to the concerns that prompted their production).

However, as well as relying on these documents and focusing on rhetoric, language, structures of feeling, and their evolution, this book also places them in a broader context, relying on a considerable body of secondary analysis. It asks a number of critical questions: Where and how was each of these texts specifically produced and circulated? How did they affect the social milieus they emanated from? Who wrote these texts? What were their stated concerns? And how was the need for a preemptive move linked to the perception of 'impending crisis'? Who read these texts and embraced their message, at times deciding to 'remove' to the settler-colonial peripheries? How did these projects operate on the ground? How did they adjust their theoretical frameworks to the realities they were encountering and shaping? Did these projects develop autonomously? Did the adherents of the 'modern imagination of settlement' read each other's works? Can we think of a widely shared 'cloud' of images pertaining to settlement – a storehouse of available, accessible, and mobilisable ideas? What were the sources on which these movements drew as they developed their various heterotopias?

The World Turned Inside Out aims to contribute to a variety of national historiographies that do not currently communicate with one another, and to trace the evolution of the political tradition they represent over time. It offers a global history of a political idea, and demonstrates that settler colonialism and the conceptualisation of settlement – a conceptualisation that involves an extraordinary variety of communal and associative undertakings – are intimately related. While some of the movements examined here gave birth to settler societies that are still

62 Typical examples include Lansford Hastings, *The Emigrants' Guide to Oregon and California* (1845), and John Mason Peck's *New Guide for Emigrants to the West* (1836). In Australia there was Nathaniel Ogle's *The Colony of Western Australia: A Manual for Emigrants* (1839). Published in London with the intention of promoting settler emigration, it included practical advice and notes on women's appropriate behaviour, sections on the 'Principles of colonisation', and a history of colonial settlements elsewhere. A German example is Gottfried Duden's *Report of a Journey to the Western States of North America* (1829). See Edward Cavanagh, '"Not Celebrated for its Agriculture": Emigrant Guides and Land Settlement in New South Wales, 1831–65', *Australian Studies* 3 (2011).

with us, others operated within them, constituting a typical expression of their operation. Displacement prompted a complex and composite political tradition and contributed significantly to the shaping of resilient political languages and their rhetorical styles. Displacement, as this book will show, begets further displacement and is inevitably predicated on violently displacing and dispossessing indigenous peoples and previous inhabitants, something the advocates of the world turned inside out rarely considered (a focus on perpetrators and their imaginings should not distract from this fundamental fact).

Finally, it should be noted that this political tradition has a significant contemporary dimension, and that the prospect of enacting change some place else is still often hailed as a preferable alternative to emplaced transformation. My aim in this book is to contribute to current debates about forthcoming crises, and the possibility of renewed voluntary relocations. We collectively face unprecedented crises, and displacement is routinely proposed as a possible solution. One of this book's premises is that the notion of settlement is not exhausted by settler-colonial conquest (or by the end of the 'settler revolution'); the politics of volitional displacement have persisted beyond an originary colonial settlement, and remain as a method, a reflex, and indeed – as Wolfe noted – a 'structure'.[63] The persistent influence of settler-colonial ideology requires decolonising practices and analytical strategies specific to the operation of this political tradition.

While a diachronic exploration can sustain an original interpretation of its contemporary manifestations, decolonising requires that the relationship between indigenous and non-indigenous collectives must change. Likewise, the persisting allure of solutions predicated on relocating elsewhere should be understood and interrogated. Relocating somewhere else still often means displacing someone else; at the same time, the contradictions one hopes to escape by relocation always catch up. The establishment of hipster republics in areas that can be gentrified necessitates the displacement and dispossession of local residents.[64]

63 Wolfe, *Settler Colonialism*, p. 3.

64 For an understanding of gentrification as 'ongoing settler colonization', see Liza Kim Jackson, 'The Complications of Colonialism for Gentrification Theory and Marxist Geography', *Journal of Law and Social Policy* 27 (2017), p. 53. Jackson concludes that, while gentrification 'can be seen to have a homological relationship to colonialism . . . [d]ispossession and displacement are logics that drive both colonialism and gentrification' (pp. 78, 55).

Thus, the place becomes bland in any case. The move into cyberspace was meant to herald an era of Jeffersonian democracy, but instead brought us unprecedented centralisation and 'surveillance capitalism'.[65] Decolonisation also means committing to emplaced transformation – to changing the way we live without moving. Karl Marx famously noted that capital strives for an ever 'greater annihilation of space by time'.[66] Aiming to manage contradictions that develop through time, settler-colonial migration strives for the annihilation of time by space. Clearly, rather than annihilating either, we should enjoy both.

65 Shoshana Zuboff, *The Age of Surveillance Capitalism: The Fight for a Human Future at the New Frontier of Power* (New York: Hachette, 2019).

66 Karl Marx, *Grundrisse: Foundations of the Critique of Political Economy*, Notebook V (1857) – available at marxists.org.

1

The World Turned Inside Out up to The Beginning of the Global Settler Revolution

The world turned inside out was imagined before it was established. Adventurer and member of parliament Humphrey Gilbert had argued in 1583 that England should seek to 'populate' the 'pagan or barbarous countries which are not really possessed by any Prince or Christian people'.[1] A 'gentleman educated at Eton and Oxford', Gilbert 'enunciated the doctrine, carried it into practice', and was instrumental in the establishment of a colony in Newfoundland 'to which England would send its unemployed citizens'.[2] 'Populate' is crucial in this formulation, especially considering its explicit link with an alleged lack of sovereignty; Gilbert's statement can be seen as the beginning of a new colonial tradition. It was presented as an alternative to other ways of colonising (the Iberians did colonialism differently), but it would not be an exclusively English-speaking tradition. The Jesuit 'reductions' in what would become today's Paraguay and elsewhere in the Americas, for example, would achieve a remarkable autonomy – a de facto independence from the colonial world that surrounded them – and were predicated on the seclusion of a particular collective from a secularising world.[3]

1 Cited in Marc Ferro, *Colonization: A Global History* (London: Routledge, 1997), p. 47.

2 Ibid.

3 See, for example, Philip Caraman, *The Lost Paradise: The Jesuit Republic in South America* (New York: Seabury, 1976); Bronwen McShea, *Apostles of Empire: The Jesuits and New France* (Lincoln, NE: University of Nebraska Press, 2019).

Secularism was a kind of revolution. The Jesuits never approved of either.

And neither was settler colonialism an entirely new idea. The ancient Greeks had already opted for colonisation as an alternative to revolution, political discord and civil strife, after the emergence of the political structures of the *polis*.[4] They had typically settled as refugees, or as traders residing in nonsovereign settlements that resembled 'foreign concessions'; but then, as resources became scarce and aristocratic rule became entrenched, the poor, as well as many wealthier families excluded from 'political privilege', had become discontented.[5] The solution was often a pre-emptive move, resulting in colonisation in all directions: Africa, Magna Graecia, the Black Sea. In some places these settlements were successful; in others they were not. Where they were, they were sovereign, and would not integrate with the natives, even though at times they did assimilate them.[6] The new states established through this Hellenising wave were also immediately independent from the motherland. Eventually, however, revolution came anyway in the metropole, and tyrants took over (interestingly, revolution never came in the Greek settler colonies across the sea). The proponents of the new tradition in the sixteenth century knew very well how the ancient Greeks had enacted colonisation.[7] And they knew about Roman colonisations, too

4 See Jean-Paul Descoeudres, 'Central Greece on the eve of the colonisation movement', in G. R. Tsetskhladze, ed., *Greek Colonisation: An Account of Greek Colonies and Other Settlements Overseas* (Leiden: Brill, 2008), esp. pp. 296, 363.

5 See Mary E. White, 'Greek Colonization', *Journal of Economic History* XXI: 4 (1961), pp. 443, 445.

6 Claude Mossé's analysis of settler-colonial phenomena in classical antiquity insists that, whatever the circumstances determining the foundation of an 'agrarian' colony, the object was always the establishment of a *polis*, an autonomous polity developing independently of the originating metropole. Mossé mentions a provision in the constitution of the Theran colony of Cyrene that assures for every settler a right to join the colony, and to be allocated a plot of land and full citizenship. This was a world turned inside out: the settlers would sooner be displaced than foster social war at home. Claude Mossé, *La colonisation dans l'antiquité* (Paris: F. Nathan, 1970), esp. 37–8. See also Alexander John Graham, *Colony and Mother City in Ancient Greece* (Manchester: Manchester University Press, 1964).

7 On references to the Greek settler 'empire' through history, see Robert Garland, *Wandering Greeks: The Ancient Greek Diaspora from the Age of Homer to the Death of Alexander the Great* (Princeton, NJ: Princeton University Press, 2014). See also Eric Nelson, *The Greek Tradition of Republican Thought* (Cambridge: Cambridge University Press, 2004).

– public programmes explicitly designed to increase military manpower while reducing the likelihood of social unrest.[8]

Richard Hakluyt's *Discourse of Western Planting* (1584) can be seen as another possible starting point for this political tradition. It listed the reasons for colonisation, and insisted on the need to prevent trouble for a kingdom 'swarminge at this day with valiant youthes rustinge and hurtfull by lacke of employment'.[9] The principal aim of this colonialism was intrinsically different from that of previous colonial experiences. Rather than riches or glory, the main driver now was a desire to pre-empt social unrest:

> By makinge of shippes and by preparinge of thinges for the same: By makinge of Cables and Cordage, by plantinge of vines and olive trees, and by makinge of wyne and oyle, by husbandrie and by thousands of thinges there to be don[e], infinite numbers of the englishe nation may be sett on worke to unburdenynge of the Realme with many that nowe lyve chardgeable to the state at home.[10]

The main purpose of this colonisation was not the exaction of tribute or the production of specific commodities to be traded in developing international networks (even though this would definitely be a welcome secondary outcome, and Hakluyt later emphasised that experienced artisans must be part of any successful expedition); rather, it was the 'unburdening' of the social body. A new economy was producing social tension and multiplying the discontented. But this colonial endeavour would ease social tension on a continental scale: 'Wee shall by plantinge

8 In Rome colonial land allotments transformed *proletarii* into *assidui*, relieving demographic pressure. Jeremia Pelgrom and Tesse Stek note that agrarian reform could have achieved the same results, but point out that 'the advantage of colonization was that it did so without upsetting the status quo in Rome and threatening *concordia*', and that 'colonization of newly conquered lands left existing property claims untouched'. These authors conclude that there is a 'correlation between recorded instances of social unrest in Rome and the intensity of colonial foundations'. Jeremia Pelgrom and Tesse D. Stek, 'Roman Colonization Under the Republic: Historiographical Contextualisation of a Paradigm', in Tesse D. Stek, Jeremia Pelgrom, eds, *Roman Republican Colonization: New Perspectives from Archaeology and Ancient History* (Rome: Palombi editori, 2014), pp. 17, 29.

9 Richard Hakluyt, *Discourse of Western Planting* (London: Hakluyt Society, 1993), pp. 4–7, 114–29, esp. p. 116.

10 Ibid., p. 116.

there inlarge the glory of the gospel and from England plante sincere religion, and provide a safe and fine place to receave people from all partes of the worlde that are forced to flee for the truthe of gods worde'.[11] Non-English Protestants would also be part of the colonising enterprise. Indeed, Hakluyt understood colonisation as a dissipator of tension that could help to ease all conflicts, including international ones. 'Old World' strife would not emerge in the 'New Worlds' created by the new colonialism, while, Hakluyt added, the colony would be an exceptional manufacturer of good soldiers: 'If frontier warres there chaunce to aryse, and if therevpon wee shall fortifie, yt will occasion the trayninge upp of our youthe in the discipline of war and make a number fitt for the service of the warres and for the defence of our people there and at home'.[12] Concluding his *Discourse*, Hakluyt returned to the need to avoid impending social unrest: 'Many men of excellent wittes and of divers singular giftes', who 'are not able to live in England', may 'be raised againe' in the colonies, 'and doo their Contrie goodd seruice: and many nedefull uses there may (to greate purpose) require the savinge of greate numbers that for trifles may otherwise be deuored by the gallowes'.[13]

The possibility of easing social tension sustains Hakluyt's rhetorical climax: 'the wanderinge beggars of England that growe upp ydly and hurtefull and burdenous to this Realme, may there be unladen, better bredd upp, and may people waste Contries to the home and forreine benefite, and to their owne more happy state'.[14] The poor would be relocated, and through labour recover their virtue elsewhere. They were burdensome and restive in one place, but would eventually provide the Queen with 'toll, excises and other duties, which without oppression may be raised' in another.[15] Hakluyt then concluded: 'This Norumbega', the provisional name of this potential colony, 'offreth the remedie' – displacement was thus the remedy against a world turned upside down. His project of North American colonisation insisted on

11 Ibid., p. 117.

12 Ibid.

13 Ibid., p. 118.

14 Ibid.

15 Richard Hakluyt, *The Principal Navigations, Voyages, Traffiques and Discoveries of the English Nation Made by Sea and Overland to the Remote and Farthest Distant Quarters of the Eart at Any Time within the Compass of These 1600 Years* (London: J. M. Dent, 1928 [1599]), p. 98.

the benefits for the metropole and on the possibility of avoiding revolutionary disturbances.

Closer to home, it was Ireland that became a veritable early laboratory of the world turned inside out. The concerns that prompted its recolonisation were similar. The notion that England was overpopulated was widely held, and with overpopulation came the prospect of social unrest. In 1619, an English writer urged transporting to Ulster 'the superfluous multitudes of poor people which overspill the realm of England to the weal of both kingdoms; relatively underpopulated and underdeveloped, Ulster offered prospective colonists access and legal title to land.[16] A reference to the 'weal of both kingdoms', however, marked a conceptual shift: the project was no longer only about relieving the metropole; attention was now focused on the receiving location too.

Crisis

Even closer to home, increasing revolutionary tensions had prompted similar imaginings and practices in England. The enclosures and a new economic dynamism were transforming society.[17] Social tension was rising. New class antagonisms were an outcome of a new economy, but economic crisis in the years between 1620 and 1650 had exacerbated conflict.[18] The 'world turned upside down' was indeed a real prospect during the fateful decades of the seventeenth century Christopher Hill

16 Cited in Jonathan Bardon, *A History of Ulster* (Belfast: Blackstaff Press, 1992), p. 127.

17 See, for example, Robert C. Allen, *Enclosure and the Yeoman* (Oxford: Clarendon, 1992). Allen sets out to explode the myth of 'agrarian fundamentalism' – the notion that improved farming, modern agrarian institutions, increasing inequality and the industrial revolution are linked. For Allen, agrarian fundamentalism has two (Tory and Marxist) factions: one thinks that large farms and enclosures increased employment and productivity; the other insists that they reduced farm employment while raising productivity. Allen argues that there were two agricultural revolutions in England: the yeomen's, and the landlords' (p. 13). The yeomen had been ascendant in the seventeenth century, but eventually lost out as a result of the landlords' agricultural revolution. It is significant that one response to the landlords' revolution in the eighteenth century was the renewal of a settler-colonial tradition in America.

18 Christopher Hill, *The World Turned Upside-Down: Radical Ideas During the English Revolution* (London: Penguin, 1972), p. 21.

explored. But if the prospect of revolution was rising, the politics of volitional displacement were also growing. Hill refers to a 1594 pamphlet advocating the colonisation of Ireland noting that it would remove out of the city 'people poor and seditious, which were a burden to the commonwealth' by drawing them 'forth'.[19] Widespread Anabaptist ideas were both revolutionary and supportive of the prospect of displacement: if baptism was to be the voluntary act of an adult, no national church could legitimately exist. This understanding of community had crucial implications for understandings of sovereignty, which became both diffuse and disconnected from place. According to this logic, voluntary congregations could legitimately constitute themselves anywhere. Anabaptism is the original religion of modern settler colonialism, but not the only one. Hill notes, for example, that Calvinists could not have 'confidence in democracy' because their religion 'was for the elect, by definition a minority'.[20] But, should Calvinists settle a 'new' locale, a country that could be represented and understood as empty, democracy and election would coexist seamlessly, and even reinforce each other.

Revolutionary ideas spread in 'heath and woodland' areas, often located outside of the parish system. Revolutionary leader Gerrard Winstanley knew that these were the areas where revolutionaries could 'live out of sight or out of slavery'.[21] And yet, if settler colonialism is born with revolution, revolution is also born in a new type of geographical mobility: 'forest squatters, itinerant craftsmen, and building labourers, unemployed men and women seeking work, strolling players, minstrels and jugglers, quack doctors, gipsies, vagabonds, tramps' all moved.[22] Facing new social experiences, many thought that 'masterless people', but also placeless ones and the poor in general should be 'settled on new holdings carved out of the waste'.[23] Most could agree on reclamation: no land would be forcibly acquired if ther agricultural land that was to be distributed was to be reclaimed from 'wastes'. Only genuine reactionaries objected.

The St George's Hill Digger 'colony', located just outside London, ostensibly targeted unimproved land, and it was only one of many such

19 Ibid., p. 20.
20 Ibid., p. 160.
21 Cited in ibid., p. 46.
22 Ibid., pp. 48–9.
23 Ibid., p. 53.

colonies. Winstanley thought that 'from a half to two thirds of England was not properly cultivated', and wanted to 'go forth and declare it' by organising 'us that are called common people to manure and work upon the common lands'.[24] He wanted to improve common land collectively; but it was a commonly held idea that the poor should be resettled elsewhere. William Covell, a conservative, and Milton also pleaded for the 'just division of waste commons'.[25] But there was an essential ambiguity about where change should happen. The last line of the Diggers' Song called for 'Glory here, Diggers all', envisaging no or little displacement.[26] The Ranters, a radical wing of the revolutionary movement, had no doubt: change was to be enacted right where they were – indeed, inside their very body and soul.

Improvement and commons are indeed central to understanding the evolving relationship between displacement and change. As Hill stressed, 'The Revolution began with Oliver Cromwell leading fenmen in revolt against court drainage schemes; its crucial turning point was the defeat of the Leveller regiments at Burford, which was immediately followed by an act for draining the fens; it ended with the rout of the commoners and craftsmen of the south-western counties in the bogs of Sedgmoor'.[27] Mobility was also crucial; Hill remarked on the 'importance of social and physical mobility in expanding the possibility of freedom'.[28]

Bunyan's *The Pilgrim's Progress* was, for Hill, the 'greatest literary product of this social group, the epic of the itinerant'; those uprooted by social and economic upheaval dreamt of progressing (that is, literally moving forward), and eventually settling down.[29] It is the story of a displacement, individual and collective; and it is the pilgrim's family that travels to the Celestial City – 'that which is to come'. It is the tale of a permanent migration from the City of Destruction, the story of a pre-emptive move; it is the prospect of damnation that prompts a decision to remove, and it seems important that Christian, the main character, does not plan to return. Unlike similar travels, this is a literal

24 Cited in ibid., pp. 128–9.

25 Cited in ibid., p. 346.

26 Cited in ibid., p. 150.

27 Ibid., p. 360.

28 Ibid., p. 316.

29 That is, those who were, to use Bunyan's words, 'in danger of being removed like a cottage'. Cited in ibid., p. 406.

displacement, the story of a collective movement through real places – the 'Slough of Despond', the 'Hill Difficulty', the 'Valley of the Shadow of Death', the 'Doubting Castle', the 'Enchanted Ground' – rather than an allegory of a soul's path to salvation. Itself highly mobile, Bunyan's text would be incredibly successful in the American colonies.[30]

The alternative to turning outward was to turn inward. The Quakers toyed with revolution, but ended up espousing pacifism and non-involvement. William Penn, who understood this tension, established a settler colony and its administration for the Quakers who would go to America, but mandated quietism and withdrawal for those who would stay put.[31] In Hill's summation, these alternative stances were 'simply the consequence of the organized survival of a group which had failed to turn the world upside down'.[32] Both were non-revolutionary stances. Strategic defeat shaped this group's options: the 'openness of the religion of the heart' was, for Hill, at first a 'vehicle of revolutionary transformations of thought', but after the Restoration had the 'opposite effect'.[33] The revolution had been defeated, and the world turned upside down was no more (except for a few surviving and minoritarian undercurrents). But it eventually re-emerged in America; and 'The World Turned Upside Down' (the tune) was played when Cornwallis surrendered to Washington, and by the Shakers, 'a Lancashire group who were "commissioned of the Almighty God to preach the everlasting gospel to America" in 1774'.[34] Displacement was seen in this context as a remedy both to the prospect of a coming social war and to its outcome.

James Harrington's *Oceana* (1656) also advocated displacement. In *Oceana*, Harrington envisages a complex political system ensuring a fairer distribution of landed property.[35] The 'Commonwealth of Oceana'

30 See Christopher Hill, *A Turbulent, Seditious, and Fractious People: John Bunyan and His Church, 1628–88* (Oxford: Oxford University Press, 1989).

31 Hill, *World Turned Upside Down*, p. 253. See also Shuichi Wanibuchi, 'William Penn's Imperial Landscape: Improvement, Political Economy, and Colonial Agriculture in the Pennsylvania Project', in Andrew R. Murphy and John Smolenski, eds, *The Worlds of William Penn* (New Brunswick, NJ: Rutgers University Press, 2019).

32 Hill, *World Turned Upside Down*, p. 256.

33 Ibid., p. 371.

34 Ibid., p. 380.

35 See J. G. A. Pocock, 'Editorial and Historical Introductions', in James Harrington, *The Political Works of James Harrington* (Cambridge: Cambridge University Press, 1977).

is an 'equal commonwealth' founded on a distributive agrarian law that limits the size of landholdings to a defined threshold; this is, in Harrington's account, the only genuinely stable form of government. Harrington was seeking stability in a world massively upset by revolution and civil war.[36] But *Oceana* was not only about internal stability (even though the scholarly literature has focused on its domestic prescriptions); stability was ultimately predicated on an ability to expand constantly: Oceana needed an outside.[37] Indeed, Harrington distinguishes fundamentally between 'a commonwealth for preservation' and 'a commonwealth for increase'.[38] It is the commonwealth of increase that is most stable, but only if what is increased is a particular type of citizenry defined by freehold. The commonwealth's ability to 'increase' was thus predicated on the possibility of ongoing displacement, and Harrington was generally enthusiastic about displacement, suggesting, for example, that, since the Irish lacked 'industry', the Jews should be settled in Ireland instead. And it is significant that this is not a utopian text; Harrington's Oceana remains politically attached to England (even if territorial contiguity is not necessary).[39] Oceana was a really existing place with room to expand.

Massachusetts

Besides Ireland, the most obvious elsewhere in seventeenth-century England was America. The early literature regarding the colonisation of America imagined Virginia as a non-revolutionary utopia where Indians would become the colony's plebeian classes.[40] The Puritan settler-colonial world had several failed precursors. After failure on Roanoke Islands in 1585–87, Ralph Lane emphasised privateering and the mining of

36 J. G. A. Pocock, 'Introduction', in James Harrington, *The Commonwealth of Oceana and A System of Politics* (New York: Cambridge University Press, 1992 [1656]), p. xix. Pocock remarks that Harrington saw the English Civil War as a revolution.

37 See Charles Blitzer, *An Immortal Commonwealth: The Political Thought of James Harrington* (New Haven, CT: Yale University Press, 1960).

38 Harrington, *Commonwealth of Oceana and A System of Politics*, p. 7.

39 See Pocock, 'Introduction', p. xvii.

40 See Ethan E. Schmidt, 'The Well-Ordered Commonwealth: Humanism, Utopian Perfectionism, and the English Colonisation of the Americas', *Atlantic Studies: Global Currents* 7: 3 (2014).

precious metals as purposes for which to set up colonising ventures, but Thomas Hariot's *A Briefe and True Report of the New Found Land of Virginia* (1588) stressed timber products, silk grass, animal furs and medicines. The aim of colonial activity had shifted from the exclusive enrichment of individuals situated in the metropole to the new community's reproduction on site: colonising endeavours in the future would involve women, farmers and craftsmen.

The settlement of Providence Island in the Caribbean (1625–30) had been another failure. Promoted by the cream of Puritan society, it was radically different from what would become Massachusetts. Investors remained in England, while the colonists had to sign 50 per cent of their profits away. Power also remained in England; since this made communication difficult and governance inflexible, tobacco was the only really successful crop. A corporate monopoly of shipping hindered growth. Labour was scarce, indentured labourers were reluctant to emigrate, and the land remained underutilised. Slaves were then imported.[41]

Advocates of displacement as an alternative to revolution in the seventeenth and eighteenth centuries include the promoters of Puritan New England. They envisaged the constitution of a 'city on the hill', and were horrified at what they perceived as worrying signs of impending social upheaval. John Winthrop promoted and practised displacement. Son of a country gentleman, he had converted to Puritanism and exercised the legal profession before migrating to Massachusetts as governor of the Massachusetts Bay Company (he had considered Ireland as a site for his migration before becoming involved with Massachusetts). Winthrop had realised that relocation would precipitate a specific state form and its particular sovereign prerogatives.[42] That specific state was born out of displacement in the face of growing revolutionary tensions. Many left England as they expected upheaval, but many returned and embraced the revolution (for more than a third of the ministers who returned to England between 1640 and 1660, America was a staging

41 See Ed Wright, *Ghost Colonies* (Sydney: Murdoch, 2009), p. 140.

42 Agnes Delahaye foregrounds settler colonialism and Winthrop's awareness of having been put in charge of the 'creation of a state formation of a new kind'. Agnes Delahaye, *The Good Land: Governance and Promotion in John Winthrop's New England (1630–1650)* (Leiden: Brill, 2020), p. 168.

point, not a final destination).[43] When the Commonwealth was terminated in England, many decided to move across the ocean, in another great migratory wave. Thus the dialectical relationship between emplaced and displaced transformation played a crucial role in New England.[44]

Winthrop's 1629 letter to his wife epitomises the sensitivity that had led to this world turned inside out. After complaining about the 'evil' times that had engulfed England, he offered a prognosis:

> I am veryly persuaded, God will bring some heavye Affliction upon this lande, & that speedylye: but be of good comfort, the hardest that can come shall be a meanes to mortifie this bodye of corruption, which is a thousand tymes more dangerous to us then any outward tribulation, & to bring us into nearer communion with our Lord Jesus Christ, & more assurance of his kingdome. If the Lord seeth it wilbe good for us, he will provide a shelter & a hidinge place for us & others.[45]

This is not a persecuted man considering exile; rather, his concern is for what he sees coming. Some of the colonists of the Massachusetts Bay Company had suffered religious persecution, but it was the sense of an impending calamity and the perception of a changing world that was crucial in shaping the choice of many others. The latter had alternatives, but decided to relocate.[46]

---

43 See Susan Hardman Moore, *Pilgrims: New World Settlers and the Call of Home* (New Haven, CT: Yale University Press, 2008).

44 Dealing with Ann Hutchinson's challenge, a diatribe that broke the unity of the colony, led Winthrop to distinguish between 'moral' and 'natural' liberty. In Winthrop's reconstruction, moral liberty adopts displacement and refuses revolutionary transformation; natural liberty, on the contrary, follows a loss of organising principles, a loss that amounts to a revolution. See Tiziano Bonazzi, *Il sacro esperimento* (Bologna: il Mulino, 1970), pp. 232–3.

45 Cited in Loren Baritz, *City on a Hill: A History of Ideas and Myths in America* (Westport, CT: Praeger, 1980), pp. 7–8.

46 Sacvan Bercovitch noted that Massachusetts was one out of three possible options: the Puritans who emigrated to America 'represented one of three Puritan groups of the time. The largest, most eclectic of these were the Presbyterians, who sought to purify the country at large to a state worthy of its special calling. The smallest of the three groups, the Separatists, took the opposite course. They purified their faith to the point where they refused allegiance to any institutional authority, including that

Crucially, Winthrop's justification for the settlement enterprise included both a realisation that keeping up had become difficult, and the conviction that God had given the whole earth to men, and that it would be folly to remain in one place when others were available. 'We are growne to that height of Intemperance in all excesse of Ryot, as noe mans estate allmost will suffice to keepe saile wth his aequalls', he wrote.[47] Winthrop understood social transformation as a revolutionary process, and a determination to protect his social status was expressed in a desire to appropriate land elsewhere. This had to be justified, as admittedly the indigenous peoples were 'other sonnes of Adam'. Winthrop had very little knowledge of Indian life. And yet he maintained:

> 1. That which is com[mon] to all is proper to none, these salvadge peoples ramble over muche lande without title or property; 2. there is more than enough for them and us; 3. God hathe consumed the natives with a miraculous plague, whereby a greate parte of the Country is left voyde of Inh[abita]ntes; 4. We shall come in with good leave of the natives.[48]

It is telling that, in his rendition, peaceful relations only *follow* dispossession, appropriation and elimination.

In *Reasons to be Considered* (1629), Winthrop again emphasised the expectation that God's wrath is about to fall on England, and the notion that Massachusetts would be the shelter for those he has decided to spare (it was to be a site-specific godly wrath). Winthrop's notes on the economy expressed discomfort:

> This Land growes weary of her Inhabitants, soe as man, whoe is the most precious of all creatures, is here more vile & base than the earth we trade upon, & of lesse prise among us then an horse or a sheepe:

---

of the English Protestant church, whether Anglican or Presbyterian. Instead, they hoped to join the progress of the "universal invisible church" in small congregations, modelled after the first Christian communities. Some remained in England, others fled persecution to Amsterdam, and then, in the case of the Plymouth Pilgrims, to the New World. The Massachusetts Bay immigrants sought a "middle way" between these extremes'. Revolution, reaction, and displacement – three options. Bercovitch, *The Rites of Assent*, 73.

47 Cited in Baritz, *City on a Hill*, p. 9.

48 Cited in ibid, p. 10.

> masters are forced by authority to entertaine servants, parents to mainetaine there owne children, all towns complaine of the burthen of theire poore . . . & thus it is come to passe, that children, servants & neighboures, especially if they be poore, are compted the greatest burdens, wch if thinges weare right would be the chiefest earthly blessings.[49]

The new economy, and especially the new estate-management policies, had resulted in two interlinked and in his view detrimental consequences: an increase in the number of paupers and a dangerous tendency towards upsetting social hierarchies. Nonetheless, his invocation of '[t]his land' implicitly raised the possibility of another.

Many of the promoters of the 'Great Migration' were landowners whose families had prospered with the expropriations of ecclesiastical estates in the sixteenth century. In the early decades of the seventeenth century, this group's most pressing problem was whether they could develop their properties according to the new commercial regime. Many gentlemen of the south of England joined the Puritan movement when they were acting as estate administrators, and yet were rejecting on moral grounds the *consequences* of the new regime. It was an unsolvable contradiction, but displacement offered a possible synthesis. The idea that a properly organised migration would provide the mechanisms by which England's social problems could be relieved was already widespread. Winthrop concluded that it could solve his problems, too.

His discovery of the falling price of a man is also an essential element in the constitution of the world turned inside out. Economic forces were subverting the social order; 'goodness' and 'honesty' were no longer sufficient for a man to live with dignity, and this was bound to bring forth God's wrath. Migration seemed like a suitable solution especially because it would offer the opportunity for *selective* displacement: nothing unwanted would be carried over to the new location. Thus, this migration had to be associated with a particular form of government: a government by and for the colonists. Other colonial ventures had failed, but the new Puritan enterprise was to be different. Previous endeavours were 'carnall and not religious; [and] aymed chiefly at profit, and not the

49 Ibid.

propagation of Religion', Winthrop noted.[50] Most importantly, the human material and organisation of the migration would be qualitatively different: previous endeavours had 'used unfit instruments, a multitude of Rude and misgoverned persons the verye scomme of the lande [and] they did not establish a right forme of Goverment'.[51] The new enterprise would arrogate this right to itself.

Winthrop's realisation of impending disaster, his consequent decision to relocate, and the direct relationship between the former and the latter are crucial:

> My means here are so shortened (now my 3 eldest sons are come to age) as I shall not be able to continue in this place and employment where I now am . . . and with what comfort can I live with 7 or 8 servants in that place and condition where for many years I have spent 3 or 400 li. per ann. and maintain as great a charge?[52]

'My means here', 'where I am now', and 'in that place' are all remarks that foreshadow the possibility of an elsewhere. Winthrop is asking a rhetorical question: If there is no comfort in a specific location, and revolution is foreclosed, what alternative remains other than relocation? It is precisely because Winthrop cannot keep his station that he feels he cannot be stationary.

And yet mere displacement by itself cannot be enough; the new society must be properly organised. Only a sovereign and constitutive capacity would make it possible. In *Modell of Christian Charity* (1630), Winthrop would explicitly and famously proclaim a law-making ability: 'Thus stands the case between God and us. Wee are entered into Covenant with him for this worke [i.e. relocating and constructing the 'city on the hill']. Wee have taken out a Commission. The Lord hath given us leave to drawe our own articles'.[53] That 'leave' was, however, crucially predicated on actually leaving. This was a crucial transition from metaphorical to literal departure. Whether Puritan New England

50 Cited ibid., pp. 10–11.

51 Cited ibid., p. 11.

52 Cited in Richard Pares, 'The Economic Factors in the History of the Empire', *Economic History Review* 7: 2 (1937), p. 119.

53 Cited in Francis Jennings, *Conquest of America* (New York: W. W. Norton, 1976), p. 180.

constituted 'America' has been fiercely debated; that it strongly shaped the world turned inside out is undeniable.[54]

This was not the realisation of one individual alone. John Cotton delivered *God's Promise to His Plantations* to those about to leave for America in the spring of 1630. It is an exploration of the ways in which a man could determine whether he is called by God to Massachusetts (nobody was asking women). It is an important question since, once ascertained, a 'calling' to settle in New England was, Cotton argued, a vocation superior even to the duty of being Christian. Cotton defined the colonists as the new people of Israel, the people of God, and a collective that would go wherever God commands. It was the Lord that wanted their departure. Cotton emphasised that the actual location of any people in one or another country was ultimately chosen by God and quoted the Biblical passage where the people of Israel are promised a land that will be exclusively theirs: 'Moreover I will appoint a place for my people Israell, and I will plant them, that they may dwell in a place of their owne, and move no more'.[55] Displacement was here dialectically linked to a yearning for ultimate immobility. The settlers would move in order to move no more.

If collectives are no longer fixed to their original location, ethnicity itself becomes fluid and portable. This allowed Cotton to develop a veritable anthropological geography: since God was no longer intervening in human affairs by means of miracles, one needed to inquire rationally into his 'secondary' causes – real events happened for a reason. For example, if God wanted one people to reside anywhere, he would make room for it through a sacred war, or ensure that the indigenous people might grant permission to the newcomers, or vacate the country in other ways. The very locale of the future settlement thus became charged with a messianic and sacred character. According to this logic, the

54 For a critique of a view of the constitution of 'America' from the perspective of New England, see, for example, Hugh Kearney, 'The Problem of Perspective in the History of Colonial America', in K. R. Andrews, N. P. Canny and P. E. H. Hair, eds, *The Westward Enterprise: English Activities in Ireland, the Atlantic, and America, 1480–1650* (Liverpool: Liverpool University Press, 1978).

55 John Cotton, *God's Promise to His Plantations; As it was delivered in a Sermon, by John Cotton, B. D., and Preacher of God's word in Boston* (London: William Jones, 1634), pp. i, 1. Cotton had developed a reputation as a remarkable religious scholar after defeating Boston, England's Arminian faction. He finally reached Boston, New England, in 1633.

settlers' movement was qualitatively different from that of other migrants; because the settlers had been called, they had become God's people, and had been entrusted with a special site-specific mission (not so, for example, the Pilgrim Fathers of 1620, who were migrants fleeing persecution and lack of economic opportunity). Importantly, God's people is sovereign somewhere, but not anywhere – a focus on specific locations defines the political traditions of settler colonialism.

In *A Discourse about Civil Government in a New Population whose Design is Religion* (1663), Cotton systematised the structures of a Congregationalist settler-colonial collective: church elders must be submitted to the magistrates as regards the 'external man'; conversely, as regards the 'inward man', they remain autonomous.[56] And yet, Cotton stressed that religious and social life must not be considered distinct, because it was place that united them in an indissoluble bond.[57] Of course, the Congregationalists needed an 'unsettled' country to start with; only in such a place could the two forms of life be properly articulated. In a crucial passage, Cotton distinguished between 'a Common-wealth already settled, and a Common-wealth yet to be settled . . . wherein men are free to chuse what Form [of political organisation] they shall judge best'.[58] It is a fundamental distinction, because the rules that apply to settled countries, whether Christian or not, do not apply to countries yet to be settled. For Cotton, Paul's exhortation to submit to civil authorities is thus not binding in the case of displaced collectives that have been 'called' to a new country: 'if [Paul] had written to a company of Believers in a New Plantation, where the Foundations of the Church and Civil State, and the communion of both, was to be laid out for many Generations to come, he would have advised them to take the same course which we plead for'.[59] The second part of Cotton's proposition is also critical: the settlers of unsettled locations enjoy an unconstrained freedom to

56 It was Cotton who wrote it, not John Davenport. See Isabel M. Calder, 'The Authorship of a Discourse about Civil Government in a New Plantation Whose Design is Religion', *American Historical Review* 37: 2 (1932).

57 John Cotton, *A Discourse about Civil Government in a New Plantation whose Design is Religion, Written Many Years Since, by that Reverend and Worthy Minister of the Gospel* (Cambridge, MA: Samuel Green/Marmaduke Johnson, 1663), pp. 8–9.

58 Ibid., p. 9.

59 Ibid., 10.

choose the political and ecclesiastical structure they prefer. Cotton could not have emphasised this prerogative more strongly, and he repeated twelve times in his *Discourse* that in 'new Plantations . . . men are free to chuse'. The settlers were free, but this freedom was site-specific and only obtained in polities that had resulted from a collective relocation.

Cotton's *Discourse* and Winthrop's *Modell* outlined the structures of the 'political experiment' as it was established in 1630–31; they constitute the founding political theory of Puritan Massachusetts. It was not an affirmation of oligarchy over democracy, as it has often been portrayed; rather, it proposed a system of government that could only be legitimate if and where it had been relocated. God would effectively become a sovereign – but even this sovereignty was subordinated to location. In this context, displacement trumped birth, in relation to both status and someone's origin. When Lord Say approached Cotton regarding the possible emigration of aristocratic Puritans, he was told that in Massachusetts there would be no aristocracy.[60] Understandably, Lord Say decided not to emigrate, and aristocratic interest in emigration would thereafter be concentrated on a few Caribbean islands.[61]

Winthrop's projection of a world turned inside out (he did not use the expression, of course) was ultimately based on a covenant between individual settlers. In his formulation, a displaced society immediately becomes an enclosed and exclusive body, in which only those who participate in the covenant have an interest in its realisation. Likewise, the social covenant is jointly owned by those who partake in it – all others are excluded. Massachusetts thus became an autonomous corporate body free of any external authority. Most importantly, being a corporation, Massachusetts was especially free from any obligation towards anyone who, despite residing within its jurisdiction, was not included within the covenant. This meant other English subjects, migrants, slaves, and of course indigenous peoples. Because of this succession of radical exclusions, Winthrop saw Massachusetts as existing in a continuous state of emergency. But if, internally, there was

60 See Bonazzi, *Il sacro esperimento*, pp. 232–3.

61 See K. Ordahl Kupperman, *Providence Island, 1630–1641: The Other Puritan Colony* (Cambridge: Cambridge University Press, 1993).

anxiety, externally this anxiety had to be prevented from finding expression. The strength of the settler covenant needed to be eminently visible:

> We shall find the God of Israell is among us, when tenn of us shall be able to resist a thousand of our enemies, when hee shall make us prayse and glory, that men shall say of succeeding plantacions: the lord make it like that of New England: for wee must Consider that wee shall be as a Citty upon a Hill, the eies of all people are uppon us.[62]

The Massachusetts Puritans took visibility seriously; their site-specific political theory demanded that they be visible from a distance.

The Royal Charter of 1629 established the Massachusetts Bay Company as a legal personality endowed with extensive powers of self-management and practically unlimited authority over the territory it identified. The Royal Charter also extended to Massachusetts Bay a type of tenure that was unburdened by ecclesiastical or military ties, rendering it a practically sovereign body that encompassed legislative, judicial and executive powers. Various ties still connected it with England: an oath of allegiance to the king that the governor and the magistrates had to take before attaining office; the unavoidable fact that the charter had emanated from the king; and an obligation not to pass laws and ordinances contrary to those of the English kingdom. But these dispositions could be ignored and were often circumvented. Loren Baritz observed that, with 'the substitution of God for King' in the oaths required of officials of the Company,

> the Bay saints had, through an exercise of their own will, included God in the concession which had made them into an organic whole. The King had created a trading corporation but God had turned it into a nation. The King, as a magistrate, must provide protection for the fragile colony against Indians and Catholics. For this there would be gratitude. But the saints could afford obedience to the King only when he did not interfere with their divine mission. The saints, in other words, could obey the King only when they were convinced that

62 Cited in Baritz, *City on a Hill*, p. 17.

> it would be faithful to their covenant with God to do so. The decision was theirs, as Calvin had earlier concluded it should be.[63]

God had turned a corporation into a nation by commanding its displacement. The colonists could only obey when they believed they were being faithful to an original covenant, and their belief would depend on *where* they were. The covenant was paramount but, again, place-specific.

The Royal Charter and the liberties it granted would be abolished in 1684, and then largely reinstated in 1691. But these powers could not have been enacted if the Company had resided in England and operated like other colonial ventures. Initially paramount, its commercial concerns became subordinate to the organisation of its settlement. A 1629 agreement stipulated that the members of the Massachusetts Bay Company would pledge to depart only under the provision 'alwayes that before the last of September next the whole government together with the Patent for the said plantacion bee first by an order of Court legally transferred and established to remayne with us and others which shall inhabite upon the said plantacion'.[64]

It was a veritable coup, and a major turning point: the Cambridge Agreement is indeed a crucial event in the consolidation of the world turned inside out. As it demanded that the charter and the entire government must be displaced to America, the Agreement upended the colonial relationship; the centre would now be at the margin. The leaders of the enterprise knew that this provision would prove essential to their success; the new polity was conceived as a self-governing political body carrying an inherent sovereign ability. The Cambridge Agreement had created a particular political collective, and its executors agreed 'that this whole adventure growses upon the joint confidence we have in each others fidelity and resolucion herein, so as no man of us would have adventured it without assurance of the rest'.[65] In October 1629, Winthrop became governor and the Massachusetts Bay Company, which was now instrument of the 'Great Migration', ceased to operate as a commercial body. And all this even before departure!

63 Baritz, *City on a Hill*, p. 40.
64 Cited in ibid., p. 12.
65 Cited in ibid., p. at 18.

Winthrop's *Essay of the Ordering of Towns* (1635) retrospectively rehearsed his *Modell*, but by the time it was written, the world turned inside out was actually constituted; the essay thus reads like a manual. It focused on the formation of towns and the means of partitioning land. Land had been allocated unequally, and this had created problems. How to maintain social peace? Winthrop restated that settlement had to proceed in an 'orderly' manner, and that 'comfortable communion' and 'comfort in vicinity' would promote peace. The distribution of religious and political rights would also help. But Winthrop also considered labour and economic development. Vicinity and dispersion would need to be accurately balanced. The towns were to be '6 miles each way' distant from each other; houses were to be located 'in a circle of three mile circumference', with 'outer fields and pasture to be allocated to those best able to improve them within two or three years'.[66]

Winthrop knew that failing farmers would express their discontent and 'damnify the commonwealth'; on the other hand, wealthier settlers had to rely on tenants, which was more advantageous than using 'bound labour'.[67] Tenancy 'brought more peace of conscience and less danger' to the owners, even though it might reduce profits.[68] Tenancy, and the prospect of ownership that the settlement's ability to expand indefinitely would guarantee its colonists, would promote social peace. The settlement was born in displacement, but the settlement also absolutely needed more displacement still if it was to chase the spectre of social strife away. Winthrop also acknowledged in his *Journal* that 'it would not avail by any law to redress the excessive rates of laborers' and workmen's wages, etc. (for being restrained, they would either remove to other places where they might have more, or else being able to live by planting and other employments of their own, they would not be hired at all)'.[69] What would become known as primitive accumulation was undone by the poorer colonists' ability to move and immediately acquire possession of some land elsewhere. The system was also reliant on a constant flow of immigrants – a double movement, a movement to new lands near the settlement, and from the Old Land was Winthrop's

66 Cited in Delahaye, *Good Land*, p. 192.

67 Cited in ibid., p. 194.

68 Cited in ibid., pp. 17, 194.

69 Cited in ibid., p. 200.

solution to the prospect of social unrest (as we shall see, this insight would also be achieved independently by Edward Gibbon Wakefield two centuries later).

The New England Puritans were not the only ones who were thinking along these lines. John Smith, who had extensive experience of other colonial endeavours in Virginia but was not involved in the Massachusetts experiment, advocated a similar model. For him, it was those who were best suited to succeed in 'planting', the 'middle classes', who should relocate. Displaced paupers, he knew personally, made poor settlers. His *Description of New England* (1616) argued that the settlement of New England must be different from previous colonial experiments. In his opinion it was subjection to powers located in the metropole that had doomed previous attempts to establish viable settlements. In America, he insisted, there were no 'hard Landlords to rack us with high rents, or extorted fines to consume us, no tedious pleas in law to consume us with their many years disputation for justice, no multitudes to occasion such impediments to good orders'.[70] Available land and the absence of Old World institutions meant that in America 'every man may be master and owner of his own labor and land; or the greatest part in a small time. If he have nothing but his hands, he may set up his trade; and by industry quickly grow rich; spending but half that time well, which in England we abuse in idleness, worse or as ill'.[71] Displacement would turn one thing into its opposite: social mobility was unsavoury and disruptive in England, but 'noble' and 'profitable' elsewhere.

Refuges

'America' was indeed represented as radically different. For example, the New England colonists could be 'warm in winter, warmer even than the nobility of England could be'; and if the Old World was facing an acute fuel crisis, the New World would allow everyone to be warm.[72] William Cronon quoted Francis Higginson's remark that a 'poor servant here

70 Cited in Philip Barbour, ed., *The Complete Works of Captain John Smith* (Chapel Hill, NC: University of North Carolina Press, 1985), p. 332.

71 Ibid.

72 William Cronon, *Changes in the Land: Indians, Colonists, and the Ecology of New England* (New York: Hill & Wang, 1983), p. 25.

that is to possesse but 50 Acres of land, may afford to give more wood for Timber and Fire as good as the world yeelds, than many Noble men in *England* can afford to do'.[73] Cronon also remarked that the sources consistently noted that in America rents were low and labour expensive.[74] Indians were often represented as 'rich beggars', or 'poor gentlemen': the indigenous world was a world turned upside down, and 'America' a world inverted. This pattern of reference would remain resilient – a pattern of representation that would sustain the imagination of alternative politics. If war and disruption were characteristic of the Old World, the New one could afford many refuges.

French Calvinist Nicolas de Villegaignon, for example, established *France Antartique* in what would become Rio de Janeiro in 1555. It was meant to become a Calvinist colony, and a refuge from religious war in France. He was commanding a small fleet of two ships, 600 soldiers, and a number of Huguenot colonists – the king would eliminate the 'heretics' in France, but was helping them elsewhere. They founded Fort Coligny (in honour of a Huguenot admiral who supported the expedition), and, initially unchallenged by the Portuguese, welcomed more arrivals in 1556 (mainly Genevan Calvinists, but also a few Catholics). The indigenous Tupinambás traded with the French, and relatively good relations were established; but the Portuguese were finally able to dislodge the French in 1567.[75]

Throughout the following two centuries, new revolutionary crises would prompt new settlements and new attempts to turn the world inside out. Scottish reformer James Oglethorpe lobbied for the establishment of a colony in what would become Georgia for the many bankrupt gentlemen debtors who were at the time filling London's prisons after the markets had taken a wrong turn (the 'poor gentlemen' were in England after all, not America). Oglethorpe advocated displacement rather than acceptance of what was for him an intolerable world turned upside down (back then, bankrupt gentlemen who had invested unwisely were not bailed out, and their imprisonment constituted indeed a

73 Ibid., p. 25.

74 Ibid., p. 169.

75 See Frank Lestrignant, 'La mémoire de la France Antarctique', *História* 27: 1 (2008). Lestrignant refers to a 'third solution', beyond the 'Rome' and the 'Genève' options (p. 105). This third option was predicated on displacement.

shocking instance of revolutionary upheaval).[76] The Oglethorpe scheme was one result of a parliamentary committee established to investigate prison conditions; it proved able to muster significant political support. In practice, many of those who eventually left for Georgia were artisans and craftsmen, not fallen entrepreneurs, and the actual colony was thus quite different from the original vision; but the world turned inside out had been imagined again in the face of crisis.

Oglethorpe articulated an idea that would be reiterated often: organised displacement could be an instrument to regulate the functioning of unpredictable markets and other disruptions. This idea had been articulated earlier as well. Scottish plans to settle the Darien jungle were similarly drawn up in the context of social upheaval and tension, and it was a struggling Scottish petit bourgeoisie that especially invested in the scheme.[77] William Paterson, a prominent leader of the enterprise, had called Panama 'the door of the seas, and the key of the universe', but the expeditions in 1698–99, and again in 1699–1700, were a disaster.[78] The crisis had come earlier in Scotland, while the failure of this scheme in turn further contributed to crisis. The financial disruptions associated with the Darien debacle were significant and protracted.

Oglethorpe and Paterson, of course, were not exceptions. Swiss colonial adventurer and serial promoter of failed settlements Jean Pierre Purry tried to establish settlements in Australia and South Africa, and eventually in South Carolina, where he 'planted' a few Swiss Protestants. He assumed that colonisation would be most successful at around 33 degrees latitude (this is the latitude of biblical Canaan; the location was different than that devised by Cotton, but the method for devising an appropriate location – inquiry into 'secondary causes' – was not), and expressed a theory about the legitimate dispossession of indigenous peoples' property based on a Lockean notion of 'natural law'.[79] The impulse for Purry's colonial endeavours was a response to serial failure:

76 See Phinizy Spalding, *Oglethorpe in America* (Chicago: University of Chicago Press, 1977).

77 See John Prebble, *Darien: The Scottish Dream of Empire* (Edinburgh: Birlinn, 2000); Arthur L. Herman, *How the Scots Invented the Modern World* (New York: Three Rivers, 2001), pp. 32–6.

78 Cited in Herman, *How the Scots Invented the Modern World*, p. 33.

79 See Carlo Ginzburg, 'Latitude, Slaves, and the Bible: An Experiment in Microhistory', *Critical Inquiry* 31 (2005).

his investment schemes in the 'old' land had fared miserably, and his escape was indeed a response to contradictions at home. Purry's schemes interacted with those of Oglethorpe (Purrysburg was eventually established in the 1720s across the Savannah River in South Carolina, but only after Georgia had been established), and it is significant that Purry, like the philanthropists who gathered around Oglethorpe, was especially interested in providing an escape from bankrupted debtors (which is understandable, as he was one of them).

Purry was a Huguenot. Facing revolutionary tensions in prerevolutionary France, many Huguenots had decided to move on. Jean-Louis Gibert, for example, eventually moved to New Bordeaux, South Carolina, with a few other like-minded French exiles.[80] He had fled France in the 1760s, but had previously built Protestant churches in Saintonge, and had behaved as a 'naturally seditious' man (as one bureaucrat had described him) – as a revolutionary.[81] Emigration had earlier been for Gibert a threat to force concessions from the authorities and the monarch (according to prevailing physiocratic ideas, population and labour were crucial to political economy, and anyone leaving the realm would impoverish it); but France ended up becoming for him a most undesirable location. 'Desert' and 'refuge' were the terms the Huguenots used, but it is important to note that toleration was on the rise as well as revolutionary tension. The former would have prompted a decision to remain, the latter counselled departure.

French Protestantism was thus divided between those who had stayed in the 'desert' and those who had fled. Gibert shifted from one camp to the other; but he embraced displacement especially because he foresaw coming upheaval. Indeed, toleration itself was revolution of a sort that would deprive the reconstituted French Protestant church of its militant character, and would assimilate Protestants within the state.[82] Owen Stanwood notes that

80 For an analysis of the transition of Huguenot emigration from a threat (to the wealth of the realm) to a collective attempt to turn the world turned inside out, see Owen Stanwood, 'From the Desert to the Refuge: The Saga of New Bordeaux', *French Historical Studies* 40: 1 (2017). A threat to emigrate focuses on the place of origin; the latter stance has given up on it.

81 Cited in Stanwood, 'From the Desert to the Refuge', p. 5.

82 Ibid., p.10.

> Gibert [had] explained in a letter [to the Archbishop of Canterbury] that conditions had been fairly good in Saintonge since 1755, but . . . feared that recent good treatment was just a ruse to get the Protestants to lower their guards and that he and his followers aimed to 'expatriate themselves, if it is not possible for them to gain the liberty to worship God in the kingdom'.[83]

By then, many were considering displacement not as a threat, but as a viable option. For them, France was no longer at the centre. In the 1750s, the settler-colonial impulse grew significantly in this milieu. Huguenot 'desert' leader Antoine Court also changed his mind and promoted emigration.[84]

Gibert thus switched spatial focus and began promoting his 'model' settler community. He had in mind a communal colonising endeavour; but his plan was frustrated, and New Bordeaux developed along lines that would disappoint him. The Huguenots were indeed 'natural' and model settlers; as one South Carolina colonial governor noted, they were not induced 'to leave their Country out of Penury and Want, but from a desire to live under a free Government, and enjoy the Exercise of their Religion'.[85] Stanwood sees this shift, even if he focuses on Gibert's 'global trek to find religious toleration' rather than on a quest to assert a sovereign ability.[86] Crucially, the shift away from 'building churches' in France to growing silkworms elsewhere was also a move away from an approaching revolution.

The Huguenot diaspora would constitute multiple worlds turned inside out.[87] Many abandoned 1760s France after concluding that it was an irredeemable 'desert', and committed to a series of 'New Frances'

83 Ibid., p. 18.

84 See ibid., p. 11. See also Pauline Haour, 'Antoine Court and Refugee Political Thought (1719–1752)', in John Christian Laursen, ed., *New Essays on the Political Thought of the Huguenots of the Refuge* (Leiden: Brill, 1995).

85 Cited in Stanwood, 'From the Desert to the Refuge', p. 20.

86 Stanwood, 'From the Desert to the Refuge', p. 14.

87 On the Huguenot 'new worlds', see also Owen Stanwood, 'Between Eden and Empire: Huguenot Refugees and the Promise of New Worlds', *American Historical Review* 118: 5 (2013); Michelle Magdelaine and Rudolf van Thadden, eds, *Le Refuge Huguenot* (Paris: A. Colin, 1985); Eckart Birnstiel, Chrystel Bernat, eds, *La Diaspora des Huguenots: Les réfugiés protestants de France et leur dispersion dans le monde (XVIe–XVIIIe siècles)* (Paris: Champion, 2001).

elsewhere.[88] This migration was initially seen as exile, but was eventually re-coded as 'exodus' in an American context. Exile focuses on a location of origin, Exodus on the place of arrival – a most significant reconceptualisation. As Marco Sioli has noted,

> These suddenly placeless people moved toward a new destiny, through something indefinite and uncontrollable that could be compared to the biblical 'desert'. The word 'desert' was used by Huguenots to represent their flight after the revocation of the Edict of Nantes and the consequent exile in foreign places, whether America or Protestant European countries such as England or Switzerland. In his descriptions [Daniel] Trabue [the Huguenot exile Sioli is working on], significantly, replaced it with the word 'wilderness', something he had encountered on the early American frontier, certainly much less arid and much closer to his experience.[89]

'Wilderness', of course, is a prominent segment in the Exodus story – when exile is left behind. After the Glorious Revolution of 1688, and as a result of their contribution to securing English Protestantism's ascendancy, Huguenots were offered land and incentives to settle in Virginia and the Carolinas. An international network of Protestant solidarity assisted the Huguenot families that travelled to America together with their possessions. Their migration was also promoted by a number of French tracts advertising North American possibilities.[90] For a while,

---

88 Molly McClain and Alessa Ellefson note that the 'Huguenot exodus was one of the largest population movements of early modern Europe', and that an 'estimated two hundred thousand people departed France from 1680 to 1710'. It was a movement they compare with the expulsion of the Jews and Moriscos from Spain in 1492 and 1609. The emigrants were often well off; some went to locations in Protestant Europe (especially Britain, Ireland and the Netherlands, but also Germany); some went to the New Worlds (North America, particularly South Carolina, and South Africa). Molly McClain and Alessa Ellefson, 'A Letter from Carolina, 1688: French Huguenots in the New World', *William and Mary Quarterly* LXIV: 2 (2007), p. 378.

89 Marco Sioli, 'Huguenot Traditions in the Mountains of Kentucky: Daniel Trabue's Memories', *Journal of American History* 84: 4 (1998), pp. 1,318–9.

90 See McClain a Ellefson, 'Letter from Carolina', p. 378. McClain and Ellefson analyse a Huguenot veteran settler's reflection on who exactly among the Huguenots should consider moving to the New World: 'This country is neither for those who have many goods, nor for those who want to lead an easy life, nor for those who have nothing. It is good only for those who still have some belongings, who want to work, who are resolved to suffer and who prefer peace to anything else' (cited on p. 394).

the focus of this settler migration was tidewater Virginia, but then it shifted to the 'new' lands across the mountains. Sioli also draws attention to the ways in which the Huguenot legacy 'created the premises for an articulated formulation of the concept of popular sovereignty in frontier territories'.[91] The Exodus story is about a collective movement but also about sovereignty – about the promise *in another place* of collective self-determination.

'America'

The Huguenots were officially welcomed to the British colonies in the eighteenth century, but other 'persecuted' Christians – the Armenians and Greeks residing in the Ottoman Empire, for example – were also the target of settlement schemes.[92] Who else should consider joining the incipient world turned inside out? Benjamin Franklin's *Information to Those Who Would Remove to America* (1782) aimed to discourage the 'fruitless Removals and Voyages of improper Persons'.[93] Neither aristocrats nor paupers should come. Franklin, in focusing on desirable immigrants, was in fact considering the social nature of the United States. He began by espousing the notion of a comparatively classless society:

91 Sioli, 'Huguenot Traditions', pp. 1,325–6.

92 Bernard Bailyn contends that the settlement of New Smyrna in Florida was 'the largest shipment of migrants from Europe to North America since the Puritan migration of the 1630s – and the most disastrous'. The Christians of the Near East were supposedly suited for the peopling of Florida and for cultivating exotic products – vines, olives, cotton, tobacco, madder and silk. Besides, they were currently subjected to Turkish despotism, were already migrating to Naples and Minorca, and supposedly only needed allotments of land to be convinced to relocate to British North America. Being Orthodox Christians, they would not collaborate with the French and Spanish. The recruits 'were a bizarre collection of ethnic groups drawn, largely in family units, from all over the Mediterranean' – Italians from Livorno, refugees from the southern Peloponnesus, Corsican Greeks, people from Crete, Smyrna, Melos, Santorini, and 200 Minorcan stowaways; 'all of them were refugees from political and religious oppression'. For these minorities, the prospect of national revolution would only become a reality in the nineteenth century. For the time being, displacement was the only option. See Bernard Bailyn, *Voyagers to the West: A Passage in the Peopling of America on the Eve of the Revolution* (New York: Knopf, 1987), pp. 451, 452, 454, 459.

93 Benjamin Franklin, 'Information to Those Who Would Remove to America' (1782), available at press-pubs.uchicago.edu.

'though there are in that Country [America] few People so miserable as the Poor of Europe, there are also very few that in Europe would be called rich; it is rather a general happy Mediocrity that prevails.'[94] There was no need for persons seeking civil or military offices and sinecures, or for individuals who would seek to advance their status by way of their aristocratic birth. No special incentives were needed: 'the government does not at present, whatever it may have done in former times, hire People to become Settlers, by Paying their Passages, giving Land, Negroes, Utensils, Stock, or any other kind of Emolument whatsoever.'[95] Farmers, however, were welcome, 'insomuch that the Propriety of an hundred Acres of fertile Soil full of Wood may be obtained near the Frontiers, in many Places, for Eight or Ten Guineas, hearty young Labouring Men, who understand the Husbandry of Corn and Cattle, which is nearly the same in that Country as in Europe, may easily establish themselves there.'[96]

Craftsmen, supplying farmers in the context of rapid demographic increase, were also welcome. This was a society where what would become known as primitive accumulation was undone by the labourers' ongoing ability to relocate onto cheaply available land: in America 'Hands [are] difficult to [keep] together, every one desiring to be a Master, and the Cheapness of Lands inclining many to leave Trades for Agriculture.'[97] Franklin focused especially on the effects of rapid demographic increase:

> In America, the rapid Increase of Inhabitants takes away that Fear of Rivalship, and Artisans willingly receive Apprentices from the hope of Profit by their Labour, during the Remainder of the Time stipulated [in their indenture], after they shall be instructed. Hence it is easy for poor Families to get their Children instructed; for the Artisans are so desirous of Apprentices, that many of them will even give Money to the Parents, to have Boys from Ten to Fifteen Years of Age bound Apprentices to them till the Age of Twenty-one; and many poor Parents have, by that means, on their Arrival in the Country, raised

94 Ibid.
95 Ibid.
96 Ibid.
97 Ibid.

Money enough to buy Land sufficient to establish themselves, and to subsist the rest of their Family by Agriculture.[98]

Constant expansion – displacement into an outside – would undo contradictions. Franklin agreed with both Harrington and Winthrop.

Who had actually 'removed'? Franklin's call came at the end of a century when settler colonialism had been intensely practiced. In many ways it was a retrospective analysis. The Ulster Scots, or Scots-Irish, among other collectives, had turned the world inside out for decades. Ireland, and especially Ulster, had been a testing ground – the world turned inside out was tested there, and it was exported from there. But this group's re-emigration is significant, because it confirms the choice to relocate as a political tradition. Between 1718 and 1775, more than 100,000 men and women migrated from Ulster to the North American colonies, in the largest such movement in the eighteenth century.[99] This collective is difficult to define: not English, they did not hold power; not Scottish, they often came from Ireland; not Irish, they often originated from Scotland. Why did they leave the Old World? Many feared that a 'counterrevolution', a political upheaval that would undo the Glorious Revolution, was inevitable – they felt that their privilege as Protestants in Ireland would be threatened.[100] The Ulster Presbyterians did not command the state; members of the established church did. If Presbyterians were tolerated in England and ascendant in Scotland, they could be neither in Ireland. But it was the *prospect* of regime change, the perceived likelihood of revolutionary upheaval, that contributed to creating the conditions for their collective displacement.

Moreover, the expansion of linen manufacturing in Ireland had brought opportunity, but it also brought exposure to market downturns. Many Scots-Irish families had lost whatever security they once held,

98 Ibid.

99 Patrick Griffin, *The People with No Name: Ireland's Ulster Scots, America's Scots Irish, and the Creation of a British Atlantic World, 1689–1764* (Princeton, NJ: Princeton University Press, 2001), p. 1. James Webb – who unquestioningly, and yet questionably, identified with them – called them a 'new people, strong and unfulfilled'. James Webb, *Born Fighting: How the Scots-Irish Shaped America* (New York: Broadway, 2004), pp. 116–17. See also Warren R. Hofstra, ed., *Ulster to America: The Scots-Irish Migration Experience, 1680–1830* (Knoxville: University of Tennessee Press, 2012).

100 Griffin, *People with No Name*, p. 11.

while their communities realised that families relying on their involvement in that manufacture were facing new social challenges – challenges that established Presbyterian practices could not easily accommodate (for example, new labour practices were challenging the traditional roles of male householders). This was also a revolution, a market-driven revolution, and a desire to *return* to a previous dispensation was acutely felt. This community already had a collective history of self-constitution and displacement. They had constituted institutions in Ireland immediately after migrating there, and they ostensibly exercised jurisdiction over political and ecclesiastical matters. Their sense of community and their shared experience of a foundational displacement allowed them to embrace the world turned inside out. The Williamite War had brought unsteady economic conditions. The year 1739 had been one of economic depression, further exacerbating social tensions. The Ulster Scots were not the poorest in Ulster, but they were under pressure during economic downturns. They felt that they could only retain their position by moving out.

In America, they would regain access to land, a perception of a 'truer' freedom of religion, and religious and social unity. In America, the Ulster Scots remained exceptionally mobile, and typically joined the Baptist church – a church that, in the words of Patrick Griffin, 'favored an independent form of church government' and was especially suited for 'frontier' conditions.[101] Seriality, mobility and reproducibility characterised their world.[102] Griffin concludes that they were simultaneously at the 'margins of an Atlantic world' and at 'its centre'.[103] The 'centre' was travelling with them towards a world turned inside out.

But the 'people with no name' were not the only people with no name. Bernard Bailyn has focused on 'distressed' Yorkshire 'country folk', who faced 'an uncertain economic future, many in a high state of religious agitation and eager to withdraw into a separate community of like-minded

101 Griffin, *People with No Name*, p. 165.

102 Ed White argued that seriality was a fundamental feature of early settler America: a series of colonies, a series of dispersed farms: 'Dispersal was disintegration, fragmentation, isolation, scattering'. Specifically, White refers to J. Hector St John de Crevecoeur's influential celebration of rural seriality, which he defined as 'an inactive gathering of reciprocal isolation'. Ed White, *The Backcountry and the City: Colonization and Conflict in Early America* (Minneapolis: University of Minnesota Press, 2005), pp. 29, 35.

103 Griffin, *People with No Name*, p. 173.

worshippers.'[104] Often affected by Methodist propaganda, they had a passionate desire to 'draw apart from a corrupt and abusive world and to create a refuge for themselves and their community on the far margins of the British periphery.'[105] The promotional material for emigration to America insisted on the absence of feudal obligations. Nova Scotia, for example, was represented as 'that famous and flourishing country . . . that land of liberty where there are neither game laws nor land tax', and where ordinary people, 'particularly those skilful in the husbandry business', could prosper.[106] Bailyn concluded: 'to the victims of economic instability and to people facing discouraging futures, the advertised prospects of land ownership or cheap rentals in a world free from the power of landlords were far more effective' than cautionary tales about the difficulties of a new life in a new world.[107]

Bailyn also reflected on the particular ways in which information about America was transmitted, and referred to a 'characteristic circuitry of news dissemination':

> It is as if a huge but rather inefficient communication network centered in Yorkshire and the Scottish Lowlands had been in continuous operation, spreading news of population movements randomly throughout the British world. Impulses received at any one point would eventually be felt elsewhere – not necessarily where it mattered – as the printers recirculated materials received at second, third, or fourth hand.[108]

It was an effective network of social information, and it could rely on an added driver, because a desire to avoid landlords was more and more paralleled by a desire also to escape markets (a very demanding landlord

104 See Bailyn, *Voyagers to the West*, pp. 378–9.

105 Ibid., p. 420.

106 Ibid., p. 401. Francis Jennings also noted that 'America' is fundamentally defined by imaginings about feudal orders. But it can go both ways: it is either the representation of a reconstituted (and therefore peaceful) feudal order, or, more frequently, the representation of a circumstance defined by the absence of a feudal order (and therefore by the absence of a struggle to overcome it). They do not reflect the same imaginary, but both emphasise the absence of social strife. See Jennings, *Conquest of America*.

107 Bailyn, *Voyagers to the West*, p. 404.

108 Ibid., pp. 404, 402.

indeed). One settler noted with pride that in America there 'was no need for market days since each farm did its own slaughtering and raised most of what it consumed'.[109]

Escaping markets demanded a specific mode of production and a particular social collective.[110] Allan Kulikoff insightfully defined the latter: 'Neither exploiter nor exploited, most farmers owned land and equipment and worked their farms with family labor . . . they resemble both proletarians and bourgeoisie, and are thereby located in more than one class simultaneously'.[111] These settlers had 'left a dynamically growing capitalist economy, but rejected the commodification of labor already occurring' in England.[112] 'What was exceptional about the rural United States', Kulikoff concluded, 'was not the development of capitalism, but the formation and long history of regional classes of yeomen, living in a capitalist world but not of it'.[113] This resilient formation would in the nineteenth century sustain the world turned inside out during the global settler revolution, but preceded the revolution itself.[114]

109 Ibid., p. 410.

110 See Charles Post, *The American Road to Capitalism: Studies in Class-Structure, Economic Development and Political Conflict, 1620–1877* (Leiden: Brill, 2011).

111 Allan Kulikoff, *The Agrarian Origins of American Capitalism* (Charlottesville: University Press of Virginia, 1992), p. 4. See also Allan Kulikoff, *From British Peasants to Colonial American Farmers* (Chapel Hill, NC: University of North Carolina Press, 2000). In the latter, Kulikoff insisted on crisis. The opening sentence was: 'A sense of crisis pervaded early modern England' (p. 7). The transformation of peasants in one locale into settlers in another begins with crisis, and crisis 'bred rebellion' (p. 7) and displacement, as the would-be emigrants 'looked back on a supposedly more prosperous time and sought to remake it in America' (p. 9). Kulikoff further noted: 'By the early seventeenth century, crisis permeated English society. Enclosures multiplied, peasants lost land, the textile industry faced depression, wage labor spread, and vagabonds tramped every country lane. But rural folk considered permanent wage labor (much less vagabondage) a debased status unworthy of freeborn people, because it made them absolutely dependent on others for their survival . . . wage labor turned the relation of husband and wife upside down' (p. 27). Economic cycles produced social upheaval and a determination to relocate: 'Every seventeenth-century colony was founded during a depression . . . Joint stock companies and proprietors made countercyclical investments, hoping that colonizing would make money at times when few investments were profitable' (p. 53).

112 Kulikoff, *Agrarian Origins of American Capitalism*, p. 59.

113 Ibid., p. 59.

114 In an 1859 speech delivered to the Wisconsin Agricultural Society, future US president Abraham Lincoln still emphasised that most men 'are neither hirers nor hired', but work with their families 'for themselves, on their farms, in their houses and in their

The escape was sometimes violently defended against possible reconnections. The 1767 'War of Regulation in North Carolina' provides an example of such a rearguard defence. The 'Regulators' insisted on direct representation and on binding 'instructions' – a notion that underpins a particular spatial understanding of sovereignty (representation by definition must happen in another location). The Regulators argued that the farmer embodies both the public at large and the community, but maintained that, since the farmer is dispersed, displaced, he must be represented in ways that transcended normal mechanisms. They thought spatially, and the 'instructions' were thus meant to protect a sovereign dispersal against reconcentration: the elected representatives could not change ideas as they travelled away from their remote settlements – displacement could not be undone.[115]

Local settlers had formed a political association in 1766, the Sandy Creek Association in Orange County, North Carolina, and had addressed the colonial assembly in order to express grievances regarding allegations of widespread 'corruption', anxieties about the activities of speculators, and concerns regarding taxation. The North Carolina Assembly saw these activities as tantamount to the erection of a sovereign and separate jurisdiction – an existential challenge to its prerogatives. The original Association was politically moderate, but in 1768 it had radicalised. Increased confrontation ensued, and Regulator ideas spread to other counties. The Regulators tried to elect farmers to the colonial assembly and to impose their notion of representation. Herman Husband was one of the Regulators elected to the Assembly, but he was expelled (he would later participate in the Whiskey Rebellion in Pennsylvania).[116] He had prophesised a 'New Jerusalem' of independent farmers, a 'temple' where 'the walls were the mountains, the gates the

---

shops, taking the whole product to themselves, and asking no favors of capital on the one hand, nor hirelings nor slaves on the other'. For Lincoln, the market revolution was still to be responded to by way of spatial displacement. The mode of production that would sustain this escape was by that time more than a century old. Cited in Kulikoff, *Agrarian Origins of American Capitalism*, p. 95.

115 See Loretta Valtz Mannucci, *Le radici ideologiche degli Stati uniti* (Lecce: Milella, 1981).

116 On the Whiskey Rebellion and its implications for the emerging US republic, see, for example, William Hogeland, *The Whiskey Rebellion: George Washington, Alexander Hamilton, and the Frontier Rebels who Challenged America's Newfound Sovereignty* (New York: Scribner, 2006).

gaps in them by which the roads came, and the sea of glass, the lake on the west of us'.[117] This imagined New Jerusalem was somewhere else, not exactly where he was.

More generally, the decades between 1755 and 1775 saw a remarkable number of backwoodsmen becoming farmers, settling, formalising communities, instituting town meetings and other regular administrative structures, and acquiring political experience. These are crucial moments of settler self-organisation, moments that *precede* formal incorporation in colonial administrations and reconnection. The frontiersmen were opposing a drive towards concentration of property and political power in the hands of the colonial elites. This conflict took the form of an ongoing demand for separation, and was enacted in the context of a long-lasting tradition of backcountry demands. The first draft of the constitution of Kentucky proclaimed that allowing an individual to own more land than he could cultivate would subvert the fundamental principles of a 'free' republic (this radical compact would be moderated shortly after). Vermont also adopted a radical democratic constitution; its denunciation of New England's religious intolerance and its embrace of the 'Great Awakening' followed a similar pattern. Pennsylvania's original 'democratic' constitution was also 'moderated' in later years. The land must belong to its cultivators, it was argued; any compromise on this proposition would reproduce the 'Old World' within the new.

Given this pre-existing tradition, the American Revolution itself could be seen as, among other things, an attempt simultaneously to preempt and manage reconnection.[118] It resulted in a state, and those who

117 Cited in Sioli, 'Huguenot Traditions in the Mountains of Kentucky', at p. 1,320.

118 Besides, whether it can be seen as a 'revolution' is debatable, and Edmund Morgan concluded that the Revolution 'came about not to overthrow tyranny, but to prevent it'. Edmund S. Morgan, *The Genuine Article: A Historian Looks at Early America* (New York: Norton, 2005), p. 237. See also Eric Nelson, *The Royalist Revolution: Monarchy and the American Founding* (Cambridge, MA: Belknap Press of Harvard University, 2014). For an argument about displacement as antithetical (and also indifferent) to revolution (settler North America was much larger than the theatre of the Revolutionary War on the eastern seaboard), see Claudio Saunt, *West of the Revolution: An Uncommon History of 1776* (New York: Norton, 2014). On the American Revolution as a reactionary moment, see, for example, Gerald Horne, *The Counter-Revolution of 1776: Slave Resistance and the Origins of the United States of America* (New York: New York University Press, 2014).

embraced images of Jeffersonian, self-reliant, federally enabled isolation from a contradiction-ridden North Atlantic world and projected them onto the 'Old Northwest' aimed to use this state to protect separation.[119] As Joyce Appleby has insightfully noted, 'America' was thus indeed a veritable world-project. It remained so after independence; indeed, it became even more so after independence.[120]

Appleby stressed how the putative absence of 'Old World' evils was making revolution, in the eyes of observers, simultaneously unnecessary and impossible in America:

> America, in the minds of attentive European observers of the eighteenth century, was exceptional because its healthy, young, hardworking population had won a revolutionary prize of an empty continent upon which to settle its freeborn progeny. America was exceptional because the familiar predators on ordinary folk – the extorting tax collector, the overbearing nobleman, the persecuting priest, the extravagant ruler – had failed to make the voyage across the Atlantic.[121]

It had been a selective displacement. Appleby cites Elisabeth d'Houdetot who, writing in 1790, when the violent career of the French Revolution had barely begun, remarked that 'the characteristic difference between [the American] revolution and ours is that having nothing to destroy,

119 See Peter S. Onuf and Leonard J. Sadosky, *Jeffersonian America* (Malden, MA: Blackwell, 2002).

120 Appleby called for the abandonment of 'that venerable tale about a singular national destiny' and notions of American exceptionalism. She argued that the United States 'became a political prodigy in reference to a consensus shared by Continental *philosophes*, English Dissenters, and radical pamphleteers'. Joyce Appleby, 'Recovering America's Historic Diversity: Beyond Exceptionalism', *Journal of American History* 79: 2 (1992), p. 420. 'America' would remain a world project. On the imaginary of 'the West' as a location for possible new polities (on the West as a world-project), see David Wrobel, *Promised Lands: Promotion, Memory and the Creation of the American West* (Lawrence: University Press of Kansas, 2002). On boosterist representations of the West for international audiences, see David Wrobel, *Global West, American Frontier: 19th and 20th-Century Travelers' Accounts* (Santa Fe, NM: University of New Mexico Press, 2013). On images of settler-colonial America in France, see Durand Echeverria, *Mirage in the West: A History of the French Image of American Society to 1815* (Princeton, NJ: Princeton University Press, 1957).

121 Appleby, 'Recovering America's Historic Diversity', p. 420.

you had nothing to injure'.[122] Appleby concludes that, 'by construing their own liberty as liberation from historic institutions, the enthusiasts of democracy made the United States the pilot society for the world'.[123] And yet, all the worlds turned inside out construe their liberty as a liberation from history, and all express a firm belief in their own 'pilot' role – they are all world-projects, as far as they are concerned. But America was the first to frame itself in this way.

Creole revolutions

The 'age of revolutions' was a truly global phenomenon, and each revolution prompted voluntary as well as nonvoluntary displacements. The American Revolution prompted a veritable settler colonial diaspora, as the British Loyalists were displaced to what would become Canada and to many other locations.[124] This diaspora engaged in intense polity-making. Maya Jasanoff has referred to the 'Spirit of 1783' as a global political project developing in the context of a particularly intense revolutionary conjuncture, when the Haitian Revolution loomed as large as its American and French counterparts.[125] Nova Scotia, New Brunswick, Upper Canada and Sierra Leone were all colonies established or re-established as a response to revolution elsewhere. It was a significant displacement, and the Loyalists who departed with slaves and freedmen may have been 2.5 per cent of the Thirteen Colonies' pre-revolutionary population.[126] The Black Loyalists who went to Freetown, Sierra Leone, may have been 1,200 in number.[127] The Spirit of 1783 was thus about renewed imperial growth through spatial expansion and a commitment to upholding hierarchical relations. This 'spirit' also concerned the

122 Cited in ibid., p. 420. Of course, d'Houdetot's logic only works if one neglects to consider the exclusion of slaves, women and indigenous peoples from the bounds of moral concern.

123 Appleby, 'Recovering America's Historic Diversity', p. 426.

124 See Robert M. Calhoon, *The Loyalists in Revolutionary America* (New York, Harcourt Brace, 1973); Norman Knowles, *Inventing the Loyalists: The Ontario Loyalist Tradition and the Creation of Usable Pasts* (Toronto: University of Toronto Press, 1997).

125 Maya Jasanoff, *Liberty's Exiles: American Loyalists in the Revolutionary World* (New York: Knopf, 2011).

126 Ibid., p. 6.

127 Ibid., p. 10.

sovereign prerogatives of the Loyalists. Hierarchical relations and settler sovereignty, antithetical in the forming of the United States, could be articulated in the wider British Empire through spatial expansion.

Jasanoff has emphasised that the Loyalists were not 'backward-looking reactionaries', and that they articulated their rights in ways that resonated with the claims of their revolutionary counterparts.[128] Once the decision was taken to evacuate, Sir Guy Carleton, who had been charged with organising the evacuation from New York and the other strongholds remaining in British hands, was instructed to help them move to 'whatever other parts of America in His Majesty's possession they choose to settle'.[129] The Loyalists were thus refugees, but were also endowed with rights. They could choose to locate themselves almost anywhere in the empire, but apart from a few exceptions Britain was ruled out as a destination. This was a 'diaspora' that was to gather somewhere else, so its rights were place-specific. But it consisted of settlers who travelled with rights, provisions and supplies. They could acquire title to land on arrival.

In New York, while awaiting evacuation, some Loyalists intending to emigrate to Nova Scotia had autonomously established their own association, a sign of their political independence. These settlers would prove restive in their new location, and even clash with the authorities. Their settlement (Shelbourne) would not last. Some Loyalists in East Florida even considered a coup in order to prevent the colony's cession to Spain.[130] Some Black Loyalists had been transported to Britain, where they were left to themselves; but their abject poverty and unemployment had afterwards become a 'problem'. Some asked to be transported again, and lobbied for their relocation to Sierra Leone as free colonists. In 1786, they were sent in a hastily organised expedition. That 'First Fleet' was a disaster, and the colony soon disappeared. Others planned to colonise Australia with Loyalists, or convicts.[131] The other 'First Fleet' was a disaster for the Aboriginal inhabitants of Australia. Revolution in the Thirteen Colonies prompted renewed imperial efforts in every direction. Crisis provoked further displacement.

128 Ibid., p. 33.
129 Cited ibid., p. 63.
130 Ibid., p. 105.
131 Ibid., p. 141.

All these colonial endeavours were an expression of a particular settler-colonial sensibility focusing on alternatives to revolution. New Brunswick, recently separated from Nova Scotia, was 'the closest thing Loyalists had to their own state'.[132] It could be represented as a veritable hierarchical-colonial utopia, and the local Loyalist elite enthroned itself. This was a new society, an early instance of what would become known as 'systematic' colonisation. New Brunswick was 'a chance to construct a whole colonial state along [the elite's] preferred lines'; 'a neo-feudal oligarchy'.[133] It was a Loyalist-'majority state'; as one of its promoters suggested, the 'most Gentlemanlike on Earth'.[134] Its capital city would not be near the water, a possible source of revolutionary contamination; it had to be nestled among landed estates. The elite entrenched itself, elections were annulled, repression ensued.[135]

Nearby Nova Scotia had welcomed the largest groups of Loyalist refugees, but the colony had struggled to cope as its settler population had doubled in a few months. Discontent had flared – land grants, even though they had been promised, were being allocated too slowly. In their demands, the local settlers sounded like the Patriots they were escaping from.[136] Upper Canada had been carved out of Quebec (and out of indigenous lands, of course) in a way similar to that in which New Brunswick had been carved out of Nova Scotia. Carleton (now Lord Dorchester) imagined establishing there an authoritarian multiethnic empire, but others wanted a 'New Britain in the west'.[137]

Many more displacements in the British Empire followed the European revolutionary wars ('New Geneva', for example, was once in Ireland); but displacements would follow the end of the revolutionary wars, too.[138] The organised transfer of the British 'Emigrants of 1820' to

132 Ibid., p. 152.

133 Ibid., pp. 179, 182.

134 Ibid., pp. 180, 182.

135 William Cobbett was a witness to this repression. His memories of the 1785 New Brunswick election were critical in shaping his later advocacy of parliamentary reform in Britain. In this instance, repression in the colony was displaced to become reform in the metropole. See Jasanoff, *Liberty's Exiles*, pp. 187–9.

136 Ibid., p. 170.

137 Ibid., p. 204.

138 The defeat of the Genevan Revolution of 1782 had prompted plans to establish in Ireland a colony of exiled republican Genevan exiles, mainly skilled workers employed in the watchmaking industry. The Genevan revolution had been

the Cape Colony represented a crucial turning point in this evolution: unlike the Loyalist refugees of previous decades, these emigrants participated in a thoroughly planned resettlement.[139] There were 800 families, mainly from England, organised into sixty distinct pre-organised groups. Free land, subsidised passage, and subsistence en route were additional enticements – it was a state-aided emigration scheme – but a number of very respectable emigrants were included, too. There were three types of 'group': proprietary (with indentured personnel following a proprietor), joint-stock (comprising independent applicants sharing jointly in the enterprise), and 'other' (individuals sponsored by parishes, for example). As Alan Brunger has noted, joint-stock groups 'were from the outset more communal and had in many cases signed "Articles of agreements" for mutual support or had formed cooperative societies prior to emigrating'.[140] That the societies were formed *before* departure was a marker of a specific constitutive capacity; that this scheme was explicitly linked to the need to quell domestic unrest after the shocking repression of the workers' movement at Peterloo should also be noted.

Later still, in what would become South Africa (even if in the context of a completely distinct milieu – this was an anti-British movement, even if it was prompted by a British movement), Voortrekker leader Piet Retief's 1837 'anticolonial manifesto' would articulate a world turned inside out and its justification:

---

repressed by the armies of France and Savoy, and by Swiss troops from Bern, and many had fled. The British government supported the idea – skilled Protestant labourers who opposed the French would be welcome. Southern Ireland would be preferable to England or Northern Ireland. There, the New Genevans would not compete with English watchmakers, or collaborate with Irish republicans. In the south, the newcomers would also help in countering the threat of peasant revolt. Diplomatic pressure against the prospect of resettlement, delays in approving a grant that would allow the watchmakers to establish themselves, and the reconciliation policy pursued by the new Genevan authorities convinced the 1,000 to 2,000 exiled revolutionaries to return. See F. Ferretti, 'Pioneers in the History of Cartography: The Geneva Map Collection of Élisée Reclus and Charles Perron', *Journal of Historical Geography* 43 (2014); P. Jupp, 'Genevese Exiles in County Waterford', *Journal of the Cork Historical and Archaeological Society* 75 (1970), Jennifer Powell McNutt and Richard Whatmore, 'The Attempts to Transfer the Genevan Academy to Ireland and America, 1782–1795', *Historical Journal* 56: 2 (2013).

139 See, for example, Alan G. Brunger, 'The Geographical Context of Planned Group Settlement in Cape Colony: The 1820s British Emigrants', *Journal of Historical Geography* 29: 1 (2003).

140 Brunger, 'Geographical Context of Planned Group Settlement', p. 63.

> 1. We despair of saving the colony from those evils which threaten it by the turbulent and dishonest conduct of vagrants, who are allowed to infest the country in every part; nor do we see any prospect of peace and happiness for our children in a country thus distracted by internal commotions . . .
> 6. We solemnly declare that *we quit this colony with a desire to lead a more quiet life* than we have heretofore done . . .
> 7. We make known that when we shall have framed a code of laws for our future guidance, copies shall be forwarded to the colony for general information . . .[141]

Against turbulence, vagrancy and internal commotion, the manifesto juxtaposed peace, happiness and familial relations somewhere else. This was a self-constituting settler-colonial collective that understood itself as endowed with an inherent law-making capacity linked to an ability to relocate. The conflict between the Boers and the imperial bureaucracy stemmed crucially from the latter's attempt to access *all* people subjected to settler control. The first British governor of the Cape attempted to regulate employment contracts between settlers and 'Hottentots'. In the 1830s the emancipation of slaves constituted a further acceleration of this process. An imperial arrogation of sovereignty was in a way revolutionary, and contributed crucially to framing the trekkers' decision to relocate. The Boer trekkers were escaping imperially endorsed emancipation – a development they perceived as a genuine revolution.[142]

But if revolution in the Old World was prompting displacement, displacement to the New World was prompting revolutions. According to Joshua Simon, the 'creole revolutions' are comparable with each other (they could indeed be seen as a single revolution), and resulted from an important type of displacement: the creoles' final and *political*

141 Cited in W. A. De Klerk, *The Puritans in Africa: A Story of Afrikanerdom* (London: Rex Collings, 1975), p. 22 (emphasis added).

142 See, for example, John L. Comaroff, 'Images of Empire: Models of Colonial Domination in South Africa', in Frederick Cooper and Ann Laura Stoler, eds, *Tensions of Empire: Colonial Cultures in a Bourgeois World* (Berkeley: University of California Press, 1997). Jürgen Osterhammel interprets the Boer exodus as a response to the 'social revolution brought about by the liberation of the Cape slaves in 1834'. Jürgen Osterhammel, *The Transformation of the World: A Global History of the Nineteenth Century* (Princeton, NJ: Princeton University Press, 2014), p. 354.

realisation of a permanent relocation to the New World.[143] Simon focused on the political thought of the American Alexander Hamilton, the Venezuelan Simón Bolívar and the Mexican Lucas Alamán. The creole revolutions were the revolutions of many elsewheres. They also promoted further displacements.

Displacement and revolution chased each other and proceeded together. Projects envisaging settler colonisation in the early creole republics – and even earlier, in late colonial Latin America – were designed to counter the risk of revolution. Ernesto Bassi has outlined a number of failed immigration schemes, and cited the notion, articulated in 1824, of one of Colombia's founding fathers that white, northern and western European immigration – even Protestant immigration – was especially needed to reduce the 'risk of a civil war with blacks and *mulatos*'.[144] Earlier policies were also designed to mitigate revolutionary tensions, and the Spanish colonial authorities consistently believed that northern European immigrants would enhance the loyalty of all subjects. A century later, the Spanish colonial authorities were still pursuing similar schemes, and, as Cuba burned during the first war of independence, the colonial authorities were imagining a resettled order through displacement. An official scheme in 1871 proposed to import between 40,000 and 50,000 German immigrants to the island.[145] Following a similar logic, and facing revolution during the second war of independence, they thought of displacing entire populations to strategic locations under a policy of 'reconcentration'. These were the first concentration camps.[146] But cramming the countryside with German settlers or

143 Joshua Simon, *The Ideology of Creole Revolution: Imperialism and Independence in American and Latin American Political Thought* (Cambridge: Cambridge University Press, 2017). See also Hilda Sabato, *Republics of the New World: The Revolutionary Political Experiment in 19th-Century Latin America* (Princeton, NJ: Princeton University Press, 2018).

144 Ernesto Bassi, 'The "Franklins of Colombia": Immigration Schemes and Hemispheric Solidarity in the Making of a Civilised Colombian Nation', *Journal of Latin American Studies* 50 (2017), p. 677.

145 See Luis Álvarez Gutiérrez, 'Un proyecto de colonización alemana para la Isla de Cuba en 1871', in Consuelo Naranjo Orovio and Tomás Mallo Gutiérrez, eds, *Cuba, la perla de las Antillas: Actas de las I Jornadas sobre 'Cuba y su Historia'* (Madrid: Doce Calles, 1994).

146 See Iain R. Smith and Andreas Stucki, 'The Colonial Development of Concentration Camps (1868–1902)', *Journal of Imperial and Commonwealth History* 39: 3 (2011).

emptying it entirely of unmanageable populations were two sides of the same coin. Displacement was still understood as an antidote to revolution.

Likewise, failed displacements (for example, a national bourgeoisie's sustained subordination to foreign cultural standards rather than its ability to craft autonomous ones) have been linked to failed revolutions. Argentinian novelist Osvaldo Soriano, for example, interpreted the country's difficult history as a consequence of failed revolution.[147] The revolutionary component of the independence movement was defeated, he noted, but the liberal canon later claimed the revolutionaries even as it disavowed their political project. Mariano Moreno's *Plan de Operaciones*, in which Moreno emerges as an 'expropriator of colonial fortunes', was forgotten. Cornelio Saavedra wanted independence; Juan José Castelli wanted revolution. Belgrano belonged to the revolutionary camp, and so did Rivadivia; but the former expressed an 'indigenising' position, and thought that an Inca king could be enthroned, while the latter advocated replicating European models. In the end, creole independence needed all the help it could muster, and relied on both Indian and foreign support (Castelli depended on the insurgencies of the Indios, while Carlos Maria Alvear invited annexation by the British). Ultimately, however, revolution was defeated; the landowners set up profitable trading relations with the British as they repressed the revolutionary option. In Soriano's rendition, a compromised revolutionary tradition resulted in a defective world turned inside out.

Many believed afterwards that this settler colonial deficit could be rectified. Future president of Argentina, Domingo Faustino Sarmiento, visited Algeria in 1846, where he met the French generals and was impressed by plans to attract 2 million colonists. He hoped that a similar

147 Osvaldo Soriano, *Cuentos de los años felices* (Buenos Aires: Editorial Sudamericana, 1994). Failed revolution is also emphasised in Maurice Zeitlin's analysis of Chile's nineteenth-century civil wars. Zeitlin described two failed revolutionary moments, one from below, in the 1850s, and one from above, during the presidency of José Manuel Emiliano Balmaceda (1886–91). After the final 'pacification' of the Araucanos in the early 1880s, 'settlement' had become the Balmaceda administration's priority. Balmaceda declared two new provinces, Malleco and Cautin, and 'opened up' the frontier areas to settlers of modest means. The *latifundistas* did not approve of a policy that was depriving them of cheap labour, and launched a successful civil war to remove him. See Maurice Zeitlin, *The Civil Wars in Chile (Or the Bourgeois Revolutions That Never Were)* (Princeton, NJ: Princeton University Press, 1984).

scheme could be developed 'from the Rio de la Plata to the Andes'. During the second half of the nineteenth century, all of the Latin American elites consistently tried to address a perceived deficit by 'whitening' their countries, and thus neutralising the possibility of insurgencies led by non-whites. Countless schemes designed to facilitate immigration were pursued in this context, and between 1870 and 1914 about 5 million Europeans migrated to Brazil and Argentina.[148] In these cases, unlike in the North American settler republic, political separation was established first. The political traditions of settler colonialism were to be imported subsequently.

Displaced common sense

The most successful of the creole revolutions was the North American one. Thomas Paine's *Common Sense* (1776) had advocated separation. A typical member of the 'settler classes', bankrupt and without a job, Paine had gone to London in 1774, and then to America.[149] Dissenting Protestantism (Paine hailed from a Quaker background) was a crucial element in the formation of his radicalism.[150] But that radicalism was in a sense more about displacement in general than about 'America' in particular; as Isaac Kramnick has remarked, neither America nor independence is mentioned 'until well into the pamphlet'.[151] *Common Sense* is less a manifesto for America than for the broader settler-colonialist project:

> In order to gain a clear and just idea of the design and end of government, let us suppose a small number of persons settled in some sequestered part of the earth, unconnected with the rest; they will then represent the first peopling of any country, or of the world. In this state of natural liberty, society will be their first thought.[152]

148 See Richard Gott, 'Latin America as a White Settler Society', *Bulletin of Latin American Research* 26: 2 (2007), p. 286.

149 See Isaac Kramnick, 'Editor's Introduction', in Thomas Paine, *Common Sense* (London: Penguin, 1986), p. 27.

150 See ibid., p. 41.

151 Ibid., p. 38.

152 Thomas Paine, *Common Sense* (1776), available at marxists.org

'Men' are originally disconnected from government; they are 'sequestered' in unspecific locations, spatially separate, and live in a 'state of natural liberty'. Then government comes. Paine insists: the ideal relationship between society and government requires a minimalist administration that interferes as little as possible with a spontaneously harmonious polity:

> Some convenient tree will afford them a State House, under the branches of which the whole colony may assemble to deliberate on public matters. It is more than probable that their first laws will have the title only of regulations and be enforced by no other penalty than public disesteem. In this first parliament every man by natural right will have a seat.[153]

Growth would demand ever more government. If a remote colony on the frontier was at one extreme of the simplicity–complexity spectrum of possibility, the English constitution comprised 'the base remains of two ancient tyrannies, compounded with some new republican materials'.[154] Not only were they different, occupying opposite ends of a spectrum of possibility, government and 'natural' polity were *spatially* distinct.

Most importantly, while in Britain Paine was a revolutionary, in America he was not. He chose America, arguing for its independence and for a repudiation of aristocratic and monarchic privileges; but his main argument for political separation was that the two territories were already spatially separate. Radical egalitarianism was his stance in one location, but a defence of property rights characterised his posture in another. Displacement had transformed his politics. Much later, in *Agrarian Justice* (1797), Paine suggested that fifteen pounds be paid to every person on turning twenty-one: a social entitlement that would have ensured the establishment of a yeoman republic of independent landowners. It was a proposal very similar to that found in Harrington's *Oceana*, a proposal also evoked in Lane's later 'common-hold'.

Paine feared that Britain's continued influence on America would compromise the viability of the world turned inside out (even though he

153 Ibid.
154 Ibid.

did not use these terms, of course). Should that influence persist, the settler classes – the 'persons' Franklin had singled out in his 'Considerations' – would not want to move to America, and political life of a settler-colonial world would be engulfed by revolutionary upheaval. In *Common Sense*, Paine had evoked the possibility that 'some Massanello may hereafter arise, who laying hold of popular disquietudes, may collect together the desperate and the discontented, and by assuming to themselves the powers of government, may sweep away the liberties of the continent like a deluge'.[155] He feared upheaval, and he knew that, '[s] hould the government of America return again into the hands of Britain', upheaval would be inevitable.[156] His common sense recommended the avoidance of one revolution through the embrace of another.

155 Ibid.
156 Ibid.

2

The World Turned Inside Out up to The Peak of the Global Settler Revolution

During the nineteenth century, and in conjunction with the global 'settler revolution' the political traditions of the world turned inside out flourished spectacularly. This was the global 'age of revolutions'; but the search for alternatives to revolution proceeded at a fierce rate, too.[1]

'Captain Swing' heralded a major revolutionary crisis in post-1815 England. By then, as Eric Hobsbawm and George Rudé have noted, the 'typical English agriculturalist was a hired man', and the demand was for wage rises, not land.[2] The main social problem in rural Britain was not the enclosures, but an oversupply of labour and chronically depressed wages. The social and economic gulf between tenant farmer and labourer had widened, and they were no longer sharing the same social space. As one of Hobsbawm and Rudé's sources noted, 'the Masters and the Labourers [had] parted'.[3] English rural workers were tied to specific parishes, where they could access relief; it was the poor-relief system that meant many would find it easier to migrate to Tasmania than to the next county. At the origin of this agrarian crisis was the market 'revolution'. Aristocrats, squires and farmers had embraced it; they were

1 Eric J. Hobsbawm, *The Age of Revolution, 1789–1846* (New York: New American Library, 1962).

2 Eric J. Hobsbawm and George Rudé, *Captain Swing: A Social History of the Great Agricultural Rising of 1830* (New York: W. W. Norton, 1975). Connecting metropole and settler colony, the book includes a chapter on colonial Australia.

3 Cited in ibid., p. 46.

pursuing a new economy, and yet 'did not want it to disrupt a society of ordered ranks'.[4]

Predominantly rural and disconnected from the towns, the agricultural poor would not formally organise, but they fought back in traditional ways. Still, their fight had important consequences, even if it was ruthlessly repressed. Hobsbawm and Rudé emphasised the authorities' sense of panic, and linked the social legislation of the early 1830s and the 1832 Reform Act to this struggle.[5] But the most prominent outcome of this rural uprising may be the emergence and subsequent ascendancy of the colonial reform movement. By the 1830s, the transportation of a rural proletariat to Australia was no longer simply about offloading unwanted human material. Some of the convicts as well as the free settlers were even deemed appropriate for an embryonic world turned inside out. Tasmania's governor, Colonel Arthur, called them convicts of 'the better sort'.[6] The Van Diemen's Land Company sought these convicts especially – they were the ones suitable for its expansionary designs. Some of the transportees were even reunited with their families at the government's expense; many did very well in the Australian colonies.

Edward Gibbon Wakefield was crucially concerned with the possibility of revolution, and even wrote a pamphlet on 'Captain Swing'.[7] He knew that, in 1830, news of the French and Belgian revolutions had been crucial in promoting rural agitation in England, and he also knew that the crisis was hitting farmers and rural labourers more than anyone else. He intended to pre-empt a revolutionary crisis he felt was imminent, and endeavoured to promote a general movement for colonial reform. Like him, the British 'colonial reformers' and those who promoted his schemes throughout the British Empire were responding to the rising prospect of revolutionary agitation in the metropole.[8] But, in the wider British Empire,

4 Ibid., p. 47.

5 See ibid., pp. 296–7.

6 Cited ibid., p. 248.

7 Edward Gibbon Wakefield, *Swing Unmasked, or the Causes of Rural Incendiarism* (London: E. Wilson, 1831).

8 In *Responsible Government* (1840), Charles Buller had argued that, lacking a government that would be responsible to the settlers, the settler colonies were 'always verging on revolution'. Charles Buller, *Responsible Government* (London: James Ridgway, 1840), p. 10. The colonies had to be stabilised against possible revolutionary convulsions, and the radicals argued that the government there should be made responsible to public

as Jane Lydon has suggested, his schemes were a response to another revolutionary process: the abolition of slavery.[9]

In more abstract terms, Wakefield had discovered the operation of capitalism (as Marx would point out) and detected its tendency to accumulate contradictions.[10] However, Wakefield believed that the displacement of labour and capital could undo growing contradictions. He was explicit about his counterrevolutionary aspirations:

> for a country now situated like England, in which the ruling and the subject orders are no longer separated by a middle class, and in which the subject order, composing the bulk of the people, are in a state of gloomy discontent arising from excessive numbers; for such a country, one chief end of colonization is to prevent tumults, to keep the peace, to maintain order, to uphold confidence in the security of property, to hinder interruptions to the regular course of industry and trade, to avert the terrible evils which, in a country like England, could not but follow any serious political convulsion.[11]

But circumstances in the colonies concerned him, too. Labour was scarce there, and the availability of cheap or free land resulted in a subsistence economy that he perceived as a kind of 'agrarian barbarism'.

He thus saw degeneration abroad and revolution at home, and imagined many worlds turned inside out instead: the settler colonies were to become agrarian appendages of the industrial metropole, separate spatially but united economically and politically. The 'sufficient price' of

---

opinion. For them, government should be displaced, too – a radical departure from colonial doctrine.

9 Citing promoter of settler colonies Edward Gibbon Wakefield, Lydon concludes: 'Settler colonialism itself can in this sense be seen as a response to the loss of the "human trade in flesh"'. Jane Lydon, 'A Secret Longing for a Trade in Human Flesh: The Decline of British Slavery and the Making of the Settler Colonies', *History Workshop Journal* 90 (Autumn 2020), p. 191.

10 See Mark Neocleous, 'International Law as Primitive Accumulation; Or, the Secret of Systematic Colonization', *European Journal of International Law* 23 (2012); Gabriel Piterberg and Lorenzo Veracini, 'Wakefield, Marx and the World Turned Inside Out', *Journal of Global History* 10: 3 (2015).

11 Cited in Duncan Bell, 'John Stuart Mill on Colonies', *Political Theory* 38: 1 (2010), p. 46.

land, the cornerstone of his 'system', was to ensure that labour in the colonies would remain available and relatively cheap. He was a most unorthodox political economist; Malthus had argued that social distress would find a natural solution – namely, death and starvation; but Wakefield realised that social distress would likely result in revolution instead. He had discovered primitive accumulation (even if he did not use the term), and intended to reproduce it even where it was undone by the availability of cheap or free land on expanding frontiers. Unlike Marx, he approved of primitive accumulation – but, like Marx, he understood its consequences.

Most importantly, as Marx would, Wakefield believed that capitalism tended to produce the conditions for its own demise. Wakefield was a critic of capitalism, even though his was a critique from within.[12] Pauperisation was not the only problem; the sons of the lesser gentry were finding no career opportunities, and small capitalists were downwardly mobile – he would have known, as he was one of them. This was the social revolution that most concerned Wakefield, because, if the conditions of the labouring poor would necessarily deteriorate before they could improve, an imminent revolutionary crisis was inevitable. A 'ruined man is a dangerous citizen', Wakefield sourly noted, before adding, 'there are at all times in this country more people who have been ruined than in any other country'.[13] But Britain's post-war distress was also one result of capitalism's diminishing rate of profit – a decline that was damning the 'middle or uneasy class'. Wakefield was thus sure that a 'servile war' was coming.[14] A disastrous outcome would be inevitable: if the working classes lost, they and therefore the economy that relied on them would be destroyed; if they won, there would be 'a revolution of property'.[15] The crisis was coming; the world turned inside out beckoned.

12 As Bernard Semmel observed, Wakefield had anticipated the Marxian analysis with regard to both the growing contradictions of capitalism and the inevitability of social disruption. Bernard Semmel, *The Liberal Ideal and the Demons of Empire: Theories of Imperialism from Adam Smith to Lenin* (Baltimore: Johns Hopkins University Press, 1993), p. 31.

13 Edward Gibbon Wakefield, 'A View of the Art of Colonization' (1849), in M. F. Lloyd Pritchard, ed., *The Collected Works of Edward Gibbon Wakefield* (Glasgow: Collins, 1968), p. 799.

14 Cited in Bernard Semmel, 'The Philosophic Radicals and Colonialism', *The Journal of Economic History* 21: 4 (1961), p. 517.

15 Ibid.

Wakefield deployed an expanded understanding of revolution; for him, the universal franchise, for example, would indeed represent a revolution, because laws promulgated by the representatives of a poor and discontented multitude would invariably target private wealth. His solution was not class warfare or repression – the reactionary option – but the displacement of both capital and labour. To avoid revolution, Wakefield suggested turning the imperial possessions into sites for social experimentation – a move that required a significant paradigm shift, because emigration was still regarded at the time either as a net loss to the national economy, or, as Charles Buller had noted in parliament in 1834, as primarily a means of 'shovelling out paupers to where they may die without shocking their betters with the sight or sound of their last agony'.[16] Either way, before Wakefield's interventions, the focus was still fixed on the metropole, not on his distant 'laboratories'.[17]

For Wakefield, revolution was regression in the metropole and regression on the frontier. America was the degenerative template in this context, but Wakefield detected such a tendency in South Africa, in Canada, in Australia, and in Argentina: 'barbarism', whereby every colonist 'gradually learns to like the baser order of things, takes a pleasure in the coarse licence and physical excitement of less civilized life', was inevitable unless undone by 'systematic colonisation' and organised displacement.[18] If revolution in the metropole would take the shape of property confiscation, in the colonies it would take the shape of population dispersion. The end-result was the same: subsistence production was the antithesis of the wage relation, or what Wakefield called 'capitalist civilisation'. For him, the American backwoodsmen and the world's indigenous people were ultimately the same (they dwelled equally outside 'capitalist civilisation'), and the 'white savages of Kentucky' – 'a people without monuments, without history, without local attachments . . . without any love of birthplace, without patriotism' – had definitely regressed to the

16 Cited in Onur Ulas Ince, *Colonial Capitalism and the Dilemmas of Liberalism* (Oxford: Oxford University Press, 2018), p. 128. Donald Winch also emphasised the crucial shift in public discourse from a rejection of the benefits of emigration to an embrace of 'colonization'. Winch highlighted Wakefield's crucial contribution to promoting this transition. See Donald Winch, *Classical Political Economy and Colonies* (London: Bell, 1965).

17 See Simon Barber, 'In Wakefield's Laboratory: Tangata Whenua into Property/Labour in Te Waipounamu', *Journal of Sociology* 56: 2 (2020).

18 Wakefield, 'View of the Art of Colonization', p. 873.

state of 'English Tartars'.[19] Subsistence farming was undoing 'capitalist civilisation'; this regression was marked by indolence. And yet, according to his plan, 'systematic colonisation' – displacement to the colony without dispersion – would reconnect Britain with its dependencies through a sustained stream of capital, labour and commodities, drive a wedge between labour and land, reproduce the wage relation in the colony while protecting it at home, and result in a new society free from the social 'evils' characterising the old one. He had in mind especially the urban proletariat and a parasitic aristocracy.

British liberalisms

Those who agitated to repeal the Corn Laws wanted to turn England into a polity comprising a metropolitan core and several colonising settler peripheries.[20] Imported corn from the settler colonies would mean, in practice, adding land to the polity – repeal would in practice establish a polity resembling Harrington's 'Oceana' as a 'commonwealth of increase'. The prospect of revolution, and the need to pre-empt or defuse it, was also one driver of this movement: one repealer, a prominent Benthamite, noted that repealing the Corn Laws and 'proper schemes of colonization' would 'render the inevitable progress of democracy in this country as safe and peaceable as it is in America'.[21] The alternative to this displacement? Reaction or revolution, and possibly both: Wakefield and the radicals had argued, as Bernard Semmel has remarked, that 'without a positive program to "extend the field of production", England faced disastrous social revolution'.[22]

'Happy Englands abroad' was the slogan of the British 'colonial radicals' – those especially influenced by Wakefield. Anthony Trollope's 'English life all over again' turned the Tory myth of a 'merry England' in the past into the myth of a Merry England somewhere else. Displacement could thus even undo time. Duncan Bell has argued that the colonial

19 Edward Gibbon Wakefield, 'A Letter from Sydney' (1829), in M. F. Lloyd-Prichard, ed., *The Collected Works of Edward Gibbon Wakefield* (Glasgow: Collins, 1968), p. 134.

20 See Semmel, 'Philosophic Radicals and Colonialism'.

21 Cited in ibid., p. 520.

22 Ibid., p. 514.

reform movement 'put forward a new system for extending British colonization which they claimed would alleviate social malaise and economic stagnation at home and ensure rapid development in the colonies and that the reformers formulated a liberal concept of empire which the Durham Report did much to make a reality by laying the foundation for a self-governing commonwealth'.[23] This imperial concept was settler-colonial. 'The Colonial Reform movement', Bell concluded, 'was itself an off-shoot of philosophical radicalism; an attempt to transplant Benthamite political ideas in a new setting'.[24] But, crucially, the validity of the new ideas was place-specific – they only applied to the imperial peripheries (not all of them, of course).

After 1830, the colonial reform movement had its chance, and New South Wales became a testing ground for the ideas of systematic colonisation: crucial policy innovations included assisted emigration funded from the land revenue and efforts to equalise the relative proportion of male and female emigrants. The effort was coordinated under the Australian Waste Land Act of 1842. In South Australia in 1834, and later in New Zealand, the old seventeenth-century idea was revived of a joint-stock company established for the purpose of colonisation. The link between emigration and convict or pauper transportation was now broken: turning the world inside out had become official policy.

Colonial bureaucrat and administrator George Grey's antipodean career epitomised this policy. While, in the words of Alan Lester, Grey 'helped reconcile settler colonialism with humanitarian governance', he remains an ambivalent figure: for some, an autocratic and conservative influence; for others, an influential liberal and even a radical reformer.[25] He was not inconsistent, however; he was simply taking different stances depending on his location. He had seen Ireland during his first posting in the early 1830s, had seen abject poverty, and had sensed Ireland's revolutionary potential. He thought that displacement to various parts of the British Empire might be a solution, and his decision to pursue a career in the colonial service, he admitted, was linked to this epiphany.

---

23 Duncan Bell, *Reordering the World* (Princeton, NJ: Princeton University Press, 2016), p. 20.

24 Duncan Bell, 'The Dream Machine: On Liberalism and Empire', in Bell, *Reordering the World*, p. 22.

25 Alan Lester, 'Settler Colonialism, George Grey and the Politics of Ethnography', *Environment and Planning D: Society and Space* 34: 3 (2016), p. 492.

Unlike Wakefield, Grey recognised the existence and importance of indigenous collectives. He had actually been involved in colonial administration, and knew that the Aboriginal 'question' could not be avoided. Indigenous peoples were in the way of colonisation, but their elimination was not appropriate either (he saw the settlers' recurring calls to exterminate them as one example of the re-barbarising tendencies of the frontier Wakefield was also decrying). Like many of the humanitarians administering colonial policy in the 1830s, Grey knew that societies founded on criminal behaviour could not produce regenerate polities; most importantly, he also knew that settlers who had killed Aborigines with impunity were dispersed over vast areas. This was a Wakefieldean observation, and Grey agreed that settler dispersion was undoing 'civilisation' in the colonies. His *Report on the Best Means of Promoting the Civilization of the Aboriginal Inhabitants of Australi*a (1840), based on his observations on the ground in Western Australia, became enormously influential. It envisaged indigenous assimilation (Grey called it 'amalgamation'), a policy based on the acquisition of ethnographic knowledge and the recognition that indigenous individuals (though not indigenous collectives) retained inherent rights.

In his opinion, this recognition would promote a 'systematic' type of colonisation by sustaining a 'sufficient' price of land (Aboriginal stakeholders' acquiescence to colonisation had to be purchased, and this would make land more expensive). It was a variation on the Wakefieldean 'system' of colonisation, and Grey proposed the partial substitution of imported labourers with indigenous ones, enabling all immigrants immediately to become landed settlers, rather than having to wait for a specified period of time (as the Wakefield scheme envisaged). It was a type of settler colonialism that did not demand the temporary subjection of the new settlers that Wakefield proposed: the recognition of indigenous rights would suffice to reintroduce primitive accumulation. Like the immigrant labourers of Wakefield's schemes, the Aborigines who would work for wages for three years would then be allocated land *as settlers*. In Grey's estimation, this would further reinforce the settler colonial project by creating efficiencies. Grey assumed that Aborigines embedded in the colonial regime would not resist the expansion of colonial control. Rapid development could then enable the colonial regime to rapidly displace revolutionaries away from wherever they were. The origins of Grey's amalgamationist settler colonialism thus lie in his perception of revolution in the metropole; Grey frequently claimed that his Irish experience had been foundational.[26] In Grey's vision, 'amalgamating' indigenous people rather than physically eliminating them would sustain a world turned inside out (and save the Empire's conscience).

The main issues in British public debates during the 1810s and 1820s were overpopulation, unemployment, pauperism, growing agitation and political militancy – especially in Ireland. The Horton schemes of government-assisted emigration, promoted between 1823 and 1830, were concerned primarily with relief, not with turning the world turned inside out. As Bell observed, Horton intended to '"locate" or "plant" emigrants on the land', and 'favoured selecting mainly agricultural labourers' for the prospected social benefit of the colony.[27] It was an intermediate position, but the link between displacement and revolution clearly emerges when the Horton schemes are seen in the Irish context in particular: Horton's objective was to remove agitators more than anything else (associating colonisation with pauperism, Horton had insisted that respectable people should not emigrate).

Conversely, Malthus, David Ricardo and both James and John Stuart Mill all expressed scepticism and 'doubts as to the suitability of paupers as settler material', and maintained an opposition to 'continued public assistance to emigrants'.[28] J. S. Mill concluded that he had 'no faith in the efficiency of any plan of emigrating, which for every labourer whom it removes, implies the permanent alienation of a portion of the national wealth' (though his position would change in later years).[29] But a minority of economists had supported Horton's schemes because they assumed that addressing the potential for civil disturbances was more urgent than the prospect of losing workers to the national wealth. The turning point in the story of the global settler revolution was when schemes for the assisted emigration of paupers became schemes for the assisted emigration of a section of the whole of society – that is, when Wakefield's theory of systematic colonisation rearticulated the world turned inside

26 See ibid., p. 494.
27 Bell, 'Dream Machine', p. 54.
28 Ibid., pp. 55–64.
29 Cited in ibid., p. 64.

out. Specifically, Wakefield broke the Ricardian orthodoxy of the political economists, advocating colonisation as a solution for an unprecedented crisis of overcapitalisation. Wakefield had envisaged state intervention as a solution for the crises of capitalist development almost a century before Keynes.

Nineteenth-century British liberalisms considered the politics of volitional displacement with some care. Bell's analysis has located settler colonialism squarely in the context of liberalism: 'Settler colonialism played a crucial role in nineteenth-century imperial thought, and liberalism in particular, yet it has largely been ignored in the burst of writing about the intellectual foundations of the Victorian empire', because it 'was in the settler colonies, not India, that many liberals found the concrete place of their dreams'.[30]

J. S. Mill's definition of settler colonialism in *Principles of Political Economy* (1848) recapitulates the world turned inside out as a political project, referring to its fundamental characteristics: 'a stage of civilisation', a racial and gendered order, a classless condition, and a non-revolutionary circumstance (that is, a dispensation where all contradictions are pre-emptively neutralised):

> The northern and middle states of America are a specimen of this stage of civilization in very favourable circumstances; having, apparently, got rid of all social injustices and inequalities that affect persons of Caucasian race and of the male sex, while the proportion of population to capital and land is such as to ensure abundance to every able-bodied member of the community who does not forfeit it by misconduct. They have the six points of Chartism, and they have no poverty . . .[31]

For Mill, of course, colonialism and colonisation were entirely distinct propositions, and Mill distinguished between 'dependencies' that were 'capable of, and ripe for, representative government', and those that remained 'a great distance from that state'.[32] 'Distance' here was used

30 Ibid., pp. 2, 15.

31 John Stuart Mill, *Principles of Political Economy* (London: J. W. Parker, 1848), vol. II, pp. 308–9.

32 Bell, 'John Stuart Mill on Colonies', p. 35.

metaphorically, to describe not spatial disconnection, but stages of development. The colonies inhabited by progressive settlers were thus 'close' to the motherland no matter where they were; and it was this closeness that sustained appropriate displacements, because one could move great distances and yet still inhabit the highest level of civilisation. Mill thus believed that metaphorical 'progress' would be sustained by spatial progress.

But if Wakefield wanted to create new countries, replicating socially the old one in order to avoid revolution (and, indeed, Britain would not be subject to the pan-European insurrections of 1848, thanks largely to its vast empire), Mill saw the new countries as opportunities for testing the social experiments that would pre-empt revolution by eventually making the old country look like the new ones.[33] Pre-emption of contradictions by way of displacement was one option, but Mill went a step further, hoping for the development of technologies that would ultimately undo the need for displacement in the first place.[34] The settler colonies presented opportunities to establish new and 'progressive' political communities, as Mill would say. In these colonies, the political transformation that was inadvisable at home (or the political transformation that would have required a revolution at home) could finally be realised. The Canadian rebellions of 1837–38, Mill believed, offered a chance to establish anew what had become a corrupted polity; a model colony would emerge. He thus counselled Lord Durham to legislate the *tabula*

33 See Miles Taylor, 'The 1848 Revolutions and the British Empire', *Past and Present* 166: 1 (2000). Taylor concludes that 'Metropolitan Britain's relatively safe passage through these troubled times was impossible without the empire. It was the Cape and Australian settlements to which English and Irish political prisoners were transported after 1848. It was the empire as a whole that was forced to downsize its military resources in order to allow for drastic government retrenchment at home, the single most important factor in ensuring the loyalty of the British taxpayer in 1848. And it was the West Indies and Canada in particular which bore the brunt of the free trade reforms which fueled consumer prosperity in Britain' (p. 152).

34 In the 1830s Mill had aimed to form a Radical group in parliament, and to consolidate a lobby outside it – a body of reformers especially concerned with the settler colonies. But Mill's radicalism by this time was much softened after the 1830 revolution in France (which he had supported before changing his mind). Focusing on locations somewhere else after (and instead of) revolution seemed appropriate for this group of colonial reformers who dreamt of polities established elsewhere. See Alexander Brady, 'Introduction', in John M. Robson, ed., *Collected Works of John Stuart Mill* (Toronto: University of Toronto Press, 1977), p. xiv.

rasa necessary for progressive experimentation (of course, Wakefield was advising Durham, too).

Mill was excited about South Australia, too:

> Like the Grecian colonies, which flourished so rapidly and so wonderfully as soon to eclipse the mother cities, this settlement will be formed by transplanting an entire society, and not a mere fragment of one. English colonies have almost always remained in a half-savage state for many years from their establishment. This colony will be a civilized country from the very commencement.[35]

He believed in coordinated state-sponsored efforts to displace entire communities rather than individual displacements on dispersed frontiers; but displacement remained a constant.

With regard to Ireland and the Irish, Mill entertained a more conservative position. It was 'a serious question', Mill considered, 'whether, in laying the foundation of new nations beyond the sea, it be right that the Irish branch of the human family should be the predominant ingredient'; on the contrary, it was the 'English and the Scotch' that were 'the proper stuff for the pioneers in the wilderness'.[36] The Irish would probably carry revolution with them. He eventually shifted from enthusiasm to disillusionment, becoming progressively disappointed by the settler policymakers' failure to enact progressive legislation after self-government had been granted. The self-governing settlers had also failed to support free trade, or simply to behave humanely towards indigenous peoples. Ironically, it was the settlers' very recently won political autonomy that had stunted their potential progressivism: they had been free, and freely decided to enact protectionist legislation.

Greater Britains

Mill was to be disappointed, but James Froude remained enthusiastic about the settlers and explicitly referred to Harrington's *Oceana*. He had seen what he considered a truly revolutionary development up close, the

35 Cited in Bell, 'John Stuart Mill on Colonies', p. 39.

36 Cited in ibid., pp. 49–50.

end of the aristocracy of 'character', and convened with Harrington that a commonwealth of increase was now absolutely needed. In 'England and her colonies' (1870), he focused on the degrading industrial cities of the nineteenth century:

> The life of cities brings with it certain physical consequences, for which no antidote and no preventive has yet been discovered. When vast numbers of people are crowded together, the air they breathe becomes impure, the water polluted. The hours of work are unhealthy, occupation passed largely within doors thins the blood and wastes the muscle and creates a craving for drink, which reacts again as a poison. The town child rarely sees the sunshine; and light, it is well known, is one of the chief feeders of life. What is worse, he rarely or never tastes fresh milk or butter; or even bread which is unbewitched.[37]

But these cities, Froude considered, held an enormous colonial outside:

> England at the same time possesses dependencies of her own, not less extensive than the United States, not less rich in natural resources, not less able to provide for these expatriated swarms, where they would remain attached to her Crown, where their well-being would be our well-being, their brains and arms our brains and arms, every acre which they could reclaim from the wilderness, so much added to English soil, and themselves and their families fresh additions to our national stability.[38]

Thus the conurbations and their outside were intimately related. Transforming the latter would reconstitute and avert revolution in the former. In Harringtonian terms, the latter would constitute the 'increase' of a reformed 'commonwealth'. English strength and vitality, now being dissipated in squalid industrial conditions, will be regained, and expansion, that is, displacement to an outside, would prevent the explosive growth of resentment between social 'superiors' and 'inferiors'. Froude's

37 James A. Froude, 'England and Her Colonies', *Fraser's Magazine: New Series* I (1870), p. 11. It seems significant that Friedrich Engels, in *The Condition of the Working Class in England* (1845), also focused on the industrial city. The appraisals were similar, but Engels advocated revolution as a solution rather than displacement.

38 Froude, 'England and Her Colonies', p. 1.

'aristocracy' of character would be safe from loss of character and external challenges equally.

The 'Manchester school' had argued that the settler colonies were a burden, a source of expenditure and an outlet for emigration, a phenomenon that deprived the industrialists of what Marx would call an industrial reserve army and therefore required that they forfeit a proportion of the surplus value they could otherwise obtain. The industrialists and the political economists resented displacement, but Froude embraced it. Unlike Mill, he argued that the Irish should be resettled in Canada and Australia, and thus prevented from escaping to America or starve to death. In 1884, Froude would actually circumnavigate the globe and personally connect with what he could imagine as an actually existing global 'Oceana'. South Africa, Australia and New Zealand, and then San Francisco, Salt Lake City, Denver, Chicago, Buffalo, New York. It is significant that Froude started reading Harrington only after his circumnavigation had begun; he had been Harringtonian almost without knowing it. South Africa was disappointing because it was mired in contradictions. The 'history of Ireland is repeating itself, as if Ireland was not enough', he noted, and besides, he felt that the Boers were the only truly settler colonists. South Africa was replete with revolutionary tension, but the rest of 'Oceana' was greatly relieving. Froude saw the whole world turned inside out as an existing global network of settler colonies, and was especially enthusiastic of the US, which he saw as an efficient and vibrant settler commonwealth of increase.

Froude was primarily opposed to the consequences of urbanisation, industrialisation, and modernity: a polarised society characterised by the protective acquisitiveness of the ruling classes and the revolutionary acquisitiveness of the poor. Settler colonial displacement, Froude argued, was the answer: 'Greater Britain' – 'the unity of Britain and the settler colonies' – colonies that were somewhere else and needed Britons to displace there.[39] 'Greater Britain' required the displacement of Britain itself. But Froude still needed to demonstrate that the settlers were selected human material and the settler locales were regenerative sites.

39 Duncan Bell, 'Republican Imperialism: J. A. Froude and the Virtue of Empire', *History of Political Thought* XXX: 1 (2009), p. 177. See also Theodore Koditschek, *Liberalism, Imperialism and the Historical Imagination: Nineteenth-Century Visions of Greater Britain* (Cambridge: Cambridge University Press, 2011).

Many remained unconvinced. The settler 'revolution' remained unfinished; thus the promoters of 'Greater Britain', promotions to which Froude was a crucial contributor, attempted a comprehensive rebranding. The colonies were now to be represented as organic to the 'mother country' and the colonists as loyal patriots.

In this rebranding leading to further displacement, Froude was equally against the left and the right, against the Liberals and against the Tories. He dreamt of a world turned inside out – of a return to an uncorrupted world that depended on a forward movement. The settler colonial option was thus a non-revolutionary escape, a physical displacement leading to chronological one – a move forward in space and a return in time. The settler colonies would self-govern themselves: '[o]ne free people cannot govern another free people', he noted.[40] It was a pre-emptive response to the prospect of corruption (also a form of revolution). To preserve or recover their virtue and self-determination, the English should embrace the open spaces of Oceana and constitute a polity 'united as closely as the American states [were] united'.[41]

For Froude then, it was a case of settler colonialism *or* debasement. If

> the millions of English and Scotch men and women who are wasting their constitutions and wearing out their souls in factories and coal mines were growing corn and rearing cattle in Canada and New Zealand, the red colour would come back to their cheeks, their shrunken sinews would fill out again, their children, now a drag upon their hands, would be elements of wealth and strength [reproduction is turned into a resource, it is no longer leading to a burden] while here at home the sun would shine again, and wages would rise to the colonial level, and land would divide itself, and we should have room to move and breathe.[42]

It was disgust with modernity that prompted settler colonial imaginings. Froude had focused on anxiety at home but had seen the possibility of regeneration on the outside:

40 Cited in Bell, 'Republican Imperialism', p. 181.

41 Ibid.

42 Cited in Bell, 'Republican Imperialism', p. 189.

> Amidst the uncertainties which are gathering round us at home [. . .] it is something to have seen with your own eyes that there are other Englands besides the old one, where the race is thriving with all its ancient characteristics.[43]

In the end, Froude had managed to relocate England 'from the past to elsewhere' – a displacement indeed.[44]

Many others were arguing for a 'Greater Britain' too. With a book of the same title, Charles Dilke became the recognised prophet of 'Anglobalization', a transnational form of belonging for the 'Anglo-Saxon highway round the globe'.[45] For Dilke, Englishness was a feeling, something eminently portable. Like Froude's Oceana, Dilke's 'Greater Britain' included the US, where 'the peoples of the world are being fused together' while being 'run into an English mould'. 'Through America, England is speaking to the world', he had concluded.[46] Dilke's idea of a Federation uniting a British Empire of racial identity was part of a larger federation movement, and it is significant that 'Greater Britain', consistently enjoyed bipartisan support.[47] 'The movement advocating Greater Britain', Bell has argued, 'appealed to people across the political spectrum, though they defended it for different reasons':

> For radicals, always in the minority, colonial unity would help simultaneously to democratise Britain and the international system as a whole. It would constitute part of a progressive multi-lateral

43 Cited in Robert J. C. Young, *The Idea of English Ethnicity* (Malden, MA: Blackwell, 2008), p. 220.

44 Ibid., p. 221.

45 Cited in ibid., p. 198.

46 Cited in Paul A. Kramer, 'Empires, Exceptions, and Anglo-Saxons: Race and Rule between the British and United States Empires, 1880–1910', *Journal of American History* 88: 4 (2002), p. 1,324.

47 Symptomatically, E. A. Freeman's powerful critique of J. R. Seeley's argument for imperial federation did not contest the ability of Englishmen to move across space and organise politically. Freeman emphasised 'Anglo-Saxonism', a notion equally focusing on the identity of Britons and settlers, while foregrounding political separation. Seeley and Freeman agreed on English sovereign displacement, even though they disagreed on the specific form of the English global imperial polity they were imagining. See Duncan Bell, 'Alter Orbis: E. A. Freeman on Empire and Racial Destiny', in Jonathan Conlin and Alex Bremner, eds, *Making History: Edward Augustus Freeman and Victorian Cultural Politics* (Oxford: Oxford University Press, 2015).

> institutional order. [. . .] The dominant view, however, was that Greater Britain provided a way of securing British power while dampening the threat posed by radicalism. Through a process of systematic emigration, the disruptive, degenerative potential of democracy would be neutralised as 'excess' population was channelled from Britain (and in particular from its overcrowded and festering cities) into the huge open spaces of the colonies. This movement, it was argued, would simultaneously defuse the dangers of urban radicalism while populating the colonies with individuals who, as a result of a transformation in their natural and cultural environments, would be transmuted into rugged imperial patriots, citizen-subjects of the most powerful polity on earth.[48]

'Greater Britain' was thus about enacting or defusing radical reforms, not the same aim, but the approach was consistently about displacement. It 'required a significant cognitive shift': recognising that the 'distant and scattered colonies (and colonists) were an integral part of the British polity'.[49]

Many philanthropists also supported domestic and transmarine colonies. Caroline Chisholm's activism for women's emigration – she published *The ABC of Colonisation* in 1850 – also aimed to turn the world inside out. Chisholm consistently and influentially advocated for the sponsored emigration of 'respectable' poor farmers and especially single women. The latter would enable colonial fathers of working-class families to become respectable manly breadwinners. Her insight was that it is appropriate reproduction that turns the world inside out and she called for the systematic 'population' of Australia, which she saw as 'the future England of our Southern Hemisphere'.[50] William Booth's *Labour and Life of the People* (1889) was also extremely influential, and his Salvation Army aimed to literally 'colonise' the urban poor (i.e., to transport them to colonial locations). Booth developed a comprehensive plan,

48 Duncan Bell, 'Imagined Spaces: Nation, State, and Territory in the British Colonial Empire, 1860–1914', in William Mulligan and Brendan Simms, eds, *The Primacy of Foreign Policy in British History* (Houndmills: Palgrave, 2010), pp. 293–4.

49 Ibid., p. 303.

50 See Margaret Kiddle, *Caroline Chisholm* (Melbourne: Melbourne University Press, 1990); Carole Walker, *A Saviour of Living Cargoes: The Life and Work of Caroline Chisholm* (Melbourne: Australian Scholarly Publishing, 2009).

a world turned inside out plan, comprising of city shelters, followed by preparatory domestic farm colonies, and then by actual emigration towards the settler societies.[51]

Even those who resented colonial adventurism advocated settler colonial expansion. John Hobson, for example, feared that despotism trained and strengthened in the colonies may be reimported in the metropole, furthering social and political antagonism. He complained against 'our unfree Empire', but also contended that 'freedom', trained and strengthened in the settler colonies, could be reimported to Britain to defuse social and political contradictions.[52] There was an extraordinary convergence: Hobson would protest against the Boer War, while Robert Baden-Powell would fight in it (his Boy Scouts, an outcome of his experience in that war, were an eminent instance of the politics of volitional displacement, upholding discipline and obedience against urban chaos, while literally taking the youth on preparatory excursions somewhere else). But both Hobson and Baden Powell agreed that the crisis was real, and both believed that displacement may be a solution.

Later, in the Spring of 1917, the British Empire could be seen as approaching a revolutionary crisis. The Western Front was all consuming while anticolonial nationalism was on the rise in Ireland, Egypt, and India. Facing a system-wide crisis, the newly installed Prime Minister, David Lloyd George, turned decisively to the settler colonial Dominions. The premiers of Canada, Australia, New Zealand, and South Africa were to contribute to a new 'Imperial War Cabinet', a veritable committee of imperial public safety. They collaborated, but demanded a substantive say in the shaping of British foreign policy, a commitment to enforcing the 'colour bar' globally, and a global political realignment and partnership with the US. This was a forming global settler colonial polity, one result of growing revolutionary

51 Though the Salvation Army is known primarily for its urban work, it sent more than 250,000 emigrant settlers to the colonies. Booth embraced domestic and settler colonialism, and saw them as part of a continuum. He tried to promote his schemes in the United States as well, but his project there ultimately failed (even though he was able to recruit powerful allies). In the United States there were already settlers on the land, and moving the urban poor to rural areas was ultimately contrary to the interests of industrialists. See Barbara Arneil, *Domestic Colonies* (Oxford: Oxford University Press, 2017), p. 245.

52 Bell, *Reordering the World*, pp. 341–62.

contradictions; a global 'commonwealth' dedicated to upholding white supremacy in the face of disruption and modernity.[53]

And yet the British liberals neglected the world turned inside out in the twentieth century, after they had engaged so intensely with it in previous decades, and even if British migration to the Dominions remained significant.[54] Perhaps it would be more correct to say that they did not focus on it as much as they had done in the previous century. The world turned inside out remained a viable option in British political cultures.[55] Perhaps the ascendancy of global revolution in the 'short' twentieth century contributed to this forgetting: evasion was no longer an option, and in the twentieth century they fought a total struggle against 'totalitarianisms'.[56] And yet the tradition remained, and J. G. A. Pocock's work since the 1970s can be seen as a neo-Seeleyan plea for restoring the world turned inside out (especially because Pocock saw British secession from Empire and its membership in the European Common Market as a type of revolution). For Pocock, as Richard Bourke has noted, 'balkanization [was] a consummation of revolutionary anti-politics'.[57] For Pocock, only settlers, as they exercise their sovereignty through displacement, genuinely abandon revolution *and* secession. In this sense, Pocock is indeed an advocate of a world turned inside out.[58]

Federalists, antifederalists, and their descendants

The 'Old North West' was once a possible world turned inside out. The American Revolution had won the war, but competition between very

53 See John Mitcham, *The Empire Club: Imperial Politics, White Supremacy, and the Making of the Commonwealth* (Oxford: Oxford University Press, forthcoming).

54 See Stephen Constantine, *Emigrants and Empire: British Settlement in the Dominions between the Wars* (Manchester: Manchester University Press, 1990).

55 For an analysis of British social imperialism between the wars and its specific insistence on overseas settlement, see Neil Redfern, *Social-Imperialism in Britain: The Lancashire Working Class and Two World Wars* (Leiden: Brill, 2018).

56 Domenico Losurdo makes this argument in *War and Revolution: Rethinking the Twentieth Century* (London: Verso, 2015).

57 See Richard Bourke, 'Pocock and the Presuppositions of the New British History', *Historical Journal* 53: 3 (2010), p. 768.

58 Gabriel Piterberg, 'J. G. A. Pocock's Antipodean Gaze from the Standpoint of a Fellow Colonist', in Lorenzo Veracini and Susan Slyomovics, eds, *Race, Place, Trace: Essays in Honour of Patrick Wolfe* (London: Verso, forthcoming).

different political projects ensued almost immediately. The faction supporting displacement initially lost – the centralising Federalist elites won comprehensively – but did not disappear.[59] At least since the 1780s, settler 'squatters' in what would become Ohio were opposed to Congress. Land distribution and the organisation of society, the squatters demanded, had to be governed by local rules, not directed by a distant national government. It was an opposition framed primarily in terms of location rather than other ideological determinants. The squatters claimed the right of Americans 'to pass into every vacant country, and there to form their constitution'.[60] As well as disagreeing with 'outsiders' on the source and location of political authority, however, the squatters were opposed to visions of a Federalist West – and the Federalists had plans for the West.[61]

This political struggle, of course, was fought through propaganda as well, and the frontiersmen were often represented as inherently lacking – resembling, as one commentator suggested, 'white Indians of no character'.[62] The nuclear family survived migration, but other institutions were less portable. As Andrew Cayton noted, a strong current of opinion characterised frontiersmen as uncultured and uncivilised.[63] In 1786, Founding Father Benjamin Rush had described the typical stages of frontier settlement: the first settlers 'quickly acquired the manners of the Indians'; the second wave were lazy and lacked 'republican' virtues; only the third wave were organised in a satisfactory way.[64] The Federalists wanted to send only the right kind of settlers to the 'new' lands – a move that would bypass Rush's two earlier stages. Lobbying for the Ohio Company, speculator Manasseh Cutler insisted that 'systematic

59 See Andrew R. L. Cayton, *The Frontier Republic: Ideology and Politics in the Ohio Country, 1780–1825* (Kent, OH: Kent State University Press, 1986); R. Douglas Hurt, *The Ohio Frontier: Crucible of the Old Northwest, 1720–1830* (Bloomington: Indiana University Press, 1996).

60 Cited in Cayton, *Frontier Republic*, pp. 9, 78.

61 See Peter S. Onuf, 'Liberty, Development, and Union: Visions of the West in the 1780s', *William and Mary Quarterly* 43: 2 (1986); Kristopher Maulden, *The Federalist Frontier: Settler Politics in the Old Northwest, 1783–1840* (Columbia, MO: University of Missouri Press, 2019).

62 Cited in John R. Van Atta, *Securing the West: Politics, Public Lands, and the Fate of the Old Republic, 1785–1850* (Baltimore: Johns Hopkins University Press, 2014), p. 41.

63 Cayton, *Frontier Republic*, pp. 5, 8.

64 Ibid., pp. 14–15.

settlement' be adopted in this instance (Wakefield would also talk about 'systematic colonization').[65] His insight is telling; for him, the Northwestern Territory was a possible site for immediately regenerating social life because it enjoyed 'one advantage which no other part of the earth can boast and which probably will never again occur – that in order to begin right, there will be no wrong habits to combat, and no inveterate systems to overturn – there is no rubbish to remove before you can lay the foundation.'[66]

The Federalists planned cities, and wanted agriculture to be immediately complemented by manufacture and commerce. In Cayton's summation, they had a 'nationally controlled, urban vision of the West.'[67] But, despite their efforts, the Federalists could not decisively win against other tendencies, and the Federalist Party would lose power and influence as squatters and Jeffersonian Republicans would forcefully propose their own vision instead. Nonetheless, contradictions remained, and, as Cayton observed, there were always two sources of political authority on the frontier and in the new states: 'the white males residing in the state', and the 'government of the United States.'[68]

After independence, anxieties about potential settler-led secessions had prompted serious concerns in Federalist circles. This was not only fear of settler independence; it was also social fear deriving from the elites' belief that unregulated settlement was producing a society of 'white savages' that was also fundamentally unregulated. Talking about the stream of settlers entering Tennessee and Kentucky, President Washington warned Congress that, without a proper policy, the 'settling, or rather overspreading of the Western Country will take place, by a parcel of *Banditti* who will bid defiance to all Authority.'[69] For decades before the Jacksonian turn, which was hailed by its supporters as a revolution, the federal government tried to foster the growth of a 'commercial economy' in frontier zones, and to reproduce a 'well-regulated

65 Cited in ibid., p. 25.

66 Cited in Andro Linklater, *Measuring America: How the United States Was Shaped by the Greatest Land Sale in History* (New York: Plume, 2003), p. 82.

67 Cayton, *Frontier Republic*, p. 31.

68 Ibid., p. 83. White universal male suffrage was enacted in 1792.

69 Cited in Linklater, *Measuring America*, p. 63. John Weaver refers to 'co-operating groups of small American squatters who, in the 1780s and 1790s, attempted frontier social revolutions by occupation.' *The Great Land Rush and the Making of the Modern World, 1650–1900* (Montreal: McGill-Queen's University Press, 2003), p. 59.

society' there.[70] Elite concerns had been significant, and their control minimal; they felt they should promote 'nation building by design'.[71] Internal improvements were often prospected as a solution; they would promote a steadily expanding and densely connected agricultural republic – a 'world within itself' – and not a series of dispersed ones.[72] The Jefferson administration was initially against too rapid expansion, but the Old Jeffersonians also eventually came to favour internal improvements, a policy that became known as the 'American System'. Federalists and Jeffersonians thus fundamentally agreed on the need for systematic colonisation. Internal improvement, however, required taxation, and increased taxation disproportionally punished subsistence farmers, so the two camps remained opposed.

The crisis that followed the 'panic' of 1819 prompted renewed displacement. Jeremiah Morrow and George Robertson were the first outspoken defenders of a 'radical' West, and launched, as John Van Atta noted, a 'strident, multifaceted campaign to undercut the national government's regulation of western social and economic development'.[73] Three ideas eventually coalesced, all promoting displacement against centralisation: Thomas Hart Benton's plan for the 'graduation' of land prices (no 'sufficient' price for land, to use a Wakefieldean expression, was therefore envisaged – if land remained unsold, prices would need to decrease); pre-emption (the legalisation of squatters' claims); and cession – the idea promoted by Ninian Edwards and many others that land within a forming state should belong to that state (and therefore not to the federal government).

Land price graduation provided one important way to offer relief to indebted settlers. Graduation and pre-emption promised to undo previous policies and to facilitate settlement. Allowing settlement before purchase was also proposed. The idea was to allow poor settlers to acquire land. The promoters of this settler colonial response to crisis argued that access to property somewhere else would improve the 'general morals' of America, and that it would turn potential troublesome individuals into a virtuous citizenry with a proper stake in society.

70 Van Atta, *Securing the West*, p. 5.
71 Ibid., p. 6.
72 Ibid., p. 71.
73 Ibid., p. 93.

Many in New England resented all emigration, as it was restricting profits, but many also felt that it might act as a safety valve against emerging contradictions, and noted that the prospect of emigration to the West was keeping wages high and people well fed. Many ended up arguing that land should be granted to settlers for free 'without money and without price'.[74] Displacement was again powerfully on the agenda in the face of rising social tension and economic crisis.

Significant opposition to the interests of the settler farmers remained. Mathew Carey was a promoter of industrialisation and argued for protectionism and against land-price reductions, and hoped that industry would fill the void created by the crisis. Hezekiah Niles also thought that agriculture and industry should be 'coordinated' (coordination is, after all, the very opposite of separation), while President Madison lamented that vacant land drew away labouring classes and frustrated 'the spontaneous establishment of manufactories'.[75] Likewise, powerful politician Henry Clay consistently championed the American System; his determination to sell lands has often been explained in terms of a desire for revenue, but his intention was also to counter more egalitarian tendencies. He was not against new land being 'opened up' (he consistently thought that opening new lands would allow the United States to avoid becoming a new Europe, riddled with contradictions); but he was against opening new land in ways that would upset established orders elsewhere.[76] It was a matter of timing. Clay, however, did not partake of the rhetoric of the 'settler revolution'; for him, the settlers were invariably irresponsible, and internal improvements were especially needed because they would convert subsistence farming into commercial production. His general plan was to reconnect, not to disconnect.

In the 1820s and 1830s, however, the balance of power was gradually shifting in favour of the settlers, and even many speculators realised that keeping squatters around rather than asking the authorities to dislodge them was good business practice. Their presence kept land prices up. The American System's central tenet was that diversification of employment would prevent a 'demoralization of society'.[77] Clay never condoned

74 Cited in ibid., p. 158.
75 Cited in ibid., p. 113.
76 Ibid., p. 124.
77 Cited in ibid., p. 204.

squatting; but the public had moved on, and the squatters could now be represented as 'the finest portion of republican citizens'.[78] The 'preemption act' sanctioned the squatters' transition from the 'fringes of civil life' to the mainstream'.[79] The US version of the global settler revolution was born in the panic of 1819, while a further acceleration would take place after the crisis that followed 1837.

For decades, the Antifederalist settler world had evolved in dynamic tension with the Federalist one, and each with their successors (and yet both camps had fundamentally agreed on the need for ongoing displacement, wrestling chiefly on its modalities and timing). According to Woody Holton, the Federal Convention had been motivated primarily by the need to restrain state legislatures for having been too responsive to the needs of debtors and taxpayers (many of the Framers were also land speculators). The Convention acted to curb a 'prevailing rage of excessive democracy', and to ensure a sustained flow of overseas investment.[80] It did so in a variety of ways, but the most important one was to establish massive electoral districts. Representation would become less direct; as the Regulators had once feared, and as outlined in the previous chapter, the political power of displacement was thus undermined by electoral reconnection.

Farmers in cash-strapped rural districts (there was little currency where a subsistence economy still prevailed) had responded to increased taxation designed to service interests paid to investors and speculators in government securities by demanding that state legislatures print money, delay payments and protect debtors through other legislative means. This agitation, Holton has argued, had been quite effective. In the peculiar circumstances of the early US Republic, threatening unrest, or threatening to remove further west, proved convincing arguments. The critics of harsh fiscal and monetary policies claimed that taxes were rendering 'normal' familial relations impossible; but they especially resented taxation because it introduced a form of primitive accumulation where there previously was none (the farmers had to labour for a

78 Cited in ibid., p. 205.

79 Ibid., p. 213.

80 Woody Holton, *Unruly Americans and the Origins of the Constitution* (New York: Hill & Wang, 2007), p. 5. See also Jackson Turner Main, *The Anti-Federalists: Critics of the Constitution, 1781–1788* (Chicago: Quadrangle, 1964).

wage, or to produce for markets, if they wanted to obtain the currency that could be accepted as tax). Taxes in this context were not just something one had to pay; they were undoing an escape and the mode of production that underpinned it.[81]

Holton refers to anxious concerns in subsistence districts that, unless relief legislation was introduced, rural husbands and fathers would be unable to 'meet their families with conjugal and parental affection' (the reverse is also true, and there were suggestions that women consumed too much because their husbands and fathers had abdicated their role of patriarch).[82] Taxation and indebtedness were leading to concerns over the undermining of masculinity, and the perception of its loss of control over the familial unit. Herman Husband epitomised this sensibility. He was a 'New Side' evangelical; backcountry Regulator; supporter of paper money; theorist of a 'pre-emption right' – a right that anyone moving west should be entitled to (that is, anyone white, male, and Protestant); supporter of 'ordinary men's political abilities', abilities predicated on their status as 'minor patriarchs'; and advocate of county-based 'legislatures' that would have been expressions of a genuine settler democracy. Husband argued for decentralisation, lamenting 'Our Want of the proper Use of those lesser Joints in the Body-Politick'.[83] He was not isolated, and Holton emphasises a pattern of social unrest characterising all of the US backcountry: there 'were actually multiple revolts up and down the seaboard'; insubordination, and especially the threat of it, were endemic, he concludes.[84]

81 See Holton, *Unruly Americans*, p. 155.

82 Cited in ibid., p. 45. Honor Sachs described how a generation of settlers had failed to become landowning patriarchs after displacement to the frontier. This failure, he argued, prompted them to restore a sense of masculinity marked by the ability to control their wives' and their children's labour. It was a place-specific type of masculinity. The male settlers saw themselves losing control in the settled parts of the country, where they were coming from, and were attempting to restore it in the backcountry. But they were failing still: the governments were not defending them from Indian attacks, and the speculators also had the upper hand over them. Moreover, these fathers were often working for wages. Sachs thus links the disappointed expectations of eighteenth-century male Kentuckians with their rebellion against state authority. Honor Sachs, *Home Rule: Households, Manhood, and National Expansion on the Eighteenth-Century Kentucky Frontier* (New Haven, CT: Yale University Press, 2015). See also Stephanie McCurry, *Masters of Small Worlds: Yeoman Households, Gender Relations and the Political Culture of the Antebellum South Carolina Low Country* (New York: Oxford University Press, 1995).

83 Cited in Holton, *Unruly Americans*, p. 172.

84 Ibid., p. 145.

The synthesis in this dynamic contest pitting creditors against debtors was the West – another place. The North-Western Ordinances had enshrined some settler rights even before the Constitution did (though these rights were site-specific, and were moot in the North-east and in the South).[85] Displacement was one way out of revolutionary tension: debtors would move west and escape harsh taxation and fiscal pressure, and creditors would be paid with money stemming from speculation in Western lands. Western expansion, however, also enabled another synthesis: the Jeffersonian project.[86] Jefferson saw with exceptional clarity the conflict between a right to claim land emanating from occupation and an elite's determination to defend its right to profit from the possibility of taxing displacement. He continuously lobbied for a policy of land allocation that would thwart the speculators' schemes and waged a protracted ideological war against them.

The Jeffersonian notion of 'independence' – a category that had both an international and a social dimension – articulated this type of settler colonialism in a synthetic fashion. Jefferson's solution to ensure the substantive independence of the new Republic was to rely exclusively neither on subsistence farming nor on the country's subsumption into international networks of trade, but a mix of the two. Joyce Appleby

85 See Robert Alexander, *The Northwest Ordinance: Constitutional Politics and the Theft of Native Land* (Jefferson, NC: McFarland, 2017); Peter S. Onuf, *Statehood and Union: A History of the Northwest Ordinance* (Bloomington: Indiana University Press, 1987); Adam Dahl, *Empire of the People: Settler Colonialism and the Foundations of Modern Democratic Thought* (Lawrence: University Press of Kansas, 2018). The Ordinances were indeed crucial founding documents of settler-colonial orders. Jack Balkin and Sanford Levinson have noted that the very 'language of the Thirteenth Amendment is taken from the 1787 Northwest Ordinance', while the 'slavery' that the Thirteenth Amendment referred to was the result of a denial of the freedom to relocate to the new lands. See Jack M. Balkin and Sanford V. Levinson, 'The Dangerous Thirteenth Amendment', *Columbia Law Review* 112 (2012), p. 1,462. The definition of these fundamental settler rights was of course predicated on the displacement or extermination of the indigenous people. See also Jeffrey Ostler, '"Just and Lawful War" as Genocidal War in the (United States) Northwest Ordinance and Northwest Territory, 1787–1832', *Journal of Genocide Research* 18: 1 (2016).

86 In *Notes on the State of Virginia* (1785), Jefferson had famously argued that America should endeavour to remain an exclusively agrarian country. In 1785 separation (from Britain) required that manufactures and cities be left behind and across the ocean. Later, however, Jefferson argued that separation (across vast distances in the consolidating United States) required that manufactures be developed in the country as well. He had changed his mind, but separation remained. See Leo Marx, *The Machine in the Garden: Technology and the Pastoral in America* (Oxford: Oxford University Press, 1964), pp. 116–44.

offers an insightful critique of the literature on Jefferson's 'yeomanism' (his ideal of individual self-sufficiency), focusing on the 'myth' of Jefferson's exclusive reliance on the 'non-commercial, nonpecuniary, self-sufficient aspects of American farm life'.[87] 'It is especially the commercial component of Jefferson's program that sinks periodically from scholarly view', she noted – 'a submersion that can be traced to the failure to connect Jefferson's interpretation of economic developments to his political goals. Agriculture did not figure in his plans as a venerable form of production giving shelter to a traditional way of life; rather, he was responsive to every possible change in cultivation, processing, and marketing that would enhance its profitability'.[88]

Appleby connects population growth in Europe with growing demand for American grains – a contingency that 'created an unusually favourable opportunity for ordinary men to produce for the Atlantic trade world'.[89] Jefferson saw favourable terms of trade as potentially underpinning a polity that would resolve the tension between international trade (a trade dominated by Britain – a colonial trade) and subsistence production away from the markets' reach. He embraced both self-sufficiency and the development of a global capitalist economy, and proposed a synthesis between these two options, seeing one as predicated on the other rather than as its antithesis. The farmer would participate in international trade, and the basic unit of this mode of production would remain the self-producing family farm. Sustained expansion through displacement would provide the balancing element. In the struggle between democratising settler tendencies and Federalist mercantilist centralisation, Jefferson proposed a settler colonial solution, arguing counterintuitively that integration into international markets – an integration that only the Union could underwrite – would maintain the Republic's integrity.

The Jeffersonian agrarianist moment was a crucial passage in the development of the political traditions of settler colonialism, a prodrome to the global settler revolution.[90] It was a synthesis: the Republican-Jeffersonians

87 See Joyce Appleby, 'Commercial Farming and the "Agrarian Myth" in the Early Republic', *Journal of American History* 68: 4 (1982), p. 834.

88 Ibid., p. 844.

89 Ibid., p. 836.

90 See Patrick F. Quinn, 'Agrarianism and the Jeffersonian Philosophy', *Review of Politics* 2: 1 (1940), p. 100.

aimed to build up the federal Union in order to insulate the displaced settler republics from the Atlantic world and its imperial systems, and from the revolutionary tensions that characterised them. Facilitating the settler escape required a powerful federal state that would engage with a tumultuous wider world. A federal framework was thus needed to deal with the larger world – to engage with markets in order to ensure a degree of insulation from markets. Thus, in the words of Peter Onuf and Leonard Sadosky, the 'American farmer would not be immune to the "casualties and caprice" of the marketplace because he had withdrawn into virtuous isolation, but rather because he and his fellows used government to successfully assert their just claims.'[91] Jefferson initially argued that 'our work-shop' should 'remain in Europe' (this point had been made by Franklin too, of course).[92] But later he acknowledged the need to increase internal production. The Jeffersonians first emerged as the main opposition to the Federalist regime, and they eventually came to power in Virginia, the South and the West. In the end, they became a contender for power in the North-east as well.

This synthesis had important gendered implications. Jefferson assumed that a farmer knew what was best for his farm, and that a father knew what was best for his family. For Onuf and Sadosky, Jeffersonianism represented the 'apotheosis of the republican father and head of the household':

> Republicanism resonated most profoundly with American fathers and their sons – future fathers – as they sought both to make their households into autonomous 'little republics' and to participate freely and consensually in the business of the world. The fantasy of household independence was crucial to the conceptions of minimal government so eloquently articulated by Jefferson and his Republican colleagues. Republican politics presupposed a natural social order, with the family as its basic building block.[93]

Jefferson's notion of settler popular sovereignty thus proceeded upward, as every citizen participated in his own government:

91 Peter S. Onuf and Leonard J. Sadosky, *Jeffersonian America* (Malden, MA: Blackwell, 2002), p. 125.

92 Cited ibid., p. 125.

93 Ibid., pp. 85-6.

> His scheme for ward republics [i.e. the states] translated the abstraction of popular sovereignty into an elaborate federal scheme: household and nation would be linked in an ascending series of 'republics', each 'sovereign' in its own sphere. He thus collapsed traditional distinctions between government and society, making every family farmer his own governor. In the Jeffersonian scheme, family government was the foundation of civil order.[94]

Jeffersonian republican domesticity was secluded and, because the farmers were dispersed, also displaced. He saw many patriarchal worlds turned inside out rather than upside down.

But it was also a reaction. The erosion of traditional patriarchal familial forms (a revolutionary transformation) was engulfing America during these crucial decades at the beginning of the nineteenth century. America had once offered extraordinary opportunities to establish new households, and to do so earlier rather than later in life; but land scarcity in settled districts and the forming labour markets of the urban areas were resulting in the attenuation of traditional patriarchal authority. Evangelical Christianity was also a response to the perception of crisis. As Onuf and Sadosky conclude, 'Jeffersonianism and evangelical Christianity both flourished in a world where political and cultural authority was radically decentered and diffused'.[95] In this sense, the Jeffersonian reaffirmation of patriarchal order in turbulent times was paralleled by evangelical awakenings, not opposed to them. But that reaffirmation demanded continuous displacement.

The market revolution

Visiting English writer Harriet Martineau wrote in 1837 of the United States:

> If a man is disappointed in politics or love, he goes on and buys land. If he disgraces himself, he betakes himself to a lot in the west. If the demand of any article of manufacture slackens, the operatives drop

94 Ibid., p. 82.
95 Ibid., p. 119.

> into the unsettled lands. If a citizen's neighbours rise above him in the towns, he betakes himself where he can be monarch of all he surveys.[96]

And yet, paradoxically, precisely because contradictions could not always be defused through displacement, wherever social tension was becoming hard to contain, even more displacement was proposed as a solution. Anti-rentism in pre–Civil War America, for example, was for a while a vehicle for the articulation of displacement as ideology.[97] Hard-pressed tenants eventually denounced the long-lasting accommodation that had underpinned the developments of large seigneurial estates in New York State. In the 'Anti-Rent War' of the 1840s, the tenants challenged their landlords' titles in courts, entered the political arena, and formed bands of masked 'Indians' to protect fellow tenants from evictions and from forced sales of personal belongings to pay rents.

Eventually, the state militia was dispatched to pacify the area; it was a revolutionary crisis. Anti-rentism was ultimately contained, and the landlord–tenant system survived. But the emergence of the 'free labor' ideology espoused by northern Republicans a decade later was related to its development. Anti-rentism was a constituent ingredient of notions like 'Free Soil, Free Labor, Free Men' – all ideas fundamentally predicated on displacement. Reeve Huston concludes that, far from 'being crushed by the parties and the advocates of the emerging capitalist order, the anti-renters unleashed a dialectic that helped usher in a new social and political order'.[98] Jacksonian 'producerism', agrarianism and related rhetorical strands (all embedded in 'free soilism') were well suited for the anti-landlord sentiments of tenants. Anti-rentism and anti-slavery were inseparable; and since slavery was one crucial factor in the demise of the party system, the

96 Cited in Linklater, *Measuring America*, p. 171.

97 See Reeve Huston, *Land and Freedom: Rural Society, Popular Protest, and Party Politics in Antebellum New York* (New York: Oxford University Press, 2000); Charles W. McCurdy, *The Anti-Rent Era in New York Law and Politics, 1839–1865* (Chapel Hill, NC: University of North Carolina Press, 2001); Adam Wesley Dean, *An Agrarian Republic: Farming, Antislavery Politics, and Nature Parks in the Civil War Era* (Chapel Hill, NC: University of North Carolina Press, 2015). Dean's analysis of the ideology of the Republican Party before and during the Civil War foregrounded 'agrarianism' as a last effort to displace contradictions rather than accept the inevitability of sectional or class war.

98 Huston, *Land and Freedom*, p. 217.

anti-renters contributed crucially to the political reconfiguration that matured in the 1850s.

Eric Foner has noted that the ideal of the autonomous small producer constituted a 'full-fledged critique of early capitalism and its transformation of free labour into a commodity' in Jacksonian America.[99] Wage labour was typically associated with servility, and the economic depression of 1837–42 (and associated revolutionary tensions) further revitalised the politics of displacement. Foner points out that, in 'the aftermath of the economic depression of 1837–42, the most severe in American history to that date, a different mode of securing economic autonomy for workingmen rose in popularity: the movement for free land'.[100] For years 'the Democratic Party had advocated a policy of easy access to government land', and of 'afford[ing] every American citizen of enterprise', as Andrew Jackson proclaimed, 'the opportunity of securing an independent freehold'. But 'in the 1840s, it was George Henry Evans, a journalist and veteran of the Jacksonian labour movement, and the iconoclastic Horace Greeley, a sometime Whig, communitarian socialist, and antislavery reformer, who popularized the idea of free homesteads in the West. "Freedom of the soil", Evans insisted, offered "emancipation" to the wage slave, the only alternative to permanent dependence'.[101] This 'emancipation' was framed as a spatial escape *away* from the wage relation.

Evans's activities and writings are especially crucial in this developing tradition. Through his *Working Man's Advocate*, he sustained the 'Vote Yourself a Farm' campaign, and engaged with Robert Owen and Fanny Wright. In the *Advocate*, he noted:

> The only remedy for the workmen is for them to instruct their representatives in Congress to pass a law allowing every citizen of good character, who may wish it, his right to a portion of the Public Lands, free of expense, for cultivation. We have no doubt that enough would

99 Eric Foner, *The Story of American Freedom* (New York: W. W. Norton, 1998), p. 59.

100 Ibid., p. 63. On the movement for 'free land', see Julius Wilm, *Settlers as Conquerors: Free Land Policy in Antebellum America* (Stuttgart: Franz Steiner Verlag, 2018). Wilm contends that schemes designed to establish settlements by way of 'free' allocations in Florida, Arkansas and Oregon failed to deliver the desired outcomes.

101 Foner, *Story of American Freedom*, p. 63.

> avail themselves of the privilege to prevent such a surplus of workmen in factories as would place the whole body (as now) at the mercy of factory owners.[102]

In other words, the workmen's 'only' remedy was displacement (Evans also argued that emancipated African-Americans should be deported west, like the Indians had been).[103] Displacement was possible, and was an alternative to both conflict and poverty – that is, to revolutionary agitation on the one hand, or accepting an intolerable transformation on the other. Evans continued:

> There are Public Lands enough in the possession of the general government (leaving Oregon and Texas out of the question) to allow every family in the United States two hundred acres each, besides all the land now held in private property in the twenty-six States and Territories. Yet with the vast field of nature inviting Industry to its occupation, degraded men are begging employment of their fellow men, striking and turning out for better wages: and poor, ragged, dirty, half-naked, half-famished children are walking the streets of Republican cities, begging for bread.[104]

Alienated labour was no longer entirely alienated if displacement remained a viable alternative: 'If the people have free access to the land, the laborer would not be dependent on the employers, and would consequently rise to his proper rank in society, instead of being debased in proportion to his influence. He would receive the full value of his labor, because he would have the ready alternative of laboring for himself'.[105] *Potential* worlds turned inside out, yet alone actually existing ones, would thus reform the Old World.

Then again, displacement served the function of keeping other revolutions at a safe remove too. Caleb Cushing argued in 1839 that

102 Cited in Carter Goodrich, Sol Davison, 'The Wage-Earner in the Westward Movement', *Political Science Quarterly* 51: 1 (March 1936), p. 175.

103 See Greg Grandin, *The End of the Myth: From the Frontier to the Border Wall in the Mind of America* (New York, Henry Holt, 2019), p. 80.

104 Cited in Goodrich and Davison, 'Wage-Earner in the Westward Movement', p. 175.

105 Cited in ibid., p. 176.

displacement was a way to prevent social tension and the need to repress it, which would have required extending the powers of the federal government. 'Empire' was a 'safety valve for all the pent up passions and explosive or subversive tendencies of an advanced society', he noted. Robert Walker similarly argued that displacement could be a way to solve the slavery issue – freed former slaves could then go west.[106] Leader of the New England Emigrant Aid Company, Eli Thayer, on the contrary, believed that the problem of slavery could be solved by promoting the emigration of white settlers to Kansas (spatially constraining slavery as an institution would in turn lead to its gradual abolition).[107] For Thayer, deferral in time, a chronological compromise, would be prompted by a radically uncompromising spatial fix. Class, racial, and constitutional conflicts could all be solved through displacement. Displacement would keep all revolutions at bay. But where was all this social tension coming from?

There was one revolution that could not be spatially constrained: the 'market revolution' that was engulfing 1820s and 1830s America (even though it might have engulfed it earlier).[108] This revolution promoted displacement too: as the cash economy progressively penetrated the rural life of a settler society, smallholders found themselves progressively subjected to market discipline, or alternatively could move further away. Harry Watson contends that there was a market revolution everywhere in North America at some point in time, because everywhere, eventually, 'the balance between household and market production tipped in favor of the latter'.[109] Farmers had to abandon aspirations to self-sufficiency and shift to cash crops or petty commodity production. Improved transport was the way in which the 'revolution' penetrated American life, typically rendering subsistence farming unsustainable.

The tension between self-sufficiency and production for markets informed American life 'throughout the antebellum period'.[110] New York

106 Grandin, *End of the Myth*, pp. 78–9, 82.

107 See Courtney Buchkoski, '"Luke-Warm Abolitionists": Eli Thayer and the Contest for Civil War Memory, 1853–1899', *Journal of the Civil War Era* 9: 2 (2019).

108 See Charles Post, *The American Road to Capitalism: Studies in Class-Structure, Economic Development and Political Conflict, 1620–1877* (Leiden: Brill, 2011), pp. 184–93.

109 Harry L. Watson, *Liberty and Power: The Politics of Jacksonian America* (New York: Hill & Wang, 1990), p. 262.

110 Ibid., p. 28.

state was a crucial site of this struggle, and it was this region that suffered more than most from the sustained attack the market revolution brought against the traditional subsistence economy. It was here that 'democratic' sentiments, as they were called, coalesced in the context of a threatened social milieu and a settler colonial moral economy. Economic booms and hard times, and the stresses of capitalist transformation, had produced upheaval in politics and religion. It was in this region that displacement as a political tradition emerged most forcefully during this phase. Anti-masonic political sentiments and Mormon revelations both emerged from this region; many felt that they were losing control and responded by displacing their frustrations if not their families.[111]

The transformation that had begun with the crash of 1819 resulted eventually in the democratic Jacksonian insurgency, and in the re-emergence of Old Republicanism. The National Republicans did not recognise this shift, and initially found themselves left behind (literally, in the settled areas, and metaphorically, politics had moved on). All these tensions coalesced in the Jacksonian 'revolution', which was first felt at the state level but eventually transformed federal politics. The change that had not come in 1824 arrived in 1828. The Jacksonian Democrats' political ideal was aptly articulated by Orestes Brownson: 'instead of one man's working for another and receiving wages therefor, all men will be independent proprietors, working on their own capitals, on their own farms, or in their own shops'.[112]

These farms and shops were to be somewhere else; capital could be easily transported there. And this somewhere else could be within the recognised borders of the Republic or without. It is significant that the Democrats from the North and the South both supported foreign adventurism, and David Wilmot famously argued in Congress that he pleaded 'the cause and the rights of free men', and that he intended to 'preserve to free white labor a fair country'. And all that could be wrested from Mexico. Conversely, the Whigs in the East aimed to prevent rapid population movements; focusing on 'improvements', they tried to prevent rapid expansion.[113]

---

111 See Lorenzo Veracini, 'Mormonism, Primitive Accumulation, Preaccumulation', in Lorenzo Veracini and Susan Slyomovics, eds, *Patrick Wolfe: A Festschrift* (London: Verso, forthcoming).

112 Cited in Watson, *Liberty and Power*, p. 238.

113 Cited in ibid., p. 243.

The Market Revolution was revolutionary indeed.[114] Predicated on other revolutions – including the transport, legal, and industrial revolutions – and on unprecedented economic development and a commercial boom, initially in wheat and cotton, it prompted many worlds turned inside out.[115] Charles Sellers set the scene of ongoing culture wars between opposing subcultures. 'Arminian' market confronted 'antinomian' land:

> Profound cultural differences arose from these contrasting modes of production. The market fostered individualism and competitive pursuit of wealth by open-ended production of commodity values that could be accumulated as money. But rural production of use values stopped once bodies were sheltered and clothed and bellies provided for. Surplus produce had no abstract or money value, and wealth could not be accumulated. Therefore the subsistence culture fostered family obligation, communal cooperation, and reproduction over generations of a modest comfort.[116]

The advocates of displacement supported hard-money circulation because banks, paper money and 'money-changers' were all perceived as part of the market revolution from which the settlers were escaping in the first place. The settlers were also against developmentalist agendas and the taxes they would generate (they liked inflation, though, which is ultimately a form of debt relief). Taxation and debt were especially damaging to a subsistence economy, but tax and debt were also the harbingers of the market revolution – many, many settler homes and farms were lost to tax and debt.[117] No wonder that banks and speculation were typically seen by subsistence settlers as inherently fraudulent. Sellers observed that often 'the subsistence culture answered taxes with violence.'[118]

---

114 Charles Sellers, *The Market Revolution: Jacksonian America, 1815–1846* (New York: Oxford University Press, 1991).

115 On the dynamics of the settler revolution in the United States, and on the Jacksonian 'moment', see also Arthur M. Schlesinger, *The Age of Jackson* (Boston: Little, Brown, 1945). Schlesinger emphasised the 'end of [Jeffersonian] arcadia': that 'paradise of small farms, each man secure on his own freehold, resting under his own vine and fig-trees, was already darkened by the shadow of impending change' (p. 8). Contradictions were emerging; Jacksonianism was a response.

116 Sellers, *Market Revolution*, p. 5.

117 Ibid., p. 15.

118 Ibid., p. 73.

Taxes, credit, banks and courts were anathema to these constituencies. The subsistence farmers' mode of production required land, at least land available somewhere else, as it was ultimately pitted in an unequal struggle against the market revolution. It was an unequal struggle because, as Charles Post has argued, this mode of production was producing the conditions for its own demise.[119] There was a 'rolling' agrarian crisis in the older settlements, Sellers remarks, as 'the market assailed traditional ways, shrinking farms were spawning more people than they could feed'.[120] A rising age of marriage, declining birth rate, and erosion of patriarchal authority followed – all indications of significant social stress. And the agrarian crisis was matched by an urban crisis: urban workers were also subjected to increasingly precarious conditions. They had had security, tools, skills, and shops; but deskilling and proletarianisation were now a reality or a threat for most urban workers (even though some shop owners did become successful manufacturers).

In the context of these rising contradictions, Sellers notes, 'a historic surge of religious fervor crested to nerve [rural people's] stressful passage from resistance through evasion to accommodation. Only religious intensity could reconstitute intrapsychic/intrapersonal life to the imperatives of competitive effort'.[121] Sellers notices psychological displacement here (physical displacement, however, also proceeded at a fierce rate). A whole social world was being shattered. Manufactured cloth and dresses, introduced in the 1820s in rural areas, were important vehicles of the market revolution because patriarchal honour was susceptible to 'emulative consumption', and store goods were important transformers of rural household consumption patterns. The Second Great Awakening (unlike the moderate revival of the urban centres) was one result of these tensions. The Baptists, Sellers avers, 'institutionalized most fully the egalitarian localism of the subsistence culture'.[122] They had already done so for a long time.

119 Post focuses on 'the transformation of Northern agriculture before the Civil War from independent household production, a social form relatively impervious to market-forces, to petty-commodity production, a social property form dependent upon competitive markets'. See Post, *American Road to Capitalism*, p. 73.

120 Sellers, *Market Revolution*, p. 17.

121 Ibid., p. 29.

122 Ibid., p. 159.

'Moderate Light' and 'New Light' fought especially bitter culture wars in Upstate New York, and this is also where the Mormon prophet Joseph Smith had his visions. The Smiths had been tenants, had moved frequently, and had lost farms. The family-based mode of subsistence reproduction had been violently disrupted in their case. Rural settlers' communities had traditionally survived capitalist dislocations through enhanced familism and displacement, but this social milieu developed by the 1820s a genuinely apocalyptic imagination. The Mormon religion and the Mormon collective displacements can indeed be seen as settler colonial response to crisis.[123] The *Book of Mormon* (1830) tells the story of a 'Jewish' clan that populated America: they were the original displaced. This religion also reinstated patriarchal authority in the face of the market challenge. As a generation of young fathers saw their manhood threatened by their inability to meet traditional familiar obligations, as Sellers notes, 'patriarchal utopia arose from male panic'.[124] Richard Lyman Bushman concludes that the *Book of Mormon* was the work of a 'rural visionary'.[125] Indeed, it was the work of a *settler* rural visionary facing an existential crisis. A revelation commanded: 'Go to the Ohio'.[126] The same revelation said: 'I will give unto you my law, and there you shall be endowed with power from on high'.[127] A sovereign capacity, 'law', is thus only validated through displacement ('there', of course, means 'not here'). Accordingly, the sovereign ability of a community on the move becomes place-specific.

Unprecedented migratory flows were occurring: from East to West, from South to North-west, and from town to city. The community lost its traditional role, and the isolated nuclear household became a 'final refuge'.[128] Nuclear households were mobile; displacement was still the answer, but the 1820s were also years of growing revolutionary movements and organising. Society, especially in the swelling urban centres, was becoming class-conscious, a crucial prerequisite of political

123 See Veracini, 'Mormonism, Primitive Accumulation, Preaccumulation'.

124 Sellers, *Market Revolution*, p. 225.

125 This expression recurs several times in the book. See Richard Lyman Bushman, *Joseph Smith: Rough Stone Rolling – A Cultural Biography of Mormonism's Founder* (New York: Vintage, 2007), pp. 58, 72, 111, 127, 143.

126 Cited in ibid., p. 124.

127 Cited ibid., p. 156.

128 Sellers, *Market Revolution*, p. 242.

confrontation. And there were workers' movements against proletarianisation. Working-class militancy ushered in a potentially revolutionary moment, and these were years of increasing repression – repression, for example, of alcohol consumption and of sexual behaviour: the 'psychodynamics of personal transformation increasingly demanded a teetotal purification that radicalized and politicized collective repression'.[129] A settler colonial moment, a settler colonial revolution and many associated displacements, emerged out of increasing revolutionary contradictions.

President Jackson mobilised 'patriarchal democracy' and 'egalitarian hopes' against 'money power', and the 'Bank War' was one crucial focus of this mobilisation. William M. Gouge's *Short History of Paper Money and Banking in the United States* (1833) had been an instant classic. It argued that banking was destroying republican virtue, and warned that the banks would 'recolonise America' if its ambition was not constrained.[130] Jackson's anti-banking veto ostensibly claimed to be aimed at saving 'frontiersmen' from subjection to Eastern interests, and this claim should be taken seriously. The Democratic insurgency focused on the National Bank because its speculations were removed from scrutiny, and because the consequences of its activities and power were everywhere.[131] More generally, while the market revolution and industrialism were producing social discontent in the North-east, and the South also begun resenting the American System and the ascendancy of the commercial interests it favoured (it especially resented the protective tariff), increasing contradictions produced a situation in which, as Arthur Schlesinger noted, 'the dissatisfied classes' everywhere 'found themselves gathering behind the doctrines sustained so long by the lonely devotion' of the Jeffersonians.[132] It was a revolutionary moment; the 'flour riots struck terror in the hearts of the conservatives', Schlesinger remarked.[133]

One response to the Jacksonian crisis was intense experimentation with radical transformation in secluded locations. This included the Fourierist experiments promoted by Arthur Brisbane, Robert Owen's

129 Ibid., p. 265.
130 Cited in Watson, *Liberty and Power*, p. 144.
131 Sellers, *Market Revolution*, p. 359.
132 Schlesinger, *Age of Jackson*, p. 34.
133 Ibid., p. 219.

New Harmony, the Oneida community, the Shakers, and many further communitarian endeavours.[134] The other response was a right-wing restatement of settler colonialism – what Schlesinger called the 'Whig Counter-Reformation'.[135] The Whigs eventually adjusted to the new political dispensation and the renewed politics of displacement, and rebranded their own politics. They took a new ostensible interest in the 'frontier': the older-style Whig and Federalist language disappeared, and, as Schlesinger remarked, a 'whole flock of neo-Jeffersonians appeared, led by Horace Greeley and Daniel D. Barnard of New York, to stage a boarding party against Democratic principles and rally the business community under the stolen banners'.[136] William Henry Harrison, their presidential candidate, and his 'invented' public profile were the outcome; the 1840 election marked the conservative embrace of the political traditions espousing worlds turned inside out. 'Hard cider' and the 'log cabin' became powerful symbols, and they were somewhere else. As in previous decades, both sides of politics now embraced displacement, albeit in different ways and for different reasons: it was an 'empire of the people', and this people was mobile.[137]

Greeley was especially important in this context: a Whig, an anti-Jacksonian, and a public intellectual especially concerned with finding alternatives to revolution.[138] He would argue in 1854 in the *New York Tribune*:

> Make the Public Lands free in quarter-sections to Actual Settlers and deny them to all others, and earth's landless millions will no longer be orphans and mendicants; they can work for the wealthy, relieved from the degrading terror of being turned adrift to starve. When employment fails or wages are inadequate, they may pack up and strike

134 See Robert V. Remini, *The Jacksonian Era* (Wheeling, IL: Harlan Davidson, 1997), pp. 101–8.

135 Schlesinger, *Age of Jackson*, p. 267.

136 Ibid., p. 281.

137 Dahl, *Empire of the People*.

138 There has been a general emphasis on Greeley the reformer, but Schlesinger focused on Greeley the anti-democrat and supporter of conservative economics. See Schlesinger, *Age of Jackson*, pp. 294–5. He was a 'safe' radical, Schlesinger concludes, who 'invariably forgot socialism in favor of Whig economics when the chips were down' (p. 367). See also Coy F. Cross, *Go West, Young Man! Horace Greeley's Vision for America* (Albuquerque: University of New Mexico Press, 1995).

> westward to enter upon the possession and culture of their own lands on the banks of the Wisconsin, the Des Moines or the Platte, which have been patiently awaiting their advent since creation. Strikes to stand still will be glaringly absurd when every citizen is offered the alternative to work for others or for himself, as to him shall seem most advantageous. The mechanic or laborer who works for another will do so only because he can thus secure a more liberal and satisfactory recompense than he could by working for himself.[139]

The public lands were elsewhere; contradictions could and should be displaced. This was trickle out economics.

And there was even more land beyond the limit of the expanding American Republic. Thomas Richards has noted a continent-wide 'Texas Moment', when many settlers groups abandoned the United States and established alternative if ephemeral forms of settler self-governance. While 'Texas became a language through which to understand the future geopolitics of the continent', there were several 'breakaway Americas' beyond Texas, as settlers from the Great Lakes attempted to establish a republic in British Canada, Mormons settled the Salt Lake Valley, many Cherokees embraced the prospect of an Indigenous republic in Indian Territory, and many settlers trekked towards Mexican California and Oregon.[140] Many were moving beyond the internationally recognised borders of the United States. 'Filibustering' originally referred to hostile actions carried out by United States citizens beyond these borders, but if the Republic expanded, filibustering could be retrospectively recoded as Manifest Destiny.[141]

Settling American communities outside the borders of the American Republic, however, demanded that the question of sovereignty be addressed. The Republic was aggressively expansionist, but the settlers

139 Cited in Goodrich and Davison, 'Wage-Earner in the Westward Movement', p. 179.

140 Thomas Richards, *Breakaway Americas: The Unmanifest Future of the Jacksonian United States* (Baltimore: Johns Hopkins University Press, 2020), p. 7.

141 On William Walker's Central American 'empire', see, for example, Michel Gobat, *Empire by Invitation: William Walker and Manifest Destiny in Central America* (Cambridge, MA: Harvard University Press, 2018). The scholarship on Walker focused on his imperialist design for Latin America, but he was escaping a convulsing social body as well as the prospect of war. Gobat sees Walker's Nicaraguan project as specifically promoting a particular type of settler colonisation.

also did important conceptual work in order to proclaim an inherent right to relocate. To preserve his colony, 'Empresario' Stephen F. Austin wrote *Translation of the Laws, Orders, and Contracts, on Colonization* (1829).[142] Austin's 'Introduction' and 'Advertisement' articulated a doctrine of settler sovereignty. He insisted that the laws of Mexico were valid, and indeed the foundation of the colony's legitimacy (Mexico's *empresario* programme was predicated on a substantial devolution of self-governing capacities); but he also clarified that an underlying settler sovereignty remained, and that the local settler community must be self-governing. It was a declaration of irreducible autonomy with respect to the local sovereign, but that the Anglo-Texans were escaping the US Republic should also be noted. They were less interested in American Manifest Destiny than in freeing themselves from the constraints they were leaving behind, and their declarations of loyalty to Mexico should be taken seriously (their subsequent secession was a response to Mexico's renewed centralism, not evidence of a pre-existing determination to accede to the United States).[143] Texas was, after all, the 'default frontier', populated by many individuals fleeing from creditors and economic 'busts further north'.[144]

The Oregon Trail was also an instance of the politics of displacement. The Trail enabled many to 'return' by way of a forward movement. Richards has suggested that one of the ingredients of the overland migration to Oregon was a desire to return to the 'so-called "patrimonial family"', and the 'traditional agrarian family', which derived from the settlers' ability to bestow land to their sons and provide for their wives and daughters.[145] The 'market revolution' of the 1820s and 1830s and the

142 Stephen F. Austin, *Translation of the Laws, Orders, and Contracts, on Colonization* (1829), available at texashistory.unt.edu/ark. See also Adam Nemmers, 'Colony at the Crossroads: The "Translated" Settlement of Texas Under Stephen F. Austin', in Yu-ting Huang and Rebecca Weaver-Hightower, eds, *Archiving Settler Colonialism: Culture, Space and Race* (London: Routledge, 2018).

143 See Sarah K. M. Rodriguez, '"The Greatest Nation on Earth": The Politics and Patriotism of the First Anglo American Immigrants to Mexican Texas, 1820–1824', *Pacific Historical Review* 86: 1 (2017).

144 James Belich, *Replenishing the Earth: The Settler Revolution and the Rise of the Anglo-World, 1783–1939* (Oxford: Oxford University Press, 2009), p. 241.

145 Thomas Richards, '"Farewell to America": The Expatriation Politics of Overland Migration, 1841–1846', *Pacific Historical Review* 86: 1 (2017), p. 120. On the familial structures of these settlers, see also Kathleen Neils Conzen, 'A Saga of Families', in Clyde A. Milner, Carol A. O'Conner and Martha A. Sandweiss, eds, *The Oxford History of the American West* (New York: Oxford University Press, 1994).

'Panic of 1837' had made this impossible, but the settlers were leaving the United States also because they had given up on a polity they perceived as riddled with contradictions. Many 'longed for a western republic of their own'.[146] Writing to relatives in the Ohio, an early Oregon settler cited by Richards insightfully noted that, in the old settlements, 'you are a slave to your property, your labor is principally spent for [others]', while in Oregon 'a man's property will support him'.[147] Property that looks after its owner is a good definition of a directly accessible means of subsistence. These settlers were escaping primitive accumulation where they hoped it would not reach them (it did). Foreshadowing the Homestead legislation, the Oregon Donation Act of 1850 had granted 320 acres of land to every white adult male who had cultivated his claim for four years.

But expansion, the annexation of Texas, war with Mexico, the Oregon dispute and Manifest Destiny brought into the foreground a crucial question: Which worlds were to be turned inside out and expand? Were they to be the South's or the North's? The Wilmot Proviso of 1845 and the Compromise of 1850 had stipulated that slavery would not be allowed to expand spatially. This was a spatial fix, and the Civil War would be fought on the issue (as well as on several others).[148] North and South were projecting two mutually exclusive worlds, and both depended on continued expansion. It was on this issue – whose displacement, not whether it should occur – that the Jacksonian coalition finally fragmented.

John Ashworth has argued that class must be reckoned with in order to understand the evolution of American politics and ideology: 'it was possible for southern slavery and pre-capitalist free labor in the North to coexist, but increasingly difficult, and finally impossible, for slavery and capitalism to coexist'.[149] Coexistence had been predicated on

146 Richards, 'Farewell to America', p. 114.

147 Cited in ibid., p. 120.

148 Stephen Maizlish has argued that the issue of the expansion of slavery into the West had remained 'the most critical issue' after the Compromise of 1850. The spatial fix was temporary. See Stephen E. Maizlish, *A Strife of Tongues: The Compromise of 1850 and the Ideological Foundations of the American Civil War* (Charlottesville: University of Virginia Press, 2018), p. 27.

149 John Ashworth, *Slavery, Capitalism, and Politics in the Antebellum Republic – Volume 1: Commerce and Compromise, 1820–1850* (New York: Cambridge University Press, 1996), p. 115. See also John Ashworth, *Slavery, Capitalism, and Politics in the Antebellum Republic – Volume 2: The Coming of the Civil War, 1850–1861* (New York: Cambridge University Press, 2007).

displacement. Ashworth sees the Jacksonian Party as a coalition designed to keep slavery out of politics, and its ultimate failure to do so as one result of economic developments – the capitalist outcome of the market revolution. Contradictions had caught up with the Jacksonian 'revolution'; if it had been a response to crisis and social tension, a crisis that prompted the imagination of spatial alternatives, the expansions it engendered precipitated a war to save the viability of one displacement over another.[150] After war and defeat, displacement remained. While many migrated west, numerous Confederate colonies were established in many countries south of the border.[151]

Displacing socialists

Ideas about settler colonial displacements emerged also where the revolution was not coming, or where it was unclear whether it would come. Epitomes of this approach during the early decades of the nineteenth century include the Icarians, who followed French 'protosocialist' leader Étienne Cabet to Texas, and departed only weeks before the revolution took place in Paris.[152] The Icarian movement epitomises the

150 Charles Post also sees the Civil War as a crucial turning point. He detects no capitalist relations in colonial America (initially the subsistence farmers of the trans-Allegheny West were not compelled to integrate into markets, and even the slave plantations of the South were largely self-sufficient, as they produced commodities for international markets but could rely on locally produced food and tools). The Civil War brought an end to both modes of production. Massive immigration and railroad land grants destroyed the 'independent mode', ushering in the era of large-scale capitalist production. But before the Civil War, independent farming had already resulted in capitalist relations: the family farms had constituted a massive market for capitalist-produced and locally produced industrial goods like farm machinery, tools, meat, leather and flour. For Post, subsistence farming had already become 'petty-commodity production', a form of production transitional to capitalism. Contradictions had not caught up; they had developed in situ, but if you are trying to escape them this is ultimately a moot point. See Post, *American Road to Capitalism*, esp. pp. 17–23.

151 See Lawrence F. Hill, 'The Confederate Exodus to Latin America', *Southwestern Historical Quarterly* 2, 3 and 4 (1935–36); Donald C. Simmons, *Confederate Settlements in British Honduras* (Jefferson, NC: McFarland, 2001); Mimi Dwyer, 'The Brazilian Town Where the American Confederacy Lives On', *Vice*, 5 February 2015.

152 Cabet authored *Voyage en Icarie* (1840), *Douze lettres d'un communiste à un réformiste sur la Communauté* (1841–42), *Almanach icarien* (1843), and *Le vrai Christianisme* (1848).

contradiction between the world turned inside out and the world turned upside down; Christopher Johnson's analysis outlined its shift in the 1840s from revolutionary outfit to sectarian group committed to displacement (the movement had never been quite committed to revolutionary transformation anyway, and Cabet's reading of class antagonism consistently emphasised cooperation and 'respectability' rather than intractable opposition).[153] The Icarian movement had 'bound together anticapitalist emotion and faith in technological progress'.[154] Johnson has called Cabet a 'utopian' socialist, and 'the nebulous and not very literate author of a communist plan called *Voyage en Icarie* who later went off into the American wilderness for yet another try at community building'.[155] Yet the Icarians are important; and while Johnson concludes that, despite their strength, they 'had little direct influence on the development of the European socialist movement', Cabet was able at one point to represent the political attitudes, as Engels noted in 1847, 'of the great mass of the French Proletarians'.[156]

The Icarians focused on displacement. After years of internal turmoil (the poorer militants tended to abandon the movement), Cabet announced that, rather than pursuing a revolutionary project in France, it was better to create a new 'nation' of Icarians in America. Johnson has called this predicament the 'bitter choice between the promotion of working-class revolution and escape'.[157] True, not many followed Cabet across the ocean (the Icarian emigrants were supposed to pay their way), but many responded enthusiastically to his call. Those who remained, after the internal conflict of the preceding years and the departure of many comrades, still rejected revolution. The revolutions of 1848 sealed the movement's fate, and the organisation rapidly disappeared.

Cabet had almost no rural following (there was no threatened class of small proprietors at this stage in France), and his supporters were concentrated in provincial cities (Reims, Vienne, Lyon), and in Paris. Transformations in the technologies of production had altered working conditions, greatly reducing the status of workers in traditional trades.

153 Christopher H. Johnson, 'Communism and the Working Class before Marx: The Icarian Experience', *American Historical Review* 76: 3 (June 1971).

154 Ibid., p. 644.

155 Ibid., p. 642.

156 Ibid., p. 643; cited at p. 647.

157 Ibid., p. 657.

Johnson has noted that these transformations were pre-industrial, and that there was no concentration of industrial workers in areas where the Icarians were strong. In Paris, the commercialization and 'ready-made' production was 'moving apace' in older industries; Lyon, however,

> was dominated by the silk industry, which exhibited a highly capitalistic putting-out system of production marked by intense antagonism between *canut* [Lyonnais silk worker] and *fabricant*. Traditional craft industry held sway in the other towns where Icarian communism showed strength . . . [T]his correlates well with the occupational analysis of the movement. The virtual absence of Icarians in the rapidly industrializing cities of the Nord, such as Lille and Roubaix, is indicative.[158]

This 'market revolution' also resulted in contradictions; displacement in this case was a likely response especially because the possibility of revolutionary action was still unavailable, or was pre-emptively rejected by these urban workers:

> Thus increased efficiency, marked by concentration of ownership, ruralization of labor resources, and experiments with mixed cloths, became the hallmark of Lyonnais entrepreneurship. Prices fell, the *fabricants* turned the screw, and the *canuts* were faced with downward pressure on their wages and higher rates of unemployment than had existed in the halcyon days gone by. This frustrating experience fell upon the most skilled and literate working-class population in France, a population also renowned for its sobriety and its sensitive, often rather mystical mentality. Icarian communism took Lyon by storm.[159]

The perception of social upheaval was widespread: '[F]or all the old-line handicraftsmen, still thinking in terms of quality of workmanship and enjoying the dignity of independence, the mass-production climate created by *confection* (ready-made production) must have had devastating psychological effects'.[160] In other words, the Icarians were

158 Ibid., p. 653.
159 Ibid., p. 658.
160 Ibid., p. 660.

experiencing proletarianisation during the 1830s and 1840s. Handicraft artisans, especially tailors, weavers and shoemakers, made up the bulk of the Icarian movement.[161] Johnson remarked that a 'married man was hard pressed to stay above water unless his wife and children were employed' (in France, too, the market transformation seemed to threaten 'manhood').[162] The obvious responses would have been accommodation or genuine revolutionary organising. But the prospect of a spatial escape was more appealing in this milieu.

Cabet's displaced utopia envisaged a return to a lost 'Golden Age' – he imagined a movement through time as well as space. His plan envisaged a communal society dwelling in an imaginary new country: Icaria. This prospect captured the imagination of working-class communities and individuals who were especially anxious about their future, and suspicious of revolutionary and conspiratorial politics, preferring Cabet's pacifism, legalism and emphasis on civil courage (and apparent religiosity). Moreover, Cabet's doctrines insisted on familial orders: he was interested in the reproduction of a particular community, not in the violent overthrow of society.

Women were especially drawn to the Icarian movement. They resented the masculinised politics of other revolutionary milieus (though Johnson notes that while Cabet 'wrote at length about the domestic, economic, and sexual oppression of women, he did not believe in women's suffrage and showed scant regard for their rights').[163] The *Almanach icarien pour 1846* touched on the gendered politics of the Icarians:

> Before Icarian Communism appeared, our husbands were nearly all in secret societies . . . neglecting their work, spending all their money, always uneasy and upset, often arrested and prosecuted; and we were always abandoned, always in misery and anxiety. Since Icarian Communism, on the contrary, everything has changed; our husbands have renounced secret societies, and we no longer fear those dreadful *visites domiciliaires*, those terrible arrests, that ruined us in the past; they take us with them to their meetings with their friends to discuss

161 Ibid., p. 656.
162 Ibid., p. 665.
163 Ibid., p. 676–7.

> things; the women thus find themselves meeting together along with their husbands and their children.[164]

The Icarian communities were thus reasserting a 'truer' form of manhood, while civil courage 'provided the militant with a manly alternative to violence and conspiracy'.[165] One source recalled the Icarian meetings as social events:

> The Lyonnais Icarians formed several groups of which the most important met at the home of M. Garqon, rue Saint Rose, in the Croix Rousse. I often attended these meetings, which were composed of men, women, and children. Evenings there passed agreeably. We recited fables. We sang politico-socialist songs that were, for the most part, written by young Icarians. We discussed all sorts of political and social questions. It was an excellent way for men to get used to public speaking. To please the women and children, the evenings usually ended in playing games.[166]

This was a self-constituted collective without a territory, a people without a land.

It was Icarian *families* that eventually migrated to America – Johnson describes the typical Icarian as 'a family man of middle age who had already endured considerable hardship and who was frustrated by his own lack of mobility'.[167] Then, in May 1847, came the announcement: '*Allons en Icarie!*' ('Lets' go to Icaria!').[168] A social movement dedicated to the transformation of society was turned into a separate body politic committed to its reconstitution elsewhere: 'a heightened spirit of exclusivism and of religious enthusiasm grew among those Icarians who remained loyal'.[169]

The Icarians, of course, were not alone in dreaming of reconstituted community elsewhere. Like Cabet, Robert Owen also engaged systematically with the prospect of turning the world inside out. He founded a

164 Cited in ibid., at p. 674.
165 Ibid., p. 674.
166 Cited in ibid., at p. 680.
167 Ibid., p. 677.
168 Ibid., p. 680.
169 Ibid., p. 686.

colony for his workers away from his factories, then another on another continent, and then another still further away.[170] Owen had initially devised a 'Home colonization Plan' for Britain, but as his 'Villages of Cooperation' came to nothing in the old country, he turned to America, in particular to New Harmony, Indiana, where the built architecture resembled that of Van den Bosch's Colonies of Benevolence.[171] The distinction between internal and external colonialism was not relevant to him, and he then focused again on Britain, again proposing a home colonisation scheme for the idle poor.[172]

Owen is widely seen as the father of British socialism, but he was as much a conservative as a socialist, and never approved of militancy (indeed, as V. A. C. Gatrell has noted, he initially saw himself as 'the spokesman of tory philanthropy').[173] His communities would opt out and relocate, and Owen specified every detail pertaining to their relocation, including appropriate home furnishings, dress, and even heating systems. These communities would change society by example, not revolution. Owen yearned for a return to the social peace he thought had reigned in rural Wales, where he had grown up. He embraced displacement, but never really specified where exactly his communities should be established; his projects were not site-specific. And yet, in an important sense they were: while he focused on these communities' organisation more than anything else – he paid attention to the quality of the land, its size, its distribution and its spatial organisation – as his communities were to be established in ways that did not upset existing sociopolitical arrangements, they had to be somewhere else: anywhere else.

New Harmony was his most ambitious experiment. That it should be in the 'New' world after his political project had been defeated in the

170 See Robert Owen, *A New View of Society, and Report to the County of Lanark* (Harmondsworth: Penguin, 1969).

171 See Michelangelo Sabatino and Ben Nicholson, eds, *Avant-Garde in the Cornfields: Architecture, Landscape, and Preservation in New Harmony* (Minneapolis: University of Minnesota Press, 2019).

172 See John F. C. Harrison, *Robert Owen and the Owenites in Britain and America: The Quest for the New Moral World* (London: Routledge, 2009); Phillip Newell, *A New Harmony: The Spirit, the Earth, and the Human Soul* (San Francisco: Jossey-Bass, 2011); José Maria Herrera, 'Vision of a Utopian Texas: Robert Owen's Colonization Scheme', *Southwestern Historical Quarterly* 116: 4 (2013), pp. 343–56.

173 See V. A. C. Gatrell, 'Introduction', in Robert Owen, *A New View of Society, and Report to the County of Lanark* (Harmondsworth: Penguin, 1969), pp. 15, 21.

'Old' one is also significant. But the original development of his project should be placed in the context of increasing revolutionary tensions, luddite activism, the Peterloo Massacre, and the comprehensive transformation of society that accompanied the industrial revolution (he knew especially about this latter transformation – he was a keen observer and a successful industrialist). The ascendancy of a repressive disposition in the ruling classes and militant recalcitrance in the emerging working class both worried him. He remained consistent in his non-revolutionary stance, and in later years opposed Chartist agitation as much as any conservative. 'Reason' was his proposed solution, not 'parliamentary reform, revolution, class conflict'.[174]

Owen recommended a pre-emptive move. There was urgency, he argued, and if his model was not adopted, then 'general disorder must ensue'.[175] He did not aim to return to a preindustrial world, but thought that the interdependence and social harmony that he believed had been typical of pastoral Britain in the past could be reconstituted. The end of war with France had produced a genuine revolutionary crisis, and the succeeding economic slump had highlighted unprecedented social cleavages. He prepared his proposal for reform in the expectation that his record of managing his industrial estate at New Lanark would convince the powers that be to endorse his project. It did not happen: in 1817 his project was finally rejected. He had been snubbed; his report was not even considered. The pre-emptive move he advocated was rejected in favour of a repressive stance. It was a turning point in his career. He then became isolated, and was never able to regain his influence in conservative circles.

Believing that a good society could be instituted one small-scale community at a time, beginning with New Lanark, he therefore proceeded alone. The Owenite small communities, the Villages of Cooperation, embraced spade cultivation rather than the plough (displacement, rather than food production or efficiency, were the main point). The *Report to the County of Lanark of a Plan for Relieving Public Distress* (1821) condemned the capitalist ethic and heralded a harmonious society. Owen framed the *Report* as a response to Robert Torrens, who had savagely attacked him in 1819 in the *Edinburgh Review*. Torrens had rehearsed the

174 Ibid., p. 22.

175 Cited in ibid., p. 34.

political-economy argument, noting that Owen had 'excluded a consideration of rent and profit, landlord and capitalist from his theory entirely'.[176] This was no theory, Torrens had concluded; but that was Owen's main point: he had assumed that his communities would be entirely separate from society, and that they would not need to consider rent and profit. Owen had embraced displacement, and his solutions 'were to be implemented outside the existing social system'.[177] They ultimately failed, but primarily because the envisaged separation could not be sustained, not because integration had not been considered.

Owen argued that, while industrialisation and overpopulation were devaluing manual labour, manual labour properly directed elsewhere could retain or regain its value. Insisting on the increased yields of spade cultivation, Owen argued that Britain was actually underpopulated, and that one could therefore colonise at 'home'.[178] His main argument was that the change he was advocating would not happen in urban and industrial locales. It was to happen somewhere else first, and would then be brought back – two successive displacements were thus envisaged. Owen's agricultural villages were to be separate: someone would populate these communities, and someone else, somewhere else, would look at them from some distance and decide to join or emulate them. Importantly, everyone had an interest in establishing these villages: the 'landed proprietors', the 'large capitalists', the 'established companies', the 'parishes and counties', and even the 'associations of the middle and working classes of farmers, mechanics, and tradesmen'.[179]

This model was eminently non-revolutionary. The 're-arrangement of society', Owen emphasized,

> will be effected in peace and quietness, with the goodwill and hearty concurrence of all parties, and of every people. It will necessarily commence by common consent, on account of its advantage, almost simultaneously among all civilized nations; and, once begun, will daily advance with an accelerated ratio, unopposed, and bearing down before it the existing system of the world.[180]

176 Cited in ibid., p. 73.
177 Ibid., p. 79.
178 Owen, *New View of Society*, p. 201.
179 Ibid., p. 252.
180 Ibid., p. 253.

Owen later restated his non-revolutionary proposition, cautioning that 'not any part of the existing system shall be prematurely disturbed'.[181]

Despite his political isolation, Owen contributed to a significant public debate. As we have seen, he was not alone in proposing displacement as a possible solution to growing contradictions. Jeremy Bentham, who had remained a committed anticolonialist between the 1790s and the 1830s, also considered displacement at the end of his career. Many have pointed out that utilitarianism was an excuse for despotism in the colonies, but, as Jennifer Pitts has convincingly demonstrated, it was not Bentham but his disciples – and especially the Mills – who were committed colonialists.[182] And yet, while Bentham consistently made no distinctions between Europeans in the colonies and their descendants and colonised others, he made an exception for 'systematic' colonisation.[183] It was Wakefield who had convinced the old man.[184] Bentham thus wrote in 1831 the framework for a charter of a society dedicated to settling parts of Australia. Like Owen, he focused on every detail, including the physical exercises the colonists should perform during their outbound voyage. It was a scheme aiming at 'transferring individuals in an unlimited multitude from a state of indigence to a state of affluence'.[185] This shift in economic condition was crucially predicated on relocation.

Likewise, whereas Charles Fourier himself was ultimately interested in emplaced change, his followers in Britain and America were often committed advocates of settler colonialism.[186] Britain's Fourierists were especially interested in colonial issues, and saw the colonies as locations

---

181 Ibid., p. 268.

182 See Jennifer Pitts, 'Legislator of the World? A Rereading of Bentham on Colonies', *Political Theory* 31: 2 (2003).

183 Jeremy Bentham, 'Emancipate Your Colonies', in Philip Schofield, Catherine Pease-Watkin and Cyprian Blamires, eds, *The Collected Works of Jeremy Bentham* (Oxford: Oxford University Press, 2002); Jeremy Bentham, 'Rid Yourselves of Ultramaria', in Philip Schofield, ed., *The Collected Works of Jeremy Bentham* (Oxford: Oxford University Press, 1995). The former was an appeal to the French Republican Assembly, the latter to the Latin American Creoles rebelling against Spain.

184 See Pitts, 'Legislator of the World?', p. 226.

185 Cited in Semmel, 'Philosophic Radicals and Colonialism', p. 519.

186 For Britain, see Lloyd Jenkins, 'Fourierism, Colonization and Discourses of Associative Emigration', *Area* 35: 1 (2003). For the United States, see Carl J. Guarnieri, *The Utopian Alternative: Fourierism in Nineteenth-Century America* (Ithaca, NY: Cornell University Press, 1991); Jonathan Beecher, *Charles Fourier: The Visionary and His World* (Berkeley: University of California Press, 1986).

where Fourierist principles could best inform social organisation – 'Emancipation, Emigration, and Colonization' was one of their slogans.[187] According to these advocates, colonisation could relieve the worker from the tyranny of isolation in the workplace and from oppression – some even praised the associative character of convict life in New South Wales over the alienation of the new industrial mills.[188] But it was in the 1840s in the United States that Fourierism would benefit from what Schlesinger calls several 'outbursts of Utopian enthusiasm.'[189] Owenite and Fourierist movements there adopted the 'patent-office model', believing that 'communal and cooperative settlements could serve as social laboratories and that by experimenting on a small scale the reformers might teach the larger world some lessons.'[190] Fourierism was propagated in the United States by Albert Brisbane as 'Associationism'; it expressed a 'vigorous disavowal of class conflict' and emphasised 'class harmony and pastoralism.'[191] The idea of 'homesteadism' developed in this context.

Horace Greeley embraced this mode of social change. Writing about New Harmony, he proclaimed that there would be 'no paupers and no surplus labor [and no] inefficiency in production and waste in consumption', that 'in association the future may be assured', and that the whole of society would thereby be reformed.[192] Creating a society devoid of pauperism and class divisions, allowing an outlet for all surplus labour by constantly 'opening' new land, ensuring that commodities could be effectively traded by a population of virtuous settler republicans, and that a

187 Cited in Jenkins, 'Fourierism, Colonization and Discourses', p. 87.

188 Ibid., p. 89.

189 Schlesinger, *Age of Jackson*, p. 361.

190 Robert S. Fogarty, *All Things New: American Communes and Utopian Movements, 1860–1914* (Chicago: University of Chicago Press, 1990), p. 10. The Brook Farm community, active in the 1840s just outside Boston, was very influential, albeit ephemeral. It was a crucial site of political experimentation (Nathaniel Hawthorne was a member and wrote about it). Initially organised in accordance with Transcendentalist precepts, eventually it became Fourierist. Henry James, Ralph Waldo Emerson, Horace Greeley, Margaret Fuller and David Thoreau visited the community and liked what they saw. Its organising principles revolved around pooling labour and considering all labour, including that of women, equally valuable.

191 Detecting a non-revolutionary stance, Schlesinger insightfully noted that Fourierism 'appeased' the consciences of 'sensitive men' without 'committing them to any very drastic action'. Schlesinger, *Age of Jackson*, pp. 363–4.

192 Cited in Robert P. Sutton, *Communal Utopias and the American Experience: Secular Communities, 1824–2000* (Westport, CT: Praeger, 2004), p. x.

community of settlers could reshape the whole of society through their own example – all of these priorities were predicated on displacement. The idea that separate, regenerated communities would eventually reform the whole of society is especially telling. No action was needed other than relocation – Greeley, after all, posed as a radical but recommended that 'young men' should 'strike westward' rather than go on strike.

The stark choice between turning the world turned inside out and revolution was especially obvious to the German socialist revolutionaries of 1848, who were exiled to the antebellum United States and left revolution behind.[193] They did not think New York was an 'empty land', but they thought that the young republic had an enormous capacity for expanding on 'free', 'empty' lands. Some of them had very successful military careers, defending the Union's prerogatives against the challenges generated by the expansionary needs of a different mode of domination. These revolutionary exiles were escaping defeat in Europe; but many European revolutions were defeated in the nineteenth century, and as defeat or its likelihood sunk in, relocation had often emerged as an alternative. This was especially so in Britain, where the ongoing prospect of moving to the colonies of settlement allowed Chartism to focus on emigration as well as on land reform.[194]

But the nexus linking colonisation overseas with labour militancy in Britain, as we have seen, had preceded Chartism, and the mass protests surrounding the deportation of the 'Tolpuddle Martyrs', when six agricultural labourers from Dorset were convicted and sentenced to penal

193 On the German post-1848 exiles in the United States, see Robin Blackburn, *An Unfinished Revolution: Karl Marx and Abraham Lincoln* (London: Verso, 2011); Bruce Levine, *The Spirit of 1848: German Immigrants, Labor Conflict, and the Coming of the Civil War* (Urbana: University of Illinois Press, 1992); Alison Clark Efford, *German Immigrants, Race, and Citizenship in the Civil War Era* (Cambridge: Cambridge University Press, 2013); Mischa Honeck, *We Are the Revolutionists: German-Speaking Immigrants and American Abolitionists after 1848* (Athens: University of Georgia Press, 2011); Andrew Zimmerman, 'From the Second American Revolution to the First International and Back Again: Marxism, the Popular Front, and the American Civil War', in Gregory Downs and Kate Masur, eds, *The World the Civil War Made* (Chapel Hill, NC: University of North Carolina Press, 2015). On republican democratic European revolutionaries turning settler colonialists in the Americas and especially in Argentina, see Alessandro Bonvini, Stephen Jacobson, 'Democratic imperialism and Risorgimento colonialism: European legionnaires on the Argentine Pampa in the 1850s', *Journal of Global History* (2021).

194 Taylor, 'The 1848 Revolutions and the British Empire', p. 159.

transportation to Australia in 1834 for organising a friendly society, are now celebrated as the origin of the modern British workers' rights movement. The labourers were pardoned two years later and returned to England; but five of them later voluntarily migrated to London, Upper Canada.[195] In this instance, relocation was not the issue – the question was whether it should be voluntary. But the workers who embraced Chartist leader Feargus O'Connor's 'Land Plan' and broke the unity of the movement also insisted on the advisability of voluntary relocation.[196] Unlike Cabet, O'Connor never recommended moving abroad; but he did propose relocation as a solution – the movement was to be away from the industrial districts of Northern England and towards rural settings (importantly, O'Connor did not cause the movement to fail; on the contrary, it was his project that was born out of the defeat of a revolutionary movement). Born into a prominent Irish Protestant radical family (his brother had fought with Bolívar and his father was a United Irishman), O'Connor was elected to parliament, but was subsequently disqualified. He had joined the Chartist movement early and had become one of its leaders.[197]

O'Connor travelled extensively through the English north and Midlands, addressing huge meetings, denouncing the new Poor Law, and advocating the 'Five Cardinal Points of Radicalism' – a genuinely revolutionary manifesto. After the movement's defeat, he spent time in prison and changed his mind: revolution was no longer needed if change could be enacted elsewhere. In prison, he wrote a series of letters for the *Northern Star* under the heading 'Letters to the Irish Landlords', in which he advocated a scheme of peasant proprietorship. After the first wave of Chartism was crushed, he established the Chartist Cooperative Land Company in 1845. The Company sought to buy large agricultural

195 See Peter Jones, 'The Tolpuddle Martyrs Museums and Related Sites', *Labour History Review* 67: 2 (2002).

196 See David Lloyd, *Irish Culture and Colonial Modernity* (Cambridge: Cambridge University Press, 2011), pp. 76–84. On the Land Plan and Chartism, see also Dorothy Thompson, *The Chartists: Popular Politics in the Industrial Revolution* (New York: Pantheon, 1984); James Epstein, *The Lion of Freedom: Feargus O'Connor and the Chartist Movement, 1832–1842* (London: Croom Helm, 1982); James Epstein and Dorothy Thompson, eds, *The Chartist Experience: Studies in Working-Class Radicalism and Culture, 1830–60* (London: Macmillan, 1982); David Jones, *Chartism and the Chartists* (New York: St Martin's, 1975).

197 Paul A. Pickering, *Feargus O'Connor: A Political Life* (Brecon: Merlin, 2008).

estates in order to subdivide them into smallholdings that could be let to individuals.

Like Owen, O'Connor saw industrialism in unvaryingly negative terms. If machines were now emptying the land (he saw land as the ultimate source of all wealth and wellbeing), the first mistake had been the movement away from it:

> [T]he poor countryman who gave up his house and home under the compulsion of the Poor Law Amendment Act, in the hope of going to a permanent situation, was unconscious in the 'hey-day' of manual labor, as then applied to infant machinery, that each improvement in the one would be a nail in the coffin of the other. Estates were cleared of willing immigrants seduced by the spirit of the moment, and when anticipation had failed, they then framed the stringent rules under which the hellish law had placed them, when they sought for an asylum in the parish of their fathers. Had it not been for machinery, the Poor Law Amendment Act never would have passed – nay, never would have been ventured upon, because the whole force of popular indignation would have been directed against the general plunder, while opposition was much mitigated in consequence of the casual provision which machinery offered as a substitute; thus has the Poor Law Amendment Act been another direct effect upon machinery.[198]

Industrial machinery, O'Connor argued,

> opens a fictitious, unsettled, and unwholesome market for labor, leaving to the employer complete and entire control over wages and employment. As machinery becomes improved, manual labor is dispensed with, and the dismissed constitute a surplus population of unemployed, system-made paupers, which makes a reserve for the masters to fall back upon as a means of reducing the price of labor. It makes character valueless. By the application of fictitious money, it overruns the world with produce, and makes labor a drug. It entices the agricultural laborer, under false pretenses, from the natural and

198 Cited in Frank F. Rosenblatt, *The Chartist Movement: In Its Social and Economic Aspects* (London: Routledge, 2013), p. 51.

> wholesome market, and locates him in an unhealthy atmosphere, where human beings herd together like swine.[199]

If the problem was increasingly located in an unhealthy atmosphere, O'Connor's plan aimed to raise wages by reducing the pool of surplus labour by way of a fundamental relocation. This time, however, the movement would be away from the industrial districts. O'Connor now rejected revolutionary means, which made his position in the Chartist movement untenable (William Lovett, the drafter of the Charter, considered O'Connor a 'misleader'). 'I have always been a man of peace', O'Connor argued:

> I have always denounced the man who strove to tamper with an oppressed people by any appeal to physical force. I have always said that moral force was the degree of deliberation in each man's mind which told him when submission was a duty or resistance not a crime; and that a true application of moral force would effect every change, but in case it should fail, physical force would come to its aid like an electric shock – and no man could prevent it; but that he who advised or attempted to marshal it would be the first to desert it at the moment of danger. God forbid that I should wish to see my country plunged into horrors of physical revolution. I wish her to win her liberties by peaceful means alone.[200]

This statement is probably genuine; O'Connor was unaware of the events that would lead to the disturbances of the Newport Rising.

By the time he was writing *A Practical Work on the Management of Small Farms* (1843), he was explicitly advocating relocation as a solution to all social ills.[201] Like Owen, he called for a return to the 'good old days' of spade husbandry. At the same time, he was now opposed to socialism:

> I have ever been, and I think I ever shall be opposed to the principles of communism, as advocated by several theorists. I am, nevertheless,

199 Cited in ibid., p. 110.

200 Cited in ibid., p. 111.

201 Feargus O'Connor, *A Practical Work on the Management of Small Farms* (London: John Cleave, 1843).

> a strong advocate of cooperation, which means legitimate exchange, and which circumstances would compel individuals to adopt, to the extent that communism would be beneficial. I have generally found that the strongest advocates of communism are the most lazy members of society – a class who would make a division of labor, adjudging to the most pliant and submissive the lion's share of work, and contending that their natural implement was the brain, whilst that of the credulous was the spade, the plough, the sledge and the pickaxe. Communism either destroys wholesome emulation and competition, or else it fixes too high a price upon distinction, and must eventually end in the worst description of despotism . . . whilst, upon the other hand, individual possession and co-operation of labor creates a wholesome bond between all classes of society.[202]

His plan proposed to spread peasant proprietorship, which would have allowed his peasants to meet the property qualifications enabling them to vote. *A Practical Work on the Management of Small Farms* set forth his plan to resettle surplus factory workers on smallholdings of up to four acres. O'Connor held that the only possible way to raise wages peacefully was to remove surplus labour out of the manufacturers' reach, and thus compel them to offer higher wages to those who would remain.

The land was to be subdivided, the soil improved, and farm buildings and cottages provided, together with advance sums to purchase stock. But it was an expensive proposition. Besides, industrial workers might not make good farmers, and the more land was bought, the higher the price of future purchases would be.[203] The plan was predicated on the assumption that land could be bought in unlimited quantities, and that all subscribers would become successful farmers and promptly repay all advances. The viability of farming on such a small scale and with

202 Cited in Rosenblatt, *Chartist Movement*, p. 109.

203 And yet David Lloyd argues that the plan was not necessarily doomed to failure, or a throwback to an earlier life that had become impossible by the time it was proposed. He sees it as a genuine alternative to capitalism, and cites Eileen Yeo, who considers the Land Plan 'the most extended development of the principle of Chartist self-provision, promising not only escape from the wage contract but also total independence from all the subordinating relationships of capitalist social life'. Cited in Lloyd, *Irish Culture and Colonial Modernity*, p. 80.

primitive methods was also uncertain. Nonetheless, O'Connor abandoned the Charter and vigorously promoted his Land Plan.

The Chartist Cooperative Land Company, later known as the National Land Company, acquired six small estates in 1846. In May 1847 the first of the estates was opened at Herringsgate (renamed O'Connorsville). Subscriptions came in handsomely, especially considering the poverty of most subscribers. Allocations were by ballot; the initial beneficiaries were to pay back with interest, and ultimately all subscribers would be settled.[204] Soon hundreds of households were resettled, notwithstanding objections from hostile Chartists, the press and the authorities. For a while, world turned inside out Chartism appeared to be winning over world turned upside down Chartism, and the Land Plan offered more immediate promise than the Charter. But administering the scheme proved difficult, and procuring land was a complex undertaking. Now a member of parliament for Nottingham, O'Connor proposed that the government take over the National Land Company. But the government declined, his opponents in the Chartist movement now accusing him of being 'no longer a "five point" Chartist but a "five acre" Chartist'. The new farmers were having difficulties making a living, let alone repaying their debts; and those who had paid but had not been settled yet were clamouring. A parliamentary investigation found that the National Land Company was an unlawful scheme, and that it could not fulfil the expectations it held out to its shareholders. The Land Plan was discontinued. Meanwhile, the Chartist movement itself also declined rapidly.

But this was not the end of the cooperative movement and its attempts to turn the world turned inside out in the British Isles. Decades later, Anglo-Irish (but also 'American') land reformer Horace Plunkett influentially promoted cooperative organisation to defuse revolutionary

204 Since the 1990s, several studies of the Chartist Land Company have advanced more positive interpretations of the Land Plan. See Malcolm Chase, '"We Wish Only to Work for Ourselves": The Chartist Land Plan', in M. Chase and I. Dyck, eds, *Living and Learning: Essays in Honour of J. F. C. Harrison* (Aldershot, Scholar, 1996); Jamie L. Bronstein, *Land Reform and Working-Class Experience in Britain and the United States, 1800–1862* (Stanford: Stanford University Press, 1999); Andrew Messner, 'Land, Leadership, Culture and Emigration: Some Problems in Chartist Historiography', *Historical Journal* 42: 4 (December 1999); Malcolm Chase, *Chartism: A New History* (Manchester: Manchester University Press, 2007); Malcolm Chase, '"Wholesome Object Lessons": The Chartist Land Plan in Retrospect', *English Historical Review* 118: 475 (2003).

potential in Ireland. A well-connected aristocrat, Plunkett had been a successful rancher in Wyoming for ten years and then a member of the Irish Congested Districts Board. Serving in it, he had witnessed the dismaying condition of the Irish rural districts in the 1890s. Plunkett was a consistent advocate of rural and agricultural development and of a settled and secure peasantry. Relying on American settler farming models, he endeavoured to establishing the Irish cooperative movement, contributed to *The Irish Homestead* journal, and argued that the 'industrial revolution' demanded redress through an 'agricultural revolution'. He initially believed that the economic development of the rural areas more than Home Rule was to be a solution to Ireland's problems, but later became convinced that independence (without partition and as an integral part of the British Commonwealth) would be the best way to ensure the economic development and demographic viability of the rural areas. After the nationalist revolution and after his estate was burned down by IRA revolutionaries in 1923, Plunkett chose exile and moved to England where he continued to promote rural cooperatives.[205]

Displacing endangered nationalities

Modernity is a great destroyer of nationalities as well as a fierce creator of them. Several endangered nationalities sought refuge in other places. Some sought to preserve the Welsh nation from the ravages of modernity by establishing a Welsh-speaking, self-governing 'new Wales' overseas (many had felt similarly with regard to Scotland).[206] It did not matter where, but it had to be far away, and Palestine and Vancouver Island were considered before they settled (literally) upon the Chubut Valley in Patagonia.[207] Chubut thus became a Welsh world turned inside

205 See Margaret Digby, *Horace Plunkett: An Anglo-American Irishman* (Oxford: Basil Blackwell, 1949).

206 See Sarah Sharp, 'Exporting "The Cotter's Saturday Night": Robert Burns, Scottish Romantic Nationalism and Colonial Settler Identity', *Romanticism* 25: 1 (April 2019).

207 Lucy Taylor, 'Welsh–Indigenous Relationships in Nineteenth Century Patagonia: "Friendship" and the Coloniality of Power', *Journal of Latin American Studies* 49: 1 (2017); Lucy Taylor, 'Global Perspectives on Welsh Patagonia: The Complexities of Being Both Colonizer and Colonized', *Journal of Global History* 13: 3 (2018); Lucy Taylor, 'The Welsh Way of Colonisation in Patagonia: The International Politics of Moral Superiority', *Journal of Imperial and Commonwealth History* 47: 6

out. Hugh Hughes, one of the leaders of the colony and movement, wrote the guide for the prospective settlers, the *Handbook of the Welsh Colony* (1862), stating that the movement's aim was to recognise the rights to the land held by indigenous people, and to acquire a right to it through friendship with them.

Indeed, the Welsh settlers sought to defend indigenous autonomy during the Argentinean military advance southwards – especially because protecting indigenous sovereignty was also a way for the settlers to assert their own autonomy against Argentina's incursions. Like the New England settlers two and a half centuries before, these settlers emphasised in their representations of the surrounding landscape a world socially transformed, and noted that, while in Wales hunting was 'the closed privilege of the squires and rich landlords' and game 'was reserved for the gentry', in Patagonia 'the settlers are privileged to enjoy it in abundance and variety'.[208] By moving, the colonists had claimed a right to 'speak and organise, pray and learn in Welsh'.[209] This was an arrogation of sovereignty without conflict.

Leaders of this enterprise included Lewis Jones, Michael Daniel Jones – a Congregationalist minister and father of modern Welsh nationalism – and Edwin Cynrig Roberts, who had been an emigrant to the United States, and had realised there that the Welsh language would be doomed unless it could prosper in isolation. Nationalist and preacher Michael D. Jones had advocated the idea of a Welsh-speaking colony in South America, and had called for a new 'little Wales beyond Wales'. He proposed setting it up away from the influence of the English language; he then recruited settlers and provided financing. He had also spent years in the United States, seeing Welsh immigrants quickly assimilating. Assimilation was the great enemy of endangered nationalities in the nineteenth century – but assimilation was also a type of revolution, relentlessly turning one identification into another.

(2019); Ester Whitfield, 'Empire Nation and the Fate of a Language: Patagonia in Argentine and Welsh Literature', *Postcolonial Studies* 14: 1 (2011); Glyn Williams, *The Desert and the Dream: A Study in Welsh Colonization in Chubut, 1865–1915* (Cardiff: University of Wales Press, 1975).

208 Cited in Taylor, 'Welsh–Indigenous Relationships in Nineteenth Century Patagonia', p. 158.

209 Ibid., p. 159.

Other nationalities sought salvation elsewhere. Many Polish nationalists attempted to preserve Polish nationality in the Americas while various revolutions consumed the country on the inside (one such attempt would be captured by Florian Znaniecki and William I. Thomas in their classic *The Polish Peasant in Europe and America*, which, as well as being a classic of sociology, is a book about remaining the same despite and indeed because of displacement).[210] But there had been other new Polands, such as Nowa Polska, founded in Brazil in 1871, when the Polish territories were subjected to occupation by the German, Austro-Hungarian, and Russian empires. Polish interest in colonial enterprises was thus a response to fears of cultural extinction, and Poland's nineteenth-century 'Brazil fever' was one result of such anxieties (as well as economic opportunities).[211] Subjected to foreign rule and the revolutionary transformations that it promoted, many believed that genuine national life could only be sought elsewhere.

There was also a Finnish world turned inside out. Sointula, British Columbia, was an 'ethnically homogeneous, utopian socialist commune' established in 1901.[212] An intense campaign of Russification had already eroded the Finnish old regime; but at the end of the nineteenth century industrialisation and urbanisation – both fateful revolutionary transformations – were also rampant. Socialism grew in this context, but also did its world turned inside out counterpart, and Matti Kurikka, Sointula's future leader, had shifted away from revolutionary agitation to advocate relocation instead. Active in the Finnish labour movement, Kurikka was staunchly opposed to the Lutheran Church, but also interested in Tolstoy's politics and in Madame Blavatsky's theosophy. With 200 comrades, Kurikka tried to establish a self-sufficient New Finland in Queensland, but then moved on to British Columbia, Canada. He had given up on Finland and on Finnish socialism.[213]

210 Florian Znaniecki and William I. Thomas, *The Polish Peasant in Europe and America*, 5 vols (Chicago: University of Chicago Press, 1918–20).

211 See Silvia G. Dapía, 'The Polish Presence in Latin America: An Introduction', *Polish American Studies* 69: 1 (2012); Márcio de Oliveira, 'Origins of Southern Brazil: The Importance of Polish Immigration in Paraná, 1871–1914', *Estudos Históricos* 22: 43 (2009).

212 Mikko Saikku, 'Utopians and Utilitarians: Environment and Economy in the Finnish-Canadian settlement of Sointula', *BC Studies* 154 (Summer 2007), p. 3.

213 See ibid., p. 11.

In Sointula, relationships with the indigenous people were also friendly, especially because the newly established community was not self-sufficient and needed to rely on local trade. Kurikka even believed that 'there existed a close common ancestry between Finns and First Nations in Central Asia'; but, once again, protecting indigenous autonomy was a way of affirming the settler community's independence from a progressively more assertive Canadian state.[214] Even a 'New Iceland' was envisaged in Manitoba (Canada was a site of intense experimentation with group settlements).[215] Emigration from the island was happening anyway, but the Canadian government sought to establish a group settlement after 1875 – a 'white settler reserve'. New Iceland was also a world turned inside out of sorts, while limited political opportunities – an impossible transformation in the old land – were one crucial factor prompting emigration.[216]

Many further collectives needed other places – the Doukhobor religious community, for example.[217] In 1897 the prominent Russian anarchist Peter Kropotkin had travelled from Toronto to the Pacific coast. He had already written about Canada, and appreciated its potential as a site for segregated colonies and displaced social experimentation.[218] Kropotkin believed that Doukhobor's communities could successfully resettle in Canada, and that they would effectively challenge the Russian state by escaping to somewhere outside its territorial sovereignty.

214 Ibid., p. 15.

215 John C. Lehr and Yossi Katz, 'Crown, Corporation and Church: The Role of Institutions in the Stability of Pioneer Settlements in the Canadian West, 1870–1914', *Journal of Historical Geography* 21: 4 (1995).

216 See Ryan Eyford, *White Settler Reserve: New Iceland and the Colonization of the Canadian West* (Vancouver: University of British Columbia Press, 2016); L. K. Bertram, *The Viking Immigrants: Icelandic North Americans* (Toronto: University of Toronto Press, 2020).

217 They received support from Leo Tolstoy and Peter Kropotkin. See Leo Tolstoy, 'A Letter to those Doukhobors who have migrated to Canada' (1900) – available at multiculturalcanada.ca; and Peter Kropotkin, 'Some of the Resources of Canada', *Nineteenth Century*, March 1898. Kropotkin argued that colonies are about control, but that control is either external or internal – either exercised on behalf of an external agency (as in normal colonialism) or retained by a colonising and separate sociopolitical collective (as in anarchist colonialism). As it relies on separation, the latter formation could be seen as a variant of settler colonialism.

218 See Paul Avrich, 'Kropotkin in America', *International Review of Social History* 25: 1 (1980).

Negotiating with the Canadian government on their behalf through an intermediary, he insisted: '1. No obligation of military service 2. Full independence in their inner organization 3. Land in a block; they cannot live in isolated farms'.[219] He was embracing displacement, and demanded a sovereign status for the future colonies.

Away from Russia and Canada, Mennonite nationalist endeavours eventually focused on Paraguay.[220] This group had a long tradition of autonomous self-rule and pioneering; Catherine the Great had invited their ancestors to Russia in the eighteenth century after the Prussian state had insisted on their conscription. They had been seen as 'Germanic pioneers', part of a diasporic *Auslandsdeutsche* – a semi-sovereign quasi-German settler-colonial movement characterised by an ability to retain important elements of self-rule. In Russia, Mennonite communities had once been self-determining, and were largely in control of their economic institutions.[221] Between the wars, Mennonite Zionism sought to establish a 'state', in an international diasporic effort responding to revolutionary transformations in Russia and Canada, where the traditional isolation and autonomy of Mennonite settlements was also being challenged.

Many Mennonites moved to Paraguay to 'establish an ideal Mennonite state', as one colonist noted, and to escape both revolution and modernity.[222] In this instance, 'state' formation, even if it was meant to be a state within a state, was an escape from rather than an embrace of modernity. The Paraguayan state did not interfere – it had neither the inclination nor the ability to do so. The Mennonites were escaping revolutions where the revolutions could no longer reach them; both Stalinist Russia and assimilationist Canada were left behind. The Jesuits in the seventeenth century, the defeated Australian revolutionaries who followed

219 Cited in Arneil, *Domestic Colonies*, pp. 184–5.

220 See Benjamin W. Gossen, 'Religious Nationalism in an Age of Globalization: The Case of Paraguay's "Mennonite State"', *Almanack* 14 (September–December 2016); Benjamin W. Gossen, *Chosen Nation: Mennonites and Germany in a Global Era* (Princeton, NJ: Princeton University Press, 2017).

221 See Bradley Naranch, 'Inventing the *Auslandsdeutsche*: Emigration, Colonial Fantasy, and German National Identity, 1848–71', in Eric Ames, Marcia Klotz and Lora Wildenthal, eds, *Germany's Colonial Pasts* (Lincoln, NE: University of Nebraska Press, 2005); Stefan Manz, *Constructing a German Diaspora: The 'Greater German Empire,' 1871–1914* (New York: Routledge, 2014).

222 Cited in Gossen, 'Religious Nationalism in an Age of Globalization', p. 76.

William Lane to New Australia, and the followers of Friedrich Nietzsche's brother-in-law Wilhelm Förster, who had gone to Paraguay in order to preserve an 'authentic' German racial stock threatened at home by the revolutionary prospect of Jewish assimilation – all had hoped that Paraguay, at the end of the world, would be a suitable proposition for their world turned inside out.[223]

223 On Nueva Germania, see John F. Williams, Daniela Kraus and Harry Knowles, 'Flights from Modernity: German and Australian Utopian Colonies in Paraguay, 1886–1896', *Journal of Australian Studies* 69 (2001). The authors conclude that 'Lane's utopian, agrarian socialism (rooted in mateship) and the mystical racial socialism of the Volksgemeinschaft – that was central to Nueva Germania – were based on similar reactions to modern urban society' (p. 49). These projects also shared a determination to relocate as an alternative to revolution.

3

The World Turned Inside Out up to The End of the Global Settler Revolution

During the latter decades of the nineteenth century, and anticipating the end of the 'settler revolution', Henry George and his many followers throughout the 'Angloworld' promoted the 'single tax' as a revolutionary way to avoid the need for revolution altogether.[1] George published *Our Land and Land Policy* in 1871.[2] It was an immediate success because 'homesteadism', despite sustained efforts, had not been the social success it was expected to be – George made a lot of sense to his readers. The 'limitless' domain of the United States, George argued, was running out; population was increasing and would soon approach European densities; eventually, the new world would resemble the old one.

George's essay opened with the perception of crisis: '[N]o child born this year or last year, or even three years before that, can possibly get him-self a homestead out of Uncle Sam's farm, unless he is willing to take a mountain-top or alkali patch, or to emigrate to Alaska'.[3] The

1 See Charles A. Barker, *Henry George* (New York: Oxford University Press, 1955); John L. Thomas, *Alternative America: Edward Bellamy, Henry George, Henry Demarest Lloyd and the Adversary Tradition* (Cambridge, MA: Harvard University Press, 1987); Edward Nell, *Henry George and How Growth in Real Estate Contributes to Inequality and Financial Instability* (Houndmills: Palgrave Macmillan, 2019).

2 Henry George, *Our Land and Land Policy: Speeches Lectures, and Miscellaneous Writings* (East Lansing, MI: Michigan State University Press, 1999).

3 Ibid., p. 5.

problem was not absolute land scarcity, or the prospect of land scarcity; for George the problem lay with land monopolies. It was monopolisation that was making land and settling expensive. If a frontier is defined as a locale where land is bloody cheap (this is no unnecessary swearing – it is a literal description), George was announcing the passing of the frontier a couple of decades before Frederick Jackson Turner would. The global settler revolution had peaked.

Moreover, George continued, land was being allocated to speculators who did not intend to use it themselves (to profit, they were planning to 'tax' those who would cultivate it). Expensive land was ultimately a tax on settlement, he reckoned – nobody likes taxes, and subsistence settlers, as we have seen, dislike taxes more than anyone else. And, despite the promise of homesteadism, land was becoming ever more expensive. Despite the achievements of settler independence and settler democracy, George argued, it

> was not until 1820 that the minimum price [for an acre of land] was reduced to $1.25 cash, and the Government condescended to retail in tracts of 160 acres. And it was not until 1841, sixty-five years after the Declaration of Independence, that the right of pre-emption was given to settlers upon surveyed land. In 1862 this right was extended to unsurveyed land. And in the same year, 1862, the right of every citizen to land, upon the sole condition of cultivating it, was first recognized by the passage of the Homestead law . . . But this growing liberality to the settler has been accompanied by a still more rapidly growing liberality to speculators and corporations, and since the pre-emption and homestead laws were passed, land monopolization has gone on at a faster rate than ever.[4]

Relatively speaking, the new settlers had been treated unfairly, even though, and George did not consider it, it was the dispossessed indigenous nations that had been treated more unfairly than everyone else. Speculators and corporations had outpaced the settlers. By definition, displacement is no solution if your relative speed does not exceed that from which you are escaping. For George, land grants – all land grants distributed to any interest rather than settlers: to states, to educational

4 Ibid., p. 8.

institutions, to railroad corporations – were ultimately a tax on bona fide settlers. George realised that the possibility and appeal of relocation was disappearing fast, if it had not disappeared already. A major war to maintain its viability had just been waged; but if one enemy of the possibility of turning the world inside out had been eliminated (slavery), another (monopolies) had been given free rein.

Besides, land grants for railways, George noted, despite arguments to the contrary, were actually *retarding* settlement. The grants, like the 'sufficient price' Wakefield had argued for the British colonies of settlement, ensured that primitive accumulation would be immediately transferred to the 'new' lands; but, whereas Wakefield had intended to extend primitive accumulation as a way to reconnect metropole with peripheries, George was lamenting this transfer. George was interested in the sustained possibility of an escape:

> While there is plenty of uncultivated land in the older States, we are giving away the land in the Territories under the plea of hastening settlement, and when the time comes that these lands are really needed for cultivation, they will all be monopolized, and the settler, go where he will, must pay largely for the privilege of cultivating soil which since the dawn of creation has been waiting his coming. We need not trouble ourselves about railroads; settlement will go on without them – as it went on in Ohio and Indiana, as it has gone on since our Aryan forefathers left the Asiatic cradle of the race on their long westward journey.[5]

A felicitous constellation of circumstances – available land, and a possible escape away from growing contradictions – had been discontinued. George thus proposed a return to a happier situation: he wanted to make America great again.

George focused on California because it was, in his estimation, the worst-affected state; California was where it had all ended, geographically as well as sociopolitically. The powerful Lockean fantasy of property arising from mixing one's labour with unclaimed land had ended there:

---

5 Ibid., p. 23.

> Across many of these vast estates a strong horse cannot gallop in a day, and one may travel for miles and miles over fertile ground, where no plough has ever struck, but which is all owned, and on which no settler can come to make himself a home, unless he pay such tribute as the lord of the domain chooses to exact.[6]

Settler property could not emerge there because its original formation had been pre-empted:

> Nor is there any State in the Union in which settlers in good faith have been so persecuted, so robbed, as in California. Men have grown rich, and men still make a regular business of blackmailing settlers upon public land, of appropriating their homes, and this by the power of law and in the name of justice. Land grabbers have had it pretty much their own way in California – they have moulded the policy of the general Government; have dictated the legislation of the State; have run the land offices and used the courts.[7]

And yet California could have been the most suited of all the states for denser settlement (the notion of 'denser' settlement was a necessary development in this context: if less land was needed for settler 'competence', displacement would still be possible even after the public domain had been depleted). Instead, California had been a mecca of grants: bogus grants, Mexican grants, railroad grants, scrip originating from other states and issued for a variety of purposes (half-breed scrip, educational scrip, and so on). Land monopolisation had proceeded unchecked.

And it was not only about taxing settlers with land grants and associated speculations, which amounted to an invisible tax; speculators were routinely robbing actual settlers of their properties: '[B]ad as the railroad grants are, the operations of these speculators are worse. The railroad companies can only take half the lands; the speculators take it all. The railroad companies cannot easily disturb previous settlers; but the speculators take the settler's home from under his feet.'[8] George saw a world turned 'backwards', a world that

6 Ibid., p. 25.
7 Ibid.
8 Ibid., p. 42.

> has already impressed its mark upon the character of our agriculture – more shiftless, perhaps, than that of any State in the Union where slavery has not reigned. For California is not a country of farms, but a country of plantations and estates. Agriculture is a speculation. The farmhouses, as a class, are unpainted frame shanties, without garden or flower or tree. The farmer raises wheat; he buys his meat, his flour, his butter, his vegetables, and, frequently, even his eggs. He has too much land to spare time for such little things, or for beautifying his home, or he is merely a renter, or an occupant of land menaced by some adverse title, and his interest is but to get for this season the greatest crop that can be made to grow with the least labour. He hires labour for his planting and his reaping, and his hands shift for themselves at other seasons of the year. His plough he leaves standing in the furrow, when the year's ploughing is done; his mustangs he turns upon the hills, to be lassoed when again needed. He buys on credit at the nearest store, and when his crop is gathered must sell it to the Grain King's agent, at the Grain King's prices.[9]

The farmer now relied on the market for his provisions, his labour and his produce, and on credit markets to sustain his productive units. These markets were not sustaining a putative 'harmony of interests', as Henry Carey had influentially argued; they were spawning monopolies.[10] And this was not all – George worried about the *anthropological* consequences of this state of affairs. There was 'another type of California farmer', he argued:

> He boards at the San Francisco hotels, and drives a spanking team over the Cliff House road; or, perhaps, he spends his time in the gayer capitals of the East or Europe. His land is rented for one third or one fourth of the crop, or is covered by scraggy cattle, which need to look after them only a few half-civilised vaqueros; or his great wheat fields, of from ten to twenty thousand acres, are ploughed and sown and

9 Ibid., p. 47.

10 See Lorenzo Veracini, 'Henry Carey's "Entire Bad Joke" and Henry George's "Idle Taunt": Displacement and Revolution in Nineteenth-Century America', *Settler Colonial Studies* 10: 3 (2020).

> reaped by contract. And over our ill-kept, shadeless, dusty roads, where a house is an unwonted landmark, and which run frequently for miles through the same man's land, plod the tramps, with blankets on back – the labourers of the California farmer – looking for work, in its seasons, or toiling back to the city when the ploughing is ended or the wheat crop is gathered. I do not say that this picture is a universal one, but it is a characteristic one.[11]

George then concluded: California was a *classed* society (and, he noted worriedly in relation to Chinese immigration, soon to be a raced society as well). A classed society, he foretold, must result in social disruption and revolution; but voluntary displacement was no longer an option because the land had been locked away. There was even a landed aristocracy in California – the crucial social marker of the 'Old World' had preceded the settler there. At least speculators typically aim to sell the land (dearly); a landed gentry is much worse: they are intent on holding on to it.

Revolutionary measures were thus needed to pre-empt revolution: to 'break' monopolies, open the land, and enable bona fide settlers to get secure title. George proceeded dialectically: if a tax, albeit an invisible one, had been socially detrimental, a countertax would be socially beneficial. Tax property in land, he concluded – tax the tax. If settler property had been pre-empted, it could be reasserted after the fact. The tax on the tax would reconstitute the appropriate land–labour nexus. The tax was not about increasing the role of government; on the contrary, it was about undoing the consequences of its nefarious interference. Importantly, George's land tax was predicated on a specifically land-centred theory of labour:

> The value of land and of labour must bear to each other an inverse ratio. These two are the 'terms' of production, and while production remains the same, to give more to the one is to give less to the other. The value of land is the power, which its ownership gives to appropriate the product of labour, and, as a sequence, where rents (the share of the landowner) are high, wages (the share of the labourer) are low. And thus we see it all over the world, in the countries where land is

11 George, *Our Land and Land Policy*, p. 47.

> high, wages are low, and where land is low, wages are high. In a new country the value of labour is at first at its maximum, the value of land at its minimum. As population grows and land becomes monopolised and increases in value, the value of labour steadily decreases. And the higher land and the lower wages, the stronger the tendency towards still lower wages, until this tendency is met by the very necessities of existence. For the higher land and the lower wages, the more difficult is it for the man who starts with nothing but his labour to become his own employer, and the more he is at the mercy of the landowner and the capitalist.[12]

Land must be cheap; indeed, it must be free, but only to bona fide settlers, and only in limited quantities – that is, in parcels large enough to ensure a comfortable subsistence for a man and his family, his own reproduction, but also small enough to ensure that no unearned profit, no tax on future settlers, would ensue. Likewise, land that is acquired for speculation must be taxed. Thus, George's land tax reconstituted 'nature' by enabling the settler to exercise again his 'natural' and inalienable right to relocate.

With George's land tax, there would no longer be cause or need for revolutionary action or any reactionary response; the land tax would make relocating possible again, and relocation was for George a much, much better alternative than revolution. And revolution was indeed on George's mind. The United States was turning into Europe, and Europe was engulfed by revolution. George prophesised: '[W]e shall find ourselves embarrassed by all the difficulties which beset the statesmen of Europe – the social disease of England; the seething discontent of France.'[13] But it was not too late; reconstituting a world turned inside out was still possible! If only land were reallocated to actual settlers and in limited quantities, an 'orderly' settlement would ensue (George was concerned about dispersion, as Wakefield had been):

> There would be no necessity for building costly railroads to connect settlers with a market. The market would accompany settlement. No one would go out into the wilderness, to brave all the hardships and

12 Ibid., p. 55.
13 Ibid., p. 62.

> discomforts of the solitary frontier life; but with the foremost line of settlement would go church and schoolhouse and lecture-room. The ill-paid, overworked mechanic of the city could find a home on the soil, where he would not have to abandon all the comforts of civilisation, but where there would be society enough to make life attractive, and where the wants of his neighbours would give a market for his surplus labour until his land began to produce; and to tell those who complain of want of employment and low wages to make for themselves homes on the public domain would then be no idle taunt.[14]

The land tax could reconstitute a world that was being lost. Bona fide settlers and residents of city lots would be tax-exempt, land prices would inevitably fall, and all taxes on productive activities and exchanges could then be abolished.

In a final note, George reiterated that his proposed reform was absolutely necessary because the alternative was revolution, as the example of Paris demonstrated. For him, revolution was civilisation's death:

> This great problem of the more equal distribution of wealth must in some way be solved, if our civilisation, like those that went before it, is not to breed seeds of its own destruction. In one way or another the attempt must be made – if not in one way, then in another. The spread of education, the growth of democratic sentiment, the weakening of the influences which lead men to accept the existing condition of things as divinely appointed, insure that, and the general uneasiness of labour, the growth of trade-unionism, the spread of such societies as the International prove it! The terrible struggle of the Paris commune was but such an attempt. And in the light of burning Paris we may see how it may be that this very civilisation of ours, this second Tower of Babel, which some deem reaches so far towards heaven that we can plainly see there is no God there, may yet crumble and perish.[15]

In a footnote possibly added as news from the 'Old World' were coming in, George restated his argument and pleaded that revolution

14 Ibid., p. 71.
15 Ibid., pp. 86–7.

could be made impossible only by wide distribution of the property of land:

> And this French struggle also shows the conservative influence of the diffusion of landed property. The Radicals of Paris were beaten by the small proprietors of the provinces. Had the lands of France been in the hands of a few, as the first revolution found it, the raising of the red flag on the Hôtel de Ville would have been the signal for a Jacquerie in every part of the country. So conscious are the extreme reds of the conservative influence of property in land that they have for a long time condemned as a fatal mistake the law of the first Republic which provided for the equal distribution of land among heirs, not because it has not improved the condition of the peasantry, but because the improvement in their condition and the interest which their possession of land gives them in the maintenance of order dispose them to oppose the violent remedies which the workmen of the cities think necessary.[16]

George's restored world turned inside out would offer a viable alternative to both monopolistic reaction and revolutionary adventurism.

The French worlds turned inside out

George underscored the link between voluntary displacement and revolution by reference to the Communards; but the Communards themselves did so through their exile following defeat – at least those who survived. Kristin Ross's *Communal Luxury* reconstructs the history of the Commune after the Commune – her book is thus about displacement, about the Commune's 'centrifugal effects', even if the Commune was as emplaced a revolutionary event as could be.[17] Defeated revolution produced serial displacements, Ross argued, as the exiled Communards and their comrades begun theorising the

16 See ibid., p. 87.

17 Kristin Ross, *Communal Luxury: The Political Imaginary of the Paris Commune* (London: Verso, 2016), p. 2.

possibility and necessity of anarcho-communist 'decentralised communities'.[18] Decentralisation – a type of displacement – was a theoretical response to defeat and repression; but repression too, of course, had produced displacements, and, unlike the deported insurgents of 1848, the Communards were typically not sent to Algeria, but to New Caledonia, 'as far away as possible'.[19]

Thousands of exiles dispersed in all directions; some ended up thinking that the colonies could be the solution to stubborn contradictions and embraced the politics of displacement in Algeria (as many of the German exiles of 1848 had done in America). Luis Riel commented that the colonies could save the 'French genius', and become stepping-stones leading to a 'Universal Republic' (they did not).[20] Then again, most anarcho-communists did not abandon their revolutionary choice, and did not embrace displacement. Elisée Reclus, who would write against anarchist colonies and other intentional communities, symptomatically recommended that, whenever bourgeois people suggested that anarchists should move to an island where they could establish a communist society (that is, when bourgeois individuals suggested displacement as an alternative to revolution), they should have responded 'yes . . . we want the Île-de-France'.[21]

Ross also focused on the ways in which the Commune became a turning point in Marxian theory. Marx had supported it, and after its defeat considered that traditional Russian villages could function as cornerstones in achieving socialism. After arguing for decades that his former comrades of 1848 should return from America and fight the next revolutionary struggle in Europe, even Marx now agreed that revolution might be displaced.

But Ross also followed William Morris and Peter Kropotkin, finding the Commune in unexpected places – Iceland and Finland, respectively. Morris and Kropotkin looked elsewhere because the centre had been overtaken by reaction. Kropotkin concluded that 'agricultural self-sufficiency' was the key, and that this could possibly be achieved in Paris but would be more easily accomplished away from industrial centres.[22]

18 See ibid., pp. 113–16.

19 Ibid., p. 33.

20 Cited in ibid., p. 35.

21 Cited in ibid., p. 122.

22 See ibid., p. 71.

Likewise, Morris realised that Iceland could be an ideal location for social experimentation because it had developed in isolation from Europe.[23] They both sought alternatives elsewhere, and both concluded that factory workers should reconnect with the land. Kropotkin especially appreciated how factory workers in St Petersburg had 'retained the spirit of the Russian village', and regularly returned home for several months a year.[24]

But, by then, there was already a long history of French colonial displacement in the face of crisis and defeat; I have mentioned the Huguenot migrations and socialist Icaria, but there were many more. Even Korou, French Guyana, was established primarily to compensate for the loss of Canada after 1763.[25] It was meant to be a 'wonderful revenge', even if the colony floundered. During the nineteenth century, and despite a supposedly typical French reluctance to embrace emigration, French settler colonialism prospered.[26] The many Saint Simonian French colonial officials who promoted both New Caledonia and Algeria as propitious sites for the recuperation of 'fallen' revolutionaries after the revolutionary outbursts of 1848 and 1871 were thinking about turning the world inside out rather than facing a world turned upside down.[27] It was an age of revolution, and revolution was repeatedly a catalyst for French emigration: 28,000 French had gone to California after the revolution of 1848, and Algeria had become a settler colony after that revolutionary year. New Caledonia was turned into a settler colony after 1871.

Turning urban revolutionaries into farmers had been a longstanding ambition of French social experimentation, especially in Algeria. To

23 See ibid., p. 73.

24 See ibid., p. 115.

25 See Marion Godfroy, *Kourou and the Struggle for a French America* (Houndmills: Palgrave, 2015).

26 Colonial governments had to counter this 'natural' inclination. See Isabelle Merle, 'Drawing Settlers to New Caledonia: French Colonial Propaganda in the Late Nineteenth Century', in Tony Chafer and Amanda Sackur, eds, *Promoting the Colonial Idea: Propaganda and Visions of Empire in France* (Basingstoke: Palgrave, 2002).

27 See Isabelle Merle, *Expériences coloniales. La Nouvelle Calédonie (1853–1920)* (Paris: Belin, 1995); David Prochaska, *Making Algeria French* (Cambridge: Cambridge University Press, 1990); Jennifer E. Sessions, 'Colonizing Revolutionary Politics: Algeria and the French Revolution of 1848', *French Politics, Culture and Society*, 33 (2015). See also Pamela M. Pilbeam, *Saint-Simonians in Nineteenth-Century France: From Free Love to Algeria* (Basingstoke: Palgrave Macmillan, 2013); Osama Abi-Mershed, *Apostles of Modernity: Saint Simonians and the Civilizing Mission in Algeria* (Stanford, CA: Stanford University Press, 2010).

make this point, shortly after his coup d'état, in 1851 Louis-Napoleon Bonaparte exiled about six thousand political opponents there. For the future emperor, this mass deportation was primarily about purging France of small-town republicans; but French colonial administrators in Algeria – often Saint Simonians who opposed Bonaparte at home but faithfully served him overseas – espoused a politics that was place-specific, and saw in the deported the opportunity to establish a new type of agricultural colonialism. The convicts were moved to partially established villages, and were included in a scheme whereby prisoners could win freedom and ownership of agricultural land through hard work. Their families were then to be shipped free of charge to Africa.[28]

These experiments were deemed successful. Benjamin Stora observes how a revolutionary tradition was profoundly transformed through colonialism:

> Successive deportations of republicans hostile to Louis-Philippe and then Napoleon III were needed to strengthen the colony. The exiles of 1848, the deportees of the Second Empire, and penniless immigrants all claimed the heritage of liberal republicanism. These first French of Algeria, a mixture of peasants left behind by the industrial revolution in France and of exiled 'forty-eighters' and Communards, gradually acquired the mentality of small land owners. And the old Republican tradition, an amalgam of peasant individualism and attachment to liberty, flourished in this section of Algeria's European population.[29]

It is significant, however, that the French world turned inside out was interwoven with carceral colonialism, whether internal or external, and with the need to pre-empt revolution.[30] The *bagne*, convict colonialism

28 S. R. Ravis, 'Turning French Convicts into Colonists: The Second Empire's Political Prisoners in Algeria, 1852–1858', *French Colonial History* 2 (2002).

29 Benjamin Stora, 'The "Southern" World of the *Pied Noirs*: References to and Representations of Europeans in Colonial Algeria', in Caroline Elkins and Susan Pedersen, eds, *Settler Colonialism in the Twentieth Century: Projects, Practices, Legacies* (New York: Routledge, 2005), p. 230.

30 See Stephen A. Toth, *Beyond Papillion: The French Overseas Penal Colonies, 1854–1952* (Lincoln, NE: University of Nebraska Press, 2006). On French 'agricultural colonies' for 'impoverished, orphaned, abandoned, and/or delinquent children and youth', see Ann Stoler, 'On Archival Labor: Recrafting Colonial History', *Diálogo Andino*

– a well-developed practice in nineteenth-century France – was born in fantasies of regenerative work in a location that was 'other' (primarily in its lack of resemblance to congested urban settings).[31] Stephen Toth has remarked that critiques of the urban environment in a rapidly urbanising society were 'an almost visceral reaction to the "modern" world in which the city's differences from the countryside were perceived as pathological'.[32] The most prominent element in this relationship was revolution: the city bred revolutions, and Toth referred to the widespread perception that 'criminal recidivists' were merely future revolutionaries.[33] One bureaucrat he cited noted: 'it is through agricultural work and the spectacle of nature that the spirit is calmed. Ownership, marriage, paternity: these are the means by which one is influenced; transportation brings about the regeneration of men because it takes them away from our degraded and infamous metropolitan society, to make them pioneers of a new colonial society'.[34] In other words, settler colonialism in one location would pre-empt revolution in another.

Much later, but not dissimilarly, the response to revolutionary crisis during the French Third Republic – a polity itself born in a revolutionary crisis – was still more settler colonialism.[35] Victor Hugo,

46 (2015). Stoler described how children 'would be sent first to "preparatory colonies" from ages one to twelve (colonies with nursemaids), then to "colonies of transition" for those aged 12 to 14, where adolescent bodies might be first "bronzed by the sun of Provence" and finally to "colonies of application", for those aged 14 to 21, primed to be cultivators and equipped with a disciplined cultivation of the self' (p. 160).

31 Tocqueville himself had been an ardent domestic colonialist. He was an ardent imperialist, too, and saw the two enterprises as intimately related. For him, Algeria had to become a world turned inside out, and the penal institutions located there, which were antithetical to it, had to be brought back to the metropole. But this was not the end of the story. The settler-colonial project needed bodies. Tocqueville thought that the domestic colonies would manufacture republican citizens who would then move to Algeria. One colonialism was thus propaedeutic to the other. Scholars have noted the apparent contradiction between his simultaneous support for and antagonism towards colonialism and imperialism, and his liberal politics in America, as opposed to his authoritarian stance with regard to Algeria. Barbara Arneil, however, finds consistency in his politics. See Barbara Arneil, *Domestic Colonies* (Oxford: Oxford University Press, 2017), p. 41.

32 Toth, *Beyond Papillion*, p. 29.

33 Ibid., pp. 31, 32.

34 Cited in ibid., p. 34.

35 See Margaret Cook Andersen, *Regeneration through Empire: French Pronatalists and Colonial Settlement in the Third Republic* (Lincoln, NE: University of Nebraska Press, 2014).

who famously knew about the potential for social conflict but was always careful not to endorse revolutionary change, proclaimed in 1879 that to 'make old Africa fit for civilization' was 'the problem', and that 'Europe [would] resolve it'. 'Go, peoples, take this land!' He added: 'Who owns it? No one! Take this land that is God's land. God gives land to men. God offers Africa to Europe. Take it! . . . Pour your surplus into Africa and, at the same time, solve your social problems. Transform your proletarians into property-owners'.[36] This was the expression of a French republican common sense, a sensibility that would be persistent and long-lasting. Recurring crisis – indeed, a succession of compounding defeats, 1871, near defeat in World War I, and then debacle in 1940 – was consistently responded to with this well-known reflex: relocate and turn proletarians into property-owners somewhere else. In each instance, defeat in the metropole enabled the colonial empire to figure more prominently as a symbol of national regeneration.

As crises periodically engulfed France, paradoxically, even widespread concerns about depopulation in the French metropole prompted arguments in support of settler emigration. This attested to the myth of the 'prolific settler': allegedly Frenchmen became more prolific and more virile in the settler colonies, away from the degenerating influences of the modern urban metropole. One commentator remarked: 'by touching the African land [Algeria] our race has acquired a new vitality. Let us encourage emigration: for some thousands of French people that Europe would lose, there will be millions of Neo-French people that Africa will return to us one day'.[37] This myth would persist even in the face of evidence of declining birth rates. In the imagination, and in colonial rhetorics, empire and demography were intimately linked, and French pro-natalists consistently saw the colonies as indispensable social laboratories. For them, it was a matter of remasculinisation through displacement (the urban revolution – like the 'market revolution' in North America, and before that the English 'new' economy of the seventeenth century – was challenging masculinities). This alternative was typically framed as a choice between degeneration in the metropole or regeneration in the

36 Cited in Achille Mbembe, *Critique of Black Reason* (Durham, NC: Duke University Press, 2017), p. 72.

37 Cited in Cook Andersen, *Regeneration through Empire*, p. 59.

colonies. For colonial apologists, this was a dilemma that answered itself. Besides, regeneration in the colonies could then be reimported by way of promoting variously conceived versions of a 'Greater France'.

Before 1871, the French settlers of Algeria were generally seen as re-barbarised, de-cultured Frenchmen, not as suitable material for a regenerated society. After 1871, however, a new paradigm was advanced: a new Latin–Algerian–Mediterranean race primarily characterised by renewed virility.[38] Algeria therefore became a world turned inside out. This happened retrospectively, too: Algeria was then imagined as a return. Patricia Lorcin has remarked on the ways in which Algeria's 'Roman legacy' was used to create 'a tradition of [French] regionality', which simultaneously bound and separated French Algeria and France.[39] Louis Bertrand would become the 'ideological champion' of the '"Latins of Africa", a new "race" formed of the intermingling of the peoples of the northern shores of the Mediterranean'.[40] Bertrand would mobilise a specific ideological narrative that would subvert the traditional subordination of colony to metropole. For Lorcin, the Tipasa Roman necropolis, near Algiers,

> was the architectural, cultural, and linguistic manifestation of the true North Africa, a Latin Africa, whose existence he had hitherto only imagined. It was, however, at the site's necropolis that Bertrand had his most trenchant revelation. It was not just stones he encountered there but living beings, human forms whose contours were etched in the funereal strata: Christians, men of his faith, who shared the same sacraments and rites. The learned men of the Church of Carthage had shaped the churches of the West and, on the eve of the barbarian invasions, the city had been an important seat of intellectual activity. When the barbarians did eventually invade, the elite of the land had emigrated to Italy, to Spain, to Sardinia, to Corsica, and to Gaul, taking with them their libraries, their relics, and the memory of their martyrs. Now the descendants of those very people had returned to

38 See Patricia Lorcin, *Imperial Identities: Stereotyping, Prejudice and Race in Colonial Algeria* (London: I.B. Tauris, 1995).

39 Patricia Lorcin, 'Rome and France in Africa: Recovering Colonial Algeria's Latin Past', *French Historical Studies* 25: 2 (2002), p. 297.

40 Ibid., p. 312.

> reclaim their lost patrimony. It was a spiritual homecoming as much as a physical one.[41]

The descendants of the founders of Western civilisation were returning to the location of their origin; they would revitalise France and turn the world inside out. Lorcin emphasised Bertrand's personal history:

> The homecoming that Bertrand attributed to the 'Latins' of Algeria was not just a refashioning of contemporary themes. It was also the ideological manifestation of his own spiritual rebirth in the necropolis of Tipasa. Raised in a reactionary and highly religious family from Lorraine, the youthful Bertrand had rebelled, assuming an indifference to religion and a firm republican stance . . . Like Maurice Barrès's deracinés, the provincial Bertrand felt dislocated and disillusioned in Paris, where he was cut off from his native traditions.[42]

In a way, Bertrand was moving out rather than joining a revolutionary struggle, or remaining in a France that was struggling to recover from a revolutionary war. His personal rebirth in the settler colony was the result of a pre-emptive counterrevolutionary move. By extension, the 'Latins of Africa' were to be the 'regenerating force of France':

> 'French Africa,' he declared, was a rejuvenated land where a vigorous strain of humanity was developing with great promise. Bertrand's Latins, the immigrants from the northern shores of the Mediterranean, had intermarried and produced a handsome, hardworking, ardent race. Bertrand had discovered the merits of these quick-witted, pragmatic people in the months following his arrival when he had fully explored Algeria. In total contrast to 'the indolent Orientals who succumbed to laziness and an endless pursuit of pleasure', the Latins were the colony's life force. The product of both environment and blood, they were invigorated not enervated by the taxing climatic conditions. The 'harshness of the African steppes, the burning sun and sand, and the mysterious influence of ancient Latin imperialism, with its love of pomp and ostentation, its authoritarianism, its

41 Ibid., pp. 316–17.
42 Ibid., p. 318.

> individualism, and its cult of the family'; these were the formative forces of Bertrand's Latin race.[43]

If Bertrand was the instigator of an Algerian variant of the global settler revolution, the 'Algerianism' of the 'school of Algiers' was its literary–ideological expression, even though by the time of the Algerian War of Independence in the 1950s, as Albert Memmi noted, only reaction remained.[44]

Albert Camus agreed with Bertrand that settler-colonial Algeria had been born as an alternative to revolution, and narrated the history of its foundation: the revolution of 1848, further unrest, unemployment, the Constituent Assembly's decision to establish a colony of settlers, dreams of a 'Promised Land'. 'Such were the Spaniards of Mahón, ancestors of Jacques's mother, or those Alsatians who in '71 had rejected German rule and chosen France, and they were given the land of the Arab rebels of '71, who were dead or imprisoned – dissidents taking the places kept warm by insurgents, persecuted-persecutors from whom his father descended.'[45]

This was a narrative that Camus intended to expand on but did not get the chance to.[46] For Camus, enduring poverty and persecution in one location ultimately justified inflicting poverty and persecution on someone else in another. He was not the first to advance this argument and would not be the last. For him, unless revolution was to come, only elsewhere could Frenchmen be equal and inhabit a classless society. In Algeria, he noted, 'It was not even differences of class that set [Frenchmen] apart. In this country of immigration, of quick fortunes and spectacular collapses, the boundaries between classes were less clear-cut than between races.'[47] Class, however, could only be rendered moot by emphasising racial difference. In such a place, if there was to be a revolution, it would be anticolonial – and it was.[48]

43 Ibid., p. 319–20.

44 On Algerianism, see Fréris Georges, 'L'Algérianisme, le mouvement du Méditerranéisme et la suite . . .', *Méditerranée: Ruptures et Continuités* 37 (2003); Albert Memmi, *The Colonizer and the Colonized* (New York: Souvenir, 1974).

45 Albert Camus, *The First Man* (London: Penguin, 1995), p. 149.

46 See ibid., p. 245.

47 Ibid., p. 158.

48 The tension between displacement and revolution is especially apparent in the history of the Algerian Communist Party. The national liberation struggle produced an

Black worlds turned inside out

On the other side of the Atlantic, another revolution had been crushed and remained uncompleted. After the Civil War, Reconstruction had given way to Jim Crow. In a 1912 essay titled 'The Rural Negro Community', Booker T. Washington articulated the possibility of turning the world inside out as a response to defeat. There were 'rural Negro communities' in the North, and there was Liberia across the ocean; but, for Washington, these experiences 'merely represented a widespread movement among Negroes, who had escaped slavery' – an escape devoid of sovereignty.[49] For 'the first twenty years of freedom', he noted, 'there was no great disposition . . . on the part of Negro farmers to become landowners'.[50] This was the revolutionary period of Reconstruction. Now this period was over, and, Washington added, 'the masses of the Negroes lost their influence in politics'.[51] The 'more thoughtful members of the race', he argued, were finding

> that in communities where there was very little encouragement for a Negro to vote there was nothing which prevented him from owning property. They learned, also, that where their white neighbors were opposed to a Negro postmaster they had not the slightest objection to a Negro banker. The result was that the leaders of the race began to turn their attention to business enterprises, while the masses of the people were learning to save their money and buy land.[52]

Land had been the turning point, and would be so again. Black farmers were acquiring some land and establishing new communities, Washington noted. These communities hosted a few institutions, crucial sites of self-constitution, and were claiming a degree of sovereign

---

unbridgeable distance between the Algerian and the French communist parties. It was the national revolution that turned what was essentially a subsidiary of a French party into an Algerian outfit. Revolution and the world turned inside out remained incompatible in the settler colony. See Allison Drew, *We Are No Longer in France: Communists in Colonial Algeria* (Manchester: Manchester University Press, 2014).

49 Booker T. Washington, 'The Rural Negro Community', *Annals of the American Academy of Political and Social Science* 40: 1 (1912), p. 81.

50 Ibid.

51 Ibid., pp. 81–2.

52 Ibid., p. 82.

autonomy: they had previously had only the church, but now they had the school, which had 'to a large extent, taken the place of the church as the center of life in the rural districts'.[53] Thanks to the school, Washington remarked, 'there is a greater disposition among the people, in spite of the attraction of the city, to settle down upon the land and make themselves at home in the country districts'.[54] The local school was for Washington the institution that would enable relocation after the end of the revolutionary period that followed emancipation.

For example, he noted, in Macon County, Alabama, where Washington's Tuskegee Institute was located, black farmers had purchased cheap land and 'settled as the class of poor whites before them had done, upon the light soil and cheap lands in the northern half of the county'.[55] These farmers had then formed 'little communities made up, for the most part, of men who owned their own lands'.[56] Many more had followed: 'Colored farmers began to move in from the adjoining counties. Many of them came to obtain the advantages of a good country school for their children. Others came not merely for this purpose but to buy land. The effect was to bring in a more enterprising class of Negro farmers and to increase the price of land'.[57] This was one model of the politics of displacement that Washington was advocating. Many black towns were being established in the South and in the West; sometimes they were 'declared', sometimes they were not.[58]

The other model he proposed involved tenants and 'enlightened' plantation owners:

> The majority of the Negroes, who were not willing or able to acquire lands of their own, remained as tenants on the large plantations in the

53 Ibid., p. 83.

54 Ibid., p. 84.

55 Ibid.

56 Ibid.

57 Ibid., p. 86.

58 See Thad Sitton and James Conrad, *Freedom Colonies: Independent Black Texans in the Time of Jim Crow* (Austin: University of Texas Press, 2005); William H. Pease and Jane H. Pease, *Black Utopia: Negro Communal Experiments in America* (Madison: State Historical Society of Wisconsin, 1963); Roger D. Hardaway, 'African American Communities on the Western Frontier', in Stephen Tchudi, ed., *Community in the American West* (Reno, NV: Nevada Humanities Committee, 2009).

> southern part of the county. As might be expected there is a good deal of moving about of tenants on these big plantations. In the early days a Negro tenant felt he must move about more or less, merely in order to assure himself that he was actually free. This disposition has not yet, I am sorry to say, entirely disappeared. The result is that except in those cases where tenants have become attached to the plantation on which they work and made to feel at home there, Negro communities of tenant farmers have not been very permanent.[59]

But there were positive exceptions, and Washington referred to 'several model plantation communities' where 'something like a permanent tenant community exists'.[60] It was this permanency, paradoxically, that would enable a project of displacement. A benevolent plantation owner would promote the community and distribute prizes 'among those who had made the most progress during the year'; the local school would allow people to remain, and the community would remain separate as it developed.[61]

Washington knew that African-Americans from the South were by then inhabiting a vast migratory space, a veritable diaspora. They were moving out of the South, and his embrace of displacement was aimed at bringing them back, and at keeping them there – hence his famous advice to 'cast down your buckets where you are'.[62] Washington's stance has been the subject of extended critique. Andrew Zimmerman noted Washington's 'apparently inscrutable politics'; but his politics are not inscrutable if his advocacy for displacement is taken into consideration.[63] Washington was interested in displacement, had become involved in projects in Liberia and Togo, and in his landmark Atlanta Address in 1895 had talked about different 'races' remaining separate 'as the fingers'

59 Washington, 'Rural Negro Community', p. 84.

60 Ibid., pp. 84, 87.

61 Ibid., p. 87.

62 Cited in Andrew Zimmerman, *Alabama in Africa: Booker T. Washington, the German Empire, and the Globalization of the New South* (Princeton, NJ: Princeton University Press, 2012), pp. 18–9.

63 Ibid., p. 10. Zimmerman asks rhetorically: Did Washington oppose or cooperate with 'southern racism'? Probably neither – Washington *disregarded* it, and promoted displacement instead. He functionally cooperated with it in one place but systematically opposed it in another.

of a hand.[64] 'Separation' was logically predicated on the possibility of spatial distinction – a form of displacement.

Washington's stance at the beginning of the twentieth century was part of a venerable tradition – and one that would continue.[65] In the nineteenth century, the forced relocation of freed slaves had been repeatedly proposed in numerous schemes. 'Colonization' – deporting free slaves – was routinely framed as the possibility of turning the world turned inside out.[66] Benjamin Rush had already proposed domestic colonies for freed slaves in 1794. His 'negro farm settlements' and 'model farm colonies' in Bedford County, Pennsylvania, represented one attempt to face contradictions related to slavery in the early republic. Jefferson had considered domestic colonies for freed slaves, too, and also proposed deportation. 'Colonization' was for a long time the preferred option for many, and the American Colonization Society, founded in 1816, provided a venue for collaboration between abolitionist and pro-slavery sentiments through the pursuit of relocation.[67] Lincoln had embraced the prospect of colonisation, too. Kentucky, southern Indiana, southern Illinois and southern Ohio: this was 'colonization' territory, and indeed Lincoln's territory, and his political formation included giving speeches at ACS meetings.[68] For Lincoln,

64 In this he was contributing to a long tradition of African-American thought. Martin R. Delaney, for example, had promoted a scheme in 1859–60 to grow cotton in the Niger Valley with African-American labour. See Zimmerman, *Alabama in Africa*, pp. 12–13, cited at 18. But there was a long tradition of opposition to 'colonization', too: W. E. B. Du Bois, who liked revolution, thought it was a sellout. Both Washington and Du Bois argued for the civil rights of black people; they disagreed on how to achieve them, and especially on *where* they could be achieved.

65 See Robin D. G. Kelley, '"But a Local Phase of a World Problem": Black History's Global Vision, 1883–1950', *Journal of American History* 83: 3 (1999).

66 See Sebastian N. Page, *Black Resettlement and the American Civil War* (Cambridge: Cambridge University Press, 2021).

67 See Arneil, *Domestic Colonies*, p. 85.

68 See Philip Magness and Sebastian Page, *Colonization after Emancipation: Lincoln and the Movement for Black Resettlement* (Columbia, MO: University of Missouri Press, 2011). 'Colonization', as far as Lincoln was concerned, meant the government-sponsored resettlement of freed slaves. References to 'colonization' recur in Lincoln's speeches and activities throughout the 1850s and until well into the Civil War. He thought that 4 million African-Americans could be transferred somewhere in Africa or Latin America. 'Colonization', however, was an integral part of anti-slavery discourse – a truly 'Atlantic' idea with supporters in the UK, the Caribbean and Africa, and there were precedents for government-sponsored ethnic cleansing in an American context (the

emancipation and colonization went hand in hand. As president, he even established colonies in Panama and Haiti for this purpose (they failed).[69] While Lincoln remained interested in colonisation until his death, after 1862 and abolition he became more circumspect.

It was black hostility to colonisation and displacement that had spurred the emergence of radical abolitionism.[70] Colonisation, however, also had many black supporters, and never disappeared as a political option.[71] Even African-American leader Frederick Douglass toyed with it before the Civil War (he supported black colonies, but only within the United States; otherwise, he famously noted, it would be 'extermination').[72] Douglass thought that the farm colonies might be a possible 'Canaan', but he appreciated them especially for their revolutionary potential. They had to be in the South – there would be no displacement – and they had to be autonomous. It was a revolutionary demand.

Displacement, however, was largely unavailable to free blacks. During and after the Civil War and during Reconstruction, some radical Republicans had recognised that freedpeople could enter pre-emption claims; they thus imagined a sovereign displacement as a solution. But, after the end of the war, the Johnson administration resolved against this possibility, and opted against redistributing land to emigrating blacks.[73] Confiscation never became a part of the Reconstruction Acts of 1867, and emancipated blacks were largely prevented from moving west. The constitutions of the newly forming states in the West often explicitly stated that blacks could not claim land. In the South, Reconstruction was discontinued. Thus, what Foner understood as the

---

Indian removals, for example). See Eric Foner 'Abraham Lincoln, Colonization, and the Rights of Black Americans', in Richard J. Follett, Eric Foner and Walter Johnson, *Slavery's Ghost: The Problem of Freedom in the Age of Emancipation* (Baltimore: Johns Hopkins University Press, 2011).

69 See Arneil, *Domestic Colonies*, p. 89.

70 Ousmane K. Power-Greene, *Against Wind and Tide: The African American Struggle against the Colonization Movement* (New York: New York University Press, 2014).

71 See Nicholas Guyatt, '"An Impossible Idea?" The Curious Career of Internal Colonization', *Journal of the Civil War Era* 4: 2 (2014).

72 Cited in Arneil, *Domestic Colonies*, p. 94.

73 See Ira Berlin, Barbara J. Fields, Steven F. Miller, Joseph P. Reidy and Leslie S. Rowland, *Slaves No More: Three Essays on Emancipation and the Civil War* (New York: Cambridge University Press, 1992), p. 155.

'unfinished revolution' was paralleled by the impossibility of turning the world inside out.[74] What Ikuko Asaka has perceptively described as 'racially separate spaces of freedom' remained.[75]

Black freedom, emancipation, at least since the War of Independence, had been an unmistakably revolutionary demand; 'forty acres and a mule' was a revolutionary proposition especially because the acres and the mule were to be in the South, and because freed slaves were to be settled on the properties of expropriated landlords. In an important sense, Reconstruction was the antithesis of relocation as a political possibility because it envisaged emplaced change. But Reconstruction did not last, and a settler-colonial body politic reacted violently against a revolutionary experiment. Jim Crow was the reactionary outcome of defeated emplaced change. Displacement was then considered again, and re-emerged as an alternative. The black 'Exodusters' of 1879–80 were fleeing the South after the end of Reconstruction. They aimed for Kansas. Their 'great migration' of 1879 involved some 50,000 individuals.[76]

But there had been other exoduses. Liberia itself was imagined as a possible world turned inside out: an alternative to revolution, and an alternative that was appealing both to those who feared and loathed revolution and to those who yearned for it but believed it was unlikely. On the one hand, House Speaker Henry Clay would say

74 See Eric Foner, *Reconstruction: America's Unfinished Revolution, 1863–1877* (New York: HarperCollins, 2011); Henry Louis Gates, Jr, *Stony the Road: Reconstruction, White Supremacy, and the Rise of Jim Crow* (London: Penguin, 2019).

75 Ikuko Asaka, *Tropical Freedom: Climate, Settler Colonialism, and Black Exclusion in the Age of Emancipation* (Durham, NC: Duke University Press, 2017), p. 19. Asaka outlined how the response to the prospect of black freedom was primarily spatial. This response lasted the whole of the nineteenth century, and it was transnational: British, Canadian and US thinking developed along similar lines. Conceptually, 'colonization' foreshadowed successive segregationist practices. Spatial dislocation, the establishment of different spaces of freedom for different racially construed people – in Asaka's formulation, 'spatializing freedom in racial terms' – was the antidote to emancipation. Asaka demonstrates that settler colonialism is intimately linked with the expulsion of blacks, as well as the acquisition of indigenous land. 'Free soil' expansion and colonisation were 'fused', she concludes: 'the constellation of ideas and practices later labelled Manifest Destiny included Liberian colonization as part of its semiotic and material apparatus' (pp. 19, 24, 29, 41).

76 Nell Painter, *Exodusters: Black Migration to Kansas after Reconstruction* (New York: Norton, 1976).

that displacement to Liberia would 'rid our country of a useless and pernicious' population (in other words, it would neutralise a possible revolution); on the other, as one freedman who would move there noted in a letter, 'We love this country [the United States] and its liberties, if we could share an equal right in them; but our freedom is partial, and we would have no hope that it will ever be otherwise here'.[77] The two positions could not have been more different – and yet they would converge on displacement.[78]

The American Colonization Society did not promote a self-sovereign experiment; it was, after all, primarily in the business of deporting people. But the black settlers always had a very clear understanding of their sovereign prerogatives, which they saw as emanating from their collective displacement. They even drew up a compact on the first ship in 1820 (it was quashed). The ACS retained dictatorial powers, but the prospect of asserting the settlers' sovereignty was on the table even before arrival. In the 1840s and 1850s there was a shift, and migration by freedmen and 'mulattoes' was then paralleled by the migration of slaves manumitted for the purpose of 'colonization' to Africa.[79] These latecomers were, in a sense, immigrants to Liberia, not settlers: uneducated, unlike their predecessors, and poorer. The original settlers had even often paid for their passage. By the 1850s, Liberia had emancipated itself from ACS oversight and indigenous strategic threats, and a settler society had emerged.

Britain recognised Liberia's independence immediately and assumed that recognition would facilitate favourable terms of trade; but the United States only recognised Liberia fifteen years later. Then again, settler independence was no revolution, and the ACS was ultimately prepared to relinquish its responsibilities. Obscuring the existence of indigenous Liberians, the declaration of independence began: 'We the people of the republic of Liberia were originally inhabitants of the

77 Cited in David Brion Davis, *Antebellum American Culture: An Interpretive Anthology* (University Park, PA: Penn State Press, 1997), p. 285.

78 James Ciment, *Another America: The Story of Liberia and the Former Slaves who Ruled It* (New York: Hill & Wang, 2013); Tunde Adeleke, *Unafrican Americans: Nineteenth-Century Black Nationalists and the Civilizing Mission* (Lexington: University Press of Kentucky, 1998); Tom W. Shick, *Behold the Promised Land: A History of Afro-American Settler Society in Nineteenth-Century Liberia* (Baltimore: Johns Hopkins University Press, 1980).

79 Ciment, *Another America*, pp. 54–5, 102.

United States of North America', and concluded with the following passage: 'All hope of favourable change in our country was thus wholly extinguished in our bosoms, and we looked with anxiety abroad for some asylum from the deep degradation.'[80] All hope of change in one location had disappeared; displacement had been the alternative.

Nearby, Sierra Leone had also been imagined as a possible world turned inside out born in a revolutionary crisis.[81] Many of the colonists had come from Nova Scotia, where black Loyalists had become a landless proletariat. Disappointed promises, combined with a few racial pogroms, had made calls for their relocation ever more urgent. Displacement to Sierra Leone was on offer, and many prospective colonists embraced this possibility, believing that they would enjoy political rights underpinned by more British promises. But they wanted land and liberty under their own government, while the British abolitionists who ran the Sierra Leone Company disagreed strongly, especially on the last point. A 'second collective migration', a reverse 'middle passage' back to Africa, thus ensued.[82] The black colonists in Sierra Leone found that they had to fight for their rights – land allocation in Freetown was slow – and that their ability to represent themselves was curtailed by the Company's authority. They had been told that land would be free, but the Company expected a quitrent. Petitions followed. Some settlers eventually tried to stage a coup and take over the colony.[83] They had wanted what the revolutionaries in Haiti had also wanted, even if it was to be somewhere else, but were defeated. Other deported communities were dumped in the country afterwards: exiled Maroons from Jamaica, and 'recaptives' freed from slavers who were circumventing the British ban on the slave trade. Afterwards, Sierra Leone became yet another colony subjected to unrestricted metropolitan authority.

But Liberia still remained a possible world turned inside out. In the 1920s, Marcus Garvey had a Liberia plan. He wanted the Universal Negro Improvement Association to settle Africa by way of Liberia with up to a million migrants.[84] But the Americos (the descendants of the

80 Ibid., pp. 95, 96.

81 Maya Jasanoff, *Liberty's Exiles: American Loyalists in the Revolutionary World* (New York: Knopf, 2011), p. 7.

82 Ibid., p. 283.

83 Ibid., pp. 304–5.

84 See Ciment, *Another America*, p. 159.

original settlers then in control of Liberia) had no Garvey plan, and preferred their own rule. Likewise, W. E. B. Du Bois always liked Liberia, even though he did not like Garveyism and preferred revolution. His ironic description of Garvey's plan was: 'Give up! Surrender! The struggle is useless'.[85] Garveyism ultimately failed in its Liberia bid, as in its search for other sovereign displacements. The aim of Garveyism was a United States of Africa – a polity that would protect the interests of black people everywhere. Garveyism argued that African-American nationalists should abandon revolution in the United States and focus on Africa or another space to be carved out elsewhere as an alternative.[86]

Much later, Malcolm X's political trajectory, and his progressive alienation from the Nation of Islam, epitomised the confrontation pitting the possibility of voluntary displacement against revolution. Malcolm X's internationalist rhetoric, especially after his travels to Africa and the Middle East, had become ever more incompatible with the Nation of Islam's separatist line.[87] But the prospect of establishing a separate polity in an unspecified location somewhere in 'the South', as compensation for slavery, was still alive, and the Nation of Islam, an heir to Garveyism, was closely linked to it. Exodus – collective sovereign displacement – remains significant in this tradition, and in 2021 *New York Times* bestselling author Charles M. Blow released a call for 'as many Black descendants of the Great Migration as possible' to return to the South 'with moral and political intentionality' in order to deal with racism once and for all.[88]

Back in 1974, 'Afrofuturist' film *Space is the Place*, written by Sun Ra and Joshua Smith and directed by John Coney, also explicitly rehearsed the opposition between displacement and revolution.[89] Set in the early 1970s in Oakland, California the movie tells the fictional story of the way displacement to another planet becomes the local African

85 Cited in ibid., p. 156.

86 On black nationalist 'post–colonization' movements, see Edwin S. Redkey, *Black Exodus: Black Nationalist and Back-to-Africa movements, 1890–1910* (New Haven: Yale University Press, 1969).

87 See Manning Marable, *Malcolm X: A Life of Reinvention* (New York: Viking, 2011).

88 Charles M. Blow, *The Devil You Know: A Black Power Manifesto* (New York: Harper Collins, 2021). See also Emily Raboteau, *Searching for Zion: The Quest for Home in the African Diaspora* (New York: Atlantic Monthly, 2012).

89 See Mark Bould, *Science Fiction* (Abingdon: Routledge, 2012), p. 175.

Americans 'alter-destiny'. Sun Ra has visited an inviting and exotic alien planet and has decided to 'bring black people' there, so that they can 'thrive without white people'. He travels back to Earth and challenges the 'Overseer', a corrupt black leader. Sun Ra opens an 'Outer Space Employment Agency' in the ghetto; he is recruiting potential colonists, and uses his music to proselytise. Eventually, Sun Ra convinces some local youth. At first they are reluctant, perhaps they expect change to happen where they are, but they are finally convinced by his logic: they 'do not exist in their society' and must depart. They then help Sun Ra overcome a few white aerospace technicians from NASA. After his people magically gather on his spaceship and depart, Earth explodes. It had it coming.

Imaginary worlds turned inside out

Many indeed engaged with the possibility of voluntary displacement during the descending phase of the global settler revolution. Beyond class, oppressed and endangered nationality, and race, there was gender. Many suffragists, for example, mobilised a political imaginary in which frontier landscapes could be seen as engendering (white) women's freedoms.[90] While the 'political and social possibilities' associated with these landscapes required an elsewhere, turn-of-the-century settlement sociology also *performed* the politics of volitional displacement. It was an influential movement: it established the sociological method, shaped welfare policies for decades, and was crucially predicated on separation. These women believed that class and class-consciousness could be undone, and that 'connection' could be reconstituted one settlement at a time. The social workers who promoted this method of social intervention would themselves migrate to the settlements they had established, while simultaneously disconnecting from traditional charities and revolutionary politics.[91]

90 See Ana Stevenson, 'Imagining Women's Suffrage: Frontier Landscapes and the Transnational Print Culture of Australia, New Zealand, and the United States', *Pacific Historical Review* 87: 4 (2018).

91 See Ann Oakley, 'The Forgotten Example of "Settlement Sociology": Gender, Research, Communities, Universities and Policymaking in Britain and the USA, 1880–1920', *Research for All* 1: 1 (2017).

'Settlement sociology' embraced the politics of voluntary displacement. Its settlements, also called 'social settlements', operated for a few decades, especially in the United States and Britain. Based on a critique of urban poverty, its promoters' fundamental method was relocation: the activists were to move to distressed neighbourhoods, and there they would promote the separate settlements that would enable them to observe in order to ameliorate conditions – a type of surveillance that would then be fed back to improve their approach. Not only were there literally hundreds of such settlements; activities promoted within them were crucial to the establishment of welfare practices and legislation, and to shaping the methodologies of modern social work.[92]

Cooperative living was promoted, including participatory knowledge production – the main idea was that the settlements were crucial to re-establishing 'community' after it had been shattered by poverty and dysfunction. Promoters Henrietta and Samuel Barnett had proclaimed: 'We advocate, therefore, as steps towards social reform that people of knowledge, instead of sending missions to the ignorant, should themselves settle among them'.[93] Settlement sociology was thus predicated on the perception of growing revolutionary tension – a tension linked to ongoing social distress. Historian of settlement sociology Ann Oakley has concluded: 'At its most radical, settlement philosophy was about dissolving class inequality; at its most conservative, it could be seen as an aspect of a middle-class "mania for slumming"'.[94] But these are not contradictory stances: dissolving class inequality without revolution and by way of displacement was not a new approach.

Hull House in Chicago and Toynbee Hall in London were famous sociology settlements.[95] They were meant to reconstitute 'neighbourly relations' where class divisions and consciousness had undermined them, while neighbourly relations would in turn produce neighbourhoods. The settlements aimed to set up exemplary communities and through them to undo class – certainly not to wage class war, as many socialists were arguing instead. But traditional charity work was also rejected, as it also operated through class and the imposition of

92 Ibid., p. 21.

93 Cited in ibid.

94 Ibid., p. 22.

95 See Lucy Hartley, 'From the Local to the Colonial: Toynbee Hall and the Politics of Poverty', *Victorian Studies* 61: 2 (2019).

middle-class norms. Settlement sociology was thus neither reactionary nor revolutionary, pursuing an alternative and displaced approach. These reformers especially refused masculine politics and academia – they recognised the latter's classist nature and opted to produce knowledge in accordance with a 'different *epistemological* orientation'.[96] They spatially separated from both, deciding instead to build institutions on the ground, and to articulate their refusal to represent all external interests – they centred on their settlements. Mary Higgs, 'who had started a small settlement in her own home ... learnt about vagrancy both through the study of statistics and first-hand by dressing as a tramp and spending days and nights in the appalling conditions of the casual wards for homeless women attached to workhouses'.[97] She thus displaced the location of knowledge away from academia and towards communities. She aimed thereby to displace class itself.

And if one could relocate to parts of the city as if they were a foreign country, one could move into the future while staying put. Edward Bellamy's *Looking Backward* (1888) was an instant success, selling millions of copies, and immediately became a tool for political activism.[98] Bellamy's novel narrates the story of a man who falls into a hypnosis-induced sleep in 1887, and then wakes up in the year 2000. The novel offers a utopian representation of an imagined future, and a literary example of the politics of volitional displacement. The imagined dislocation, however, is across time rather than space. But time produces another space: Bellamy represented an antipolitical society, a pacified polity devoid of all class distinctions and all conflict. Social peace had been established without revolution.[99] As Philip Wegner has remarked, Bellamy attempted 'to walk a line between conservative desires for a retreat to the past and radical calls for the violent overthrow of the present' at a time of increasing social unrest.[100]

96 Oakley, 'Forgotten Example of "Settlement Sociology"', p. 30 (emphasis in original).

97 Ibid., p. 27.

98 Edward Bellamy, *Looking Backward* (New York: Dover, 1996).

99 See also Edward Bellamy, *The Duke of Stockbridge: A Romance of Shays' Rebellion* (Cambridge, MA: Harvard University Press, 1962), in which Bellamy also expressed his distrust of revolution. The novel deals with a settler revolutionary insurgency that shook the early US republic: the Whiskey Rebellion.

100 Phillip E. Wegner, *Imaginary Communities: Utopia, the Nation, and the Spatial Histories of Modernity* (Berkeley, CA: University of California Press, 2002), pp. xxii–xxiii.

Looking Backward opens in the middle of an existential social crisis: the old order is crumbling, and even those who once were secure now risk being 'swept up in a maelstrom of riot and poverty'.[101] The protagonist fears social disorder – what he calls 'a general overturn' (Bellamy especially feared socialism, once noting that 'the word socialist is one I never could well stomach').[102] The protagonist's very house cannot be completed because of strikes: 'neither masters nor workmen would concede the point at issue without a long struggle'.[103] As his wedded life cannot even begin, the social crisis is also one of reproduction – his masculinity is at stake. Unable to sleep, the protagonist is then induced into a hypnotic sleep. But he wakes up in a different place, and a whole century has passed.

He had fallen asleep during 'troublous times', but the future could not be more different. 'I must know a little more about the sort of Boston I have come back to', he asks Dr Leete, the protagonist's guide in the new world:

> 'You told me when we were upon the house-top that though a century only had elapsed since I fell asleep, it had been marked by greater changes in the conditions of humanity than many a previous millennium. With the city before me I could well believe that, but I am very curious to know what some of the changes have been. To make a beginning somewhere, for the subject is doubtless a large one, what solution, if any, have you found for the labor question? It was the Sphinx's riddle of the nineteenth century, and when I dropped out the Sphinx was threatening to devour society, because the answer was not forthcoming. It is well worth sleeping a hundred years to learn what the right answer was, if, indeed, you have found it yet.'
>
> 'As no such thing as the labor question is known nowadays', replied Dr Leete, 'and there is no way in which it could arise, I suppose we may claim to have solved it. Society would indeed have fully deserved being devoured if it had failed to answer a riddle so entirely simple. In fact, to speak by the book, it was not necessary for society to solve the riddle at all. It may be said to have solved itself. The solution came as the result of a process of industrial evolution which could not have

101 Cited in ibid., p. 66.

102 Ibid., p. 69; citation at 66 (emphasis in original).

103 Bellamy, *Looking Backward*, p. 194.

terminated otherwise. All that society had to do was to recognize and cooperate with that evolution, when its tendency had become unmistakable.'[104]

The solution was not revolution, but, counterintuitively, further monopolisation, further consolidation, and eventually nationalisation (nationalisation is, after all, the ultimate monopoly):

> The nation, that is to say, organized as the one great business corporation in which all other corporations were absorbed; it became the one capitalist in the place of all other capitalists, the sole employer, the final monopoly in which all previous and lesser monopolies were swallowed up, a monopoly in the profits and economies of which all citizens shared. The epoch of trusts had ended in The Great Trust.[105]

If George's single tax would abolish all taxes, Bellamy's single trust would abolish all trusts.

Change had occurred without strife – 'there was absolutely no violence.'[106] Wages had been abolished, and with the wage relation, gone were also the contradictions that it engenders.[107] It was a world turned inside out where even labour had been abolished: electricity saved labour, scientific organisation saved labour, and labour power was no longer even traded. The market was abolished, too. What did the revolutionaries do as these transformations were taking place? They allied themselves with the retrograde capitalists to fight against the new order. They were even paid by the latter, but reaction and revolution together were defeated, and the world had been turned inside out rather than upside down.[108]

William Morris's *News from Nowhere* (1890) was a direct response to Bellamy's *Looking Backward*.[109] This time, displacement had gone the other way, and it was an agrarian landscape that had peacefully

104 Ibid., pp. 204, 205.
105 Ibid., p. 209.
106 Ibid.
107 Ibid., pp. 225–6.
108 See ibid., pp. 299, 300.
109 William Morris, *News from Nowhere, or an Epoch of Rest, being some Chapters from a Utopian Romance* (London: Longmans, Green, 1908).

infiltrated a modern, urban one. Whereas *Looking Backward* emphasised labour-saving technology and urban settings, *News from Nowhere* privileged agrarian and pastoral surroundings – conditions understood as especially conducive to a 'love' for labour. In the novel, an ideal social regime is thus represented as a return: a return to a pre-industrial age, to simple forms, and to a stateless social organisation. Formal education, property, courts, politics, slums, urban overcrowding and crime are all abolished. Local inclusive assemblies provide basic political organisation. There is fear, but it is fear of missing out, of missing out on opportunities to labour and on its pleasures – it is fear of 'work-famine'. There is still displacement, of course, and in *News from Nowhere* the settler colonies – especially in North America – are a way to avoid 'work-famine': there, labour abounds, there is more to do than in the Old World. Thus displacement still undoes fear – a function that most of the projects belonging to the political tradition appraised here were meant to perform.[110] The convergences between *Looking Backward* and *News from Nowhere* are significant, and it is remarkable that both novels neglect to describe *how* the transformation that brought change forth actually happened: in both novels, 'commercial slavery' is turned into a 'communal condition', and both refer to natural, seamless, gradual processes.[111] In both cases, change happens as if in a dream, and both texts express a paradoxical desire for change without change.

H. G. Wells, another writer of science fiction, also engaged with the possibility of turning the world inside out in his novels. He had written *The War of the Worlds* (1897), a novel describing what happened when

110 On the relationship between the Arts and Crafts movement and the settler colonies as possible sites for turning the world inside out, see Felix Driver, 'In Search of the Imperial Map: Walter Crane and the Image of Empire', *History Workshop Journal* 69 (2010). Driver concludes: 'The vision of empire as a means of realizing the ambitions of socialism may fit awkwardly within our own histories of imperial and anti-imperial politics, but it does pose an important question about the extent to which intellectuals and workers in the English socialist tradition – especially in its arts and crafts manifestation – were able to connect a strongly pastoral vision of socialism with a sense of allegiance to the heroic values of labour in the settler colonies around the empire, at least before the 1890s' (p. 154).

111 On William Morris's 'utopianism', see Owen Holland, *William Morris's Utopianism: Propaganda, Politics and Prefiguration* (Houndmills: Palgrave, 2017). Holland focuses on the distinction between 'No-Where and Now-Here' (pp. 3–28), and is aware of Morris's engagements with imperialism and settler colonialism.

the Martians came and turned this world upside down, called himself a socialist (but would be very critical of the Soviet Union, which, he said, was a failed experiment), and was a prolific imaginer of new political orders. He consistently thought about ways to avoid emplaced change, and developed influential ideas about a better future and the political arrangements that would usher it in. It is significant that this regenerated regime was not in a specific place – but located in a whole world (if a single tax could undo all taxes and a single trust could abolish all trusts, a single polity could abolish all conflict). Wells routinely dismissed really existing sites of contradiction – race, class, nation, the state – and could do so because the prospect of a world-state allowed him to shift the location of struggle away from actually existing geographies.[112] 'Utopia', he believed, could be in this world (not anywhere in particular – this is one of the benefits of thinking about a world-state), or perhaps even beyond it. It did not matter, provided that revolutionary struggles – which would have been dissipated in the short term by the suite of prudential measures he was also advocating – did not result in violent confrontation.

Like Morris and Bellamy, Wells offered no specific suggestion as how utopia might be realised, even if it is notable that the inhabitants of his world-state would be English-speaking people. The new dispensation would be brought about by the 'efficients' – a group that would come into conflict equally against the 'traditional landed aristocracy' and 'the helpless superseded poor', also known as 'the people of the abyss'. This was, ultimately, Bellamy's idea, too – while the very notion of an 'abyss' implies the vertical displacement Wells was arguing against. In a world with no locality, the efficients would win not by revolution, but by 'greater organisational skills'.[113] They may have been Americans, but Wells was unsure about America, even if he certainly approved of the British Empire, and saw it as a possible instrument for the establishment of a 'post-sovereign political order'. A single empire would abolish

112 See Duncan Bell, 'Pragmatic Utopianism and Race: H. G. Wells as Social Scientist', *Modern Intellectual History* 16: 3 (2019), pp. 863–95. That Wells sided with Booker T. Washington in his polemic with W. E. B. Du Bois is significant – Washington, as we have seen, was for displaced change, too. See ibid.; Duncan Bell, 'Pragmatism and Prophecy: H. G. Wells and the Metaphysics of Socialism', *American Political Science Review* 112: 2 (2018).

113 Bell, 'Pragmatic Utopianism and Race'.

imperialism while technology would undo space itself – the ultimate displacement to end all displacements.

The future had to be planned. Ebenezer Howard's Garden Cities were directly inspired by Bellamy's *Looking Backward* and George's *Progress and Poverty*. In *Garden Cities of Tomorrow* (1898), Howard proposed a vision of towns free of slums, new places endowed with the advantages of both town and country, culture and nature.[114] Like settlement sociology, the Garden Cities movement envisaged a model of social reform that was predicated on a fundamental displacement: the new cities would be *new* settings located at a specified distance from each other and from existing urban centres. They would be *independent* towns managed and financed by their residents. They would therefore be spatially as well as politically discrete entities.

The purpose of the Garden City? To 'raise the standard of health and comfort of all true workers of whatever grade' ('true workers', of course, meant not all workers – these were not to be inclusive experiments).[115] To be properly built, Howard realised, these cities needed sovereign powers, powers similar to those that had enabled the construction of railways during previous decades. Their establishment was part of a crucial transformation; they would empty the 'old slum cities':

> Now, if Parliamentary powers were necessary for the extension of railway enterprise, such powers will certainly be also needed when the inherent practicability of building new, well planned towns, and of the population moving into them from the old slum cities as naturally, and, in proportion to the power to be exercised, almost as easily as a family moves out of a rotten old tenement into a new and comfortable dwelling, is once fairly recognized by the people. To build such towns, large areas of land must be obtained. Here and there a suitable site may be secured by arrangement with one or more landowners, but if the movement is to be carried on in anything like a scientific fashion, stretches of land far larger than that occupied by our first experiment must be obtained.[116]

114 Ebenezer Howard, *Garden Cities of Tomorrow* (London: Swan & Sonnenschein, 1902).

115 Howard, *Garden Cities of Tomorrow*, p. 22.

116 Ibid., p. 128.

How will the Garden City manage emerging contradictions? Not by growth, a harbinger of contradictions, but by replication elsewhere. The 'Garden City is built up', he imagined: 'Its population has reached 32,000. How will it grow? It will grow by establishing – under Parliamentary powers probably – another city some little distance beyond its own zone of that "country", so that the new town may have a zone of country of its own.'[117]

Howard wanted to establish Garden Cities in England, even though he agreed that his ideas might be especially suitable for a 'new country' (Howard erroneously indicated that Adelaide, South Australia – a settler-colonial city – was already a model for urban cloning). But he added that even in England land could be still obtained 'with comparatively small disturbance of vested interests' – he was definitely not interested in confiscation, eminent domain, or any such a revolutionary method. Displacement was his proposed solution: 'The simple issue to be faced, and faced resolutely, is: Can better results be obtained by starting on a bold plan on comparatively virgin soil than by attempting to adapt our old cities to our newer and higher needs?' It was a rhetorical question – the answer was an emphatic 'yes', and 'virgin soil', even though only comparatively virgin soil, he admitted, was clearly the answer.[118]

Thus, Howard's Garden Cities attempted to turn the capitalist city inside out. Previously, cities had essentially been 'private commercial venture[s]' designed to reward speculation; but by envisaging ongoing corporate and public control of all land in each of the independent Garden Cities, Howard applied to urban planning significant elements of George's nationalising proposal.[119] Historian of the urban form Lewis Mumford has noted that public ownership of utilities – municipal socialism – was not new, but remarked on Howard's introduction of public ownership of land. Mumford called it a coherent theory of 'town colonization.'[120] Howard envisaged 'the splendid possibilities of a new civilisation', a new world to be attained not through revolution but through displacement and planning.[121] And, of course, as well as being

117 Ibid., p. 129.

118 Ibid., p. 134.

119 See Lewis Mumford, *The City in History: Its Origins, Its Transformations, and Its Prospects* (New York: Harbinger, 1961), p. 426.

120 Ibid., p. 476.

121 Ibid., p. 515.

inherently superior, Howard insisted, this new world would also change the old one, by promoting decongestion, by providing a model, and by defusing social tension.

Howard explicitly referred to the colonisation practices of the ancient Greeks, who had established autonomous and independent city-states, and to the works of Wakefield and Owen, who had projected small and organic new polities or communities.[122] Mumford saw suburbia as a perversion of the Garden Cities, because suburbs are not functionally independent, but rely on the conurbation to which they belong.[123] Howard, on the contrary, was aiming for genuine independence. On the basis of this autonomy, the Garden Cities would eventually federate, and even produce a collective regional 'Social City'. The metropole would then become useless – its hierarchical pull effectively countered by way of displacement.

The Russian worlds turned inside out

If Howard saw the establishment of independent and autonomous urban polities as a way to avoid revolution, Kropotkin prophesised the establishment of independent and autonomous polities as an outcome of revolution.[124] A Russian aristocrat and geographer, and a communist anarchist, Kropotkin dedicated his life to the search for a decentralised politics.[125] He believed that, in the design of governance systems, there are always two fundamentally opposed principles: 'imperialism' (concentrated, vertical power) and 'federalism' (distributed, horizontal power). He espoused a spatial, almost geometrical understanding of power, and, like Wakefield's, his theory of a forthcoming catastrophe that had to be countered with colonising endeavours elsewhere was formulated in prison – the Peter-and-Paul fortress

---

122 See ibid.

123 Ibid., p. 519.

124 See Peter Kropotkin, *Fields, Factories, and Workshops, or Industry Combined with Agriculture, and Brainwork with Manual Work* (London: Nelson, 1919); Jim Mac Laughlin, *Kropotkin and the Anarchist Intellectual Tradition* (London: Pluto, 2015).

125 See Mike Davis, 'The Coming Desert: Kropotkin, Mars and the Pulse of Asia', *New Left Review* II/97 (January–February 2016).

in St Petersburg. Facing an increasingly reactionary court in 1862, Kropotkin had voluntarily exiled himself to Siberia. The court and the country were facing an increasingly revolutionary situation. Kropotkin had moved out and devised his theory of 'desiccation', a long-lasting process of progressive desertification. To stop desiccation, as Mike Davis has noted, only 'heroic and globally coordinated action – planting millions of trees and digging thousands of artesian wells' – would do.[126] Kropotkin's 'climatic catastrophism', the perception of a coming crisis, was 'essentially untestable', but prophetic.[127] Trees and wells needed people on the land.

Like Kropotkin, many Russian populists had embraced revolution or displacement during the nineteenth century and in the very early twentieth century. This frequently depended on where they were: they would repeatedly try to assassinate the Tsar in the European parts of his domains, but would serve him in the Resettlement Administration, a state ministry dedicated to the organised movement of peasant Slavs towards Central Asia and the Far East. These populists had not changed their politics, only their location.[128] They saw no contradiction. But the Russian imagination of voluntary displacement by then also had a long history. The historiography focuses on population shifts after emancipation, but significant population movements had occurred before that, and some resettlements had involved non-Russians – ethnic Germans had been invited to settle depopulated regions because Russia's serfs were immobilised, and by the early nineteenth century they numbered about 1.7 million.[129] Resettlement under serfdom was ultimately a type

126 Ibid., p. 31.

127 Ibid., p. 34. This theory of desiccation was also embraced by the Nazi occupiers of Eastern Europe during World War II. For them, the Slavs had failed to properly relocate (i.e., they had failed to reclaim the swamps and move there). Instead, they had embraced revolution. As far as the Nazis were concerned, 'only the master race could arrest the drying' (p. 42).

128 See Alberto Masoero, 'Territorial Colonization in Late Imperial Russia: Stages in the Development of a Concept', *Kritika: Explorations in Russian and Eurasian History* 14: 1 (2013); Niccolò Pianciola, *Stalinismo di frontiera. Colonizzazione agricola, sterminio dei nomadi e costruzione statale in Asia centrale (1905–1936)* (Roma: Viella, 2009).

129 Willard Sunderland, 'Peasants on the Move: State Peasant Resettlement in Imperial Russia, 1805–1830s', *Russian Review* 52 (1993); Roger Bartlett, *Human Capital: The Settlement of Foreigners in Russia, 1762–1804* (Cambridge: Cambridge University Press, 1979); James W. Long, *From Privileged to Dispossessed: The Volga Germans, 1860–1917* (Lincoln, NE: University of Nebraska Press, 1988).

of non-revolutionary emancipation based on displacement, but many Russian peasants had in fact already moved in unsanctioned ways as a result of severe land shortages in some areas by the early 1800s. The state had thus been forced to devise a policy providing a framework for facilitating population movements. The North Caucasus and 'New Russia' were receiving areas at first.

Independent resettlements were fiscally damaging, and, as far as the administration was concerned, only a regulated process would ensure fiscal stability. If the new communities were to be tax-exempt for a certain period, the communities where the resettlers were coming from would have to compensate the state. An 1805 decree set out a specific framework: an advance party was to be sent to the targeted area to advise on its suitability; relocation was then to be officially sanctioned; another advanced party was to be sent out to build infrastructure; and only then would families travel to their new locations in the spring. No reprieve from military obligations was envisaged; however, the decree was not made public for fear that it would further promote independent resettlements. Wealthier peasants who were prepared to take advantage of existing incentives (and could sell their belongings and other property, and thus put together enough capital to ensure their sustenance in the crucial early months) constituted a significant share of these early resettlers. Push factors are emphasised in the sources, but the prospect of a land of 'freedom' and 'abundance' somewhere else, whether it existed or not, also motivated many to relocate.[130]

The traditional Russian village was a crucial instrument in organising these movements: it selected prospective migrants, organised their petitions to the administration, and provided material assistance. And yet the resettlers left as individual peasant families, and in the new locations there was typically to be no periodic redistribution of arable land; the traditional village and its institutions were not transferred intact. Land was allocated on a family-by-family basis, not as communal tenure. Willard Sunderland has concluded that it was independent peasant action that set the pace of resettlement. The state initially attempted to contain peasant mobility, and refrained from promoting resettlement.[131] Sunderland also emphasised that the

130 See Sunderland, 'Peasants on the Move', p. 478.

131 See ibid., p. 484.

resettlers had no sense of an imperial mission – he called them 'un-imperial imperialists'.[132]

Even before this period, Russia had 'colonised itself', and while V. O. Kliuchevskii famously identified 'internal colonization' as the 'basic fact' of Russian history, David Moon's description of traditional peasant expansion emphasised how the state and the resettlers had operated in step.[133] Some peasants had moved voluntarily, often illegally, others as a consequence of state policy – the historiography separates these two movements, but they were always intimately interwoven. At times, the state even offered land grants, loans and temporary exemptions from service and taxation. Cossacks, religious dissenters, retired soldiers, foreigners and fugitives from serfdom had embraced opportunities to resettle elsewhere. Some sectarian groups had been exiled by the Tsarist state, but often they embraced their 'New Jerusalem'.[134] These groups operated largely autonomously, and yet the state came to appreciate their presence, in particular their ability to patrol local frontiers.[135] Forced resettlements and convict colonisations had also been tried. Monastic orders and nobles were sometimes induced to transfer their peasants. Moon concluded that, while 'the state secured its political frontiers militarily and set the general framework for their colonisation, to a large extent the settlement of the outlying regions depended on the initiative [of], and resources generated by, the peasants who migrated to the frontier'.[136] Displacement had been an option for a long time.

Siberia had typically been represented as a possible world turned inside out. Archpriest Avvakum and the Old Believers, for example, had already found there an escape during a time of crisis in the seventeenth century.[137]

132 Ibid., p. 912; Willard Sunderland, *Taming the Wild Field: Colonization and Empire on the Russian Steppe* (Ithaca, NY: Cornell University Press, 2004).

133 David Moon, 'Peasant Migration and the Settlement of Russia's Frontiers, 1550–1897', *Historical Journal* 40 (1997). See also Alexander Etkind, *Internal Colonization: Russia's Imperial Experience* (Cambridge: Polity Press, 2011); Michael Khodarkovsky, *Russia's Steppe Frontier: The Making of a Colonial Empire, 1500–1800* (Bloomington: Indiana University Press, 2002).

134 See Nicholas B. Breyfogle, *Heretics and Colonizers: Forging Russia's Empire in the South Caucasus* (Ithaca, NY: Cornell University Press, 2005), p. 56.

135 See ibid., p. 199.

136 Moon, 'Peasant Migration and the Settlement of Russia's Frontiers', p. 892.

137 Pierre Pascal, who wrote a crucial essay on Avvakum and edited his autobiography (*Life of Avvakum*) in the early 1920s, noted how the author and the text must be contextualised within the 'Times of Troubles' (the period between 1598 and

It was a response to revolutionary transformation: the Nikonian reforms demanded conformity to newly imported religious rites, but the reforms were also part of a comprehensive centralising project associated with an accompanying commercial revolution.[138] While Avvakum rejected this revolution, he did not rebel against it. Exiled to Siberia with his family in 1653, Avvakum contributed to its exploration and colonisation. His description of the Baikal region encapsulated a possible world turned inside out:

> From the shore rose steep hills and sheer cliffs. I have dragged myself twenty thousand versts and more, but never have I seen such high mountains. And their summits are crowned with halls and turrets, pillars and gates, and walls and courts, all made by the hand of God. In those hills grow garlic and onion, the bulbs larger than those of Romanov onions, and very sweet. And there is also hemp, sown by God's hand, and in the courts, beautiful grass and sweet-smelling flowers. There are wild fowl in great number – geese and swans floating on the lake, like snow. And there are also fish: sturgeon and salmontrout, sterlet and omul and white-fish, and many other kinds. This is a fresh-water lake, but great seals and sea-hares live in it. I never saw the like in the great ocean, when I lived on the Mezen River. And the fish is abundant; the sturgeon and salmon-trout are so fleshy, one cannot fry them in a skillet, it would be nothing but fat. And all this has been created by Christ for man, that he should find pleasure in it and praise God.[139]

'All this', of course, for his intended readers, was somewhere else. Avvakum had returned to Russia, and could only perceive 'tumult' and

1613). Pascal was French and Catholic, but the Russian Revolution found him in Moscow. He had joined enthusiastically. But after his attempt to synthetise Catholicism and Communism had been rejected, he abandoned the revolution, noting that a new bourgeoisie was taking over. He turned to displacement and discovered Avvakum and his *Life*. He saw in the Old Believers communities that had been able to escape a consolidating state through displacement, and thus a model. In 1920s Russia this spatial escape carried an especially important meaning. See Pierre Pascal, *Avvakum et les débuts du raskol* (Paris: Mouton, 1963).

138 Avvakum, *Vita dell'arciprete Avvakum scritta da lui stesso* (Milan: Adelphi, 1986), p. 31.

139 Ibid., pp. 105–6.

rebellion.[140] In 1657, the persecutions of the Old Believers began in earnest, even though penalties for their nonconformism would be further hardened after 1682. The Old Believers thus became a diaspora of 'authentic' Russians that could only be itself on the outside. They moved south and east, towards the lower Volga, the Don River, the Urals and Siberia. Many ended up eventually in Australia.

Representations of Siberia always emphasised new possibilities. In the nineteenth century, Siberian regionalist Nikolai Yadrintsev even argued that mixed marriages between Russians and ethnic Siberians (and distance from Russia) had produced a distinct and in many ways improved Siberian 'ethnic type' (contemporary Russian nationalist promulgations of 'Eurasianism' adopt a similar logic).[141] Serfdom had not been introduced there, and between 1891 and 1914 nearly 5 million peasants moved to Siberia.[142] The authorities were concerned with both foreign influences and autonomist Siberian feelings. These organised population shifts were especially meant to reunite Siberia and Russia. Anatolii Kulomzin's promotional activities were predicated on the assumption that colonisation was 'the necessary requirement for the survival of Russian civilization in the world'.[143] The Russo-Japanese war and the revolutionary crisis that followed it had been a significant catalyst for change; displacement was more than ever an alternative to revolution.

Siberia was thus intensively imagined as a possible world turned inside out. Private property was tentatively introduced there in 1901.[144] Personal peasant possession there had traditionally been more widespread than in European Russia, and even indigenous possession of land had been recognised (even though the notion that these arrangements could be changed at will by the Russian sovereign had eventually been asserted). When the state began transferring peasants at the end of the nineteenth century, and before the revolution of 1917, many

140 Ibid., pp. 107, 108.

141 See Moon, 'Peasant Migration and the Settlement of Russia's Frontiers', p. 880.

142 See Eva-Maria Stolberg, 'The Siberian Frontier between "White Mission" and "Yellow Peril": 1890s–1920s', *Nationalities Papers* 32: 1 (2004).

143 Cited in ibid., p. 167.

144 Alberto Masoero, 'Layers of Property in the Tsar's Settlement Colony: Projects of Land Privatization in Siberia in the Late Nineteenth Century', *Central Asian Survey* 29: 1 (2010).

considered transferring communal peasant landholdings, too. However, segments of the Russian state had other plans for Siberia, and hoped that private property would have attracted the right kind of resettlers and the lesser nobility, and that their migration would have produced a 'new' society, not merely an extension of Russia. At the same time, widespread anxieties about Siberia remained: autonomous settlements, questionable land deeds, and tax and military conscription evasions were all signs of a waning sovereign capacity there. Settler autonomy was weakening state rule; distance was a form of sovereignty.

Nikolai Bunge, who was the main architect of the resettlement policy between 1891 and 1895, was aware of the risks of socialism, especially after the revolutionary crisis of 1881, and keen to confront the 'social question' through displacement.[145] Siberia and Central Asia beckoned. Bunge, of course, was not alone, and various colonisation models were fiercely debated. First, the new and better human material to be manufactured in the new settlements had to ward off local revolutionary tensions: Siberian autonomists, exiled revolutionaries, ethnic autonomists and Muslims were all viewed with suspicion. Debates were framed around two distinct processes: 'resettlement' and 'colonization'. The latter emerged out of the former, and was predicated, according to Alberto Masoero, on 'a careful study of the Western colonial experience', and on the 'need to respond to the challenges created by the political and intellectual context of the postreform era', including revolutionary tensions.[146] Masoero emphasised how reformist approaches focused on Siberia as a testing ground for reforms – the reforms themselves were displaced.[147]

Peasant autonomous resettlement was 'originally viewed with suspicion' – fleeing serfs and religious dissidents were too autonomous to constitute a model the state could embrace.[148] Masoero details how the search for alternatives availed itself of 'academic' and foreign knowledge about colonialism:

145 Ibid., p. 15.

146 Masoero, 'Territorial Colonization in Late Imperial Russia', p. 60.

147 Ibid., p. 62.

148 Ibid., p. 63.

> European treatises on the colonial theme – for example, *Kolonien, Kolonialpolitik und Auswanderung* (Colonies, Colonial Policy, and Emigration) by W. G. F. Roscher (1856) and *De la colonisation chez les peuples modernes* (On Colonization among Modern Peoples) by P. P. Leroy-Beaulieu (1874) – provided Russians with a scholarly language for conceptualizing their recent territorial conquests, using terminology that was in many ways flattering and attractive. Roscher, a highly respected authority among Russian scholars of economic history, offered a classification of colonies. He saw the expanses of northern Eurasia as characterized by the gradual settlement of vast uninhabited spaces and likened Asiatic Russia to the 'new lands' of Australia, Canada, and the United States, in this respect following the geographer Karl Ritter, one of the most influential sources of Russian knowledge on the East. Large parts of the tsarist peripheries were thus assigned to 'agricultural' or 'settlement colonies', to a society which, according to Roscher, could develop more rapidly and freely than their country of origin. These colonies, one Russian interpreter claimed, offered the opportunity to 'implement new ideas' and 'create new social relations'. The idea resonated deeply among Russian intellectuals from [influential philosopher] Petr Iakovlevich Chaadaev to [revolutionary and democrat] Nikolai Gavrilovich Chernyshevskii.[149]

Revolutionaries in Russia had turned colonialists in the east in the past; as Masoero points out, 'young aristocrats and famous anarchists, such as Mikhail Aleksandrovich Bakunin and Petr Alekseevich Kropotkin' had collaborated with the authorities in the Far East.[150] After the revolutionary crisis of 1881, interest in the east had grown exponentially.

But if the authorities aimed to pursue a 'well-considered policy of peasant relocation beyond the Urals' as part of a 'complex strategy to prevent the "socialist danger" ', the socialists espoused a form of 'pioneering ruralism' that also advocated peasant resettlement.[151] Socialist leader Sergei Nikolaevich Iuzhakov, for example, believed that colonisation was 'the most powerful means to extend popular [communal] land tenure', and argued that the colonisation of Central Asia reflected the

149 Ibid., p. 66–7.
150 Ibid., p. 68.
151 Ibid., p. 70.

development of a 'nonbourgeois, noncapitalistic country'.[152] The socialists and many revolutionaries hoped that 'the borderlands would be a site of radical renewal. Resettlement was presented as an opportunity to build a better Russia, as the "new places" appeared – in theory at least – free from the burden of stifling tradition'.[153] This was even more the case after 1905 – a failed revolution.

Prime Minister Stolypin clearly stated that establishing a conflictless social body somewhere else was part of his administration's agenda: for him, western Siberia and the steppe region were to be a 'cradle still free of social conflict', while, through colonisation, a 'new and powerful Russia could grow'. For his administration, turning impoverished peasants into 'hard-working, patriotic landowners' was especially appealing because implementing change in Russia had proved impracticable.[154] It was an intense and protracted debate. Reactionaries sought to offload excess population and revolutionary tension with it; the populists, socialists and anarchists saw the new lands as opportunities to build new societies when revolution was deemed impossible or unlikely in the centre; while the Resettlement Administration and many liberals saw the east as presenting an opportunity to modernise agriculture and pre-empt revolution. Lenin, however, refused the politics of displacement, and thought that only revolution in Russia proper could then enable genuine colonisation elsewhere. For him, colonisation under 'feudal remnants' would inevitably reproduce the legacies of serfdom. For Lenin, displacement could not be a genuine alternative to revolution; on the contrary, it was revolution that was to be a prerequisite for subsequent resettlements.[155] For him, revolution needed to precede displacement.

The Semirechye Oblast, roughly corresponding with most of present-day south-eastern Kazakhstan and north-eastern Kyrgyzstan, had become an area of especially intense settler colonisation.[156] 'Old settlers' and Cossacks had settled first; they held land. The latter even used native labour to work it. The 'new' settlers who had arrived in the early years of the twentieth century, however, were often destitute. But during the revolution of 1905,

152 Ibid., p. 72.

153 Ibid., p. 76.

154 Ibid., p. 78.

155 See ibid., p. 76.

156 Alexander Morrison, 'Peasant Settlers and the "Civilising Mission" in Russian Turkestan, 1865-1917', *The Journal of Imperial and Commonwealth History*, 43: 3 (2015).

the new settlers, and especially the most recent arrivals, had mobilised and organised: they wanted lands to be allocated, and fast. They also demanded weapons to deal with the indigenous Kirghiz, who were resisting land confiscation. The Resettlement Administration, staffed by many members or former members of the Socialist-Revolutionary Party, supported them. In successive years, land confiscations proceeded apace – as did the retroactive legalisation of previous settler grabs. The new settlers were now leading the colonising efforts. World War I precipitated an unprecedented crisis – many were conscripted, and weapons were even more widely distributed. When the Kazakhs rebelled in 1916, the settlers participated directly and ruthlessly in repressing the insurgency. But at this point the destruction of indigenous life-worlds was also paralleled by attacks against old settlers and Cossacks.[157] The new settlers thus joined the Bolshevik revolution by instituting *their* regime locally.

But 1917 was not as significant a divide in Central Asian history as is usually believed. Niccolò Pianciola sees a great 'migratory cycle' of Slavs towards central Asia, beginning in 1891 (the year when a devastating famine began in Russia) and ending in 1964, when the Soviet attempt to bring 'virgin lands' into cultivation finally failed.[158] When the central authorities consolidated their hold in the early 1920s, they promoted 'indigenisation' (*Korenizatsiia*), and demanded that Muslims be included in the local structures of power. The settlers were dethroned. Bolshevik leader Mikhail Frunze, who was born a settler in the area, therefore enforced an anti-settler regime.[159] The local Soviets were 'de-settlerised'; revolution terminated a world turned inside out.[160]

---

157 For a definitive collective account of the Central Asian revolt of 1916, see Cloé Drieu, Alexander Morrison and Aminat Chokobaeva, eds, *The Central Asian Revolt of 1916: A Collapsing Empire in the Age of War and Revolution* (Manchester: Manchester University Press, 2020).

158 See Niccolò Pianciola, *Stalinismo di frontiera*. During the 'virgin lands campaign' of the 1950s, 300,000 Russians and Ukrainians moved south and east, and collectively ploughed up about 89 million acres. By comparison, the 'Great Plow Up' of the 1920s in North America had turned 5.2 million acres of grassland into farmland.

159 See Marco Buttino, *La rivoluzione capovolta. L'Asia centrale tra il crollo dell'Impero zarista e la formazione dell'URSS* (Naples: L'Ancora del Mediterraneo, 2003).

160 It may have been anti-settler, but Bolshevik rule was not pro-indigenous either. See Alun Thomas, *Nomads and Soviet Rule: Central Asia under Lenin and Stalin* (London: I.B. Tauris, 2018).

But the Soviet revolution did not end the dialectical tension linking world turned upside down and world turned inside out. For example, between the wars, many Finnish-American settlers or their descendants resettled to Soviet Karelia.[161] These migrants to the Soviet Union were not necessarily poor – many owned homes, cars and farm equipment, and many moved with their families and paid their own way. The Finnish community in America at the beginning of the century was uniquely politicised.[162] There were socialists, communists, utopians and radicals, and the institutions of the community generally promoted left-wing politics.[163] The emigrants to the Soviet Union moved to Karelia because they could be seen and identified as Finns, and because they were communist sympathisers (and yet, of course, not all Finnish-Americans departed, and not all of those who departed were communists). A recruiting speech proclaimed that settlers to America would be excellent settlers in Karelia:

> Karelia . . . needs strong workers who know how to chop trees and dig ore and build houses and grow food. Isn't that what we Finns have been doing in the United States for the past thirty years? And wouldn't it be wonderful to do that same work in a country that needs you, a country where there is no ruling class, no rich industrialists or kings or czars to tell you what to do? Just workers toiling together for the common good.[164]

The early Soviet nationality policy promoted 'indigenisation'; non-Russian nationalities and their languages were to be involved in running local affairs and local government bodies. In the specific context of the

161 Emily Weidenhamer, 'Disillusionment on the Grandest of Scales: Finnish-Americans in the Soviet Union, 1917–1939', *Vestnik: Journal of Russian and Asian Studies* 3: 1 (2005). See also I. R. Takala and I. M. Solomeshch, eds, *North American Finns in Soviet Karelia in the 1930s* (Petrozavodsk: Petrozavodsk State University Press, 2008).

162 On Finnish-Americans in the United States, see Peter Filene, *Americans and the Soviet Experiment, 1917–1933* (Cambridge, MA: Harvard University Press, 1967); Mayme Sevander, *Red Exodus* (Duluth, MN: OSCAT, 1993); Paula Garb, *They Came to Stay: North Americans in the USSR* (Moscow: Progress, 1987).

163 On the politics of Finnish Americans, see Carl Ross, 'The Utopian Vision of Finnish Immigrants: 1900–1930', *Scandinavian Studies* 60: 4 (1988).

164 Weidenhamer, 'Disillusionment on the Grandest of Scales'.

Karelian Autonomous Republic, this meant promoting the Finnish language. Finns, especially American Finns, were thus required to promote 'Karelianisation' – a notion that was based chiefly on the ethnic affinity between Karelians and Finns (that settlers from another country, and then from America, would promote local indigenisation seems far-fetched now, but this was the authorities' rationale). As the years passed, however, the Finnish-Americans who had moved to the Soviet Union were subjected to increased repression. In 1937 the Finnish language of the indigenous Karelians was officially replaced by 'Soviet Karelian' – an invented pseudo-indigenous language that incorporated Russian words and Russian grammatical structures, and used the Cyrillic script.

Many more, however, left the United States for the Soviet Union during the Depression. It was an acute crisis, and many of the Americans who moved to the Soviet Union were abandoning the struggle for local revolution in order to join a new 'frontier'. They typically saw themselves as pioneers of a new world – the epitome of an American ethos. In the first eight months of 1931 the Soviet trade agency Amtorg received 100,000 applications from US citizens intending to emigrate to the USSR.[165] Most of those who actually moved there were then betrayed by the Soviet authorities during the Stalinist repression. The American authorities did not welcome them back, as they perceived them as radicals.

Yet more Americans went to the Soviet Union, even if they did not go for ethnic or political reasons. Henry Ford had a factory built in Nizhni Novogorod, a replica of the River Rouge plant.[166] He insisted on sending American workers and their families there, and for a while a veritable American community dwelled in the Soviet Union. More generally, the New Deal itself was also a response to crisis, and many of those who were instrumental in its administration expressed a genuine interest in Bolshevik experiments. US vice president Henry Wallace visited Siberia in May 1944, and saw a potential world turned inside out: 'Siberia used to mean to Americans frightful suffering and sorrow, convict-chains and exiles. For long generations Siberia remained thus without appreciable change. Then in this generation during the past fifteen years, all has

165 Tim Tzouliadis, *The Forsaken* (London: Abacus, 2008), p. 6.

166 See ibid., pp. 30–7.

been changed as though by magic. Siberia today is one of the world's largest lands still open to pioneer settlers'.[167]

Wallace contrasted 'suffering and sorrow' against 'pioneer settlers', likened the Soviet and American experiences, and did not refer to revolution but to 'magic' (a form of displacement indeed). He also added: 'The history of Siberia and its heroic population remind me of the history of the Far West of the United States'.[168] A geography professor who travelled with Wallace on that occasion also remarked that a 'village Soviet in Siberia is a forum for open discussion like a town meeting in New England'.[169] Of course, the reality was different. Winthrop, the Planner of the towns of New England, would have been horrified; but this is what these travelling bureaucrats were seeing: a world turned inside out rather than a world turned upside down.[170] It was neither.

The German-speaking worlds turned inside out

Revolution was a serious prospect elsewhere, too. It was certainly a real possibility during the twilight years of the Habsburg Empire. Ulrich Bach's exploration of Austria-Hungary's utopian literatures and the intellectual milieu that produced them sheds light on the way the possibility of voluntary displacing found expression in a number of influential turn-of-the-century novels.[171] Leopold von Sacher-Moser, Lazar

167 Cited in ibid., p. 225.

168 Cited in ibid., p. 226.

169 Cited in ibid., p. 227.

170 Between the wars, however, many relocations had been pursued by Americans outside the United States. They included America's 'forgotten' settler colony in the Isle of Pines, Cuba, the Panama Canal Zone inhabited by 'the Zonians', and Fordlandia, deep in the Amazon jungle, part of a developing Ford transnational empire. See Michael E. Neagle, *America's Forgotten Colony: Cuba's Isle of Pines* (New York: Cambridge University Press, 2016); Michael E. Donoghue, *Borderland on the Isthmus: Race, Culture, and the Struggle for the Canal Zone* (Durham, NC: Duke University Press, 2014); Greg Grandin, *Fordlandia: The Rise and Fall of Henry Ford's Forgotten Jungle City* (New York: Metropolitan, 2009). Before the war, and also outside of the US, the US colony of Hawaii had been the focus of a pervasive 'small producer' ideology. See Jessica Wang, 'Agricultural Expertise, Race, and Economic Development: Small Producer Ideology and Settler Colonialism in the Territory of Hawaii, 1900–1917', *History and Technology* (2021).

171 Ulrich E. Bach, *Tropics of Vienna: Colonial Utopias of the Habsburg Empire* (New York: Berghahn, 2016).

von Hellenbach, Theodor Hertzka, Theodor Herzl, Robert Müller and Joseph Roth all imagined 'worlds' somewhere else as they faced the revolutionary tensions that were tearing apart their Vienna. They belonged to a bourgeois scene that feared cultural and political transformation and yet was aware of its inevitability. They were patriots, Slavists, and Zionists; their politics were very diverse, even conflicting, and yet they all promoted displacement as a solution to growing contradictions.

Their utopian visions responded to the growing reality of a variety of overlapping 'revolutions' – the nationalist revolutions, modernity's onslaught, and the rising socialist movement. They imagined colonies. Bach acknowledges that there is no history of Austrian colonialism, but he focused on imaginary colonial spaces, and concluded that the 'Austrian colonial utopian narratives from the end of the nineteenth century are saturated with conscious and unconscious aspirations for an alternative social and spatial organization.'[172] The social tension was real – fringe groups were perceived as a threat to stability; but the intellectuals Bach studied were proposing a politics that was neither revolutionary nor reactionary. The places imagined by these 'marginalized intellectuals' were to be elsewhere, but it was Vienna that these intellectuals were ultimately writing about. Bach concludes that the 'Austrian colonial utopias conjure up an idealized image of Vienna projected onto a vacant colonial space.'[173]

Leopold von Sacher-Masoch's *Paradies am Dniester* (1877) imagined a utopian pan-Slavic community located somewhere east of the empire. Conflict there would be suspended and the bordered spaces of central Europe would be overcome by new spatial arrangements, as revolutionary tensions would dissipate. Theodor Hertzka's East African utopia (*Freiland*, 1890) focused on the tensions between town and country, and resolved their opposition through democracy, land reforms, careful planning, and of course displacement (to a colony beyond Europe). Hertzka imagined 'a cheerful society inhabited by young and healthy homeowners coming together to form a productive community.'[174] In

172 Ibid., pp. 1–2.

173 Ibid., p. 5.

174 Ibid., p. 7. On Theodor Hertzka's utopia, see also Ulrich E. Bach, 'Seeking Emptiness: Theodor Hertzka's Colonial Utopia; *Freiland* (1890)', *Utopian Studies* 22: 1 (2011).

Freeland, Hertzka's colony, cultivation and production would be carried out by self-governing 'associations', and 'every inhabitant [would have] an equal and inalienable claim upon the whole of the land, and upon the means of production accumulated by the community'.[175] Similarly, Herzl's *Altneuland* (1902) diverted the Jewish question away. As Palestine would become the site of 'a communal utopia', a 'new cooperative society rising in the Land of Israel that utilizes science and technology to develop the land' was powerfully and prophetically imagined. In all these novels, displacement becomes the preferred technology for managing rising social and ethnic tension.[176]

Anxieties about 'decay' in the face of industrialisation and modernisation were a crucial discursive contributor to projects advocating relocation in the German-speaking world. The notion of *Untergang* ('decay') was a pan-European concern during the latter decades of the nineteenth century, but was especially prominent in Germany, and German nationalist discourse from the era is replete with apocalyptic ideas about an impending end, a general crisis, and the need to counter it.[177] Decay can be seen, and indeed was seen, as a type of revolution – moving out was increasingly offered as a solution.[178] Richard Wagner, who wrote the *Regenerationschriften* ('Regeneration Writings', 1881), for example, talked about emigration to fertile areas of South America, and Nueva Germania had been set up in 1896 in Paraguay by Nietzsche's brother-in-law Wilhelm Förster. The aim was to breed there pure-blooded Christian 'Aryan peasants' protected against moral, racial and urban corruption.[179] Distance would afford protection against a corrupting world.

175 Cited in Gabriel Piterberg, *Returns of Zionism* (London: Verso, 2008), p. 80.

176 Bach, *Tropics of Vienna*, p. 8.

177 See, for example, Daniel Pick, *Faces of Degeneration: A European Disorder, c. 1848–1918* (Cambridge: Cambridge University Press, 1989); John Burrow, *The Crisis of Reason: European Thought, 1848–1914* (New Haven, CT: Yale University Press, 2000).

178 For Germany, see Klaus Vondung, *The Apocalypse in Germany* (Columbia, MO: University of Missouri Press, 2000). Vondung talked about an apocalyptic 'mindscape'. For France, see Koenraad W. Swart, *The Sense of Decadence in Nineteenth-Century France* (New York: Springer, 2013). On 1870s calls for taming savage environments in the colonies as a response to economic depression and industrialisation, see Woodruff D. Smith, 'The Ideology of German Colonialism, 1840–1906', *Journal of Modern History* 46 (1974).

179 See John F. Williams, Daniela Kraus and Harry Knowles, 'Flights from Modernity: German and Australian Utopian Colonies in Paraguay, 1886–1896', *Journal of Australian Studies* 69 (2001).

The politics of voluntary displacement had by then a significant and protracted history in Germany too.[180] Germans had emigrated at a formidable rate during the nineteenth century – primarily to the Americas and Russia (but also to South Australia). In important ways, these emigrations were a consequence of worsening conditions for the 'middle classes': craftsmen and shopkeeper were disproportionately represented in the diaspora. Many had abandoned revolution and reaction in one locale, and then attempted to build 'new Germanies' elsewhere.[181] German missionary J. F. H. Wohlers's rendition of his decision to dedicate his life to preaching among the Kāi Tahu in the south of New Zealand exemplifies the dialectical relationship between revolution and displacement: 'It is well that God preserved me from people with revolutionary ideas, who want to improve the world without God and without Christianity' (and without displacement). 'If I had fallen into such hands' he added, 'they might easily have led me astray and ruined me'.[182] Born in a rural milieu in northern Germany, amid a 'decaying agrarian order' in which revolution would become a real possibility, he moved permanently to one of the New Zealand Company settlements in 1852. Afterwards, he promoted the vision of a regenerated social order that would include the descendants of indigenous peoples and settler newcomers, racially united and inhabiting a new and virtuous community.

But many 'internal' colonies in Germany had also been seen as opportunities to turn the world turned inside out. Frederick the Great of

---

180 See Aaron Spencer Fogleman, *Hopeful Journeys: German Immigration, Settlement, and Political Culture in Colonial America, 1717–1775* (Philadelphia: University of Pennsylvania Press, 1996).

181 In Germany there was Gottfried Duden's *Report of a Journey to the Western States of North America* (1829), which promoted migration to North America, extolling the virtues of settlement and of the Missouri valley (a 'new' Rhine). There were many other similar texts (over 150 titles were published in Germany between 1827 and 1856), but Duden's was the most influential. German immigrants to Missouri were often called the 'followers of Duden'. See also Suzanne Zantorp, *Colonial Fantasies: Conquest, Family, and Nation in Precolonial Germany, 1770–1870* (Durham, NC: Duke University Press, 1997).

182 Michael J. Stevens, '"A Lasting Benefit for a New Race"? Rev. J. F. H. Wohlers and Racial Amalgamation in Southern New Zealand', in Warwick Anderson, Miranda Johnson and Barbara Brookes, eds, *Pacific Futures* (Honolulu: University of Hawaii Press, 2019), p. 245.

Prussia had looked down the newly reclaimed Oder Marshes and proclaimed: 'Here I have conquered a province peacefully'.[183] The following age of reclamation was also an age of growing economic disruption and mobility. David Blackbourn describes a social body riven with revolutionary tension:

> German-speaking Europe in the last decades of the Old Regime, the years before the French Revolution, was not the static society that is sometimes depicted. In many ways it was bursting out of its corsets, as the existing social order came under strain from a newly growing population, new ways of organizing business that bypassed the guilds, new rural settlements on new land, new kinds of commercialized agriculture, new ideas.[184]

From all over Germany and beyond, 300,000 people settled in these reclaimed regions. It was a revolutionary process without a revolution; in the context of absolutist centralisation, Frederick relied on men who reported directly to him, while towns, religious orders, the nobility and the guilds all lost their autonomy in the new lands.[185]

Dörte Lerp identifies several areas of German settler-colonial practice: there were settlements of ethnic Germans located beyond German territorial control in Eastern Europe and North and South America (the so-called *Ackerbaukolonien*), and there were territories integrated within the German state: areas to the east, and German Southwest

---

183 Cited in David Blackbourn, *The Conquest of Nature: Water, Landscape, and the Making of Modern Germany* (New York: W. W. Norton, 2006), p. 5.

184 Ibid., p. 54.

185 The fen colonies in northern Germany (especially in east Friesenland and Oldenburg) were also sites for imagining the world turned inside out. Oldenburg fen colonies' advocate Ludwig Starklof was especially interested in 'the social question'. Starklof's description of ideal conditions in fen colonies relates a settler idyll: 'well-tended houses and small front gardens, the clean and orderly rooms with their well-filled larders, even the occasional Black Forest clock, and the fields of arable and meadow that stretched back behind the houses to the still unexcavated peat moor'. Fen colonists were not just agriculturalists: peat-digging, agricultural pursuits, and the need to manage a small boat offered a true escape from alienation and modern conditions. The fen colonies were geometric and ordered; reclaimed space and wilderness were clearly defined. See Blackbourn, *Conquest of Nature*, pp. 50–1, 59, 60, 75, 155.

Africa.[186] By the late nineteenth century, the 'colonisation' of West Prussia and Poznania was managed by the Settlement Commission (this was a strategic region, and the ethnic-colonising effort there could also rely on the experience of earlier reclamation projects).[187] This project envisaged a combination of German displacement to the area and associated 'depolonisation' programmes. Influential intellectuals Max Weber and Max Sering were both involved, even if they diverged on how exactly to promote sustainable populations and the permanent colonisation of territory. Weber thought that the deportation of Poles and Slavs was ultimately necessary. Sering had seen settler colonialism in practice, and had liked the Canadian approach to the Métis colonies. He thought that the Poles were like the Métis, and that they themselves could be reclaimed as well as the land.

By comparison, Germany's overseas settlement colony, Southwest Africa, and settlements elsewhere in the empire, were demographically negligible – social imperialism mobilised relatively few colonists.[188] There was some consistency, however, and the conservative settler-colonial tradition imagined German elites equally dominating non-German colonised subjects, whether African or Polish. This tradition argued against settling German farmers on small plots in both locations, because it feared that they would become an agricultural proletariat and join the socialists in one place, or fail to live up to their imperial mission in the other. On the contrary, the liberal settler tradition aimed to turn landless Germans into landowners, thereby preventing them from emigrating to the Americas or from joining the socialist movement (the question of pre-empting socialism was a constant feature of projects contemplating displacement; similarly, the Labour Colony movement had risen during the depression of the 1880s, in a moment of crisis, and many saw this movement as responding to the need 'to counter revolutionary socialism among the disaffected urban working classes').[189]

186 See Dörte Lerp, 'Farmers to the Frontier: Settler Colonialism in the Eastern Prussian Provinces and German Southwest Africa', *Journal of Imperial and Commonwealth History* 41: 4 (2013).

187 Ibid., p. 571.

188 Hans Ulrich Wehler, *The German Empire* (London: Bloomsbury, 1985).

189 Arneil, *Domestic Colonies*, p. 67. On the ways in which German South-West Africa was meant to be a veritable settler society, see Jens-Uwe Guettel, 'From the Frontier to German South-West Africa: German Colonialism, Indians, and American Westward Expansion', *Modern Intellectual History* 7: 3 (2010); Daniel Joseph Walther,

These traditions disagreed on the best way to counter revolution through displacement.

There was a third model, however. It focused on a racial version of settler colonialism. Lerp calls it the *völkish* or *Lebensraum* model:

> It was based on Friedrich Ratzel's notion that the expansion of *Lebensraum* (living space) through territorial conquest was a natural process for states – they either grew or were doomed to vanish. In German settlement discourse, though, this drive for expansion was attributed not to the nation-state but to the *Volk*, defined as an ethnic and cultural community independent of the state and its institutions.[190]

This third model became increasingly prominent:

> Throughout the implementation of the settlement programmes in the eastern Prussian provinces and in German Southwest Africa this third model gained more and more persuasiveness. It could do so, because it merged conservative notions of strict social hierarchies with the liberal idea of mass colonisation and popular agrarian and anti-urban thoughts. It solved the class conflict within the settlement discourse as it framed processes of land seizure and displacement in the language of race. Within this racial order all white German men could become masters and bearers of German culture, while non-Europeans, especially Africans, were placed into the realm of nature and permanently excluded from the main privileges of European capitalist modernity: political self-determination and property possession.[191]

Liberalism and conservatism, pitted against each other at home, could collaborate by way of displacement. Besides, many commentators perceived the impossibility or inadvisability of change within Germany. Promoters of colonial expansion like Friedrich Fabri, the 'father of the

---

Creating Germans Abroad: Cultural Policies and National Identity in Namibia (Athens, OH: Ohio University Press, 2002).

190 Lerp, 'Farmers to the Frontier', p. 575.

191 Ibid.

German colonial movement', saw colonialism as a 'solution' to all of Germany's problems: national, political, economic, and demographic. This was an external solution, and yet German colonialism remained fundamentally 'frustrated' – and not only after World War I, when it was abruptly discontinued. After that terminus, only internal solutions remained: revolution or reaction.[192]

After World War I, and the traumatic loss of all colonial possessions, the colonial imagination of the Weimar Republic was redirected towards Eastern Europe.[193] In the 1930s, the prospect of regaining extra-European colonies of exploitation lost further ground; now the prospect of turning the world inside out in the east gathered renewed strength in the context of the Nazi global struggle against revolution.[194]

The Jewish worlds turned inside out

The 'Jewish question' is bound up with the possibility of voluntary displacement, a possibility that greatly exceeds the prospect of 'Displacement in Zion'.[195] Facing an unprecedented crisis, Jewish millionaire and philanthropist Baron Maurice de Hirsch aimed to

192 See Patrick Wolfe, *Traces of History: Elementary Structures of Race* (London: Verso, 2016), p. 98.

193 See Jared Poley, *Decolonization in Germany: Weimar Narratives of Colonial Loss and Foreign Occupation* (Oxford: Oxford University Press, 2005). On the struggles between two colonial imaginations, see Willeke Sandler, *Empire in the Heimat: Colonialism and Public Culture in the Third Reich* (New York: Oxford University Press, 2018).

194 Michael Burleigh, *Germany Turns Eastwards: A Study of Ostforschung in the Third Reich* (Cambridge: Cambridge University Press, 1988). Burleigh analyses a German colonial imagination that at a particular point in time shifts away from a focus on the colonies overseas and towards the settler colonies of the future in Eastern Europe.

195 On utopian visions for Jewish worlds turned inside out – one from 1825, the other from 2007, a span that conveys the intensity of the engagement – see, for example, Justin Nordstrom, '"Strange Times to Be a Jew": Themes of Whiteness, Identity, and Sanctuary in the Imagined Jewish Utopias of Grand Island and Sitka', in Patricia Ventura and Edward K. Chan, eds, *Race and Utopian Desire in American Literature and Society* (Houndmills: Palgrave Macmillan, 2019). Nordstrom focuses on Mordecai Noah's 1825 proposition that Grand Island, New York (on the Niagara River), should become 'Ararat', a haven for world Jewry, and on Michael Chabon's 2007 successful novel *The Yiddish Policemen's Union*, which envisioned Sitka, Alaska, as a refuge for Jews fleeing Israel. On 'Displacement in Zion', see Jacqueline Rose, *The Last Resistance* (London: Verso, 2007).

transform Russian Jewish emigrants into self-supporting rural colonists outside of Europe. It did not really matter where; relocation was more important than destination. Argentina, Canada and Asia Minor were targeted – but not the United States, where a relatively high concentration of Jews, it was thought, might result in social or religious conflict. Besides, Jewish emigration to the United States was happening anyway. Hirsch's plan was a response to the Russian government's rejection of his proposals for financing the technical education of Russian Jews. Like Owen had, Hirsch embraced the prospect of displaced change after his proposals for emplaced change had been frustrated.

His Jewish Colonization Association supervised the establishment of a complex and well-funded framework of institutions, including emigration agencies, technical schools, cooperatives, model farms and savings-and-loan banks.[196] Its charter stated that the Association's purpose was 'to fit Jews for emigration and assist their settlement in various part of the world, except in Europe' – displacement was mandatory. Crucial to this scheme was a comprehensive attempt to replace charity and alms-giving practices with a programme of economic and 'moral' rehabilitation (this was a critique of 'unproductive' charity similar to that offered by Settlement Sociology and Booth's Salvation Army). 'Demoralising' relief was to be discontinued – the communities envisaged in this context had to be self-supporting (and somewhere else).

Self-supporting, but not self-determining: the settlements organisers would accompany the families of Russian Jews arriving to Argentina directly from the ships to the farms on which they were to settle – there was little trust. The farms had been stocked with cattle, seeds, implements and provisions until harvest time. Hirsch's rhetoric and use of biblical images was distinctively settler-colonial: his colonists would become part of a sturdy yeomanry, and 'sit every man under his vine and under his fig tree' (even if Hirsch confessed that his hopes rested mainly upon a second generation of settlers, since 'forty years in the wilderness might be shortened but not escaped'). And yet, he believed that even Russian Jews, if properly organised, could become colonists somewhere: 'my efforts shall show that the Jews have not lost the

196 Theodore Norman, *An Outstretched Arm: A History of the Jewish Colonization Association* (London: Routledge & Kegan Paul, 1985).

agricultural qualities that their forefathers possessed. I shall try to make for them a new home in different lands, where, as free farmers, on their own soil, they can make themselves useful.'[197] This colonising enterprise was to develop according to sound capitalist practice. It was not intended to offer sites for socialist or other social experimentation:

> It will only be philanthropic in its beginning, as it will not be successful if it is not organized and managed as a business, in which the capital investment must yield a renewable return or profit, regardless of the possibility of the yield being allocated exclusively to the development of the project, with a view to extending it to the greatest possible number of emigrants.[198]

Hirsch could see a world turned inside out following forced displacement:

> Some years ago several hundred Jewish families were exiled from Russia to the Argentine. In spite of the greatest hindrances which they encountered, they succeeded in taking root in their new homes. These same families, which a few years ago, bending under heavy burdens, appeared to be only wandering trades-people in Russia, have now become thrifty farmers, who with plough and hoe know how to farm as well as if they had never done anything else. They lay out their farms in the best manner, and build themselves such pretty little houses that every one in the vicinity employs them as carpenters in house-building.[199]

The settlers involved in this scheme would eventually own their land, but were expected to repay in full the capital outlay invested in settling them (travel, food, construction, utensils, livestock), plus interest. Contracts included regulations requiring that the land be properly managed and developed: improvements were mandatory. The settlers were to cultivate a market garden of a specified size, improve pasture for a specified amount of land, improve the land with trees, fence it,

197 Cited in Isidore Singer and Oscar S. Straus, 'Hirsch, Baron Maurice de (Moritz Hirsch, Freiherr auf Gereuth)', *Jewish Encyclopedia*, available at jewishencyclopedia.com.

198 Cited in Edgardo E. Zablotsky, 'Philanthropy vs. Unproductive Charity: The Case of Baron Maurice de Hirsch', *CEMA Working Papers* 2004, PDF available at ucema.edu.ar.

199 Cited in ibid.

and contribute to maintaining schools, synagogues, communal bathhouses, and medical services. These colonies did not generally succeed.

If Hirsch wanted the Jews to return to agricultural pursuits, Zionism aimed to 'return' Jews to a non-revolutionary world. Zionism had had to contend with revolution since its inception, as Gabriel Piterberg has observed. Piterberg focused on the opposition between Theodore Herzl and Bernard Lazare: the latter 'did not wish to "normalize" the Jews but to effect a revolutionary change of the entire society and work with Jews as they were' – and where they were.[200] In Piterberg's estimation, Lazare consistently 'emphasized the revolutionary potential of the Jewish nation, especially in its East European manifestation.'[201] Herzl, on the contrary, intended to pre-empt revolution by making Jewish men more 'manly', and erasing what he saw as exilic femininity.[202] Again, renewed masculinity was linked to displacement; we have encountered similar concerns and logics already. Becoming colonisers would make Jews 'acceptable as Western men', Herzl argued.[203] The Herzl–Lazare dialectic, Piterberg has observed, developed during a period of 'calm before revolutionary eruptions.'[204] Zionism was a pre-emptive move, but not only for the reason of growing antisemitism; revolution was also a concern. It was the Jewish bourgeoisie of Western and Central Europe, a collective that had little intention of settling in Palestine, that especially promoted Zionism. They identified East European Jews as 'primordial' and 'authentic', and therefore appropriate human material for the world turned inside out they envisaged.[205]

Reviewing Piterberg's book, Zeev Sternhell focused on Herzl, who, he insisted, had seen an approaching crisis, concluding that

> the liberal order in Western Europe was tottering and emancipation was endangered even in the country where it had been invented. He realized that the rejection of liberal democracy, the appeal to national sentiment in opposition to it, and the manifestations of anti-Semitism

200 Piterberg, *Returns of Zionism*, p. 80.
201 Ibid., p. 11.
202 See ibid., p. 35.
203 Ibid., p. 36.
204 Ibid., p. 38.
205 See ibid., p. 132.

> were all part of the same phenomenon. This was the great lesson his Parisian experience taught him.[206]

Sternhell sees Zionism as a pre-emptive move against counterrevolution, not revolution. And yet Zionism was also (and especially) about collective sovereign displacement as an alternative to a plethora of revolutionary Jewish political organisations representing several revolutionary projects – significant anti-Zionist alternatives for turn-of-the-century Jewish nationalism. Zionism could then be seen as simultaneously a move against both European revolution and European counterrevolution: displacement against crisis.[207]

Zionist leader Max Nordau's literary and political trajectory epitomises the ways in which anxieties about 'devitalisation' – another crisis – prompted an acceleration in the politics of voluntary displacement. In an insightful passage, Roger Griffin notes that Nordau

> achieved international fame with two bestsellers, *The Conventional Lies of Our Civilisation* (1883), a scathing indictment of the moral bankruptcy of modern society, and *Degeneration* (1892), an exhaustive catalogue of the symptoms of contemporary decadence. The extraordinary success of these books points to a diffuse sense of decay and degeneracy among the general reading public that extended far beyond creative elites. At the end of *Degeneration* the pervasive sense of cultural pessimism is only relieved by the prospect of the eventual eradication – actually 'clubbing to death' – of the most decadent human specimens to ensure the survival of a fitter generation. However, he was soon to find a nobler outlet for his palingenetic longing: Zionism.[208]

---

206 Zeev Sternhell, 'In Defence of Liberal Zionism', *New Left Review* II/62 (March–April 2010), p. 105.

207 In his response, Piterberg rehearses his argument: Herzl was concerned with rising antisemitism, but was also opposed to 'more progressive and less *völkisch* Jewish nationalisms in Europe at the time – Autonomism, Bundism, or Bernard Lazare's anarcho-revolutionary Judaeo-nationalism – which were not at all colonial. These currents rejected the premise that emancipation should be conditioned by assimilation – whereas Zionism, whilst rejecting assimilation, regarded the two as synonymous'. Gabriel Piterberg, 'Settlers and their States: A Reply to Zeev Sternhell', *New Left Review* II/62 (March–April 2010), pp. 115–16.

208 Roger Griffin, *Modernism and Fascism: The Sense of a Beginning under Mussolini and Hitler* (Houndmills: Palgrave Macmillan, 2007), p. 151.

Nordau understood the Zionist project as operating equally at the level of securing a new homeland for the Jewish body politic and, literally, a new body for the Zionist 'new' men.[209] Either way, for him, Jewish men must enter a new body, literally or metaphorically, and possibly both. This new body would be an alternative to revolution; and, as revolution was everywhere in Europe, the alternative had to be somewhere else. Leon Pinsker's 'Auto-emancipation' had similarly concluded in 1882 that antisemitic hatred was inevitable and eternal, and that the only solution was separation, 'the foundation of a colonial community belonging to the Jews', and thus 'the acquisition of a Jewish homeland'.[210]

During the last decades of the nineteenth century and the beginning of the twentieth, the rise of capitalism, urbanisation and modernity subjected the structures of traditional Jewish life in Eastern and Central Europe to a comprehensive upheaval. This revolutionary transformation had engendered another: Jewish socialism. The Bund struggled for 'political and civic equality', and then for 'national and cultural autonomy' – a type of revolution without assimilation.[211] One of the Bund's ideological cornerstones was 'here-ness' – as explicit a rejection of displacement as could be.[212] The communists aimed for

209 See Stefan Vogt, 'Between Decay and Doom: Zionist Discourses of Untergang in Germany, 1890 to 1933', in Steven E. Aschheim and Vivian Liska, eds, *The German-Jewish Experience Revisited* (Berlin: Walter de Gruyter, 2015). Vogt emphasises that references to 'decay' were ultimately calls for political regeneration. Zionists and German nationalists shared this discursive practice to the point that it was a 'common or co-constituted discourse' (p. 7). Zionism, however, unlike much of reactionary German nationalism, called for regeneration elsewhere.

210 Leon Pinsker, 'Auto-Emancipation', 1882, available at jewishvirtuallibrary.org.

211 See Alain Brossat and Sylvie Klingberg, *Revolutionary Yiddishland: A History of Jewish Radicalism* (London: Verso, 2017), p. 24.

212 On the Jewish Bund as an alternative to Zionist settler colonialism, see also Massimo Pieri, *Doikeyt, noi stiamo qui ora!* (Milan: Mimesis, 2017). The Bund was crucial to shaping Russian socialist traditions, and was defined by three ideological cornerstones: Socialism (i.e. revolution), *doikeyt* ('staying put'; *Doikeyt* can be translated as 'here-ness'), and nationality (and therefore internationalism). For the Bund, it was Zionism that was 'Old World' – that is, part of the old regime that would be wiped out by revolution. For Zionism, it was the Bund that was 'Old World' – that is, an outfit determined to remain in Europe. The Bund envisaged the establishment of a Jewish autonomous entity in post-revolutionary Europe; Zionism envisaged an autonomous national entity in post-displacement Palestine. Regarding this opposition, Patrick Wolfe cites Shaul Stampfer's remark that, for the Bundists and for liberal religious Jews, 'a denial of migration' was crucial to their 'self-definition'. It was a denial of displacement. The Zionists relied instead on a denial of exile. Wolfe, *Traces of History*, p. 110.

revolution and assimilation, even though in the Soviet Union during the 1920s and early 1930s – and despite contradictions and several policy shifts – there were attempts to settle 'Jewish workers' on the land. This endeavour focused in particular on Southern Ukraine and Crimea, and on the Siberian Far East. In Birobidzhan, across from Japanese-controlled Manchuria, there was a Jewish 'territorial unit', then a 'Jewish Autonomous Region', and then even a 'Republic', established before being repressed and largely discontinued.[213] The Geserd – the organisation set up by the Soviet government in 1925 – oversaw numerous attempts at Jewish territorialisation.[214] It was a type of revolutionary displacement, and some Zionists from Palestine even moved to the Soviet Union in 1928, exchanging displacement for revolution. These socialists went to colonise Crimea, and while their leader had 'championed "Zionist communism"', he now 'despaired of developing socialism' in Palestine.[215] They formed a commune, or kibbutz, in their new land; but their group was dispersed during the Stalinist purges.

Both the Bund and the communists rejected displacement, but others attempted to reconcile displacement with revolution. Zionists typically rejected revolution, assuming that it was likely in Europe, and therefore opted to move to where it could not follow them; but the militants of Poale Zion, a Marxist and Zionist outfit, and their leader Ber Borochov, argued that revolution in Europe would have been desirable, but was impossible (and therefore that socialism had to be built in Palestine). Borochov concluded that 'the social structure of the Jewish people in the diaspora formed un upside-down pyramid', and that therefore there was no chance of emancipation in the diaspora, while assimilation was an 'illusion'. For him, revolution was a chimera.[216] Poale Zion struggled with this contradiction for decades. In 1920 it broke up between those who sought to join the Communist International and those who maintained the validity of 'class Zionism' and displacement. It eventually

213 See Brossat and Klingberg, *Revolutionary Yiddishland*, pp. 205–12.

214 See ibid., pp. 187, 204.

215 Ibid., p. 205. See also Ofer Aderet, 'The Wind that Shook Prestate Israel's Emigrants to Crimea: In 1928, Around a Hundred Jews Left Mandatory Palestine for Crimea, Then an Outpost of Stalin's Russia. Not the Greatest Idea', *Haaretz*, 21 March 2014.

216 Brossat and Klingberg, *Revolutionary Yiddishland*, p. 5.

joined the Zionist Organization in 1937.[217] It was a difficult predicament. One of Alain Brossat and Sylvia Klinberg's informants noted how Poale Zion was 'shunned' by both communists and Zionists, and was caught 'between the hammer and the anvil', as it tried to maintain a balance between 'what they called *da* and *dort* ("here" and "there") – activity in Poland and propaganda for a socialist Palestine'.[218]

Zionism rejected strategically the possibility of world revolution advocated by the Bund and by the Jews who joined the revolutionary movements and parties. As Brossat and Klingberg conclude, it was 'against the traditions [of the] revolutionary movement, against its utopia, its history and its memory, that the Hebrew state was established'.[219] Seeking his help, Herzl had once reminded the German Kaiser that Zionism would 'take the Jews away from the revolutionary parties' and 'drain off the surplus Jewish Proletariat'.[220] In *Der Judenstaat* (1896), explaining why a Zionist settlement was necessary, he had argued that when 'we [Jews] sink, we become a revolutionary proletariat, the subordinate officers of all revolutionary parties; and at the same time, when we rise, there rises also our terrible power of the purse' (this power led to assimilation – another form of revolution).[221] This notion was widespread. Winston Churchill, for example, saw Jews as 'the force hidden behind every subversive movement of the nineteenth century'.[222] Churchill thought that Zionism could be an effective antidote against

217 Ibid., pp. 27, 260.

218 Ibid., pp. 57, 73–4.

219 Ibid., p. 20. After Spain, after the destruction of the European Jewry, after repression in the Soviet Union, and after facing resurgent antisemitism in the post-war socialist republics of Eastern Europe, many of the revolutionaries moved to Israel – a polity that actively repressed the very memory of their struggle. Some moved after having turned from 'revolutionaries' into 'officials' in socialist Poland, Romania, Bulgaria, Yugoslavia, Czechoslovakia and Hungary, and after becoming disillusioned; others, after fighting in Spain and in World War II, actively embraced Zionism. For the latter group, the shift towards Zionism was a veritable 'transfer of utopias': a displacement. All left after 'their native soil of Yiddishland had been wiped off the map, and along with it the social, cultural, linguistic, and historical fabric of their own existence'. Ibid., pp. 175, 129, 262; see also pp. 132, 242, 267.

220 Cited in Jacqueline Rose, *The Question of Zion* (Princeton, NJ: Princeton University Press, 2005), pp. 110–11. Rose emphasised the perception of impending crisis and an apocalyptic imagination.

221 Cited in ibid., p. 110.

222 Cited in Enzo Traverso, *The Origins of Nazi Violence* (New York: New Press, 2003), p. 103.

Jewish participation in revolutionary movements, and against Bolshevism in particular (even though they did so for obviously for different reasons, the Bolsheviks agreed).[223] In a 1920 *Illustrated Sunday Herald* article titled 'Zionism Versus Bolshevism: A Struggle for the Soul of the Jewish People', Churchill called on the 'Zionist Jew' to tempt Jews away from Bolshevism and establish the Jewish homeland in Palestine.[224]

The Balfour Declaration was to offer such a temptation. It was an imperialist text, but it especially envisaged displacement as an alternative to ongoing conflict – and in important ways it was not Britain, but 'Greater Britain', that issued the promise.[225] Dan Freeman-Maloy has insightfully followed the Declaration's genealogy to South Africa and the other British settler dominions, also highlighting John Buchan's role in its drafting and promotion. A member of Milner's 'kindergarten', Buchan was a crucial intellectual and propagandist, and a powerful promoter of the idea of turning the South African Union into a settler-colonial polity – a transformation that would have united its settler constituencies.[226] Buchan was also instrumental in setting up settler rule in Palestine. He was rabidly antisemitic (in one of his novels, for example, 'Jew-anarchists' conspire to unleash World War I), but recast Jews as 'worthy settlers in Palestine'.[227] His antisemitism was thus place-specific; displacement could undo it. Freeman Maloy concludes that 'Buchan's support for Zionist aspirations in Palestine and his disparagement of Jews in Britain are sometimes presented as contradictory tendencies of

223 In 1937 Trotsky defined Zionism as 'utopian and reactionary' – a description Churchill would have endorsed. Leon Trotsky, 'Thermidor and Anti-Semitism', February 1937, available at marxists.org. Lenin had already argued in 1903 that the Zionist idea of a Jewish nation 'is entirely false and reactionary in its essence'. The Bolsheviks generally took an anti-Zionist position on two grounds: first, they considered the idea of a Jewish nation to be against the interests of the Jewish proletariat (relatedly, the Bolsheviks argued that the Zionists were gathering 'around themselves petty-bourgeois elements and erecting a thick barrier between the Jewish masses and the Russian Revolution'); second, the Bolsheviks saw Zionism as serving British imperialism. Cited in Jamil Hilal, 'Imperialism and Settler-Colonialism in West Asia: Israel and the Arab Palestinian Struggle', *Utafiti: Journal of the Arts and Social Sciences* 1: 1 (1976), p. 67.

224 Cited in Michael Makovsky, *Churchill's Promised Land: Zionism and Statecraft* (New Haven, CT: Yale University Press, 2007), p. 85.

225 See Dan Freeman-Maloy, 'Remembering Balfour: Empire, Race and Propaganda', *Race & Class* 59: 3 (2018).

226 See Freeman-Maloy, 'Remembering Balfour', p. 5.

227 Ibid., p. 8.

his career. But if one considers his lifelong engagement with British ideas of settler colonialism, there is no contradiction.'[228] Buchan would end up as governor general in Canada in the 1930s.

Zionism was more acceptable in the dominions of the empire than in Britain itself, and many between the wars argued that Palestine itself should be settled as a British dominion.[229] The Zionist movement operated thus in a network of complex relations marked by internal suspicion and external support. While Canada was already an ardent Zionist power in the early decades of the twentieth century, many Canadian Jews believed that Zionism might turn potentially socialist immigrants to Canada into settlers in Palestine, transforming an unwanted problem into a global solution. The community's leaders were concerned about the effect these immigrants might have on Canada's revolutionary potential.[230] Money poured from Canada into Palestine, and 'Greater Britain' collectively supported Zionism way more than Britain did. When an army from the Australasian settler dominions was stationed in Palestine after the end of World War I, waiting to be repatriated, it even ethnically cleansed a Palestinian village just as the Zionist army would do after the end of World War II.[231] But this was 1918, not 1948.

Zionism advocated settlement in Palestine, but there was another world turned inside out option: territorialism. The Freeland League for Jewish Territorial Colonization, active between 1905 and the late 1940s, considered colonising a remarkable variety of locations, including Suriname, where it claimed there was an ancient Jewish presence, Canada, parts of Australia, north-eastern Libya, and Angola.[232] Like the Zionists, the

---

228 See ibid., pp. 8–9.

229 See ibid., p. 10.

230 Cited in ibid., p. 11.

231 On the Surafend massacre, when Australian and New Zealand soldiers removed all women and children from the Palestinian village of Surafend and then killed between 40 and 120 unarmed villagers, see Paul Daley, *Beersheba: A Journey Through Australia's Forgotten War* (Melbourne: Melbourne University Publishing, 2009). This was not a war crime only because the war was already over. The New Zealanders blamed the Australians; the Australians blamed the New Zealanders.

232 Adam Rovner, 'Zions Other Than Zion', *Forward*, 5 July 2011; Adam Rovner, *In the Shadow of Zion: Promised Lands before Israel* (New York: New York University Press, 2014). See also Gur Alroey, '"Zionism without Zion"? Territorialist Ideology and the Zionist Movement, 1882–1956', *Jewish Social Studies* 18: 1 (2011).

Territorialists argued that Jews could be good colonisers too, but unlike the Zionists, they insisted that Jews could be good settler colonisers everywhere, and that the ideal society they had in mind could not be established in Palestine, which was unavailable, was not 'empty', and was too 'full' of Jewish memories. Memories would make building the brand new world they had in mind impossible.

After the Zionist Congress rejected the British offer of a 'New Palestine' in East Africa, Zionism and Territorialism became antagonistic movements. It is easy to see why: the Freelanders' brand of territorialism championed Yiddish over Hebrew, Diaspora over Zion, and cultural autonomy over political sovereignty. Aware of the Palestinian presence, the Territorialists promoted a global settler colonial project instead. They believed that they could obtain special dispensations from existing authorities and organise autonomous ethnoreligious enclaves where their settlements would be endowed with a radical sovereign capacity (Austin had argued similarly in the case of Texan prerogatives). The Territorialists also believed that by remaining 'migrants' in the countries where they would settle, their colonists would not be transformed, that they would not assimilate, and would thus remain faithful to their Jewish origins. They were also concerned about the corruption that dominating colonised populations would inflict on the colonisers.

Russian-born social revolutionary leader Isaac Steinberg led the organisation. After the abortive revolution of 1905, Steinberg was arrested in Moscow and exiled to Germany. He had returned to Russia in 1910 and rose to assume a central role in the non-Marxist Left-Social Revolutionary Party. Following the 1917 Revolution, Steinberg became Lenin's first Commissar of Justice. Steinberg, however, eventually fled Russia, and resettled in Germany, before moving to London. Despite his anarchism, Steinberg had opted out of the revolutionary struggle (he parted with Lenin on the autonomy he demanded for Jews in revolutionary Russia, an autonomy Lenin would not agree to). But Steinberg also rejected the prospect of a Zionist world turned inside out in Palestine (like the Bolsheviks, he also understood Zionism as a reactionary political movement). The Territorialists were interested in 'autonomy', not sovereignty in particular, and felt that the urgency of removing eastern Jews from their locations trumped all other considerations. Refusing assimilation, for them, included a refusal to be assimilated outside of Europe as colonising Europeans. The Territorialists saw colonising displacement as a type of assimilation.

In his search for available localities, Steinberg focused on the East Kimberley region in Western Australia's north, a remote and underdeveloped region that could be represented as empty (it was not). He hoped to settle 75,000 Jewish refugees there and to develop the region's pastoral and agricultural industries.[233] The 'Kimberley Plan' envisaged a veritable Jewish homeland there. The Freeland League explored in 1938-39 the possibility of acquiring the pastoral firm of Michael Durack, covering about 16,500 square kilometres. Yiddish poet Melech Ravitch was sent out to investigate and was impressed.[234] The plan was to send out 500-600 'pioneers' to build infrastructure before others would join the settlement. Ravitch thought that the land could support up to a million settlers.

Steinberg arrived in Australia in May 1939 to enlist governmental support for the prospected group settlement. He aimed to leverage public concerns about the 'empty' north. His lobbying was somewhat successful, but Australia's Labor Prime Minister John Curtin ultimately declined to endorse it (he enjoyed bipartisan support on this matter). The fear was that communist pioneers would be involved in the project, and that they would not remain where they were to be sent and drift southward. Curtin told Steinberg that Australia would not 'depart from the long-established policy in regard to alien settlement in Australia', and that the government could not 'entertain the proposal for a group settlement of the exclusive type contemplated by the Freeland League'.[235] Steinberg left Australia in 1943 to rejoin another settler society (Canada) and wrote about Australia as the 'Unpromised Land'. But he tried once more in 1950, even after Israel had been established. Liberal Prime Minister Robert Menzies also declined. Menzies too did not approve of nationally exclusive groups settlements; he instead aimed to establish Australian (or British) group settlements. Australian settler colonialists

233 See Beverley Hooper, 'Steinberg, Isaac Nachman (1888–1957)', *Australian Dictionary of Biography* (Melbourne: Melbourne University Press, 2002), pp. 298–9.

234 This region had already been a 'Promised Land'. Novelist Mary Durack's ancestors had crossed the desert to get there in patriarchal fashion. See her *Kings in Grass Castles* (London: Penguin, 2018 [1959]).

235 Hooper, 'Steinberg, Isaac Nachman', p. 299.

would not support someone else's settler colonialism in Australia. They supported Zionism in Palestine, of course.

The Bund and Territorialism eventually vanished – Zionism got the state and got to develop its settler colonial project, but the contradiction between the revolutionary option and turning the world turned inside out remained. Many years and a few wars later, Shlomo Avineri concluded that Zionism should be seen as a national 'revolution', a movement that transformed the European Jewish society.[236] But that transformation was fundamentally premised on displacement to Palestine, a negation of revolution. Alain Badiou perceptively emphasised Zionism's ambivalence in a retrospective summation. For the French Maoist intellectual, Zionism remained 'suspended' between revolution and colonialism:

> The founding of a Zionist state was a mixed, thoroughly complex, reality. On the one side, it was an event which was part of a larger event: the rise of great revolutionary, communist and socialist projects, the idea of founding an entirely new society. On the other hand, it was a counter-event, part of a larger counter-event: colonialism, the brutal conquest by people who came from Europe of the new land where other people lived. Israel is an extraordinary mixture of revolution and reaction, of emancipation and oppression.[237]

Badiou, however, did not distinguish between colonialism and settler colonialism as distinct modes of domination, or between revolution and world turned inside out.

California as the world turned inside out

During the last two decades of the nineteenth century, California became a crucial site of political experimentation. 'Horticulture' and 'closer settlement', the catchphrases of a powerful movement advocating resettlement to California as the solution to many social ills, were predicated on a critique of the political economy of gold and wheat. Henry

236 Shlomo Avineri, *The Making of Modern Zionism: The Intellectual Origins of the Jewish State* (New York: Basic Books, 1981).

237 Cited in Slavoj Žižek, *Violence* (London: Profile, 2008), p. 105.

George, as we have seen, had produced a comprehensive critique of this overreliance. His globally influential movement had emanated from California.

Horticulture was to offer the opportunity to turn the world inside out. Ian Tyrrell described how 'smaller and middle class operators helped shape the vision of horticulture', and concluded that 'its promoters saw horticulture as a foundation for the ideal society'.[238] It was a comprehensive project of social regeneration. Temperance, health, family values and racism were also ideological components contributing to this project. The Garden Movement, which emerged in California in the 1870s, focused on smaller plots, nuclear families, cooperation and rural civility, and on the care of homes, churches and libraries. Citrus cultivation was compatible with these priorities, most unlike wheat.[239] Citrus inspired and sustained the anti-monopolist reform movements of late-nineteenth-century California. In these movements' plans, the Golden State would become a veritable 'squatter's republic' – a society of white men who claimed no more land than they could use, and who promised to uphold agrarian republican ideals and resist all monopolies, and those who made them powerful – such as eastern industrialists, immigrants, railroads and corporate interests.[240]

The horticultural dream evolved from the works of American protectionists Henry Carey and George, who both made land use and ownership central to the sustained avoidance of class struggle. As we have seen, George argued that California represented a promise unfulfilled. He had blamed agricultural specialisation, and producing for international markets. Thus, the renewal of the promise was about self-reliant diversification. The horticulturalists were convinced that 'intensive agriculture would save California from racial and class conflict' – displacement into smaller lots would save it from all conflict.[241]

238 Ian Tyrrell, *True Gardens of the Gods: Californian-Australian Environmental Reform, 1860–1930* (Berkeley, CA: University of California Press, 1999), p. 9; see also Ian Tyrrell, 'Peripheral Visions: Californian-Australian Environmental Contacts, c. 1850s–1910', *Journal of World History* 8: 2 (1997).

239 See Gary C. Sackman, *Orange Empire: California and the Fruits of Eden* (Berkeley, CA: University of California Press, 2005).

240 See Tamara Venit Shelton, *A Squatter's Republic: Land and the Politics of Monopoly in California and the Nation, 1850–1900* (Berkeley, CA: University of California Press, 2013).

241 Tyrrell, *True Gardens of the Gods*, p. 39.

Diversification would also protect the farmer and undo his dependence on distant markets. Cooperative settlements were ideal for promoting self-sufficiency, and fruit production was more about the reproduction of settlements than producing for markets; the latter was to be subordinated to the former.[242] Midwestern immigrant Protestant Anglos, who were moving away from growing revolutionary tensions in their states, found this prospect especially appealing. The formidable expansion of irrigation colonies of small growers on land that was being reclaimed through extensive waterworks should be understood in this ideological context.

Women were especially active in this movement – its ideology had a markedly gendered dimension. Even crops were understood in moral terms: citrus was 'healthy', the planted eucalyptuses were 'cleansing' and 'disinfecting' the air (and needed little labour), and flowers would keep ugly feelings away. Of course, no unions were allowed, the presence of indigenous peoples was foreclosed, and other ethnic groups were kept at bay. The 'garden' ideal was not for them. The supporters of horticulturalism also expressed a distinct anti-urban sentiment, and ultimately sought to do away with the wage relation itself; when extra labour was needed, labourers would mix with the proprietor, and nobody would be 'inferior'.[243] Like the self-sufficient household producers of the previous century, families would labour together on their small plots. The farms would be white. Ethnic and racial tensions, like social tension, would dissipate through exclusion – a form of preemptive displacement.[244]

242 See ibid., p. 40.

243 Ibid., p. 117.

244 Settler nativisms are an important expression of the political traditions of voluntary displacement: the anti-immigrant rhetoric is grounded in the perception that the immigrant masses are bringing revolution with them and are importing contradictions by making cheap labour available. Immigration undoes the separation sought by the settlers, and anti-Chinese exclusion, a policy that is shared among many settler societies of the Pacific Rim, where organised labour in the nineteenth century aimed to escape rather than shape labour relations, aimed to preserve separation. In other words, if the possibility of relocating threatens the availability of an industrial reserve army in the 'Old World', an industrial reserve army in the New World threatens the world turned inside out. See Iyko Day, *Alien Capital: Asian Racialization and the Logic of Settler Colonial Capitalism* (Durham, NC: Duke University Press, 2016); Alexander Saxton, *The Indispensable Enemy: Labor and the Anti-Chinese Movement in California* (Berkeley, CA: University of California Press, 1995).

The California Constructive League saw irrigation as absolutely central to this project. Irrigation would make closer settlement possible, and closer settlement would in turn enable a move away from both servile labour and the wage relation. This specific ideological compound aimed at 'restoration' and 'renovation'; it spawned utopian schemes promoting images of an egalitarian, racially exclusivist 'democracy'.[245] The ideology pursued a return to stability – a return that would have followed relocation to California.[246] Irrigation would create a middle-class utopia because family farms would not need to rely on hired labour. Only water was needed, because the land itself was in fact 'superior' (horticulturalism was thus a site-specific political project, like many that preceded it; irrigation as ideology only made sense in specified locations). Georgist ideas fitted very well with irrigation and horticulturalist propaganda. Irrigation had the added advantage that it would reverse the deleterious inequalities in land ownership without the imposition of a land tax, which could be seen as a type of confiscation. Horticulturalism was Georgism without its radical edge. Irrigation would also allow the politics of displacement to target otherwise unusable land. It did not require the break-up of large estates – a proposition that would have encountered significant resistance.

It is significant that this world turned inside out, too, was a response to the perception of crisis. Tyrrell noted that the irrigation frontier was promoted as a safety valve for social discontent, as a solution to 'several of the most vexing questions of political and social economy'.[247] Thus horticulturalism was not primarily about agriculture:

> The horticulturalists broke away from the State Board of Agriculture in 1883, formed their own State Board of Horticulture, and henceforth self-consciously proclaimed their own cause as distinct from and superior to general agricultural pursuits . . . Diversification into fruit was supposed to allow farmers to find a refuge from the vicissitudes of distant mass markets, in part because diversity would allow hedging, and in part because emphasis initially was not on easily spoiled crops.[248]

245 Tyrrell, *True Gardens of the Gods*, p. 13.
246 Ibid., p. 230.
247 See ibid., pp. 40, 116.
248 Tyrrell, 'Peripheral Visions', p. 281.

In the end, Tyrrell concluded, horticulture provided 'the leading sector of expansion and also became the leading "ideological sector" in the agrarian economy'.[249] It was a powerful ideology, even if it could not ultimately break the landholders' stranglehold on the land: people had to move to their irrigated plots, and the 'arid land, monopolized by the few', would be turned into a 'middle-class paradise'.[250]

Eventually, California came to embody images of a garden paradise and idealised life.[251] As settlements relied on smaller plots, rural settings became town-like settings. 'Rurban' ideals and suburban expansion were born in this ideological mix.[252] James E. Vance has argued that the 'city in a garden' was 'America's first fundamental contribution to urban form', and that the 'discrete suburb came next'.[253] Eventually 'men in Megalopolis envisaged and produced a new settlement form, that home of *urban pastoralism* that . . . has come to be called exurbia'.[254] In this context, California became 'the core area of the geography of the ideal' ('Kansas' had once performed a similar function and in some ways continued to do so, but California definitely took over).[255] Vance

249 Ibid.

250 Ibid., p. 282.

251 The historian of this vision of an idealised life connects it with America's 'ever-present search for a desirable life-style', an ideal that is typically to be achieved through a 'changing morphology of residence' – displacement. James E. Vance, 'California and the Search for the Ideal', *Annals of the Association of American Geographers* 67 (1972), p. 186.

252 The planners of countless schemes for suburban white flight to the 'crabgrass frontier' thus relied on a long tradition of voluntary displacement as a political approach. See Kenneth T. Jackson, *Crabgrass Frontier* (New York: Oxford University Press, 1985); Lorenzo Veracini, 'Suburbia, Settler Colonialism and the World Turned Inside Out', *Housing, Theory and Society* 29: 4 (2012).

253 Vance, 'California and the Search for the Ideal', p. 186.

254 Ibid., pp. 186, 191 (emphasis in original).

255 Ibid., p. 195. Kansas was once a world turned inside out. Eastern abolitionists and Free Soilers determined to prevent there slavery's western advance. Lawrence, Kansas, was founded by New England families whose passage was funded by the New England Emigrant Aid Society. It was the 'Boston of the prairies'. Boston had once been a world turned inside out, too. Nineteenth-century Kansas was later a site for intense social experimentation – in Thomas Frank's words, 'as though the blank landscape prompted dreams of a blank-slate society, a place where institutions might be remade as the human mind saw fit'. The Western Populism of the 1890s would rely on this tradition and respond to renewed crisis. Later still, the Midwest would be a hotbed of radical politics up to the 1930s, especially as regards the left-wing organisations of farmers, including the Farmers' Alliance and the Farmer-Labor Party. See Thomas Frank, *What's*

emphasised the 'spatially independent attraction of the geographical image' – it was the image of a world turned inside out.[256] California was the land of the 'restorative climate', of mental and physical health, of agricultural Arcadias – for many, 'California rather than Kansas furnished the image', a place to search for utopia and turn away from American norms, and a place where residents 'set up in towns of like-mindedness'.[257]

Colonies of all sorts, and social experimentation of many kinds, 'blossomed all over California' during most of its history.[258] Many have blossomed elsewhere in the United States, too.[259] Indeed, this was an age of intense utopian communitarianism in America.[260] In

---

the Matter With Kansas? (New York: Henry Holt, 2004), pp. 31–2. See also Craig Milner, *Kansas: The History of the Sunflower State, 1854–2000* (Lawrence, KS: University Press of Kansas, 2002). On the Western Populist movement, see, for example, Lawrence Goodwyn, *The Populist Moment: A Short History of the Agrarian Revolt in America* (New York: Oxford University Press, 1978).

256 Vance, 'California and the Search for the Ideal', p. 195.

257 Ibid., p. 199.

258 Ibid., p. 200.

259 The Ruskin Colonies of Tennessee and Georgia had attracted northern settlers during the recession that followed the 1893 crash. It was a vision of a utopia drenched in sunshine that proved attractive both to these artisans and to the American socialists who were trying alternative and non-revolutionary ventures. Fairhope, Alabama, was a Georgist practical experiment. The 'Fairhope Industrial Association', which then became the 'Fairhope Single Tax Corporation', was founded in Des Moines, Iowa, in 1894. It was to constitute a 'utopian demonstration community'. The would be settlers became a club, drew up a constitution, and moved elsewhere. Home, Washington, was an anarchist colony located on a remote Puget Sound peninsula. Founded in 1896, it dissolved in 1921. In 1869 colonists belonging to the Britain's National Reform League, founded by noted Chartist leader James Bronterre O'Brien, moved to Nemaha County, Kansas, and set up the Workingmen's Cooperative Colony. See W. Fitzhugh Brundage, *A Socialist Utopia in the New South: The Ruskin Colonies in Tennessee and Georgia, 1880–1901* (Champaign, IL: University of Illinois Press, 1996); Timothy Miller, 'The Roots of the 1960s Communal Revival', *American Studies* 33: 2 (1992), p. 78; Justin Wadland, *Trying Home: The Rise and Fall of an Anarchist Utopia on Puget Sound* (Corvallis, OR: Oregon State University Press, 2014); Gary R. Entz, *Llewellyn Castle: A Worker's Cooperative on the Great Plains* (Lincoln: University of Nebraska Press, 2013).

260 Michael Fellman's analysis of American 'Utopian communitarianism' and its long-lasting influence emphasised 'the attempt to enact the perfect vision of truth through *small model communities*'. The 'township ideal' was a powerful trope: 'Within a small settlement' atomisation could be countered, and many of the 'new settlements in the post–Civil War period were efforts to create new townships and return to a tradition that emphasized participation, shared symbols, common rituals, and common goals; the ideal of the township was the ideal of the perfected community'.

the South, interracialism advocated relocation to interracial communities as a response to rising racist aggression; but in California utopianism had been qualitatively different.[261] Vance concluded that California was 'settled in large measure by those searching for the desirable life-style and seeking the heartland of the geography of the ideal'.[262] This heartland was somewhere in particular, and the ideal required migration to it.

Halcyon, California, was an experiment, and an epitome of this heartland.[263] The great financial panic of 1893, rising social cleavages in the east, and labour struggles and revolutionary tensions in industrialised areas had contributed to the growth of the Theosophical movement in the United States. Temple Theosophy argued that the Iroquois League had been 'founded and governed' by the 'Great Lodge of Masters', and believed that the Masters were to establish a settlement that was to be 'a city upon a hill' that would 'furnish an object lesson to all'.[264] The Theosophists that gathered in Syracuse, New York, around William Dower chose 'Master Hilarion', 'patron of concrete knowledge and technology' – their strand of Theosophy was not as esoteric as it might seem. Members of this group believed that Hilarion had been reincarnated in eighteenth-century Iroquois leader Hiawatha (the Hiawatha of Henry Wadsworth Longfellow's 1855 *The Song of Hiawatha*) near the Temple's location in Syracuse (this meant that Hiawatha was not really indigenous, and that he could be appropriated for settler-colonising purposes). The Temple claimed to 'bring about a better

---

While Jeffersonian, Protestant evangelical and artisanal traditions contributed to the township model, Fellman's conclusion rehearsed the political tradition of voluntary displacement: the 'cooperative colonizers and the political pragmatists' were a 'conservative force' and countered 'the calls for class action that were heard increasingly in the 1890s'. They 'emphasised cooperation in the face of a growing Marxist emphasis on the inevitability of class warfare and social strife'. Michael Fellman, *The Unbounded Frame: Freedom and Community in Nineteenth Century American Utopianism* (Westport, CT: Greenwood Press, 1973), pp. xv–xvi, 8–9, 5, 18 (emphasis in original).

261 See Hunt Ferguson, *Remaking the Rural South: Interracialism, Christian Socialism, and Cooperative Farming in Jim Crow Mississippi* (Athens, GA: University of Georgia Press, 2018).

262 Vance, 'California and the Search for the Ideal', p. 202.

263 Paul Eli Ivey, *Radiance from Halcyon: A Utopian Experiment in Religion and Science* (Minneapolis, MN: University of Minnesota Press, 2013).

264 Cited in ibid., p. 7.

understanding between so-called savages and civilized races'. The Theosophists regularly visited the nearby reservation, and the Temple Movement remained interested in performing 'nativeness' after it moved to California.[265]

These Theosophists were politically very active. Centred in Syracuse, they were able to open autonomous 'squares' elsewhere in the United States, and became a national organisation (they also had adherents in Canada and Germany). Fascinated with electricity, they saw the powers of 'light' and 'darkness' meeting in deadly conflict. They originally conceived these terms as metaphors for socialism and capitalism, respectively, and mobilised for the presidential election of 1900 with calls for a 'collective commonwealth', for 'cooperative business' and for limiting the money supply. They supported strikers, and their leader attended socialist candidate Eugene Debs's organisational meeting in 1899. They supported Georgist calls, but after the ascendancy of Theodore Roosevelt to the presidency and the onset of repression, they embraced displacement. Defeated transformation in one setting prompted a decision to relocate.

A prophecy in 1899 proclaimed that revolutionary upheaval was coming:

> The Bear will growl at the Lion; the Eagle will alight on the Bear's Head and pluck out its left eye; the Ox and the Lion will close in a struggle to the death; the Ox, the Bear, the Lion and the Eagle will form a Square, from the centre of which will arise the Temple, the architect of which will rule the Earth.[266]

As one of their leaders noted, the animals in the prophecy could be seen as nations as well as other entities:

> Organized Labor will growl at Capital, the Spirit of true Liberty will alight on, or enter, the Labor Unions, and rid it of its lower mental forces. The Masses and Capital will close in a struggle to the death. The Masses, Organized Labor, Capital and the Spirit of Liberty will become co-ordinated – form a Square, from the

265 Ibid., p. 86.
266 Cited in ibid., pp. 53–4.

> centre of which will arise the Temple, the architect of which will rule the Earth.[267]

The appropriate response to foretold upheaval, they believed, was not striving for emplaced transformation. By 1900, the lodge had developed the idea of building a place somewhere else. It was an apocalyptic response: 'The wars and earthquakes and other seismic as well as sociological upheavals that must come prior to the advent of the next Avatar sufficiently accounts [*sic*] for the present disturbed condition of the planet and its races'.[268] In late 1900, they stated their goal: to establish 'a settlement which must eventually become a city'.[269]

These Theosophists thought in terms of dualities, and believed that dualities had to be harmonised. This applied to social phenomena, too. Class struggle was anathema to them – the classes would remain, but must become harmonised. They thought that Theosophy had to be demonstrated in practice – hence the need to build a visible place to solve the 'sociological world problem' and 'demonstrate the proposition of unity between spiritual and material planes and forces'.[270] Their experiment focused especially on restoring health: the community they established operated a sanatorium (California as a whole was often promoted as a health-restoring location). Restoring broken health and harmony was the declared social aim; displacement was the chosen method. They saw their community, Halcyon, as a 'city of refuge where the downcast and broken reed may mend itself and grow anew'.[271] They were thinking about a visible object lesson. Health would be restored through displacement.

Australia as the world turned inside out

The ideology of horticulturalism and irrigation had a significant transnational dimension, and 'the yeoman ideal of small town, orchard, and

267 Cited in ibid., p. 56.
268 Cited in ibid., p. 69.
269 Cited in ibid., p. 96.
270 Cited in ibid., p. 79.
271 Cited in ibid., p. 112.

farm' was popular way beyond California.[272] In Australia, these images were especially widespread, while the Georgist critique of broadacre farming on large estates resonated powerfully there. Tyrrell pointed out that, while these ideas 'first developed in California', they were 'then adopted across the Pacific'.[273] It was a remarkable two-way transnational exchange in irrigation technologies, ideas, ideologies, personnel and plants. But if California had been the early laboratory of this ideology, Australia gradually became a crucial site of experimentation.

American professor, politician, engineer and future head of the United States Bureau of Reclamation Elwood Mead's advocacy is significant in this transnational context.[274] He had, like many before him from the United States, travelled to Australia in an attempt to gather information on ways to promote a society of small-scale settlers. Ensuring the provision of rural credit (as well as government-backed irrigation schemes) was his suggestion for making settlement viable again in the United States – he called his proposals the 'Australian plan'. In Australia, the rural irrigation communities could only survive through significant state involvement in infrastructure-building and marketing. Mead also liked Australia's constitutionally enshrined commitment to racial exclusion, the White Australia policy, and thought that the relationship between owners and labourers could be sustained without creating a rural proletariat by allowing labourers to take over from older farmers. In this case, the politics of displacement acquired a marked generational dimension.

Eventually, California's full integration into the national US market discontinued the transpacific interchange of technologies and ideas. Land consolidation in both locations could not be avoided, and a focus on fruit-growing gave way to fruit-selling. Instead of egalitarian racial commonwealths, subsumption in international markets and agribusiness ensued. For a while, however, an Australian democracy of small-scale self-sufficient farmer-settlers had been pursued as a possibility – not many had agreed with William Lane that the only opportunity for it

272 Tyrrell, 'Peripheral Visions', p. 282.

273 Ibid., p. 282.

274 On the transnational exchange of reform ideas in the aftermath of the global crisis of the settler revolution, see Marilyn Lake, *Progressive New World: How Settler Colonialism and Transpacific Exchange Shaped American Reform* (Cambridge, MA: Harvard University Press, 2018).

lay elsewhere.[275] The crucial Australasian innovation in the crisis of the political traditions supporting displacement (New Zealand was also a crucial laboratory of the world turned inside out) was the state: once the settlers had escaped spatially beyond its reach; now they were relying increasingly on its support.[276]

---

275 Lane espoused his experiment in racial socialism in *The Workingman's Paradise* (1892). The settlers of Queensland had to organise because, as one of them comments in the novel, 'with the Chinese and the squatters [monopolist capitalist landowners] doing as they liked and hating the sight of a white man, we'd all have been cleared out if we hadn't'. 'Coloured labour has been the curse of Queensland', adds another, and yet the 'common danger for all the working classes' had given them a 'unity of feeling earlier than that [*sic*] has been acquired in the south' of Australia. It was spatial logic leading to a spatial conclusion: white men faced exclusion from a specific locale, had reacted and developed a theory of labour relations whereby, as another settler explains, the 'whole wage system must be utterly done away with'. This was to be achieved through cooperation and separation, not revolution, since revolutions merely destroy 'arts and science'. One of the protagonists in the novel argues: 'George's is a scheme by which it is proposed to make employers compete so fiercely among one another that the workman will have it all his own way', and to 'tax the landowner until it doesn't pay him to have unused land'. But 'capitalism continues competition', the protagonists concludes. For Lane, the single tax would only be a *temporary* fix before contradictions would catch up. His solution was *permanent*, not temporary isolation: 'Absolute isolation' in actually existing colonies, 'while the new conditions [for socialism] are being established'. Model colonies somewhere else will transform society. The prospect of spatial exclusion in one locale had produced a self-inflicted type of spatial exclusion. Unable to thrive in Queensland, Lane's settlers would thrive, he argued, not elsewhere in Australia but in Paraguay (they did not). The other half of Lane's proposal was women's freedom, because 'you can't raise free men from slave women'. This latter component of Lane's project is somewhat counterintuitive, because while Lane consistently feared class conflict he resented capitalism primarily because of its emasculating consequences. In his opinion, under capitalism, as Marilyn Lake concluded, workers were 'robbed of their manhood'. William Lane, *The Workingman's Paradise* (Sydney: Sydney University Press, 2009), pp. 107, 141; Marilyn Lake 'Socialism and Manhood: The Case of William Lane', *Labour History*, 1986, vol. 50 (1986), p. 54.

276 There was an exceptionally strong and long-lasting utopian and communal tradition in New Zealand, too. Its prime minister, Julius Vogel, had been the country's agent-general in London, and had written a utopian novel – he knew how to promote utopian images. On New Zealand utopianisms, see Lyman Tower Sargent, 'Utopianism and the Creation of New Zealand National Identity', *Utopian Studies* 12 (2001); Dominic Alessio, 'Promoting Paradise: Utopianism and National Identity in New Zealand, 1870–1930', *New Zealand Journal of History* 42 (2008). Sargent detected a widespread and long-lasting utopian trend in representations of settler New Zealand: 'Cockaigne', 'Arcadia', the 'Labourer's Paradise', the 'Middle Class paradise', the 'Just City', 'the farthest promised land', the 'happy colony', the 'land of promise', 'Brighter Britain', 'God's own Country', 'Godzone' (see pp. 1–2). For a related welfarist tradition, see W. B. Sutch, *The*

Australian politician Charles Pearson's writing and teaching were also crucial in this development, both in the Australian context and in that of the transnational development of ideas about settlement. Pearson had tried and failed at farming after migrating to Australia as a young man. His politics and writing were especially concerned with the local and global possibilities of rising racial and class-related antagonisms. He had foreseen the end of displacement as a political possibility, and did not want to return to England because he feared he would have to politically oppose the 'old Conservatives' and the 'Liberals of the Pall Mall Gazette type' equally.[277] He did not enjoy confrontation, and preferred distance. In *National Life and Character* (1892) Pearson had prophesied the global future in apocalyptic terms: the colonised peoples of the world would rise and challenge established racial orders. Revolution was in his mind. About the working classes of England, his American correspondent Charles Eliot Norton noted in a letter to him that 'their discontent, though smothered and ineffectual at present, might easily be wrought into a fury against which all the defences of actual institutions would be as vain as were the walls of the Bastille against the passions of the mob of the Faubourg St Antoine'.[278] Pearson expressed a global imagination shaped by racial and class revolutions to come; he thought, however, that Australia might be an appropriate locale to experiment against global degeneration.

Alfred Deakin, one of the Federation of Australia's founding fathers and a student of Pearson, sought to promote settlement, and with it a virtuous society that would have no resemblance to the 'Old World'. Deakin believed that irrigation would make this possible, and that only the state could make irrigation possible. He aimed to provide guaranteed markets for Australian capitalists, but he also wanted to allow farmers to escape the consequences of market fluctuations selectively – he was aware of the global crisis of the political traditions aiming to turn the world inside out rather than upside down and of the need to provide a sustained and coordinated policy response. In Victoria (he hailed from Melbourne), there was a particular need to overcome the consequences

Quest for Security in New Zealand (Harmondsworth: Penguin, 1942); W. B. Sutch, *Poverty and Progress in New Zealand* (Wellington: Modern, 1941) ('Poverty and Progress', of course, was an explicit reference to Henry George).

277 Lake, *Progressive New World*, p. 39.

278 Cited ibid., p. 29.

of the end of the gold rushes. Intensive farming was seen as a way to dampen the revolutionary potential of out-of-work miners. Deakin consistently espoused the social benefits of agrarian life as a counterpoint to city and industrial life in general. New South Wales leader and early proponent of federation Henry Parkes took the same view. Parkes had been a Chartist and a farm labourer before migrating to Australia, but his politics had now changed.

Deakin's irrigation policy and the displacements that it envisaged were framed as an attempt to pre-empt social tension. The late 1880s and 1890s were years of economic depression and social unrest; and the image of the 'garden' retained a significant appeal in Australia, as wheat and wool were emptying already underpopulated rural areas and filling rapidly growing cities. The depression and the strikes of the 1890s prompted renewed interest in the possibility of closer settlement. The Chaffey brothers had built Ontario, California, and would build Mildura, Victoria and Renmark, South Australia – all irrigation colonies. These were capitalist ventures, but the aim was also to quell the very possibility of social unrest by 'making workers part of the cooperative venture' – workers would not strike in these separate communities because the employee was 'a landowner on the estate, while every apprentice [was] the son of a settler'.[279] Both landowner and apprentice, of course, had to move.

Agitation for irrigation in Australia was the successor of previous movements for 'selection' (the rough equivalent of homesteading in North America), and in the 1880s irrigation leagues had already formed in Victoria. The Water Conservation Act of 1881 required amendments, and this was Deakin's real beginning in Australian politics: promoting legislation sanctioning compulsory easements relating to water. Irrigation would make rural enterprises predictable; irrigation settlements, it was argued, would allow a society genuinely to settle down. With irrigation, agriculture would be certain and stable. Decades later, Deakin proclaimed in the Federal Parliament in 1912:

> Nothing is more beautiful than the healthy and natural labour by which upright and honest people obtain a sufficient living, and even what may be termed luxuries, under conditions which our greatest

279 Tyrrell, *True Gardens of the Gods*, p. 146.

> cities cannot hope to rival. Those engaged in such employment are in touch with nature, their homes are healthy and restful, their freedom and independence making their citizenship a far greater prize than it is in city communities as we know them.[280]

As far as he was concerned, Australian Federation was not his primary achievement, even though it was an achievement. It had been a means to an end.

But Australasia was a laboratory of the politics of displacement beyond the importation and deployment of irrigation technologies. Australia's 'state experiments' achieved, as Marilyn Lake has observed, a 'high international profile' (including and especially the White Australia policy); they were seen as 'socialistic' or as 'socialism without doctrines', not socialism.[281] The turn-of-the-century transnational progressives engaged intensely with the politics of volitional displacement and its Australasian iterations.[282] This particular milieu was intent on keeping revolution – in other words, war, destruction and socialism – at bay. It is in this context that eminent Australian jurist and politician H. B. Higgins's notion of Australia as 'peace' should be understood.[283] In this ideological context, all war is revolution, and all revolutions are a type of war. As for keeping contradictions at bay, Lake quotes one American feminist's 1902 conclusion that Australia was the first 'to erect a nation

---

280 Alfred Deakin, House of Representatives, 5 September 1912, p. 2,940.

281 Marilyn Lake, '1914: Death of a Nation', *History Australia* 12: 1 (2015), p. 15. See also Albert Metin, *Socialism without Doctrines* (Sydney: Alternative Publishing Cooperative, 1977 [1901]).

282 See William Pember Reeves, *State Experiments in Australia and New Zealand* (London: George Allen & Unwin, 1902). Reeves interacted with the British Fabians, a group seeking in the settler colonies the antidote to revolution at home. The Fabians were heavily involved in settler-colonial issues, and split in 1900 on the Boer war – both an imperial and an anti-settler-colonial war. See also Victor Selden Clark, *The Labour Movement in Australasia* (London: Archibald Constable, 1907). It was an enormously successful book. Twenty-five editions followed between 1906 and 1910. Clark recognised that Australia was an important testing-ground for reform.

283 'The ideal of Australia is peace', Higgins proclaimed in the federal parliament. In the same parliament, Alfred Deakin quoted German general von Moltke: 'War is destruction', before adding: 'destruction of life, of property, of the means of happiness and progress. Lockouts and strikes equally involve destruction – destruction of labour, of machinery, of capital, of social relations and of social peace'. Cited in Lake, '1914: Death of a Nation', p. 8 and pp. 17–18.

without rebellion, revolution, war or compulsion and the first nation to give liberty to women'.[284] Lake lists the innovations that were implemented in this context: the secret ballot, salaries for members of parliament, the eight-hour day, compulsory arbitration, minimum-wage legislation, women's suffrage, and pensions and allowances for the old, invalids and mothers.[285] Together, these reforms represented a compact that would become known as the 'Australian Settlement'.[286]

Arbitration and irrigation would focus on different locales – urban and rural, respectively – but should be seen as part of an integrated system. The state was heavily involved in both. Like Deakin, Higgins, the architect of Australia's compulsory industrial arbitration legislation, had studied with Pearson. Higgins's role was crucial in defining the minimum wage as a *living* wage, and, after a landmark 1907 sentence, arbitration would become official policy. Higgins had noted: 'In other words the process of conciliation, with arbitration in the background, is substituted for the rude and barbarous process of lockout and strike. Reason is to displace force'.[287] A conflict that was occurring on factory floors was to be displaced to a court of law.

Arbitration and minimum-wage legislation were first developed in settler Australia (and settler New Zealand – as US travelling journalist Henry Demarest Lloyd had noted, New Zealand was the 'country without strikes'); but the plan was to propose their extension elsewhere.[288] Arbitration would make industrial conflict superfluous. The Arbitration Court and its operation have been seen as a search for the 'middle ground' between labour and capital, and a rejection of incipient class antagonism; but they should be understood especially as means pre-emptively displacing conflict. Higgins' logic made sense to

284 Ibid., p. 20.

285 Ibid., p. 13.

286 See Paul Kelly, *The End of Certainty: Power, Politics and Business in Australia* (Crows Nest: Allen & Unwin, 1994); Geoffrey Stokes, 'The "Australian Settlement" and Australian Political Thought', *Australian Journal of Political Science* 39: 1 (2004). Kelly had identified White Australia, Industry Protection, Wage Arbitration, State Paternalism, and Imperial Benevolence as the settlement's five constituent elements. They all contributed to, and converged in, distantiation: they were all designed to keep conflict at bay.

287 Cited in Lake, *Progressive New World*, p. 131.

288 Marilyn Lake, '"This Great America": H. B. Higgins and Transnational Progressivism', *Australian Historical Studies* 44: 2 (2013).

his American progressive interlocutors, but neither US capital nor organised American labour desired this type of mediation – the former focusing on 'freedom of contract', the latter on 'manly independence'.[289] This world turned inside out tradition could not be exported to the United States. During an explicitly reactionary phase in the 1920s, it was discontinued in Australia, too. And yet, while Australian Prime Minister Hughes embraced reaction, the Australian settlement survived until the 1990s.[290]

More generally, Australia was often represented as a 'new beginning' for humanity itself – a locale so removed from turmoil as to be almost out of history. D. H. Lawrence, for example, engaged with the world turned inside out, and in 1923 thought that Australia was especially suited for it. He had embarked on a 'savage pilgrimage' immediately after WWI, and had been searching for locales still uncontaminated by the industrial civilisation he saw emanating from England. He consistently and passionately professed an 'anticapitalist' drive, accompanied by an equally passionate rejection of revolution.[291]

Percy Reginald Stephensen, who had worked with Lawrence, agreed that Australia was a country 'still to make', but was especially concerned with Australia's need to stay out of the troubles he saw coming.[292] He had joined the Communist Party of Australia in 1924, but his sympathies would shift to the right as the 1930s progressed. One of the foundational experiences of his political life was his participation in the organisation of a failed general strike in London in 1926. A realisation of the

289 See Lake, '"This Great America"', p. 177. Leader of the American Federation of Labor Sam Gompers was consistently hostile to arbitration and its 'emasculations'. See also Lake, *Progressive New World*, pp. 206–7.

290 Cited in Lake, '"This Great America"', p. 186.

291 See David Game, *D. H. Lawrence's Australia: Anxiety at the Edge of Empire* (Burlington: Ashgate, 2015); D. H. Lawrence, *Kangaroo* (Sydney: Angus & Robertson, 1992). Lawrence also contemplated the establishment of a regenerative community in Taos, New Mexico (many American modernists clustered in the area in the early decades of the twentieth century). See D. H. Lawrence, *Mornings in Mexico and Etruscan Places* (London: W. Heinemann, 1956); Lois Palken Rudnick, *Utopian Vistas: The Mabel Dodge Luhan House and the American Counterculture* (Albuquerque, NM: University of New Mexico Press, 1996). Lawrence's search for 'regeneration' was based on his perception of widespread decay, which he understood as a kind of revolution.

292 See Dan Tout, 'Reframing "Inky" Stephensen's Place in Australian Cultural History', *Settler Colonial Studies* 7: 1 (2017).

impossibility of revolution would have important consequences for his politics. 'Foundations of Culture in Australia' (1936) was his political manifesto.

Its three instalments correspond to three moments: first, the settler's reclamation of life in Australia, an affirmation of displacement; second, lamentation at settler Australia's failure to embrace a settler-indigenising project – a failure fully to relocate psychologically, as well as physically; and, third, the existential danger implicit in Australia's involvement in world affairs – that is, the fatal risks inherent in possible reconnection. It was isolation that should primarily define the Australian polity, Stephensen argued, while the prospect of an end of isolation should be seen as a life-threatening challenge. If distance was maintained, Stephensen concluded, everything else would take care of itself. Britain would eventually collapse, and Europe destroy itself, and a restoration of distance would save Australia.[293] For Stephensen, Australia was the world turned inside out's best hope; disconnection, after all, was one result of displacement.

Between the wars, even the British Union of Fascists imagined Australia as a possible world turned inside out. Frustrated in one place, these fascists imagined regenerating locales elsewhere. In a piece entitled 'One of the Pivots of the Empire' (1937) BUF theorist A. Raven Thomson emphasised identity:

> Australia, alone of all the British Dominions and colonies, possesses the inestimable advantage of complete freedom from any racial problem, for the aborigines are entirely insignificant in numbers and culture. Here we have an entire sub-continent completely controlled by one race of people speaking one language, a factor which cannot be paralleled elsewhere in the Empire except in the Home country, for even New Zealand has her Maoris. For this reason, if for no other, Australia must inevitably form one of the two pivots of Empire, for it is about the two great blocks of pure British race that the Empire must revolve.[294]

293 Percy Reginald Stephensen, 'The Foundations of Culture in Australia' (1936), available at home.alphalink.com.au.

294 A. Raven Thomson, 'One of the Pivots of the Empire' (1937), available at hatfulofhistory.wordpress.com.

'Pivot' confirms it: sideways displacement to a racially defined 'Homeland' was here understood as the most appropriate response to crisis.

The Japanese worlds turned inside out

Still in the 1930s, but in another continent, during what Louise Young described as a 'time of global crisis', Japanese-occupied Manchuria became a crucial laboratory of 'Asian-style fascism', and a site for experimenting with alternatives to revolution and crisis.[295] By then there was already a significant Japanese tradition of displacement as politics, a tradition that even preceded the country's colonial take-off following the Sino-Japanese war of 1894. Recapping it, influential journalist and historian Tokutomi Soho had proclaimed in 1904 that Japan's 'future history will be a history of the establishment by the Japanese of new Japans everywhere in the world'.[296]

This sensitivity had developed as a response to crisis and revolution. Thomas Smith's 'Japan's Aristocratic Revolution' (1961) emphasised Japan's distinct (and in Smith's estimation 'defective') journey to modernity, but the notion of a Japanese revolution, even though an 'aristocratic' one, is relevant for an outline of the Japanese worlds turned inside out. Many samurai were facing impoverishment, and were alienated from a political order that only purportedly expressed their rule. Revolutionary tensions thus prompted the reconstitution of Hokkaido, where impoverished samurai were allocated land. This colonising scheme did not proceed as expected, and the state subsequently took over.[297] Significant borrowings from other settler-colonial traditions

295 Louise Young, 'When Fascism Met Empire in Japanese-Occupied Manchuria', *Journal of Global History* 12 (2017).

296 Quoted in Akira Iriye, 'Japan's Drive to Great-Power Status', in Peter F. Kornicki, ed., *Meiji Japan: The Emergence of the Meiji State* (London: Routledge, 1998), p. 57. On Japanese settlers, see also Kate E. Taylor, 'Japan: Colonization and Settlement', in Immanuel Ness, ed., *The Encyclopaedia of Global Human Migration* (New York: Wiley-Blackwell, 2013). Taylor recounts that 'Between 1868 and 1941 over 712,583 people migrated to Korea and 397,090 to Taiwan; Manchuria saw over 270,000 Japanese settlers prior to the end of the Pacific War in 1945'.

297 See Thomas Smith, 'Japan's Aristocratic Revolution', in Thomas Smith, *Native Sources of Japanese Industrialization* (Berkeley, CA: University of California Press, 1988).

would therefore characterise the settler colonisation of Hokkaido; many more exchanges in the context of the transnational circulation of colonial knowledge would follow in later decades.[298]

Manchuria especially was meant to be a Japanese world turned inside out. In the 1930s an acute rural crisis (what was known as the 'problem of the villages') had become intractable. Significant social tension and distress were widely felt. The 'Manchurian lifeline' – a 'spatial fix' – and the slogan 'Millions to Manchuria' condensed the ambition of displacing up to one-fifth of the Japanese rural population to the Manchurian 'New Paradise'.[299] It was in Manchuria that, according to Young, the Japanese 'technologies' of fascist governance were also developed and tested. 'Manchukuo represented Japan's first experiment with fascist imperialism', Young has concluded.[300] Crisis prompted displacement: a series of failed military coups in Japan proper were paralleled by the 'military takeover of the empire', which would later cause the army to become the 'premier power broker in Japan', too. '[R]epression at home [and] aggression abroad' were thus the 'inside' and the 'outside' of fascist imperialism.[301]

But for the left, too, repression at home promoted 'the migration of leftists to Manchuria'. The decimation of the Japanese Communist Party had by 1933 made revolutionary action impossible, so many Marxist intellectuals redirected their hopes towards Manchuria, where they sought to stage a 'revolution from above'.[302] Japanese fascists and defeated

298 See Hyman Kublin, 'The Evolution of Japanese Colonialism', *Comparative Studies in Society and History* 2: 1 (1959), p. 68. In the 1920s and 1930s, Zionism was a reference point in debates concerning Japanese colonial policy. Professor and long-time chair of colonial policy at Tokyo Imperial University, Yanaihara Tadao, provided this link. Zionist collectivist settler practice was appealing because it provided a pragmatic model for promoting Japanese settlements in densely populated settings like Manchuria and Korea. According to Yanaihara, exclusivist collectivism was the answer. His Zionist model was a 'non-capitalistic, non-profit oriented, and non-exploitative form of colonialism'. See John C. de Boer, 'Circumventing the Evils of Colonialism: Yanaihara Tadao and Zionist Settler Colonialism in Palestine', *Positions* 14: 3 (2006), p. 581.

299 See also Sandra Wilson, 'The "New Paradise": Japanese Emigration to Manchuria in the 1930s and 1940s', *International History Review* 17: 2 (1995).

300 Louise Young, 'When Fascism Met Empire', p. 284. See also Prasenjit Duara, *Sovereignty and Authenticity: Manchukuo and the East Asian Modern* (Lanham, MD: Rowman & Littlefield, 2003).

301 Young, 'When Fascism Met Empire', p. 286.

302 Ibid., pp. 289–90.

Marxists would kill each other in one location and collaborate in another. Limits on 'Japanese migration, Japanese exports, and Japanese expansion' had created an existential crisis. Manchukuo 'incubated' technologies of governance that placed controls on free markets and private industry; settlement was to be the priority.

By 1936, Manchurian colonisation was 'one of the pillars of Japanese national policy'. The large-scale resettlement programme had begun in October 1932, and the first settlers – primarily peasants from famine-ravaged parts of north-eastern Japan – had arrived in April 1933. In 1936, the 'Millions to Manchuria' campaign picked up pace, followed in 1937 by the establishment of the Manchuria Immigration Company. The settlers went to lands the Kwantung army had seized and vacated.[303] And yet, this world turned inside out ended in disaster, and it is estimated that about 200,000 settlers died in the exodus that followed the Soviet invasion.[304] The settlers eventually returned to Japan in a drawn-out process that begun after the end of World War II.[305] Still, the Japanese world turned inside out had lasted longer than the empire from which it emerged.

But there had been other new Japans, and Japanese emigrants to many locales had also attempted to build better 'new' Japans beyond the bounds of Japanese territorial control. Hawaii, Mexico, Brazil, Peru and Canada, as well as the US mainland, had all witnessed Japanese group settlement.[306] There were three Yamato colonies in the United States: one

---

303 On settler activism, see Emer O'Dwyer, *Significant Soil: Settler Colonialism and Japan's Urban Empire in Manchuria* (Cambridge, MA: Harvard University Asia Center, 2015). On the way metropolitan elites promoted emigration to Manchukuo as a solution to several crises (both industrial and rural), see Louise Young, *Japan's Total Empire: Manchuria and the Culture of Wartime Imperialism* (Berkeley: University of California Press, 1998).

304 See Emer O'Dwyer, 'Japanese Empire in Manchuria', in David Ludden, ed., *Oxford Research Encyclopedias: Asian History* (Oxford: Oxford University Press, 2017).

305 See Lori Watt, *When Empire Comes Home: Repatriation in Postwar Japan* (New York: Columbia University Press, 2002).

306 See Eiichiro Azuma, *In Search of Our Frontier Japanese America and Settler Colonialism in the Construction of Japan's Borderless Empire* (Berkeley, CA: University of California Press, 2019); Sidney Xu Lu, *The Making of Japanese Settler Colonialism: Malthusianism and Trans-Pacific Migration, 1868–1961* (Cambridge: Cambridge University Press, 2019). See also Daniel L. Masterson, *The Japanese in Latin America* (Urbana, IL: University of Illinois Press, 2004). On the Japanese settlers to the western US, see also Eiichiro Azuma, *Between Two Empires: Race, History, and Transnationalism in Japanese America* (Oxford: Oxford University Press, 2005).

in Florida (established 1904), one in Texas (established 1917), and one in California (established 1906). They thrived, even though they endured systematic and sustained repression. Kyutaro Abiko, the Californian Yamato colony founder, believed that the United States would provide freedom for the colony to develop. Abiko was a successful entrepreneur and a stalwart of the Japanese-American community. He owned a bank and a labour contracting firm offering Japanese labourers.

In 1906 Abiko began acquiring continuous tracts of 'empty' land near Livingston, California, circumventing with American partners exclusionary legislation that prevented Japanese from owning land. He then began welcoming Japanese 'pioneers' there. The settlers would buy their plots, and many were educated. It was a 'Christian colony'. The idea was to 'store' Japanese labour on the land – labour that could be sequestered from the wider labour market. Self-sufficiency and seclusion would assuage local Americans' anxieties about Japanese 'competition'. Abiko saw this as a way for Japanese farmers to acquire 'roots' in the new country. The colony would even survive wartime deportations.[307]

The world turned inside out loses the initiative

The world turned inside out persisted in North America beyond its moment of crisis. The so called Granger Laws, for example, had aimed to protect its viability in the West against relentless attack from market forces – forces that were perceived as emanating from beyond local control.[308] The relationship between eastern capitalists and the western regions of the United States during the immediate post-war period was in many ways a colonial one – Charles Francis Adams Jr, for example, thought so.[309] The settlers in the West, however, retained a significant degree of political power, which they had gained by relocating there.

307 See Kesaya E. Noda, 'Yamato Colony of California', in Jonathan H. X. Lee, ed., *Japanese Americans: The History and Culture of a People* (Santa Barbara, CA: ABC-CLIO, 2017); Valerie J. Matsumoto, *Farming the Home Place: A Japanese American Community in California 1919–1982* (Ithaca, NY: Cornell University Press, 1993).

308 See Noam Maggor, 'To Coddle and Caress These Great Capitalists: Eastern Money, Frontier Populism, and the Politics of Market-Making in the American West', *American Historical Review* 122: 1 (2017).

309 Cited in ibid., p. 58.

They had consolidated it by way of regional institution-building and state constitutional conventions.

The states had asserted their authority over water (riparian rights would not work in the West) and over industrial relations (industrial development, it was thought, would come with class conflict, which the new states did not want). Private militias were banned, and there were attempts to prevent the specific forms of class conflict that had manifested in the East from emerging in the West. Corporate lobbyists representing external interests had fought back, but the new states had acquired capacious regulatory powers, and the 'primacy of state authorities over corporate interests' was thus provisionally affirmed by the Granger Laws.[310] In the Midwest, resistance against market forces – an opposition that could be expressed in the language of 'transnational social republicanism' – had been defeated earlier.[311]

The Populists temporarily won some of these contests in the 1890s. They followed a fundamentally spatial logic when approaching conflict and imagining solutions.[312] But the relationship between the Populist Party founded in 1891 and organised labour remained fraught, even if a coalition of industrial workers and farmers seemed possible for a while (it came to nothing). The two could not find (metaphorical) common ground – one consequence of displacement was that the Eastern Socialists and the Midwestern Populists did not have any literal ground in common.[313] In 1915, the Nonpartisan League would spread widely in the US West (and parts of Canada), though it collapsed in the 1920s

310 Ibid., p. 60.

311 Brad Bauerly, 'Economic Transition, Class Formation, and the Superintendent State in the Midwest: 1850–1900', *Journal of Historical Sociology* 33: 1 (2020).

312 Minnesota senator and author of the Populist Party Platform Ignatius Donnelly wrote utopian literature, too. In *Caesar's Column* (1890), the collapse of democratic institutions, authoritarianism and a secret cabal of capitalists monopolising power epitomise the crisis. But revolution in the novel is a false promise: the revolutionaries are foreigners – Russians and Italians (the 'Brotherhood of Destruction'); they are even paid by the cabal. Revolution is not an option, but displacement is: to an isolated agrarian state to be built in the Ugandan Valley. See Wegner, *Imaginary Communities*, pp. 122–3.

313 See Michael Pierce, *Striking with the Ballot: Ohio Labor and the Populist Party* (DeKalb, IL: Northern Illinois University Press, 2010); Michael Pierce, 'The Populist President of the American Federation of Labor: The Career of John McBride, 1880–1895', *Labor History* 41: 1 (2000); Matthew Hild, *Greenbackers, Knights of Labor, and Populists: Farmer-Labor Insurgency in the Late-Nineteenth-Century South* (Athens, GA: University of Georgia Press, 2007).

during a reactionary phase. It was to be the last significant instance of a political movement challenging established party politics. The League constituted new and yet not unprecedented farmer–worker alliances – a Jacksonian synthesis advocating displacement; but ultimately it would be overcome.[314]

During these decades, life on the land was becoming ever more difficult, and settling new communities more problematic. New schemes and enticements had to be devised. The Canadian Pacific Railway (CPR) aggressively promoted a 'ready-made farm' scheme in the Canadian Prairie West in the 1910s. Railway and irrigation would make these settlements viable and profitable. The programme targeted British settlers of some means, promoting images of utopian rural life, agrarian ideals and a 'fertile wilderness' suitable for agricultural production and 'social renewal'.[315] The farms were equipped with house, barn, shed, fencing, and fifty acres of ready-ploughed and sowed land, and were offered to settlers on easy terms. Even community was also sold as ready-made: 'The irrigation farmer has greater community advantages', the CPR advertising material proclaimed; the settlement was 'confined to certain definite areas, instead of scattered over the country', and there were 'neighbors close at hand; schools, churches, telephones, mail deliveries', while 'all community organizations flourish as is not possible under other conditions'.[316] The scheme, and many similar ones, typically failed.

After World War I, the prospect of social conflict became urgent once again. The Commissioner of Immigration at the Port of New York, Frederic C. Howe, considered in 1918 the difficulties of post-war 'rehabilitation'. He saw with clarity a revolutionary circumstance:

> Any adequate program of rehabilitation must be developed by the government. It cannot be left to chance, to chaos, to private initiative.

---

314 See Michael J. Lansing, *Insurgent Democracy: The Nonpartisan League in North American Politics* (Chicago: University of Chicago Press, 2015).

315 See Elsa Lam, 'A Fertile Wilderness: The Canadian Pacific Railway's Ready-Made Farms, 1909–1914', *Journal of the Society for the Study of Architecture in Canada* 35: 1 (2010), p. 4.

316 Cited in Lam, 'Fertile Wilderness', p. 10. Ready-made farming schemes were also promoted in Western Australia at the same time. See Carnamah Historical Society and Museum, 'Ready-Made Farms', at carnamah.com.au.

> The consequences would be too terrible. Millions of men would drift to the cities. There may be a long period of unemployment. Industries will have to re-adjust themselves to peace demands. A million and a half women have taken the places of men, while upwards of twelve million men are, directly or indirectly, engaged behind the line in the production of war products. New cities have been built. Old cities have been congested with workers. These are some of the conditions which will be violently deranged on the termination of the war.[317]

Howe aimed to neutralise social tension. Looking at policies promoted in the British Empire, he advocated an integrated programme of reconstruction and demobilisation. It included unemployment insurance, education, 'emergency work on a large scale', a 'big transportation program', and, most importantly, 'returning soldiers to the land' while developing a 'new kind of agriculture . . . known as the farm colony', whereby 'ready-made farms' are 'grouped about a village'.[318] The failure of settlement was now promoting even further efforts to sustain viable settlements, while failing to release social tension.

Canada's 1919 General Strike was a largely unplanned revolutionary outburst, and it was harshly repressed; but it prompted, albeit indirectly, the rise of the Progressives in the Prairie Provinces. Their politics aimed to make life on the land viable again, to stop the rural exodus, and to effectively counter controlling monopsonies. In 1921 the Progressives elected more than sixty members to the federal parliament, becoming the official opposition. Later, during another acute crisis – the Depression – revolutionary activity in Canada grew again, and so did the repression. But so also did the Co-Operative Commonwealth Federation, an outfit declaring the need to overcome capitalism by democratic means and a regulated economy – and by displacement. This movement sought to promote life on the land.

The Saskatchewan Wheat Pool of the 1920s was another response to agrarian crisis. The Pool aimed to control the marketing of grains collectively and directly, and by the mid 1920s about half of the province's

317 Frederic C. Howe, 'A Constructive Program for the Rehabilitation of Returning Soldiers', *Annals of the American Academy of Political and Social Science* 80 (1918), p. 150.

318 Ibid., p. 152.

wheat acreage was involved in its activities. Through the pool system, farmers received two payments – an initial one, and one after their wheat had been sold on world markets. The Pool bought or built its own elevators, and by the end of the 1920s it was marketing more grain than any other company globally. If, in Australasia, the response to crisis at the turn of the century had been state involvement, cooperative mechanisation by settlers was North America's response. Saskatchewan was to be cooperative and different: it was supposed to be Canada's last chance, everybody's last chance – 'the last best west'.[319]

Canada's many wests had expressed a long tradition of social experimentation through settlement.[320] In this instance, however (as in Australia), the politics of displacement had eventually encountered insurmountable environmental constraints. The cooperatives were also a response to growing subjection to the concerns of distant capitalist corporations. A season of intense political struggle followed, and the Cooperative Commonwealth Federation won provincial office in 1944.[321] Importantly, this farmer–labour–socialist outfit saw itself as a bulwark against revolution. It did not trust the capitalists to provide such a bulwark – only distance could do so.[322]

Eventually, however, displacement became unappealing everywhere. Settler expansion was only taking place on what influential American geographer Isaiah Bowman in the 1920s called the 'pioneer fringe'.[323]

319 See Bill Waiser, *Saskatchewan: A New History* (Calgary: Fifth House, 2005); Alan B. Anderson, *Settling Saskatchewan* (Regina, SK: University of Regina Press, 2013); Bill Waiser, *Saskatchewan's Playground: A History of Prince Albert National Park* (Calgary: Fifth House, 1989).

320 See Doug Owram, *The Promise of Eden: The Canadian Expansionist Movement and the Idea of the West, 1856–1900* (Toronto: University of Toronto Press, 1980); Pierre Berton, *The Promised Land: Settling the West, 1896–1914* (Toronto: McClelland & Stewart, 1984). On the environmental failures of settlement in this region, see Curtis McManus, *Happyland: A History of the Dirty 'Thirties' in Saskatchewan* (Calgary: University of Calgary Press, 2011).

321 See Bill Waiser, *All Hell Can't Stop Us: The On-to-Ottawa Trek and Regina Riot* (Calgary: Fifth House, 2003).

322 See Seymour Martin Lipset, *Agrarian Socialism: The Cooperative Commonwealth Federation in Saskatchewan* (Berkeley: University of California Press, 1971).

323 Isaiah Bowman, 'The Pioneer Fringe', *Foreign Affairs* 6 (1927–28). Bowman had directed the American Geographical Society and led the Commission of Inquiry that briefed the American delegation to the Paris Peace Conference in 1919. He

Besides, this expansion was no longer politically autonomous. Autonomy had been a crucial feature of the global settler revolution. Negative representations of settlers on the land (the settlers of Appalachia, for example, were a source of sustained concern) prompted renewed attempts to make relocating great, or at least viable, once again.[324] Anxious representations had been unexceptional before the global settler revolution, were overwhelmed by positive representations during it, but now typically marked its end. The climate had changed. In the United States, as an historian of post–World War II agriculture noted, farm consolidation was achieved through 'a series of "anti-Homestead Act" ' policies.[325] The settler revolution was over.

In South Africa, 'remedial colonialism' had been a response to crisis.[326] The Carnegie Corporation's philanthropic activities offer a privileged viewpoint for an analysis of a transnational political tradition focused on displacement. The Carnegie Dominions and Colonies Fund was a crucial link in the development and reproduction of a global settler-colonial imagination during this phase. In South Africa, it sought to counter what it perceived as degenerative trends in the white community. 'Poor whiteism' there was a result of a localized market revolution; but, unlike previous calls to restore the possibility of displacement against the markets, in this instance it was the settlers who were deemed defective. Zine Magubane notes that,

considered work on this fringe to be perhaps as important as resolving Europe's conflicting territorial claims. Later, Bowman was involved with the Jewish Territorialist organisation, and before the outbreak of WWII US President Franklin D. Roosevelt had charged him with the task of finding 'uninhabited or sparsely inhabited good agricultural lands to which Jewish colonies might be sent'. Cited in Laura Almagor, 'Fitting the Zeitgeist: Jewish Territorialism and Geopolitics, 1934-1960', *Contemporary European History*, 27: 3 (2018), p. 359. See also Mark Monmonier, *No Dig, No Fly, No Go: How Maps Restrict and Control* (Chicago: University of Chicago Press, 2010), pp. 58–60.

324 See Wilma A. Dunaway, *The First American Frontier: Transition to Capitalism in Southern Appalachia, 1760–1860* (Chapel Hill, NC: University of North Carolina Press, 1996). Dunaway remarked that southern Appalachia 'is sometimes idealised in the literature as an agrarian myth based on "subsistent homesteaders", economic autonomy, and subsistence farming', and yet it was also 'a national tragedy' (p. 4).

325 Douglas Sheflin, *Legacies of Dust: Land Use and Labor on the Colorado Plains* (Lincoln, NE: University of Nebraska Press, 2019), p. 6.

326 See Zine Magubane, 'The American Construction of the Poor White Problem in South Africa', *South Atlantic Quarterly* 107: 4 (2008).

> murky as the definition of poor whiteism was and despite the additional problems potentially posed by issues of chronology, there was significant agreement both within and across nations as to what caused it. In both cases [in the US and South Africa] 'maladjustment' to changing economic conditions was seen as central. In summary, the Carnegie study claimed: 'The economic decline has been caused principally by inadequate adjustment to modern economic conditions among a portion of the white population of South Africa.' This population had, on the whole, been severed from European progress and development for many generations and lived chiefly under the simple conditions of a pioneer subsistence economy, with hardly any difference between rich and poor.[327]

For a number of reasons, but especially because of isolation, this settler society was seen as having turned backwards. Isolation had once been an essential component for turning the world inside out, but now its promoters were not so sure. Still, while reconnection might have been the logical response, the proposed solution was to re-establish the possibility of voluntary displacement by ensuring, in remote locations (but not elsewhere), protection from market forces. Protection was to be site-specific.

Globally, by the 1930s, the state was closely supervising the colonists in many areas of new settlement. The settlers were constrained and controlled; they had always resented external supervision, but now it was unavoidable, because the development of marginal regions required significant investment and government intervention. The soldier settlements that were promoted throughout the British Empire after World War I typically failed to thrive.[328] State-supported cooperative settlements were tried in Western Australia, too – which for a while became a veritable laboratory of state-settler socialism.[329]

327 Ibid., p. 699.

328 Bruce Scates and Melanie Oppenheimer, *The Last Battle: Soldier Settlement in Australia 1916–1939* (Cambridge: Cambridge University Press, 2016); Marilyn Lake, *The Limits of Hope: Soldier Settlement in Victoria, 1915–38* (Melbourne: Oxford University Press, 1987).

329 David J. Gilchrist, *Imperial Theory and Colonial Pragmatism: Charles Harper, Economic Development and Agricultural Co-operation in Australia* (Houndmills: Palgrave, 2017). See also C. J. King, *An Outline of Closer Settlement in New South Wales: The Sequence of the Land Laws, 1788–1956* (Sydney, Department of Agriculture, 1957); S. H. Roberts, *History of Australian Land Settlement* (Melbourne: Macmillan, 1968).

Italy and the United States also experimented with new types of domestic colonies during the 1930s.[330] As in the past, these projects were born in the shadow of an impending crisis, and the widespread perception in each country 'that they stood on the brink of terrifying, catastrophic changes'.[331] The Depression kick-started both projects. They were both anti-urban, even if in the United States efforts were directed at moving people out of urban areas, while in Italy efforts were designed to prevent people from moving to the cities. The colonists in the Pontine Marshes, south of Rome, were especially regulated, and even had to carry a *lasciapassare per l'interno* – an identity document. Their movement was controlled. It was a telling reversal – once the state had tried to prevent people from moving to the frontiers of settlements; now it tried to prevent them from leaving them. The fascist colonists and their families were to be isolated from each other, isolated from the nearby towns, and isolated from other labourers. The towns that were established to service these communities were also designed to maintain isolation through planning.

The New Deal communities in the United States followed a similar pattern.[332] The Depression was only a catalyst; Franklin Delano Roosevelt had endorsed plans to establish new subsistence homesteads for decades, including programmes 'to spread [people] around where they will have more elbow room and raise a large part of their food supply'.[333] Roosevelt favoured labour-intensive techniques for the building industry (Owen and O'Connor had also expressed a similar preference for spade-work).[334] He wanted employment more than anything

330 On the Italian traditions of volitional displacement, see Lorenzo Veracini, 'Italian Colonialism Through a Settler Colonial Studies Lens', *Journal of Colonialism and Colonial History* 19: 3 (2018).

331 See Diane Ghirardo, *Building New Communities: New Deal America and Fascist Italy* (Princeton, NJ: Princeton University Press, 1989). On the New Deal's 'Subsistence Homesteads', see Paul K. Conkin, *Tomorrow a New World* (Ithaca, NY: Cornell University Press, 1959), p. 187.

332 So did the communities established through the Land Settlement Association in England. See A. Arnall, 'Presenting Rurality: The Land Settlement Association in Interwar England', *Journal of Rural Studies* (2020).

333 Cited in Ghirardo, *Building New Communities*, p. 113.

334 Franklin Delano Roosevelt promoted farm colonies for the poor and to respond to drought and unemployment. Dyess Colony, Arkansas, was the most famous colony of this type. Johnny Cash grew up there (he often sang about displacement). See Arneil, *Domestic Colonies*, p. 78.

else, and 'had always supported rural over urban life'.[335] The resettlement towns of the New Deal were the outcome, even though they never really worked the way they were supposed to (though they did work for many of those who found refuge there).[336] The government retained the right to inspect and enter properties, and to choose what its tenants would grow, including where exactly on their property they should do so. Diane Ghirardo concludes: 'tenants were being held to a quasi-feudal contract within a system that, whatever its merits, rested on their willingness to submit to government policy'.[337] It was indeed the end of the settler revolution.

The end of the world turned inside out?

Los Angeles was once at the end of the world turned inside out. It later became 'the carceral capital of the world' – a most reactionary disposition.[338] And yet it was meant to be different. The Anglo settlers who were building Los Angeles in the 1880s knew that their attempt to build an 'Eden for the Saxon Homeseeker', or 'the 'Aryan City of the Sun', was the last opportunity of this kind.[339] Los Angeles was actively promoted by its boosters; its climate 'could cure any ailment and grow any seed' – but it *had* to work.[340] As Walt Whitman had evoked in 'Facing West from California's Shores' (1867), the widespread perception was that the cycle of displacement had now ended. In the poem, a settler looked 'off the shores' of 'western sea', while the circle of perennial Aryan migrations out of Asia was 'almost circled'.[341] Playing on a similar trope, John

335 Ghirardo, *Building New Communities*, p. 117.

336 See Robert M. Carriker, *Urban Farming in the West: A New Deal Experiment in Subsistence Homesteads* (Tucson, AZ: University of Arizona Press, 2010).

337 Ghirardo, *Building New Communities*, p. 179.

338 Kelly Lytle Hernandez, *City of Inmates: Conquest, Rebellion, and the Rise of Human Caging in Los Angeles, 1771–1965* (Berkeley: University of California Press, 2017), p. 1.

339 Ibid., p. 47; Kevin Starr, *Inventing the Dream: California Through the Progressive Era* (New York: Oxford University Press, 1985), p. 91.

340 Hernandez, *City of Inmates*, p. 48. See also, for example, Tom Zimmerman, 'Paradise Promoted: Boosterism and the Los Angeles Chamber of Commerce', *California History* 64: 1 (1985).

341 Walt Whitman, 'Facing West from California's Shores' (1867), available at whitmanarchive.org.

Steinbeck described 'a line of old men along the shore hating the ocean because it stopped them'.[342]

Paranoid repression in Los Angeles followed a spatial logic. Uncontrolled mobility was a particular concern. 'Hobos' and 'tramps' had prompted a panic, and, together with indigenous peoples, poor white men were incarcerated at a fierce rate. There was a veritable 'tramp panic' roughly between 1870 and 1910, which even produced a sociological subfield: 'trampology'. Josiah Flynt, a most prominent trampologist, had argued that tramps were 'parasites', that they had to be 'purged', that they were 'contagious', and had to be treated 'scientifically' and 'quarantined'.[343] The tramp can be seen as the anthropological undoing of the world turned inside out: the individual who continuously relocates, and yet carries revolution with him rather than embodying an alternative to it. Tramps *had* to be contained, and the authorities even developed a new form of prison – the 'stockade', a cheap, 'low-slung "rambling" facility'.[344] The word 'stockade' identifies a spatial location defined by a perimeter. In terms of political geometry, the stockade represents the very opposite of mobility, the solution espoused by the political traditions that advocated volitional displacement. In Los Angeles the world turned inside out turned reactionary.

Mike Davis began his history of Los Angeles with a typically world turned inside out rather than upside down outfit. The Young Peoples' Socialist League colonists of Llano del Rio, California, were escaping class war and repression downtown. They were escaping defeat in the city.[345] They arrived at the 'Plymouth Rock of the Cooperative Commonwealth' in 1914.[346] Davis saw a deliberate choice: 'Class war and repression are said to have driven the Los Angeles Socialists into the desert. But they also came eagerly, wanting to taste the sweet fruit of cooperative labor in their own lifetimes'.[347] It was a cooperative

342 John Steinbeck, *The Short Novels of John Steinbeck* (New York: Viking, 1953), p. 199. Similarly, Joan Didion remarked about California that 'things better work out here, because here, beneath that immense bleached sky, is where we run out of continent'. Joan Didion, *Slouching Towards Bethlehem* (New York: Farrar, Straus and Giroux, 1968), p. 172.

343 See Hernandez, *City of Inmates*, p. 51.

344 Ibid., p. 62.

345 Mike Davis, *City of Quartz: Excavating the Future in Los Angeles* (London: Verso, 1990), pp. 3–9.

346 Ibid., p. 3.

347 Ibid., p. 9.

community – it had kitchenless homes, daycare areas and built-in furniture. It was yet another attempt to transform society by example – social change would follow; it would be visible and repeatable. The community failed to consolidate, even if it was quite successful in attracting colonists, and it was relocated in 1918. Even New Llano, Louisiana, failed to grow, however, eventually folding in the 1930s.

Los Angeles politician Job Harriman supported the colony after his defeat in electoral politics (he nearly became Los Angeles mayor). Harriman had also been influenced by Bellamy's *Looking Backward* – indeed, his political transformation allegedly began with it. Close to socialism, but never committed to a revolutionary programme, Harriman was involved in the Socialist Labor Party's acrimonious split of 1899, and had joined the Social Democratic Party of America. He intended to establish a socialist community capable of effectively functioning within a capitalist system of relations (Llano colonists still had to own shares in the Llano Company). He imagined that society would then gradually convert to socialism.

Beyond Llano, and beyond left-wing politics, many believed that displacement this time would work. The so-called 'Arroyo set' (writers, antiquarians and publicists under the influence of Charles Fletcher Lummis) represented turn-of-the-century Los Angeles as the promised land and final destination of a millenarian Anglo-Saxon racial odyssey. It was 'a Mediterraneanized idyll of New England life'.[348] Representations included evocations of an 'Italianized Southern California', with sunshine reinvigorating 'the racial energies of the Anglo-Saxons'.[349] Davis remarked how they 'crusaded simultaneously for the Mission Indians, the mass planting of eucalyptus, citrus culture, the conservation of the Yosemite Valley, and Anglo-Saxon racial purity through eugenics'.[350] Their legacy was 'the ideology of Los Angeles as the utopia of Aryan supremacism – the sunny refuge of white protestant America in an age of labor upheaval and the mass immigration of Catholic and Jewish poor from Eastern and Southern Europe'.[351] For these propagandists, upheaval was everywhere, but Los Angeles was somewhere else.

348 Ibid., p. 20.
349 Ibid., p. 27.
350 Ibid., p. 28.
351 Ibid., p. 30.

The authoritarian regime of Harry Chandler, in the 1920s, '30s and '40s, was supported by a social base constituted by the 'great influx of Middle Western babbitry [newly arrived middle-class professionals] between 1900 and 1925 – one of the great migrations of American history'.[352] The emergence of homeowners' activism was reactionary but in a sense a world turned inside out takeover too; it emerged first in the 1920s with 'white mobilization against attempts by blacks to buy homes outside the ghetto', but was ultimately a mobilisation against the prospect of undoing an original separation. It would become a political reflex.[353] Mobilisation for incorporation and fiscal zoning in later decades would be for the 'protection' of 'home values and lifestyles' – a pre-emptive move, and a protection that was predicated on maintaining distance from corrupting locales. Davis's conclusion is that the 'folk maxim that gaunt men rebel while fat men sleep was neatly reversed by the historic suburban protests of 1976–9'.[354] In the past, a response to revolutionary outbursts in the class-ridden cities of the east and Europe had been the opening of parks and public spaces – safety valves to release social tension by mixing classes and ethnicities.[355] The Los Angeles that followed, after the revolutionary crisis culminating in the Watts Riots of 1965, was instead characterised by the exurban pattern. Displacement was still the favoured alternative to upheaval – but this was displacement combined with reaction, not displacement instead of it. It was 'Fortress LA' – it was war.[356]

But if Los Angeles epitomised the end volitional displacement, electricity was the catalyst that precipitated its end globally.[357] Electrification displaced people (the streetcar made suburbs possible); it left the countryside in the dark for half a century while the city was acquiring a new life; and, when it reached remote locations, it displaced even more people because it revolutionised farm productivity, and fewer people

352 Ibid., p. 114.

353 Ibid., p. 161.

354 Ibid., p. 180.

355 See ibid., p. 227. Davis links the creation of New York's Central Park to riots in 1863.

356 See ibid., pp. 223–63; cited at 230.

357 After all, electrification *is* revolution. In 1920 Lenin famously stated: 'Communism is Soviet power plus the electrification of the whole country'. See V. I. Lenin, 'Our Foreign and Domestic Position and Party Tasks' (1920), at marxists.org.

could now do the work of many.[358] More produce could be bought for less, and even more people left the land.[359] In the United States, centralisation and monopolies were the ultimate result of electrification. David Nye observes that the gap between farm and city had 'decidedly increased' by 1930.[360] Specialised production meant fewer farms, and fewer independent farmers. The Jeffersonian notion of agrarian life, which had always been more an ideal than a real polity, was further eroded. The more productivity was raised (and it was raised – an American farm fed ten people in 1940, and seventy-seven in the 1980s), the more rural subordination deepened.[361] Where electrification did not arrive, the country was left behind; and where and when it did arrive, electricity worsened local terms of trade and subjection. (Conversely, could solar power and batteries finally lead to an electrified, decentralised return to the land?) Electricity undid the settler revolution; the Dust Bowl then completed that undoing.[362] And the 'Okies' moved to Los Angeles.

And yet electrification was meant to have the opposite effect. Its irruption had invited the expectation of a 'rurban' utopia. William Dean Howells, in his influential *A Traveler from Altruria* (1894), had prophesied it: centralisation would be undone; people would be highly mobile and live on the land.[363] They did not, and not for lack of trying. Decades later, Frank Lloyd Wright and Henry Ford drafted similar plans. In 1922,

358 David E. Nye, *Electrifying America: Social Meanings of a New Technology, 1880–1940* (Cambridge, MA: MIT Press, 1990).

359 The railroad had already begun this process in the previous century. Henry David Thoreau had insightfully noted: 'We do not ride on the railroad, it rides on us'. He knew that the railroad undid the possibility of displacement because it promoted the market revolution from which the settlers were escaping. Henry David Thoreau, *Walden* (1854), at literaturepage.com. Before the railroad, 'internal improvements' had introduced this subordination. It seems significant that Thoreau's Walden was 'motivated by the desire to directly reject the civilized politics of accumulation' – a potentially revolutionary prospect, and yet a project focused on relocating to a cabin away from the city. See April Anson, '"The World Is My Backyard": Romanticization, Thoreauvian Rhetoric, and Constructive Confrontation in the Tiny House Movement', *Research in Urban Sociology* 14 (2014), p. 301.

360 Nye, *Electrifying America*, p. 303.

361 Ibid., p. 328.

362 See Donald Worster, *Dust Bowl: The Southern Plains in the 1930s* (New York: Oxford University Press, 2004).

363 Dean Howells, *A Traveler from Altruria* (New York: Harper, 1894).

Ford promised a new electrified utopia of decentralised production, even though his plans – while endorsed by many – came to nothing.[364] Wright's 'Broadacre City', while influential, also failed to reverse population shifts. Later still, during the New Deal, many believed that ruralisation and electrification could proceed in tandem. Arthur E. Morgan led the Tennessee Valley Authority, and wanted to use this opportunity for purposes of social engineering purposes.[365] He noted: 'the Tennessee Valley is the first place in America where we can sit down and design a civilization'.[366] These experiments also failed to thrive.

But if electricity emptied the land, 'organic' agriculture would replenish it. British theorist and precursor of the global organic agriculture movement, H. J. Massingham, rejected the mechanised production that emptied the land and made rural life impracticable.[367] Massingham epitomised a longstanding tradition: 'conservative, Anglo-Catholic and antimodernist, [he] was anxious to recover an old rural landscape wherein the craft tradition flourished in a well-populated countryside'.[368] Massingham advocated a return to the country – a collective displacement. The introduction to his influential *The Natural Order* (1944) can be read as manifesto advocating voluntary relocation. It begins with the current crisis, World War II: Germany was diseased, but the real cause of the disease was the 'absolute State', which was 'the creation not of the Prussians but the Socialists'.[369] For him, revolution – socialism – was ultimately to blame for Nazism: 'Germany has had two revolutions in one generation', he added, 'the Social Democratic and the National

364 Nye, *Electrifying America*, p. 298.

365 Ibid., p. 309.

366 Cited in Grandin, *Fordlandia*, p. 261.

367 See Richard Moore-Colyer and Philip Conford, 'A "Secret Society"? The Internal and External Relations of the Kinship in Husbandry, 1941–52', *Rural History* 15: 2 (2004).

368 Moore-Colyer and Conford, 'A "Secret Society"?', p. 200. Peter Mandler has outlined the ways in which the very notion of 'traditional' rural 'Englishness' was invented as a response to revolutionary modernity, and mentioned those who 'retreated, literally, into the country': 'the romantic Tory followers of W. E. Henley and the romantic socialist followers of William Morris'. See Peter Mandler, 'Against "Englishness": English Culture and the Limits to Rural Nostalgia, 1850–1940', *Transactions of the Royal Historical Society* 7 (1997), p. 166. See also Jan Marsh, *Back to the Land: The Pastoral Impulse in England from 1880 to 1914* (London: Faber & Faber, 2010).

369 H. J. Massingham, 'Introduction', in H. J. Massingham, ed., *The Natural Order: Essays in the Return of Husbandry* (London: Dent, 1945), p. 2.

Socialist, the one undoubtedly preparing the way for the other'.[370] Moreover, Nazism, he averred, was an essentially urban formation: 'Nuremberg, Munich, Berlin were its signposts'.[371]

This crisis, however, was now engulfing Britain, too, and Massingham could shift from one country to another: 'Centralization and large-scale semi-totalitarian planning have already reached lengths which would have stupefied our forefathers, and worse is promised'.[372] Massingham thus saw an impending crisis: against the Enclosures, the Industrial Revolution, rampant 'money-power', the folly of relying on food raised elsewhere, urbanisation and revolution, the answer for him was a return to the 'rootedness of our rural traditions' and 'restoring our agricultural self-sufficiency'.[373] A counter-displacement was needed (that is, still a displacement). Massingham argued that the 'primary sin' had been 'abandoning our native land' in pursuit of 'farming out foreign soils to feed or rather mis-feed the mass proletariat'; but this system had emptied the land, ruined 'our own farmers' and 'handed over all the power and credit in the community from the primary producer to the dealer'.[374] He was still lamenting the repeal of the Corn Laws! Against this modernity, 'a return to husbandry is the way out', he concluded.[375] Advocating a return to husbandry was a world turned inside out response to crisis, and organic agriculture was a by-product of this displacement.

Yet again, many who resented increasing democratisation in post-war Britain would give up on it, moving to other lands. Many frustrated would-be aristocrats went to Kenya, for example; many had gone there already. They exacerbated a brutal colonial regime as they enacted an imaginary return to order. Nora Strange's 1920s novels focused on Kenya's settlers and their allegedly exuberant sexual life. Crime, suicide, prostitution and alcoholism had long been perceived as existential crises in the metropole. The Victorian response had been repression. But

370 Ibid., p. 5.

371 Ibid., p. 3.

372 Ibid., p. 4.

373 Ibid., pp. 5, 6. He failed, and the 1947 Agriculture Act, as Richard Moore-Colyer and Philip Conford have concluded, 'committed British farming to a highly mechanised and chemically intensive future, wherein efficiency would be measured by output per man with the inevitable consequence of rural depopulation'. Moore-Colyer and Conford, 'A "Secret Society"?', p. 203.

374 Massingham, 'Introduction', p. 6.

375 Ibid., p 10.

repression had destroyed the sexual drive, as many had noted – including, famously, Sigmund Freud. In the ideology of this settler community – an ideology Strange embraced – the African landscape itself was enabling sexual liberation, a liberation that included the male settler's recovery of the ability to inflict marital rape. This libidinal economy encapsulates the world turned inside out: only displacement enables an appropriate reconnection with sexual desire; the alternatives of liberation or repression, revolution or reaction, are literally left behind in the old country.[376] The prospect of an idealised life somewhere else, a life free of the contaminations of modernity, still retained some appeal.

376 See Elizabeth W. Williams, 'Queering Settler Romance: The Reparative Eugenic Landscape in Nora Strange's Kenyan Novels', in Yu-ting Huang and Rebecca Weaver-Hightower, eds, *Archiving Settler Colonialism: Culture, Space and Race* (London: Routledge, 2018).

4

The World Turned Inside Out in The Global Present

'Decentraland' is a 'virtual world that runs on open standards'. It is a 'virtual reality platform powered by the Ethereum blockchain', and allows users to 'create, experience, and monetize content and applications' as they 'pioneer Genesis City'. The Decentraland site declares: a 'public virtual world should be ruled by open standards, shielded from the agenda of any central organization', and adds: 'In Decentraland, users have full control over the content of the land they own and keep all the proceeds from the value they generate for other users'. To enable all this, 'Decentraland uses blockchain technology as an unforgeable record of ownership'.[1] But there is no actual land in Decentraland; Decentraland is located online, its users only virtually displace there; and it is there that blockchain technology enables the seamless transfer of someone's property from one virtual location to another. In important ways, blockchain technology replicates for online transactions what the Torrens title did once for real estate dealings in settler colonies. Developed in nineteenth-century Australia and then exported elsewhere, the Torrens title contributed crucially to the ascendancy of the global settler revolution; its main characteristic was that ownership of land would survive all spatial dislocations.[2]

1 'Decentraland', at decentraland.org. See also Joanne Whalley, 'The Virtual Land Selling for Millions', BBC News, 27 August 2018, at bbc.com.

2 See Sarah Keenan, 'From Historical Chains to Derivative Futures: Title Registries as Time Machines', *Social & Cultural Geography* 20 (2019).

The roadmap to the full establishment of Decentraland involves several steps (the notion of a 'roadmap', of course, relies on a spatial metaphor). The Decentraland site outlines them: a 'Stone Age', when 'Land is modeled as a simple grid and a Bitcoin-like proof-of-work algorithm is used to allocate pixels to users'; a Bronze Age, 'when Land is modeled in a 3D space'; a 'Mana Contribution Period' (the Mana is Decentraland's virtual currency), when investing 'will allow users to claim parcels of LAND and interact with each other within Decentraland'; a 'Terraform Event', when users will enjoy the 'first opportunity to claim land'; an 'Iron Age', when users will be 'scripting on the land' they own; and finally a 'Silicon Age', when, through virtual-reality support and 'customization of the laws of physics', users will 'live in the blockchain'.[3]

The Frequently Asked Questions section of the site responds to a number of possible queries, including: 'How is land assigned to users?' ('Users can use MANA to buy any empty land parcel'); 'How large is a tile of land?' ('10m × 10m, or 33ft × 33ft. You can build upwards without any limits'); 'Who validates transactions?' ('The Ethereum smart contract validates that modifications were made by the owner of the land'); and 'Why is land scarce?' ('Without scarcity, most LAND would be left abandoned, which would hurt content discoverability and the user experience overall').[4] It is a rehearsal in a contemporary fashion of Wakefield's notion of a 'sufficient price of land' on the one hand, and George's 'land tax', on the other. Decentraland is an example of a contemporary escape in the face of crisis, and it is not an isolated example. The political traditions that aim to turn the world inside out rather than upside down are alive and kicking; and even if revolutionary prospects have been eclipsed, catastrophe, a form of revolution, defines the present dispensation.

Tech billionaires, for example, are currently very interested in exploring the possibility of an escape away from growing contradictions and other catastrophes. They are looking outward, some are even thinking beyond this planet, and many are definitely thinking that a catastrophe may be on the cards.[5] A 2017 *Salon* article noted that, while in 'the

3 'Decentraland'. Emphasis in original.

4 Ibid.

5 On the 'escape' currently pursued by tech billionaires, see Douglas Rushkoff, 'How Tech's Richest Plan to Save Themselves After the Apocalypse', *Guardian*, 24 July 2018. See also Fred Nadis, *Star Settlers: The Billionaires, Geniuses, and Crazed Visionaries Out to Conquer the Universe* (New York: Simon & Schuster, 2020).

robber-baron era, the pinnacle status symbol for the super-rich was having one's name on a library or a university, *à la* Andrew Carnegie, John D. Rockefeller or Andrew W. Mellon', these days

> that status symbol – at least for a certain segment of the Silicon Valley elite – is a radio telescope. The SETI Institute, SETI being an acronym for 'Search for Extraterrestrial Intelligence', is the premier international organization tasked with scouring the skies for potential signals from alien civilizations. Currently, the SETI Institute is funded largely by individual donors – and the list of major donors reads like a who's who of tech wealth. Among the SETI Institute's biggest contributors: billionaire luminaries like the late William Hewlett and David Packard, namesakes for the Hewlett-Packard Corporation; Gordon Moore, co-founder of Intel; Paul Allen, Microsoft co-founder; and Yuri Milner, the Russian-born venture capitalist with his fingers in many of Silicon Valley's pies. Aside from all being billionaires, all of the aforementioned work or worked in tech in some capacity.[6]

Why SETI? According to the article, such a quest can be linked to a particular strand of social reform: authoritarian and technocratic. But perhaps SETI is also about the search for alternative worlds. The ultimate world turned inside out must be literally another world.

These billionaires are looking in every direction, but Elon Musk has already found an alternative, and is focusing on Mars, the closest available alternative world.[7] He wants to colonise it, and aims to put a million people there by 2050. Like many of the promoters of volitional displacement of the past, he is thinking of sending out settlers who can afford to pay and indentured labourers ('anyone can go if they want, with loans available for those who don't have money'), and is allegedly 'accumulating assets on Earth' primarily to support this project.[8] He wants Mars to be re-engineered as 'a nice place to be', and plays a game

6 Keith A. Spencer, 'The New Hobby of the Super-Rich: Hunting Aliens', *Salon*, 27 November 2017.

7 Elon Musk, 'Making Life Multiplanetary' (2017), at spacex.com. See also Ross Andersen, 'Exodus: Elon Musk Argues that We Must Put a Million People on Mars if We Are to Ensure that Humanity has a Future', *Aeon Magazine*, 30 September 2014.

8 Cited in Amanda Kooser, 'Elon Musk Drops Details for SpaceX Mars Mega-Colony', cnet.com, 16 January 20. See also spacex.com/mars.

that represents how this may be done.[9] His vision of a corporate colonising effort for the mega rich and well-connected is ostensibly authoritarian, and predicated on the perception of some unspecified coming global catastrophe. Wakefield had devised his plan when perplexing news about a colony for the wealthy and well-connected had reached him, as he was neither wealthy nor connected (in 1829 he was in Newgate prison; the colony he had heard about was the Swan River Colony, where servants had deserted their masters).[10] Musk is fabulously wealthy and well-connected; he has already outperformed Wakefield.

Musk grew up in South Africa, and left in the late 1980s as a particular world was facing the prospect of an ultimate crisis – displacement is part of his horizon. And so is an apocalyptic imagination. Indeed, it does not matter *which* apocalypse – there are many to choose from; and Musk contends that we need to colonise Mars because we need a 'bolt-hole if A.I. [artificial intelligence] goes rogue on humanity', and because there is little we can do if 'apocalypse asteroids' hit it.[11] Of course, the actual catastrophe that may worry him is emplaced change; it is emplaced change that should be foreclosed. When an interviewer asked him in 2014, 'why do we spend so much money in space, when Earth is rife with misery, human and otherwise?', Musk's reported answer was about urgency, about an impending crisis, and even about the possible end of capitalism. Now, *that* will be the end of the world.

Turning the world inside out rather than upside down is important for Musk, even if he does not use these words:

9 See Andrew Maynard, 'Dear Elon Musk: Your Dazzling Mars Plan Overlooks Some Big Nontechnical Hurdles', *Conversation*, 2 October 2017. The London Design Museum 'Moving to Mars' exhibition (18 October 2019–23 February 2020) also imagined a suburban existence in functionally designed interiors. See 'Moving to Mars, at designmuseum.org. See also 'Occupy Mars: The Game', occupymarsgame.com. This game's title is a veritable manifesto, and the accompanying cinematic trailer even displays a western musical theme.

10 See Gabriel Piterberg and Lorenzo Veracini, 'Wakefield, Marx and the World Turned Inside Out', *Journal of Global History* 10: 3 (2015).

11 See Maureen Dowd, 'Elon Musk's Billion-Dollar Crusade to Stop the A.I. Apocalypse', *Vanity Fair*, 26 March 2017; Jasper Hamill, 'Earth Has "No Defence" against Apocalypse Asteroids, Elon Musk Warns', *Metro News*, 19 August 2019.

> I think there is a strong humanitarian argument for making life multi-planetary, in order to safeguard the existence of humanity in the event that something catastrophic were to happen, in which case being poor or having a disease would be irrelevant, because humanity would be extinct. It would be like, 'Good news, the problems of poverty and disease have been solved, but the bad news is there aren't any humans left'.[12]

Eliminating poverty was once the job of revolution – but revolution in this context and for him is linked the end of humanity!

The colonisation of Mars is framed as an insurance policy against extinction and crisis, and a pre-emptive move against a catastrophe that is possible in the short term but inevitable in the long run:

> Five hundred million years from now, the Sun won't be much larger than it is today but it will be swollen enough to start scorching the food chain. By then, Earth's continents will have fused into a single landmass, a new Pangaea. As the Sun dilates, it will pour more and more radiation into the atmosphere, widening the daily swing between hot and cold. The supercontinent's outer shell will suffer expansions and contractions of increasing violence. Its rocks will become brittle, and its silicates will begin to erode at unprecedented rates, taking carbon dioxide with them, down to the seafloor and into the deep crust. Eventually, the atmosphere will become so carbon-poor that trees will be unable to perform photosynthesis. The planet will be shorn of its forests, but a few plants will make a valiant last stand, until the brightening Sun kills them off, too, along with every animal that depends on them, which is to say every animal on Earth.[13]

The interview refers to 'cosmic manifest destiny'. Musk 'is rumoured to have a design in mind for this giant spaceship, a concept vehicle he calls

12 Andersen, 'Exodus'.

13 Ibid. Stephen Hawking, for example, agreed. Against future catastrophes like being hit by an asteroid or the Sun engulfing Earth, or current catastrophes like climate change and diminishing natural resources, and in an attempt to '[save] us from ourselves', Hawking also suggested space colonisation. See Pallab Ghosh, 'Hawking urges Moon Landing to "Elevate Humanity"', BBC News, 20 June 2017, at bbc.com.

the Mars Colonial Transporter', and to imagine people 'selling all [their] stuff, like when people moved to the early American colonies'.[14] The settlers of tomorrow will have to pay their way like the settlers of yesterday did, unless they were squatters: about 'a half-million dollars'. But Musk reckons that 'there are enough people that could afford to go and would want to go'.[15] The difficulties will be enormous, but colonising America was also not that easy either, Musk reminds us (and yet Mars would be somewhat easier, because it is unlikely that there would be indigenous peoples there):

> Cabin fever might set in quickly on Mars, and it might be contagious. Quarters would be tight. Governments would be fragile. Reinforcements would be seven months away. Colonies might descend into civil war, anarchy or even cannibalism, given the potential for scarcity. US colonies from Roanoke to Jamestown suffered similar social breakdowns, in environments that were Edenic by comparison. Some individuals might be able to endure these conditions for decades, or longer, but Musk told me he would need a million people to form a sustainable, genetically diverse civilisation . . . 'Even at a million, you're really assuming an incredible amount of productivity per person, because you would need to recreate the entire industrial base on Mars', he said.[16]

But Musk thinks that it will all be worth it. That his dream of Martian colonisation is meant to be an alternative to revolution is confirmed by the slogan 'Occupy Mars', which he has promoted in T-shirts and other merchandise.[17] Zuccotti Park, the site of the other 'Occupy' movement, is way too close to Wall Street for his liking.

If Musk is focusing on Mars, Blue Origin, the project of Amazon's Jeff Bezos, is aiming for the moon, where the intention is to establish a permanently inhabited base within the next few years. In a pre-emptive act of appropriation, the world's richest man noted in 2019: 'We have been given a gift – this nearby body called the moon', before adding:

14 Andersen, 'Exodus'.

15 Ibid.

16 Ibid.

17 Elon Musk (@elonmusk), 12 March 2020, at tinyurl.com/d4ckj36x.

'It's time to go back to the moon, this time to stay' – something that settler colonisers and builders of worlds turned inside out, unlike colonial sojourners or explorers, characteristically do. But Bezos has a larger plan, and is also determined to create spacecraft suitable for permanent colonies – floating, rotating cylinders able to sustain human and plant life. He refers to these craft as 'Maui on its best day, all year long . . . No rain. No earthquakes'. In other words: no crises. Bezos then concludes: 'People are going to want to live here' (i.e., in the cylindrical floating colonies his company is planning to send into orbit).[18]

Why move there? In a tweet Bezos noted: 'We go to space to save the Earth' – as good a summation of the political traditions outlined in this book as any.[19] But saving it from what? Also in 2019, Bezos delivered an 'astrofuturist' rendition of the world turned inside entitled 'Going to Space to Benefit Earth', in which the world's richest person confessed that he had accumulated an enormous fortune for the purpose of colonising space. If 'population' and 'economy' are to grow indefinitely, and they should, he argued, they can only do so in a system that is not 'finite' like Earth. Ultimately, rationing energy consumption is inevitable if humanity is bound to this planet, and this would be unacceptable, a 'bad way to go', he added. The only alternative to this revolution (always increasing energy consumption is needed to offset reduced rates of return on capital investment – could capital ever stop growing?) is to 'move out into the solar system' and 'colonise space'.[20]

Even closer to home, another tech billionaire, Peter Thiel, prefers floating islands and start-up countries that work like companies to be

18 See Kari Paul, 'Blue Origin: Bezos Company Aims to Take People to Moon by 2024', *Guardian*, 10 May 2019.

19 Cited in Catherine Clifford, 'Jeff Bezos: Forget Mars, Humans Will Live in these Free-Floating Space Pod Colonies', CNBC, 8 March 2019. This article also reproduces pictorial renditions of these Bezos-endorsed colonies. They envisage a rural-suburban arcadia.

20 Cited in Cait Storr, 'Space is the Only Way to Go: The Evolution of the Extractivist Imaginary of International Law', in Sundhya Pahuja and Shane Chalmers, eds, *Handbook of International Law and the Humanities* (London: Routledge, 2020). Storr focuses on 'astrofuturist fantasies of escape' – from 'sovereign regulatory oversight; from taxation; from operating in fiat currency; and from reliance on established forums of dispute resolution'.

established in international waters. He is seeking frontiers, and thinks about them '[w]ay more than is healthy', as he also admits. 'We're at this pretty important point in society', he continues: either we 'find a way to rediscover a frontier, or we're going to be forced to change in a way that's really tough.'[21] It is a well-rehearsed reasoning: the alternative for him is either displacement to a new frontier, or a major crisis. Thiel supported the Seasteading Institute, which envisages wealthy people living on platforms, not paying tax, and organising their self-governing institutions in yet unclaimed 'free' locales ('seasteading', of course, is a neologism that derives from homesteading).[22] TSI advertising refers to the need for a 'vibrant startup sector for governance' and highlights that 'the world needs a place where those who wish to experiment with building new societies can go to test out their ideas.'[23] This is a place somewhere else, and in particular, and significantly, French Polynesia, a colony. A Memorandum of Understanding was signed between TSI and the local authorities in 2017, even though the project has now stalled.[24]

At any rate, Thiel became a citizen of New Zealand in the early 2010s, and bought a large property there. In a sense, as a result of its location, New Zealand itself can be seen as a very large seastead; in the words of Marc O'Connell, it 'has come to be seen as a bolthole of choice for Silicon Valley's tech elite'. O'Connell also cites billionaire LinkedIn founder Reid Hoffman's remark that New Zealand has become a 'favored refuge in the event of a cataclysm', and concludes that 'New Zealand, the furthest place from anywhere, is in this narrative a kind of new Ararat: a place of shelter from the coming flood.'[25]

21 Cited in Jeff Pruett, 'The Billionaire King of Techtopia', at slinking-towardretirement.com.

22 See Philip E. Steinberg, Elizabeth Nyman and Mauro J. Caraccioli, 'Atlas Swam: Freedom, Capital, and Floating Sovereignties in the Seasteading Vision', *Antipode* 44: 4 (2012); Lorenzo Veracini, *The Settler Colonial Present* (Houndmills: Palgrave, 2015), pp. 79–82. Seasteading has been proposed as a solution to various crises, rising sea levels associated with climate change, and, most recently, the coronavirus pandemic. See Howard Timberlake, 'How Artificial Islands Could Help Us Adapt to Climate Change', BBC News, 27 October 2017, at bbc.com; Oliver Wainwright, 'Seasteading – A Vanity Project for the Rich or the Future of Humanity?' *Guardian*, 24 June 2020.

23 Cited in Surabhi Ranganathan, 'Seasteads, Land-Grabs and International Law', *Leiden Journal of International Law*, 32: 2 (2019), p. 207.

24 See Ibid., pp. 207-211.

25 See Marc O'Connell, 'Why Silicon Valley Billionaires Are Prepping for the Apocalypse in New Zealand', *Guardian*, 15 February 2018. O'Connell also refers to

Even closer to the Silicon Valley, cryptocurrency millionaire Jeffrey Berns is attempting to set up an entirely new government endowed with new and unprecedented powers to set up a 'smart' city in the Nevada desert. Like The Garden Cities that were proposed more than 100 years ago, this new government would arrogate for itself a monopoly of all services and secede from the existing county.[26] Separation would enable a blockchain-supported utopia. Then again, even when they appraise the concrete risk of climate catastrophe, Silicon Valley billionaires tend to prefer technological fixes that are to be implemented elsewhere. Former chief Reddit executive Yishan Wong's Terraformation, for example, is largely uninterested in saving established old growth forests, which would be a type of emplaced change. It focuses on afforestation efforts in 'new' areas.[27] More traditionally, but also systematically investing in other places, Bill Gates, the world's third richest man, has recently become America's largest farmland owner.[28] George would have been horrified.

These billionaires all agree: another 'world' elsewhere would be better, even if some of them opt for nearer destinations because they are being realistic. But what needs to happen before humans can literally colonise other worlds is that they must acquire the ability to compress, as Musk acknowledges, 'the amount of time it takes to make

---

James Dale Davidson and William Rees-Mogg's *The Sovereign Individual* (1997), which outlines a libertarian dystopian/utopian view of the future. The 'democratic nation-state' initially forces wealthy people to pay tax; the wealthy, however, are able to move online and out of the reach of the government, and as this 'cognitive elite' liberates itself through displacement and cryptocurrencies, the fiscal state fails through obsolescence. The happy ending is that the polity that will characterise the new dispensation will not be redistributive. O'Connell notes that Davidson and Rees-Mogg thought that New Zealand was an 'ideal location for this new class of sovereign individuals', and a possible 'domicile of choice for wealth creation in the Information Age'. For them, moving online might not be enough; actually moving to a different location was also contemplated. Beyond New Zealand, the 'ultra-wealthy' are also buying land in the US West. See Justin Farrell, *Billionaire Wilderness: The Ultra-Wealthy and the Remaking of the American West* (Princeton, NJ: Princeton University Press, 2020).

26 Joshua Nevett, 'Nevada smart city: A millionaire's plan to create a local government', BBC News, 19 March 2021, at bbc.com.

27 See Oliver Milman and Dominic Rushe, 'The latest must-have among US billionaires? A plan to end the climate crisis', *The Guardian*, 25 March 2021.

28 Eric O'Keefe, 'Bill Gates: America's Top Farmland Owner', *Land Report*, 11 January 2021.

the trip from Earth to our neighbour planet'.[29] Settler colonialism as a mode of domination was always predicated on the ability to annihilate space. After all, this is how displacement without dislocation can be imagined in the first place.

Back to the land

As we have seen, life on the land eventually lost the appeal it had once had. In due course, the global settler revolution ran out of steam. The 'safety valve' was no longer needed. A few older-style settler-colonial regimes were still struggling in the 1970s in Africa, but they were on their way out.[30] Settler colonialism as a mode of domination survived as a structure in the settler societies, of course, but while displacement on the land lost its lustre, the appeal of displacement after defeat, or in the face of catastrophe, did not.

The proponents of a back-to-the-land movement in the United States after the fateful repression of San Francisco's 'Summer of Love' may be interpreted in this context.[31] In that instance, too, the defeat of a genuinely transformative moment prompted a spatial escape. Hunter S. Thompson's description of the scene in Haight-Ashbury captures this shift:

> As recently as two years ago, many of the best and brightest of them were passionately involved in the realities of political, social and economic life in America. But the scene has changed since then and

29 Andersen, 'Exodus'.

30 Until 1974 Portugal was still proposing settlement in Africa as an alternative to revolution at home, and so were the other settler regimes of Africa's southern cone. Normally, displacement undoes revolution, but in the case of Portugal it was revolution that eventually undid displacement. See Jeanne Marie Penvenne, 'Settling Against the Tide: The Layered Contradictions of Twentieth-Century Portuguese Settlement in Mozambique,' in Caroline Elkins and Susan Pedersen, eds, *Settler Colonialism in the Twentieth Century: Projects, Practices, Legacies* (New York: Routledge, 2005).

31 See Timothy Miller, *The 60s Communes: Hippies and Beyond* (Syracuse, NY: Syracuse University Press, 1999); Jeffrey Jacob, *New Pioneers: The Back-to-the-Land Movement and the Search for a Sustainable Future* (University Park, PA: Pennsylvania State University Press, 1997); Rebecca Kneale Gould, *At Home in Nature: Modern Homesteading and Spiritual Practice in America* (Berkeley: University of California Press, 2005).

> political activism is going out of style. The thrust is no longer for 'change' or 'progress' or 'revolution', but merely to escape, to live on the far perimeter of a world that might have been – perhaps should have been – and strike a bargain for survival on purely personal terms.[32]

The possibility of change had given way to despair; and, while defeating that aspiration for transformation had required a concerted reactionary effort, flight to a 'far perimeter' often follows defeat.

But those who had contributed to the repression were also thinking that further settler colonialism was an alternative to revolution. In a 1972 *Life* interview, John Wayne argued that the new generations should learn from the past. He had visited East Africa in the 1960s, and scolded the youth of America, Britain and France for not pursuing their settler-colonial mission:

> Your generation's frontier should have been Tanganyika. It's a land with eight million blacks and it could hold 60 million. We could feed India with the food we could produce in Tanganyika. It could have been a new frontier for any American or English or French kid with a little gumption! But the do-gooders had to give it back to the Indians![33]

Wayne had the revolutionary generations of the late 1960s in mind. For him, settlement on some frontier somewhere else was preferable to activism and occupying universities.

The countercultural communes – established by individuals who typically had actual 'gumption' – constituted a variety of worlds turned inside out.[34] They did not give the land back to the Indians either, and

---

32 Hunter S. Thompson, *The Great Shark Hunt: Strange Tales from Strange Times* (New York: Warner, 1979), p. 459.

33 Cited in Richard Slotkin, *Gunfighter Nation: The Myth of the Frontier in Twentieth-Century America* (Norman, OK: University of Oklahoma Press, 1998), p. 513.

34 The back-to-the-land movement of the 1960s and later decades had important precursors: Helen and Scott Nearing's *Living the Good Life* (1954), Louis Bromfield's *Malabar Farm* (1948), M. G. Kains's *Five Acres and Independence* (1933) and Ralph Borsodi's *Flight from the City* (1933) were crucial texts. Borsodi was especially concerned with inflation, experimented with a commodity-backed currency called the 'constant', and, while a radical, was opposed to Marxism. See Jacob, *New Pioneers*; Timothy Miller, 'The Roots of the 1960s Communal Revival', *American Studies* 33: 2 (1992). Miller argues

Sherry Smith's study of the 'interplay' between Indians and 'counterculture types' acknowledged that hippies were often 'playing Indian', and that their assumption of indigenous cultural authenticity was largely misguided and misinformed. Nonetheless, Smith emphasised an ability to enact localised change (it was emplaced change, but it followed a foundational displacement).[35] Smith concluded that the hippies moved back to the land because they 'eventually found conflicts with legal authorities and city life so oppressive they wanted to flee', and because they 'wanted to establish land bases where they could put into practice their ideas about a new way of living and presumably become models for others'.[36] We have seen this before.

They had been defeated, and were seeking a 'sanctuary' – a 'refuge' away from the 'desert' (even if they often moved to communities in actual deserts). They established communes as they fled 'the increasingly tense racial politics of Berkeley' and entered remarkably diverse locales.[37] The 'Indians' sometimes evicted the hippies. Smith cited an incident in a reservation in New Mexico in which, responding to the 'invitation' to move along, hippies argued that 'no one owned the mountain' – a typical settler-colonial claim.[38] Some hippy communes had better press than others, and a local New Mexico newspaper reported on 'hard working young people' who were 'dissident and revolutionary only in that they are convincingly devoted to a new way of life'.[39] But the tension with the locals (Anglos, Hispanics and Indians) had structural reasons, too: the newcomers placed stress on the welfare system, took jobs from residents, inflated real-estate prices, and did not support a war

---

that the communes were not a result of the decay of 'urban hippie life', but that, on the contrary, it was 'the earliest communes [that] helped create the hippies', and that while 'American communitarianism has historically had stronger and weaker periods, it has been an ongoing theme in American life for more than three centuries' (pp. 73, 75). Miller concludes: 'Many socialists frustrated at their inability to gain a major foothold in the national political arena have turned to commune-building as the only conceivable way to put socialism into practice in America. Similarly, anarchists, in their resistance to structured governments, have often turned to cooperative communities as models for human interaction' (p. 78).

35 Sherry L. Smith, *Hippies, Indians and the Fight for Red Power* (New York: Oxford University Press, 2012), pp. 6, 13.

36 Ibid., p. 113.

37 Ibid., p. 119.

38 Ibid., p. 130.

39 Cited in ibid., p. 134.

many locals were enlisting to fight. Local revolutionaries realised that the hippy 'invasion' and its associated communes were not class allies. They needed 'fighters and supporters, not refugees with their own set of problems'; one Chicano newspaper (echoing Benjamin Franklin's rhetoric and logic) addressed them directly: 'You may see the scenery and relief from an oppressive America. We see a battleground. So, don't come, and when you do come, come as a revolutionary'.[40] This is not how turning the world inside out rather than upside down works: revolution had been left behind.

Countercultural types built colonies in a search of sanctuary; but others built colonies, too. Nearly a thousand Americans followed evangelical 'socialist' preacher Jim Jones to Guyana in the 1970s, after failure to enact change at home. Jones's story had begun during the Depression, in foreclosure, and in the struggle against racial segregation in 1950s Indianapolis; but the People's Temple had relocated to California after an apocalyptic vision related to an impending nuclear holocaust. The decision to move further away – this time to the South American jungle – likewise matured during a time of rising social tension. The Jonestown colony was meant to provide an example of practical social transformation that others might follow. The movement had consistently refrained from politically challenging stances in California, preferring to focus on controlling its members. In this instance, the failure of displacement – even the Jonestown colony in Guyana was never isolated enough – resulted in collective mass suicide: a choice that was symptomatically presented by those who advocated it as a 'revolutionary act', and an act of 'revolutionary suicide protesting the conditions of an inhumane world'.[41] Failed revolution was followed by successive displacements, then by a failed final displacement, followed by suicide-as-revolution. It did not end well; but it was the end of this colony and its location that were exceptional, not the nature of its inception.

Others also experimented with communal and separate living, sometimes in extreme ways. Biosphere 2, an ecocommunal and sociopolitical experiment, was designed to test whether people were ready to relocate even further away. The 'colony' ran from 1991 to 1993, when eight

40 Cited in ibid., p. 138.

41 See Jeff Guinn, *The Road to Jonestown: Jim Jones and Peoples Temple* (New York: Simon & Schuster, 2017), cited at pp. 441, 448.

volunteers moved into a sealed environment hosted in an Arizona facility funded by Texan billionaire Ed Bass. This community originated in late-1960s San Francisco, gathering around John P. Allen, 'a Harvard graduate, a metallurgist, a union organiser, a beat poet, and a traveller studying indigenous cultures'.[42] This group, actually a performance group called the Theatre of All Possibilities, wanted to 'change the world'. But they moved – first to New Mexico, where they established Synergia Ranch, an ecocommune that eventually became a self-sufficient homestead. The Biosphere 2 experiment came later: 'staged like a space mission', with 'gleaming white panels and ziggurats of glass'. The facility was filled with plants and animals, as well as laboratories. However, eventually food and oxygen became scarce, and rather 'than luxuriating in a Garden of Eden, the biospherians became more like subsistence farmers'. Two factions emerged: one wanted to continue the experiment without importing food or air; the other intended to continue the experiment while importing some food and air. In 1994, however, Ed Bass decided to take over Biosphere 2, and Allen and his team were evicted. The aim was to make the experiment more business-oriented. The newly appointed CEO was Steve Bannon – the same Steve Bannon who, in 2016, would become one of Donald Trump's successful presidential campaign strategists.

Forward to cyberspace

In the 1960s and early 1970s, the idea of displacing could mean back to the land, or perhaps forward to new frontiers. Looking back to that period, Richard Barbrook and Andy Cameron envisaged a genuine 'Jeffersonian moment', when many believed that displacement could indeed offer a way to reconcile 'hippies' with 'yuppies'.[43] This possible reconciliation was crucially predicated in the 1990s on displacing to

42 See Steve Rose, 'Eight Go Mad in Arizona: How a Lockdown Experiment Went Horribly Wrong', *Guardian*, 13 July 2020. This was a review of *Spaceship Earth*, a 2020 documentary film exploring the experience of the 'biospherians'. See also Natalie Koch, 'Whose apocalypse? Biosphere 2 and the spectacle of settler science in the desert', *Geoforum*, 124, 2021, 36–45.

43 See Richard Barbrook and Andy Cameron, 'The Californian Ideology', *Science as Culture* 6: 1 (1996).

'cyberspace', which was once thought of as brand new and inexhaustible *space*.[44] It has now been fenced in by global internet platforms, just as the West was once appropriated by railway corporations and grain elevators; but it was supposed to be different.[45] In a seminal 1996 article, Barbrook and Cameron remarked that the politics of the 'Californian ideology' were a hybrid – that is, nether left, nor right: 'the Californian Ideology promiscuously combines the free-wheeling spirit of the hippies and the entrepreneurial zeal of the yuppies'. They added: 'This amalgamation of opposites has been achieved through a profound faith in the emancipatory potential of the new information technologies. In the digital utopia, everybody will be both hip and rich'.[46]

The imaginary of this ideology refers explicitly to settlement, and its promoters wanted 'information technologies to be used to create a new "Jeffersonian democracy" where all individuals will be able to express themselves freely within cyberspace'. Barbrook and Cameron also noted that the 'path of technological progress didn't always lead to "ecotopia"' (a reference to an eponymous science fiction novel narrating the story of Ecotopia's successful secession from the United States).[47] It 'could instead lead back to the America of the Founding Fathers', they noted – who, after all, had also had in mind a type of 'secular utopianism'.[48] 'Cyberspace' is central to this reasoning, even if it is not such a current term today as it was then (the promise of a spatial escape is now moot). But the most significant aspect of their argument is that the Jeffersonian democracy to come (Barbrook and

44 For an analysis of this social milieu and its origins in the countercultural movement, 1960s–70s 'neo-communalism', and the back-to-the-land movement, see Fred Turner, *From Counterculture to Cyberculture: Stewart Brand, the Whole Earth Network, and the Rise of Digital Utopianism* (Chicago: University of Chicago Press, 2006). Turner convincingly traces the ways in which 'counterculturalists, corporate executives, and right-wing politicians' had come together by the 1990s (p. 7).

45 On the emergence and operation of 'platform' and 'surveillance' capitalisms, see, respectively, Geert Lovink, *Social Media Abyss: Critical Internet Cultures and the Force of Negation* (Cambridge: Polity, 2016), and Shoshana Zuboff, 'Big Other: Surveillance Capitalism and the Prospects of an Information Civilization', *Journal of Information Technology* 30 (2015). See also Shoshana Zuboff, *The Age of Surveillance Capitalism: The Fight for a Human Future at the New Frontier of Power* (New York: Hachette, 2019).

46 Barbrook and Cameron, 'Californian Ideology', p. 44.

47 See Ernest Callenbach, *Ecotopia* (New York: Bantam, 1975).

48 Barbrook and Cameron, 'Californian Ideology', p. 49.

Cameron repeat this expression several times in their article) was to be the result of a displacement: cyberspace is space.

It is significant that Barbrook and Cameron detected the origin of this 'ideology' in the defeat of a particular revolutionary movement:

> On 15th May 1969, Governor Ronald Reagan ordered armed police to carry out a dawn raid against hippie protesters who had occupied People's Park near the Berkeley campus of the University of California. During the subsequent battle, one man was shot dead and 128 other people needed hospital treatment. On that day, the 'straight' world and the counter-culture appeared to be implacably opposed.[49]

And yet this opposition was indeed eventually reconciled by way of displacement, they argued. It was this particular moment of violent repression that produced the Californian ideology: the hippies relocated to communes or, eventually, to cyberspace, or both, because revolution had been defeated; the yuppies moved because they had rejected revolutionary change. In both cases, cyberspace was the alternative to revolutionary transformation.

Barbrook and Cameron then rhetorically asked: 'Who would have predicted that, in less than 30 years after the battle for People's Park, squares and hippies would together create the Californian Ideology? Who would have thought that such a contradictory mix of technological determinism and libertarian individualism would become the hybrid orthodoxy of the information age?'[50] When framed in the context of the political traditions that advocate voluntary displacement, this question is less paradoxical than it appears: since it focuses on location, the Californian ideology does not need to care about a 'hybrid orthodoxy'. 'As a hybrid faith, the Californian Ideology happily answers this conundrum', Barbrook and Cameron continued; the opposition between the electronic agora (an escape from subjection) and the electronic marketplace (an embrace of subjection) could be evaded 'by believing in both visions at the same time – and by not criticising either of them'.[51] The opposition could be evaded then; it cannot be evaded now, when we are

49 Ibid., p. 47.
50 Ibid., p. 49.
51 Ibid., p. 52.

witnessing the contemporary obliteration of the agora. But the ideology was about displacement and 'anti-statism', which 'provides the means to reconcile radical and reactionary ideas about technological progress'. In Barbrook and Cameron's words, the ideology was 'Extropian', focusing on utopias located elsewhere. Most importantly, this ideology did not believe in actual change – a point they emphasised in observing its fundamental 'pessimism'.[52] It believed in displacement, however; pessimism was one of the arguments for relocation.

The internet and digital technologies enabled the imagination of several new worlds turned inside out, including the possibility that self-organised 'peer-to-peer production' might lead to 'telecommunism' – a type of communism that could be practised literally 'at a distance'.[53] This notion was not only about space that one could move to; it was also about the displacement of contradictions. Labour extracted in the context of the digital economy, for example, was for some a type of labour that might escape contradictions. In a prophetic 2000 essay, Tiziana Terranova outlined the ways in which the new digital economy relied on the notion of 'free labour' – a type of labour that is detached from the wage relation. Like many in the autonomist Italian tradition also did, when emphasising notions of a 'social factory', or of 'collective knowledge', Terranova recognised that 'free labor' has important affective dimensions: 'Collective knowledge work . . . is also not about employment. The acknowledgment of the collective aspect of labor implies a rejection of the equivalence between labor and employment, which was already stated by Marx and further emphasized by feminism and the post-Gramscian autonomy. Labor is not equivalent to waged labor'.[54] Terranova then concluded: 'Free labor, however, is not necessarily exploited labor'.[55] 'Free', unalienated labour, as we have seen, is exactly what calls to relocate are most likely to be about – the United States even had a Civil War on the question of whether 'free' or slave labour would expand in the West (it is

52 Ibid., pp. 62–3.

53 See Dmytri Kleiner, *The Telekommunist Manifesto* (Amsterdam: Institute for Network Cultures, 2010). See also McKenzie Wark, *Capital is Dead* (London: Verso, 2019), pp. 71–2.

54 Tiziana Terranova, 'Free Labor: Producing Culture for the Digital Economy', *Social Text* 63: 2 (2000), p. 46.

55 Ibid., p. 48.

significant that the internet was originally a space for virtual 'homesteading', and for the exercise of a type of freedom that would eventually be superseded, but was nonetheless a possibility for a while).[56]

Terranova saw free labour articulating with 'late capitalism' in a variety of ways:

> Such a reliance [on free labour], almost a dependency, is part of larger mechanisms of capitalist extraction of value which are fundamental to late capitalism as a whole. That is, such processes are not created outside capital and then reappropriated by capital, but are the results of a complex history where the relation between labor and capital is mutually constitutive, entangled and crucially forged during the crisis of Fordism. Free labor is a desire of labor immanent to late capitalism, and late capitalism is the field that both sustains free labor and exhausts it. It exhausts it by subtracting selectively but widely the means through which that labor can reproduce itself: from the burn-out syndromes of Internet start-ups to underretribution and exploitation in the cultural economy at large.[57]

Does the internet (and its 'free labor') embody 'a continuation of capital or a break with it'? Terranova's answer is typical of the political traditions appraised here: 'neither'.[58]

Space is crucial in this line of thinking (even though the internet is not space, we routinely represent it as such). Tim Berners-Lee, who crucially contributed to the creation of the original internet, relies on an analogy involving space when describing the breakthrough that led to its creation as a 'single global information space'.[59] We think of internet domains as analogous to real estate, but a better analogy is to see data centres as landlords leasing data space to 'landless' users. Some data centres even applied to become Real Estate Investments Trusts (to pay less tax – George would have been horrified).[60]

---

56 See, for example, Howard Rheingold, *The Virtual Community: Homesteading on the Electronic Frontier* (New York: Harper Perennials, 1994).

57 Terranova, 'Free Labor', p. 51.

58 Ibid., p. 54.

59 Cited in John Pollack, *Shortcut: How Analogies Reveal Connections, Spark Innovation, and Sell Our Greatest Ideas* (New York: Random House, 2014), pp. 104–5.

60 Ibid., p. 174.

But cyberspace is a type of space, and we are now relocating into it. Founder of *Wired* Kevin Kelly is an influential contemporary advocate of displacement. He has consistently argued that microprocessors and personal computers will lead to a new society characterised by radical individual freedom and shared prosperity. His 1994 *Out of Control* even prophesied that the net would become a superorganism endowed with a specific personality – a quasi-living being.[61] *Out of Control* explicitly rejected revolution (even if it did recognise crisis). 'Evolution' was the preferred mode of transformation, and as individuals moved into cyberspace and collectively constituted a sovereign organic entity there, Kelly saw them as *settling* within it.[62] For Kelly, humans are settlers, and settlers are the normative standard. His book even had a chapter titled 'Homesteading hyperlife territory'.[63] For Kelly, life itself, including 'hyperlife', the new life that will develop in cyberspace, 'homesteads'. His more recent *The Inevitable* (2016) confirms this approach: freedom is still achievable, even after platform capitalism has turned cyberspace into privatised silos, and surveillance capitalism has acquired unprecedented and unfathomable powers. Freedom is still achievable, only a little bit further away. We just need to relocate once more.[64]

Turning the world inside out today

As in the past, right-wing and left-wing sensitivities are equally engaging with fantasies of displacement. Expressions of left-wing movements advocating displacement include, for example, the Brazilian Movimento dos Trabalhadores Rurais Sem Terra (MST), a political organisation whose objective is to regenerate farming collectives, provided they relocate and live off the land.[65] The MST was originally focused against

61 Kevin Kelly, *Out of Control: The New Biology of Machines, Social Systems and the Economic World* (New York: Basic, 1992).

62 Kelly talks about the 'Revolution of Daily Evolution'. See ibid., pp. 300–2.

63 Ibid., pp. 296–9.

64 Kevin Kelly, *The Inevitable* (New York: Viking, 2016).

65 See Alex Flynn, 'Transformation and "Human Values" in the Landless Workers' Movement of Brazil', *Ethnos* 80: 1 (2015), pp. 52, 54; Alex Flynn, 'Aesthetic Gestures, Moral Frameworks: Performing Landlessness in Brazil', *Critique of Anthropology* 38: 2 (2018); Wendy Wolford and Angus Wright, *To Inherit the Earth: Brazil's Landless Movement and the Struggle for a New Brazil* (Oakland, CA: Food First, 2003); Miguel

latifundia and landowners, but has more recently redirected its politics to counter neoliberal land-grabs, corporate agribusiness and other unsustainable practices, including the destruction of small peasant life.[66] It is significant that the movement primarily advocates displacement, and recruits increasingly from the *periferias* of large conurbations, representing ever more people from urban backgrounds.[67] It has traditionally focused on subsistence and the planting of food, thereby escaping markets; but it has recently sought to engage in niche capitalist markets through its cooperatives. 'Agro-ecology' is now enabling the commercialisation of goods produced in MST encampments and settlements; in turn, this commercialisation sustains its settlement activity. Engagement with the wider economy is a means to the end of sustaining further displacement.

The MST was born during a revolutionary crisis in the early 1980s: runaway inflation, an enormous foreign debt, and a massive rural exodus associated with tumultuous processes of modernisation, industrialisation, and frontier expansion were rapidly transforming the country.[68] The movement sees the cities as sites of permanent crisis; the response is to move people out. It focuses on land it identifies as 'unproductive' (a classic settler-colonial attitude), and the MST settlers typically 'come to stay'.[69] Alex Flynn detected a 'strong territorial' element in its activities and ideology, as its members 'seek to live and work on land that they have won, perhaps for an entire lifetime'.[70] The movement envisages a two-pronged reclamation process. Both the land and the human material are to be reclaimed equally: 'first, the creation of *acampamentos* (encampments), which then create the possibility for

---

Carter, ed., *Challenging Social Inequality: The Landless Rural Movement and Agrarian Reform in Brazil* (Durham, NC: Duke University Press, 2015).

66 Flynn, 'Transformation and "Human Values"', p. 63.

67 Flynn, 'Aesthetic Gestures, Moral Frameworks', pp. 52, 54.

68 On MST militants as 'settlers', see Leonilde Servolo de Medeiros, 'Rural Social Movements in Brazil in the Second Half of the 20th Century: From the Peasant Leagues to the Landless Workers' Movement', *Oxford Research Encyclopedia of Latin American History*, 28 February 2020, at oxfordre.com, p. 10. Servolo de Medeiros describes the 'settlers' cooperative system', the *Sistema Cooperativista dos Assentados* (p. 13), but notes how contradictions did catch up, and even ran ahead of the settlers. Servolo de Medeiros concludes by noting that agribusiness expanded dramatically, especially in frontier areas (p. 15).

69 Flynn, 'Aesthetic Gestures, Moral Frameworks', p. 173.

70 Ibid.

subsequent, legalised, *assentamentos* (settlements). These phases are also reflected in the MST's vocabulary: members in encampments are termed *acampados* (occupiers), while those who have won land are termed *assentados* (settlers)'.[71]

Flynn concludes his analysis of the MST's mode of operation by noting that land is eventually allocated to those who are deemed to *deserve* it, not necessarily those who have *occupied* it. The MST members must 'demonstrate that they deserve land in the encampments by showing that they are disciplined, orderly and productive subjects', he remarks.[72] The 'encampment' phase then follows displacement: 'The movement promises land and a fresh start and it is precisely in the encampment, a space of reciprocity and obligation, that MST leaders envisage the departure point of a transformative process'.[73]

The 'encampment' conforms to a specific aesthetic; it is a moral space:

> Widely reproduced, the aesthetic of the MST encampment has become iconic and has come to visually represent the very essence of MST landlessness. In the encampment, one of the functions of those that 'organise themselves well' is fulfilling this aesthetic expectation and part of this is having a well-kept tent. The polythene should ideally be tightly wrapped. In the south, with its cold winters, there should be a wood-burning stove with a chimney that protrudes safely from the roof. The environs, as well as the inside of the tent, should be kept clean. In this manner, MST occupiers are not just judged on quantitative criteria, such as how long they have been encamped, how old they are, or how many mobilisations they take part in. There is also a dimension of how they enact a very specific vision of landlessness for a certain audience, the audience being in this instance, regional and state leadership of the movement to which they belong. The manner in which they construct their tent or the clothes they choose to wear are just some of the diverse facets that add up to the performance of a role, the success of which will have a direct bearing on their securing a plot of land. In this sense therefore, MST leaders

71 Ibid., p. 174.

72 Ibid.

73 Ibid., p. 177.

> act to filter out people who they deem as not being deserving of 'winning' land.[74]

To get land, one first needs to be recognised as 'landless' – a definition that goes beyond literally not owning land. 'Landlessness' is a moral attribute, and it is a status bestowed by the MST. As Wendy Wolford has noted, a majority of MST members have actually won access to land, and could be better described as *com terra*, while the movement invests systematically in its 'imagined' communities of 'new man and woman'.[75] In MST discourse, the encampments are 'transformational spaces'. The MST focuses less on the specific nature of the eventual settlements – they can be constituted, for example, as cooperatives or comprise separate familial plots – than on transformation as process.

Significantly, while the target is the 'landowner', there is little recognition in MST discourse of indigenous claims or presence. Malcolm McNee describes an essentially double identity – an identity that is

> diasporic and post-traditional: diasporic in the location of Landless identity between cities as places of dispersal and exile and the countryside as the unifying place of lost origins; and post-traditional in terms of the rediscovery, reinvention and defence of the often fragmented elements of rural, 'peasant' practices and knowledge, generally identified as 'traditions', as constitutive elements of agency in an alternative, anti-capitalist modernization.[76]

The MST occupiers can thus be seen as returning from a diaspora (the urban setting) and moving towards a location of origin: 'the land'. They are also simultaneously moving forward to an alternative modernity – a form of modernity that is not characterised by permanent crisis. And they are also 'indigenising' in their new locations, appropriating rural

74 Ibid., p. 179.

75 See Wendy Wolford, 'Producing Community: The MST and Land Reform Settlements in Brazil', *Journal of Agrarian Change* 3: 4 (2003), p. 508.

76 On the ideology and imaginary of the MST, see also Malcolm K. McNee, 'A Diasporic, Post-Traditional Peasantry: The Movimento Sem Terra (MST) and the Writing of Landless Identity', *Journal of Latin American Cultural Studies* 14: 3 (2015), p. 336.

peasant practices. The MST recovers 'local rural knowledge and cultural practices, including the medicinal uses of plants, organic methods of cultivation, regional dances and festivals, storytelling and music, cooking and food preservation, crafts and architecture, etc. In this way, the MST proposes the rescue of dimensions of local rural difference viewed as threatened by capitalist modernization'.[77]

The city is chaos, crisis; its growth deruralises the country, emptying the land and subordinating it to the city. The rural exodus is one of the crises the MST responds to; but there are actually two population flows moving in opposite directions: towards the conurbations, and towards the new frontiers and the land-grabs of the Brazilian Northeast. Both migrations empty the land; and, in the lands that neoliberal agribusiness appropriates and clears, only labourers are needed, not farmer-peasants. Against both flows, the MST proposes no less than an alternative modernity. The development and repopulation of the 'stubbornly barren regions of Brazil' would make them productive.[78] It is a modernity that is alternative to crisis, and a modernity that takes place elsewhere – a veritable world turned inside out.[79]

There are also more theoretically conceived contemporary instances of a world turned inside out in left-wing sensitivity, including radical calls for a 'horizon of horizontality' as political practice, with an associated rejection of vertical relationships. Murray Bookchin's project

77 Ibid., p. 343.

78 Ibid., p. 344.

79 The Brazilian right also has traditionally embraced displacement. After seizing power in 1964, the armed forces of Brazil planned to settle up to 200,000 families in the centre-west and the Amazon Basin, and talked about 'men without land' for a 'land without men'. Displacement and brutal repression were their response to rural unrest in the north-east and south of the country (the planned colonisation projects typically failed). Today, underpinned by paranoid conspiracy theories including the prospect of a 'Chinese invasion' and a coordinated 'globalist' campaign to undermine Brazil's sovereignty over the Amazon, the Rio Branco Project, developed by the military (again) and supported by the Bolsonaro administration, aims to occupy and populate the Amazon border region in order to pre-empt external and internal threats: NGOs, environmentalists, the Catholic Church, indigenous communities and the *quilombos* – the communities descended from escaped slaves. This semi-secret project was uncovered in September 2019. See Tatiana Dias, 'Operation Amazon Redux', *Intercept*, 20 September 2019. On the rural policies of Brazil under military rule, see Wolford, 'Producing Community', p. 504.

of revolutionary change without revolutionary rupture, for example, fits in with this framework (as has been seen with the 'Commune after the Commune' explored by Kristin Ross, and with Kropotkin's anarchist articulation of the politics of displacement, this is not a new proposition).[80] Bookchin's advocacy of libertarian municipalism and ecological decentralism embraced displacement (scaling down, after all, is a form of displacement); and besides, Bookchin's ecological thinking tellingly focused on organic agriculture rather than wildness preservation (Massingham, ultraconservative and antimodernist, would have agreed). These voices have collectively reasserted the need to disengage and build 'outside' both state and capitalism (where this 'outside' is to be located, or whether this is only a metaphor, remains unspecified).

Richard Day has pointed out how the 'newest social movements' have sought to undermine previous hegemonic conceptions of social change, and to move beyond appeals to the state in order to 'create alternatives to state and corporate forms of social organization, working "alongside" the existing institutions'. Disengagement and reconstruction are offered as alternatives to reform or seizure (in other words, revolution), the end being that of creating not a new knowable totality – a revolutionary counter-hegemony – but, rather, 'space', enabling experiments and the emergence of new forms of subjectivity.[81] The notion of 'prefigurative politics' – a rejection of centrism and vanguardism popularised in the 1980s in relation to the US New Left – and the prospect of 'creating communal embodiments of the desired society' somewhere else also recapitulate the difference between emplaced transformation and the politics of displacement.[82]

80 See Alberto Toscano, 'A Structuralism of Feeling?' *New Left Review* II/97 (January–February 2016), esp. p. 87. See Murray Bookchin, *Urbanization Without Cities: The Rise and Decline of Citizenship* (Montreal: Black Rose, 1992); Robyn Eckersley, 'Divining Evolution: The Ecological Ethics of Murray Bookchin', *Environmental Ethics* 11 (1989), p. 112.

81 Richard J. F. Day, 'From Hegemony to Affinity: The Political Logic of the Newest Social Movements', *Cultural Studies* 18: 5 (2004), p. 740; Richard J. F. Day, *Gramsci Is Dead: Anarchist Currents in the Newest Social Movements* (Toronto: Between the Lines, 2005).

82 See Wini Breines, *Community and Organization in the New Left, 1962–1968: The Great Refusal* (New Brunswick, NJ: Rutgers University Press, 1989); Christian Scholl, 'Prefiguration', in Kelly Fritsch, Clare O'Connor and A. K. Thompson, eds,

In this context, Gilles Deleuze and Félix Guattari's *A Thousand Plateaus* (1980) already envisaged an escape from what the authors had perceptively seen as the 'new capitalism' – a new mode of accumulation that was beginning to emerge triumphant through its vanquishing of the revolutionary movements of the 1960s and 1970s. This was a catastrophe, they believed: the formidable struggles of the 1970s were followed by the great 'normalization' of the 1980s – what would become known as the neoliberal revolution.[83] Like other revolutionaries facing defeat, Deleuze and Guattari opted for a spatial escape. Their *Anti-Oedipus* (1972) had emerged from a revolutionary context, but *A Thousand Plateaus* responded to the prophetic realisation that the struggle was over.[84] Deleuze and Guattari thus embraced the new phase: they cherished, for example, the opportunity finally to abandon oppositional logics; if the struggle was over, they were literally moving on, leaving oppositionality behind while seeking 'lands' that remained 'virgin of Oedipus'. They envisaged no struggle in the new land – a familiar approach.

Thus, if *Anti-Oedipus* is a 'critical' text, *A Thousand Plateaus* aims to build, to create, and to experiment elsewhere. 'Nomadology' is Deleuze and Guattari's response to strategic defeat – and if neoliberal capital systematically seeks an outside for the purpose of accumulation by dispossession, so does nomadology seek an outside for the purpose of liberation. Neoliberal capitalism supersedes, for example, national states

---

Keywords for Radicals: The Contested Vocabulary of Late-Capitalist Struggle (Chico, CA: AK, 2016), p. 323.

83 Even Ayn Rand's *Atlas Shrugged* (1957) can be seen as an advocation of the politics of displacement (as well as a contribution to the neoliberal revolution). In Rand's novel, the 'Prime Movers' move out instead of fighting the 'second-handers'; the world then spirals into chaos. Faced with revolution (the government's hostile 'takeover' of society), a group of selected objectors moves out to a secret location. Rand's novel is thus about a strike – a strike that takes the form of a displacement. A redistributive government is exploiting society's most important and creative minds, but they do not directly fight back. John Galt, the novel's protagonist, has organised a collective movement towards a secret Atlantis. Displacement enables survival, and then, after collapse, the reconstitution of an appropriate social order. See Ayn Rand, *Atlas Shrugged* (New York: Penguin, 1992).

84 Gilles Deleuze and Felix Guattari, *Anti-Oedipus: Capitalism and Schizophrenia* (Minneapolis: University of Minnesota Press, 1983); Gilles Deleuze and Felix Guattari, *A Thousand Plateaus: Capitalism and Schizophrenia* (Minneapolis: University of Minnesota Press, 1987).

and their bordered spaces, Deleuze and Guattari note; it now filters and controls production and communication flows, whereas once it sought vertical integration, command and obedience. It now no longer seeks unity. Deleuze and Guattari saw a mobile and destructuring capitalism that captures and blocks flows; and much of what they described actually came to be. Their invitation was to relinquish nostalgic longings for traditional revolutionary subjects and their homogenising tendencies. They derided those who thought that, against this capitalism, one could re-centre the state (and yet, nomadology's search for yet another 'outside' is probably no match for algorithmic governmentality either). They embraced displacement; nomads, after all, undergo displacement by definition.

The idea of escaping traditional labour forms through voluntary displacement has indeed received a renewed impetus in recent decades. In the face of extreme casualisation and capital concentration, the appeal of escaping has gained strength. Michael Hardt and Antonio Negri have, for example, called for a politics of 'subtraction' rather than seizure, and for a deliberate exodus away from traditional forms of labour exploitation. They advocate 'exodus', a displacement: 'The multitude must flee the family, the corporation and the nation but at the same time build on the promises of the common they mobilize'; it will be a 'process of subtraction from capital and the construction of autonomy'. For them, too, as 'exodus is the primary form class struggle takes today', and revolution is no longer an option, displacement remains the only alternative.[85]

But the world turned inside out persists beyond the left and its disappointed revolutionaries. The Israeli settler movement should be mentioned in this survey. Its religious settlers are often described, and describe themselves, as 'contrarians' and oppositionalists; but their organisations have cooperated with all Israeli governments, and continue to benefit from that cooperation up to the present.[86] They

85 Michael Hardt and Antonio Negri, *Commonwealth* (Cambridge, MA: Harvard University Press, 2009), p. 164.

86 See Yinon Cohen and Neve Gordon, 'Israel's Biospatial Politics: Territory, Demography, and Effective Control', *Public Culture* 30: 2 (2018), p. 210. See also David Weisburd, *Jewish Settler Violence: Deviance as Social Reaction* (University Park, PA: Pennsylvania State University Press, 1989); Idith Zertal and Akiva Eldar, *Lords of the*

move on Palestinian lands beyond the Green Line. It is not that they say one thing and do another (even if they do exactly that); as far as they are concerned, there is no real contradiction, because the contradiction is in one locale, and the collaboration in another. And it seems significant that the messianic settlements that were established in the 1970s were themselves a response to crisis. As Gershom Gorenberg concluded, a 'movement confidently declaring that Israel was striding toward redemption was ignited not by the mania of 1967, but by the depression of 1973'.[87]

Religious movements responding to crisis with calls to relocate, however, are not limited to Western or Zionist traditions. The Anastasia, or Ringing Cedars movement, which emerged in the aftermath of the post-Soviet 'hungry nineties', is indeed a response to the perception of a moral and environmental crisis. Based on Vladimir Megre's 'Ringing Cedars' book series, and on an archive of images about Siberian 'freedom' and a return to religious authenticity (at times the Anastasians are inaccurately referred to as 'Old Believers'), this New Age movement advocates 'nationwide land reform and a society based on self-sufficient, multigenerational homesteads practicing small-scale agriculture', and a return to a Slavic 'native' faith.[88] It currently comprises a network of about two hundred 'ecovillages', each housing several hundred people. The Anastasian colonies are organised in 'kin estates', where individuals are allotted a hectare of 'nature' and create their own 'space of love'.[89] These spaces are meticulously regulated, and, as Veronica Davidov has remarked, must include a 'lineage tree', a 'grove, a garden,

Land: The War over Israel's Settlements in the Occupied Territories, 1967–2007 (New York: Nation, 2007).

87 Gershom Gorenberg, *The Accidental Empire: Israel and the Birth of the Settlements, 1967–1977* (New York: Henry Holt, 2006), p. 266.

88 Veronica Davidov, 'Beyond Formal Environmentalism: Eco-Nationalism and the "Ringing Cedars" of Russia', *Culture, Agriculture, Food and Environment* 37: 1 (2015), p. 3. See also Julia Andreeva, 'Verbal Clichés of Followers in the "Anastasia" New Religious Movement', *Anthropology and Archeology of Eurasia*, 57: 2 (2018).

89 The Anastasian colonies aim to build alternative spaces but, even if on a completely different scale, a 'Eurasian perspective' promoted by influential proto-fascist intellectual Aleksandr Dugin is part of a search for an old/new neotraditional Russian space outside Russia. In Dugin's formulation, 'Eurasia' is located in a geopolitical elsewhere that is defined negatively as not Europe, not Russia, not the Atlantic world, and not the Far East. Eurasia is a world on the outside. See Alexandr Dugin, *Eurasian Mission: An Introduction to Neo-Eurasianism* (Budapest: Arktos Media, 2014).

a subsistence agriculture plot, and a pond, and have to be surrounded with a live fence made from a mixture of cedars, other coniferous and deciduous trees, and shrubs'.[90] Davidov's analysis emphasises how 'the Anastasian belief system positions its followers *vnye* (outside), and allows them to relate to the state as an entity that is, ultimately, "uninteresting" (*neinteresno*)'.[91] While these projects are predicated on the perception of a moral crisis in contemporary Russia, the Anastasians disengage – they position themselves on the 'outside' as they build their eco-conservative utopias. They are not the only ones moving to the land in this context, and in the 2010s the state-supported Far Eastern Hectare Program began allocating 2.5-acre freehold plots to 'pioneer settlers' in remote locations. By early 2020, 78,000 Russians had taken up land through this programme.[92]

These are examples of a widespread disposition; more generally, it should be noted that spatial distantiation also results from specific technologies, as well as from actual displacement. Intentional gated communities, for example, are a growing phenomenon that characterises many contemporary societies.[93] Evolving from suburbia, which once was an expression of the politics of displacement, intentional gated communities have survived its demise as they re-enact its displacements.[94] In these instances, the gate and other barriers manipulate space; even if there is no actual or significant displacement, various technologies are deployed to produce distancing effects.[95] Relying on this distancing, intentional gated communities often opt out of a society that is perceived

90 Davidov, 'Beyond Formal Environmentalism', p. 4.

91 Ibid., p. 5.

92 Andrew Higgins, 'Here I Can Be My Own Dictator', *New York Times*, 16 March 2020.

93 The Fellowship for Intentional Community manages a directory of communities in the United States and Canada. See also the Foundation for Intentional Communities, at ic.org.

94 As John Rennie Short noted, the 'division between work and home, which was such an essential feature of Suburbia, no longer holds' – this is even truer after the global pandemic of 2020. John Rennie Short, 'The End of the Suburbs', in Bernadette Hanlon and Thomas J. Vicino, eds, *The Routledge Companion to the Suburbs* (Abingdon: Routledge, 2018), p. 339.

95 See D. Hook and M. Vrdoljak, 'Gated Communities, Heterotopia and a "Rights" of Privilege: A "Heterotopology" of the South African Security-Park', *Geoforum* 33 (2002).

as irretrievably damaged, and reorder social relations.[96] Fortified enclaves are a response to perceived crisis, on the one hand, and represent the possibility of an alternative world brought into existence in an act of displacement, on the other. At the same time, the developing technologies of spatial and access control, and their ability to manipulate space systematically and selectively, displace individuals and communities even when they are not actually moved on.[97] Pushing out and moving in are two sides of the same coin.

Still further ways of manipulating space include scalar shifts: zooming in and focusing on the local also produces significant displacement effects, and decentralised local governance and other diffuse systems are often proposed as solutions to current global challenges.[98] The 'tiny homes' (dwellings that occupy less than 37 square meters of floor area), a building trend that emerged after the 2008 global financial crisis (even if it had precursors), fit well into this context. Not only do they enable their dwellers to move away from the macmansions they cannot afford; they also respond to an 'apocalyptic anxiety' by being relocatable to safer ground and potentially out-pacing 'climate disasters'.[99]

Then again, more traditional displacements are still being pursued, and many state-sponsored land settlements are even now being promoted in several countries.[100] In Australia, for example, current

---

96 Similarly, 'semigration' (a concept developed to describe Afrikaner responses to the undoing of apartheid) is a form of displacement that follows revolutionary transformation. See Richard Ballard, 'Assimilation, Emigration, Semigration, and Integration: "White" People's Strategies for Finding a Comfort Zone in Post-Apartheid South Africa', in Natasha Distiller and Melissa Steyn, eds, *Under Construction: 'Race' and Identity in South Africa Today* (Sandton: Heinemann, 2004).

97 David Lloyd and Laura Pulido, 'In the Long Shadow of the Settler: On Israeli and US Colonialisms', *American Quarterly* 62: 4 (2010).

98 See Bart Grugeon Plana, 'Want to Change the System? "Become the System"', *Shareable*, 4 October 2017, at shareable.net.

99 April Anson, '"The World is my Backyard": Romanticization, Thoreauvian Rhetoric, and Constructive Confrontation in the Tiny House Movement', *Research in Urban Sociology* 14 (2014), pp. 296–7. See also Crystal Colombini, 'The Rhetorical Resistance of Tiny Homes: Downsizing Neoliberal Capitalism', *Rhetoric Society Quarterly* 49: 5 (2019). Colombini refers to a 'coherently motivated movement to *displace* (from) big homes and *emplace* tiny houses as a sustainable alternative' (p. 450 – emphasis in original).

100 Roy Jones and Alexandre M. A. Diniz, eds, *Twentieth Century Land Settlement Schemes* (London: Routledge, 2018).

housing affordability concerns have prompted calls to enable people to move more freely. In its inaugural five-year Productivity Review, released in October 2017, the Australian government's Productivity Commission devoted an entire chapter to ways of making land use more 'efficient'. The Commission was concerned with a rapidly growing population, undersupply of new homes, mobility constraints in urban areas, high housing prices, and increasing social segregation between high-income inner-city dwellers and lower-income outer-urban dwellers. It envisaged a crisis: 'Left unaddressed, the efficiency of cities and their liveability are likely to deteriorate'. The Commission's proposed solutions? Reforming excessively prescriptive zoning laws (in other words, make residential land available for development), abolishing approval delays (make residential land available for development immediately), and considering a new land tax. This tax would replace stamp duties on residential property sales, enabling people to buy into new developments. It would make displacement possible once again.

Proposals for a land tax, of course, are not new; George's land tax was already designed to enable displacement after misallocation and monopolisation. Taxing transactions rather than land, the Commission observed, '[adds] to the price of houses, and can discourage people from moving to locations that may be closer to preferred jobs, family networks and schools'. Increased 'commuting times and costs' and 'retention of land for relatively unproductive purposes' are the unwanted results. Finally, the Commission concluded (again echoing George): 'Taxes based on land values avoid the imposition of penalties for moving, and the inequity of tax burdens falling disproportionately on those who choose to move'.[101] The Commission endorsed displacement as a solution to growing contradictions: the social tension arising from profoundly divided urban areas and increasing wealth disparity should be addressed by making displacement tax-free. A land tax would make land cheap: the Australian government has caught up with 1870s political economy.

101 Productivity Commission (Australian Government), 'Chapter 4: Better Functioning Towns and Cities', in *Shifting the Dial: 5 year Productivity Review* (2017), at pc.gov.au.

Apocalyptic displacements

As the possibility of revolution receded, the politics of voluntary displacement returned to their apocalyptic origins. Catastrophic thought is experiencing a veritable golden age, and interest in apocalypses and civilisational collapse has arguably never been greater (this does not mean the concerns associated with them are unfounded – alas, they probably are).[102] Meanwhile, the American super-rich are preparing for the collapse of orderly governance, and are investing in 'the mechanics of escape' and focusing, as we have seen, on New Zealand – a locale with a long history as a world turned inside out. In their imagination, New Zealand compares favourably with the locales they are acquainted with and are preparing to give up on. Political turmoil, 'including racial tension, polarization, and a rapidly aging population', as mentioned by Evan Osnos, are often cited as a catalysts for this shift.[103] Others are focusing on the US mountain West, and imagine settler colonial and libertarian, racially exclusive (and patriarchal) utopian enclaves enduring in the midst of social chaos.[104]

---

102 For an argument identifying the present era as fundamentally defined by the prospect of collapse, see Yves Citton and Jacopo Rasmi, *Générations collapsonautes: Naviguer par temps d'effondrements* (Paris: Seuil, 2020). Ultraconservative conspiracy theorist Alex Jones also relentlessly repeats that the 'signs of collapse are all around us'. See Matthew Phelan, 'The Menace of Eco-Fascism', *New York Review of Books*, 22 October 2018.

103 Evan Osnos, 'Doomsday Prep for the Super-Rich', *New Yorker*, 30 January 2017. See also O'Connell, 'Why Silicon Valley Billionaires are Prepping for the Apocalypse'.

104 See Brittany Henry, 'Survivalism, the Jeremiad and the Settler Colonial Utopian Imaginary in James Wesley Rawles's *Survivors: A Novel of the Coming Collapse*', *Western American Literature* 55: 1 (2020). Henry focuses on right-wing survivalist blogger and novelist James Wesley Rawles. Rawles envisages 'redoubts' located in pre-prepared survivalist retreats; his protagonists move there. Less fictionally, for an analysis of an episode of armed settler takeover of public lands – part of the larger 'sagebrush rebellion' – see Joshua F. J. Inwood and Anne Bonds, 'Property and Whiteness: The Oregon Standoff and the Contradictions of the US Settler State', *Space and Polity* 21: 3 (2017). Interestingly, one of the individuals involved in the takeover wrote survivalist fiction. See Alex Trimble Young, 'The Necropolitics of Liberty: Sovereignty, Fantasy, and United States Gun Culture', *Lateral*, 9: 1 (2020). All these authors emphasise how settler colonialism is the defining characteristic of both the fictional narratives and the real events they analyse.

But, if the wealthy always evince such concerns, anxiety is much more widespread in an age of extensive downward mobility. Popular culture is responding to this disposition, and an unprecedented interest in the zombie apocalypse can be seen as a way of facing the prospect of losing one's status.[105] While a zombie takeover can be seen as revolution of a sort – it shatters the world, and emerged historically as a global genre in response to Haiti's revolution, an event that has haunted the imagination of settler colonisers in very special ways – the proposed responses conform to a predictable pattern: imagining a way to restore order, or imagining a new settler-colonial frontier after displacement to safer ground. In the television series *iZombie* and *Santa Clarita Diet*, for example, the protagonist turns into a zombie and risks losing her status, but then finds a way to manage and possibly reverse the contagion.[106] The alternative is to rebuild elsewhere. Katherine Sugg, in an insightful article on *The Walking Dead*, noted how the 'narrative options of the zombie apocalypse [move] "back" to a brutal settler colonial logic or "forward" to an alternative, perhaps more ethical, "zombie logic", but without humans.'[107] In the imagination, the zombie revolution wins, and there is no obvious way out; but the humans of *The Walking Dead* dramatise 'processes of community formation and individual psychic and physical adaptation that have to take place under these conditions of survival.'[108] Before all this, of course, one has to get to safer ground. It all begins with displacement after crisis.[109]

Imagining apocalyptic futures, however, involves nonfiction as well as fiction. One crucial text that shaped international politics in recent decades in the context of the catastrophic imagination was Robert D. Kaplan's 'The Coming Anarchy' (1994).[110] This essay was incredibly influential; crucially, it informed US foreign policy shifts

105 On zombies, *The Walking Dead*, and the antinomy of revolution and voluntary displacement, see Katherine Sugg, '*The Walking Dead*: Late Liberalism and Masculine Subjection in Apocalypse Fictions', *Journal of American Studies* 49: 4 (2015).

106 See *iZombie* and *Santa Clarita Diet*, both at imdb.com.

107 Sugg, '*The Walking Dead*', p. 793.

108 Ibid., p. 800.

109 On zombie apocalypses, see also Gerry Canavan, '"We Are the Walking Dead": Race, Time, and Survival in Zombie Narrative', *Extrapolation* 51: 3 (2010); Evan Calder Williams, *Combined and Uneven Apocalypse* (Winchester: Zero, 2011).

110 Robert D. Kaplan, 'The Coming Anarchy: How Scarcity, Crime, Overpopulation, Tribalism, and Disease Are Rapidly Destroying the Social Fabric of Our Planet', *Atlantic Monthly*, February 1994.

during a comprehensive transition to a new geopolitical posture. It relies on a clearly defined moral geography. It is apocalyptic, but Kaplan's apocalypse moves: refugees, migrants, urbanising peasants and other contagions are all on the move. Kaplan saw people abandoning rural areas and joining dysfunctional megalopolises, dispossessed individuals on the move, resource scarcity, war, and even more movements following upheavals. In Kaplan's rendition, West Africa is already anarchic, and the rest of the world is sure to follow. Lagos, Nigeria, is an exemplar of 'Third World urban dysfunction'; the cities 'keep growing'; people keep fleeing the countryside; there are mass migrations, refugee flows. One gets the point: if it moves, it carries the coming anarchy with it.

But then there is an inflection point in the essay: Kaplan tells readers that Canadian Thomas Fraser Homer-Dixon wrote a crucial article in 1991. Entitled 'On the Threshold: Environmental Changes as Causes of Acute Conflict', the article made a key point, according to Kaplan: understanding the physical environment is central to understanding future conflicts.[111] Kaplan stresses the relationship directly linking geography and conflict, and wants the United States to prepare well for coming clashes (it did not). Against the coming anarchy, Kaplan says, salvation will come from the 'frontier' – from a tradition of displacement:

> Tad Homer-Dixon is an unlikely Jeremiah. Today a boyish thirty-seven, he grew up amid the sylvan majesty of Vancouver Island, attending private day schools. His speech is calm, perfectly even, and crisply enunciated. There is nothing in his background or manner that would indicate a bent toward pessimism. A Canadian Anglican who spends his summers canoeing on the lakes of northern Ontario, and who talks about the benign mountains, black bears, and Douglas firs of his youth, he is the opposite of the intellectually severe neoconservative, the kind at home with conflict scenarios. Nor is he an environmentalist who opposes development. 'My father was a logger who thought about ecologically safe forestry before others', he says. 'He logged, planted, logged, and planted. He got out of the business just as the issue was being polarized by environmentalists. They hate changed ecosystems. But human beings, just by carrying seeds

111 Ibid.

> around, change the natural world'. As an only child whose playground was a virtually untouched wilderness and seacoast, Homer-Dixon has a familiarity with the natural world that permits him to see a reality that most policy analysts – children of suburbia and city streets – are blind to.[112]

Homer-Dixon is not smart because he explored the environment-conflict nexus – he explored the nexus because he is a 'pioneering' expert. Pioneers by definition inhabit frontiers; for Kaplan, settler colonialism and displacement were literally still the solution to the coming crisis.

Then Kaplan shifts back to the peril: New York is in danger, 'American inner cities' are 'troubling'; China's large-scale population movements towards the seaboard will lead to catastrophe; 'Indian cities, like African and Chinese ones, are ecological time bombs' – degradation, scarcity, conflict, and tribalism. But Kaplan now sees a new weapon to impose order against the coming anarchy. Besides, 'shantytowns', he remarked, 'are not all bad'.[113] In Turkey, Kaplan went to a shantytown that was 'a real neighborhood', and visited a 'home' there. He saw 'order . . . bespeaking dignity'.[114] How? After all, the shanty he was talking about was also populated by the urbanising peasants he is so concerned about. One of his informants from an Ankara shantytown told him the secret: 'We brought the village here'.[115] Kaplan saw the people moving to the Ankara metropolitan region moving backwards as they were moving forwards – this displacement was different from all the other ones he surveyed. In this case, culture travelled with the displacees. They were, in his rendition, 'squatters' – a venerable appellation in US settler and Jacksonian traditions.

Kaplan saw displacement taking place in Turkey in a virtuous fashion, unlike elsewhere, because it resembled the movement of settlers – people who by definition carry a cultural universe with them and the sovereign ability to enact it wherever they go. This is what US policy should support, Kaplan argues: a displacement that is 'painfully and

112 Ibid.
113 Ibid.
114 Ibid.
115 Cited in ibid.

awkwardly forging a consensus with modernization, a trend that is less apparent in the Arab and Persian worlds (and virtually invisible in Africa)'.[116] Kaplan was advocating many worlds turned inside out rather than enduring a world turned upside down, a moving-forward of urbanising Turks that was also a movement back to religious piety. We now know that things went differently. China did not collapse, the Third World did not bring anarchy to the first, Turkey did not escape contradictions, and it was America that unleashed anarchy in the Middle East, not the other way around. Kaplan's prophecy was bogus; unlike the authors of zombie stories, he was selling fiction without saying so, but his mix of policy prescriptions, including border fortification against refugees and other dislocations, was bought wholesale. One does not need to be right to make an impact.

Then again, catastrophising thought now crops up in many forms and locations, at times in entirely justified ways; certainly more so now than in the mid 1990s. There are countless examples. In a very influential 2017 essay, Gerardo Ceballos, Paul Ehrlich and Rodolfo Dirzo talked convincingly about 'biological annihilation'.[117] These scientists focused on 'population losses' and on these populations' massively reduced 'range'; they focused on geographic distribution rather than mere numbers, and concluded: 'today's planetary defaunation of vertebrates will itself promote cascading catastrophic effects on ecosystems, worsening the annihilation of nature'.[118] This is definitely not fiction. And yet, counterintuitively, the implied solution is that it is only by shifting *their* own range – that is, by moving somewhere else – that humans can reduce their impact. The prospect of apocalyptic futures still prompts displacement, from an embrace of 'social distancing' rather than social solidarity as a response to the Coronavirus pandemic that began in early 2020 (as if they were mutually exclusive), to widespread and systematic withdrawal into imaginary fantasy worlds and niche cultures.[119] Many moved out of cities in 2020, the year of the

116 Ibid.

117 Gerardo Ceballos, Paul Ehrlich and Rodolfo Dirzo, 'Biological Annihilation via the Ongoing Sixth Mass Extinction Signaled by Vertebrate Population Losses and Declines', *Proceedings of the National Academies of Sciences* 114 (10 July 2017).

118 Ibid.

119 Exploring the 'Great Fantasy Migration' hypothesis, Jessica McCain, Brittany Gentile and W. Keith Campbell have recently and influentially postulated that 'geek

Covid-19 pandemic, and fantasised about more natural lifestyles somewhere else.[120]

Displacement as a central political idea continues to emerge in numerous forms. Indeed, discussion of the 'anthropocene', climate change and other disasters is often still a way to argue for new settler-colonial futures (as some scholars have pointed out, the environmental and climate crises are also, and especially, crises of settler colonialism).[121] Australia-based geographer Tony Fry has talked about a coming 'age of unsettlement', by which he means a coming age of renewed collective sovereign displacements.[122] Across the Pacific, Giles Slade has even identified a new Promised Land: climate change will make it particularly promising, especially considering that other places will become uninhabitable as a result of coming catastrophes.[123] According to Slade, lands around the forty-ninth parallel in North America are sparsely populated now, but people will move there in pursuit of 'cooler climes and higher ground', and as a response to economic and environmental collapse.[124] In all these instances, the scientific evidence is embraced

culture' enables contemporary modes of displacement away from contradictions. Jessica McCain, Brittany Gentile and W. Keith Campbell, 'A Psychological Exploration of Engagement in Geek Culture', *PLOS One* 10: 11 (18 November 2015).

120 On distancing trumping solidarity in the age of Coronavirus, see Eric Klinenberg, 'We Need Social Solidarity, Not Just Social Distancing', *New York Times*, 14 March 2020. On actual displacement in the age of Coronavirus, see, for examples, Justin Farrell, 'Where the Very Rich Fly to Hide: Wyoming's Jackson Hole Has Become a Redoubt against the Coronavirus', *New York Times*, 15 April 2020 (Teton County, Wyoming, where Jackson Hole is located, has become the richest county in the United States). See also Kevin Quealy, 'The Richest Neighborhoods Emptied Out Most as Coronavirus Hit New York City', *New York Times*, 15 May 2020. On post-Covid-19 displacements and the way they have reproduced past dislocations in the face of crisis, see Hephzibah Anderson, 'Why We Look to Nature in Uncertain Times', BBC News, 21 August 2020, at bbc.com.

121 For a call based on Indigenous perspectives to see settler colonialism as the 'historical and conceptual terrain in which to understand climate change', see Candis Callison, 'The Twelve-Year Warning', *Isis* 111: 1 (2020), p. 133. See also Bruce Erickson, 'Anthropocene Futures: Linking Colonialism and Environmentalism in an Age of Crisis', *Environment and Planning D: Society and Space*, 22 October 2018; Hannah Holleman, *Dust Bowls of Empire: Imperialism, Environmental Politics, and the Injustice of 'Green' Capitalism* (New Haven, CT: Yale University Press, 2018).

122 Tony Fry, 'Urban Futures in the Age of Unsettlement', *Futures* 43 (2011).

123 Giles Slade, *American Exodus: Climate Change and the Coming Flight for Survival* (Gabriola Island, BC: New Publishers Society, 2013).

124 Ibid., pp. 219–30.

rather than foreclosed; and yet crisis is met with a determination to enact further displacement.[125]

'Asgardia' is the first actual extraterrestrial 'nation'. In November 2017, it proclaimed its sovereignty.[126] One can become a citizen by applying for it – it is an entirely volitional polity, and one can send one's files there. It is an orbiting satellite. As files physically move there (into orbit), they escape any recognised jurisdiction, and are endowed with a sovereign status they previously did not have. Asgardia's space 'settlers' are knowingly defying current international legislation about outer space; but an assertion of a sovereign capacity is precisely their point, and, as Asgardia's website observes, 'Asgardia-1 [the orbiting satellite containing the new 'country'] contains Asgardia's Constitution, national symbols and other documents, as well as files uploaded by Asgardians'.[127] Unlike Decentraland, Asgardia occupies actual space; like Decentraland, Asgardia aims to escape all 'central organizations'. Asgardia-1 dwells outside any sovereign claim: outer space.

'Head of Nation' is Russian space scientist Igor Ashurbeyli. Files can escape sovereignty, but 'space' is limited in Asgardia: 'After they have accepted the Constitution, Asgardians are encouraged to send their files to space. The first 100,000 people who became Asgardian citizens can send up to 500KB each to Asgardia-1. The next 400,000 Asgardians can

125 There are countervailing tendencies as well: range reduction for humans and retrofitting, both envisaging emplaced rather than displaced change. Australian permaculturist David Holmgren advocates retrofitting suburban settings: 'staying where you are but radically reorganising and retrofitting the place, and reforming personal and household behaviour'. The metaphor he adopted for his book's subtitle, 'downshifting', also conveys a determination to stay put. In a similar fashion, assuming that 'a climate-induced form of economic and social collapse is now likely', Jim Bendell does not recommend that 'you drop everything now and move somewhere more suitable for self-sufficiency', '"Running for the hills" – to create our own eco-community – might backfire'. On the contrary, Bendell advocates a 'deep adaptation agenda' made up of 'resilience', 'relinquishment' ('people and communities letting go of certain assets, behaviours and beliefs'), and 'restoration', as well as a 're-localisation of economies', while shifting 'livelihoods and lifestyles'. None of this demands that people relocate somewhere else, while 'deep' also conveys a sense of rootedness. See David Holmgren, *Retrosuburbia: The Downshifter's Guide to a Resilient Future* (Hepburn, VIC: Melliodora, 2018), p. 61; Jim Bendell, 'Deep Adaptation: A Map for Navigating Climate Tragedy', IFLAS Occasional Paper 2 (2018).

126 See asgardia.space.

127 Ibid.

send up to 200KB. The next million citizens can send up to 100KB each. After that, free storage will be closed.'[128]

Asgardia is conflictless; history has been left behind, and does not enter the new 'Space Kingdom'. The preamble to Asgardia's Constitution even states that Asgardia finally 'resolves . . . inequality and imperfections in human history', while Article 9 states that 'Asgardia has no place for political parties'. Article 12 even proclaims that there is 'no place for the history of Earthly conflicts in Asgardia'. Its Constitution mentions Asgardia's 'supreme values', including as the first item 'peace in space and peaceful settlement of the Universe'. Importantly, Article 5 of the Constitution envisages the possibility of expanding on Earth (crucially, this only happens *after* constituting a sovereign body on the outside). Paragraph 3 regulates how this expansion may occur: 'Asgardian localities on Earth are peacefully and lawfully acquired natural hard and liquid surfaces on Earth, and man-made platforms situated on such surfaces'. Paragraph 6 states: 'Asgardia expands its territory by obtaining new localities on Earth, in space and on celestial bodies'.[129] Asgardia sees itself as a Harrigtonian commonwealth of increase.

128 Ibid.

129 Ibid. See also Bill Harby, 'Asgardia: The Problems in Building a Space Society', *BBC Future*, 3 August 2018, at bbc.com.

Conclusion

Revolution rather than the World Turned Inside Out

Revolution begets displacement. In 'The Eighteenth Brumaire of Louis Bonaparte' (1852), Karl Marx highlighted the double link connecting revolutionary tensions (and the need to defuse them) with the world on the outside. Displacement is one response:

> On December 20 Pascal Duprat interpellated the Minister of the Interior concerning the Gold Bars Lottery. This lottery was a 'daughter of Elysium'. Bonaparte with his faithful followers had brought her into the world and Police Prefect Carlier had placed her under his official protection, although French law forbids all lotteries except raffles for charitable purposes. Seven million lottery tickets at a franc-a-piece, the profits ostensibly to be devoted to shipping Parisian vagabonds to California. On the one hand, golden dreams were to supplant the socialist dreams of the Paris proletariat, the seductive prospect of the first prize, the doctrinaire right to work. Naturally the Paris workers did not recognize in the glitter of the California gold bars the inconspicuous francs that were enticed out of their pockets. In the main, however, the matter was nothing short of a downright swindle. The vagabonds who wanted to open California gold mines without troubling to leave Paris were Bonaparte himself and his debt-ridden Round Table.[1]

1 Karl Marx, 'The Eighteenth Brumaire of Louis Bonaparte' (1852), available at marxists.org.

In Marx's analysis, Louis-Bonapartism embraced displacement, even if the 'vagabonds' wanted to 'open California gold mines' without 'leav[ing] Paris.'

But displacement undoes revolution – after all, in psychoanalytic terms, displacement is an unconscious defence mechanism in which the mind focuses on a new object or a new aim as it shifts away from goals that it deems unacceptable (in the case of the political traditions appraised here, as we have seen, land somewhere else is literally and psychologically one result of displacement).[2] The trajectory of Dadaism, for example, characterises this dynamic: an artistic movement committed to revolutionary transformation in Europe, and a dispossessory experience after displacement to Israel. Marcel Janco had been a crucial contributor to Dadaism. He was active during the Zurich foundation of the movement, performed Dada art in Romania, and eventually moved to Israel, where he set up an artist colony in a Palestinian village that had been evacuated of its inhabitants but not physically destroyed. He claimed continuity with his revolutionary past, but he was now sustaining a dispossessory regime. Dadaism as an artistic movement had been revolutionary in Europe (for example, in its anti-war stance and its attacks against bourgeois conventions), while, outside Europe, it was organic to the settler-colonial project. In Europe, appropriating 'primitive' artistic tropes was an act of rebellion against received forms – an attempt to outrage and insult a stultified public; in Israel, appropriation served the purpose of settler-indigenising Israeli art.[3]

But displacement also pre-empts revolution. The Sombart 'question' – Why is there no socialism in the United States? – is pertinent, as we have seen, to the whole of the worlds built by settler colonialism, not just America. The question was first formulated in 1906, but in a way had already been posed by Marx, who was engaging with Henry Carey and had his 1848 comrades in mind, whom he feared would not return to Europe to fight the forthcoming revolutionary battles. Engels had also rehearsed the question in his 'Preface' to the American edition of *The Condition of the Working Class in England* (1887).[4] Indeed, the question

2 See Sigmund Freud, *The Interpretation of Dreams* (London: Allen & Unwin, 1961).

3 See Susan Slyomovics, *The Object of Memory: Arab and Jew Narrate the Palestinian Village* (Philadelphia: University of Pennsylvania Press, 1998), pp. 29–81.

4 Karl Marx, 'Bastiat and Carey' (1857), available at marxists.org. See also Friedrich Engels, 'Preface to the American Edition,' in Friedrich Engels, *The Condition of the Working Class in England* (London: ElecBook, 2000), pp. 19–32.

had already been posed in a way by Tocqueville, who in 1835 saw the state of law emerging alongside the state of nature in the early American Republic, rather than replacing it. It was an incomparably smoother process: for him, the consolidation of that state did not amount to a revolution – what was happening in America was for Tocqueville the very antithesis of the French revolutionary experience. The 'equality of conditions' had been one of the stated aims of the revolutionary struggle, but in the United States, on the contrary, a social revolution appeared 'almost to have reached its natural limits', as 'it took place in a simple, easy fashion, or rather one might say that this country sees the result of the democratic revolution taking place among us, without experiencing the revolution itself'.[5] A revolution without a revolution that happens through displacement, of course, is a good definition of the political traditions appraised in this book; and, while Tocqueville's aristocratic relatives had remained committed Royalists throughout the revolutionary years, Tocqueville dreaded revolution as much as he embraced 'liberty'. He articulated the two by way of his temporary displacement to America, and believed that France could coordinate the two by way of the Algerian enterprise.[6]

The world turned inside out was a simplified social space as well as a social space located somewhere else. Canadian geographer Cole Harris's analysis of settler colonisation emphasised the circumstances at the destination. For Harris, the 'structure of northwestern European societies overseas had more to do with the nature of access to land in colonial settings than with the particular backgrounds of emigrating Europeans'. Besides, he added, 'often, and probably characteristically, the mechanism of simplification had less to do with the particular fragment of Europeans who came to a given colony than with the conditions any Europeans encountered when they got there'.[7] Harris's 'simplification' was deliberately opposed to Louis Hartz's 'fragmentation', but the two processes are not mutually exclusive:

5 Alexis de Tocqueville, 'Introduction', in Alexis de Tocqueville, *Democracy in America* (Chicago: University of Chicago Press, 2000), p. 18.

6 See Leo Damrosch, *Tocqueville's Discovery of America* (New York: Farrar, Straus & Giroux, 2010).

7 R. Cole Harris, 'The Simplification of Europe Overseas', *Annals of the Association of American Geographers* 67: 4 (1977), pp. 469, 481.

> The human landscapes of these settlements were European in detail but not in composition. There had been little borrowing from native people, very little invention. Most of the elements of material life were European, although the mix was not that of any particular European place. The rural landscapes had been enormously simplified. Gone were the extremes of wealth and squalor of the European countryside – the mansions, walled estates, and landscaped gardens; the hovels and miniscule garden plots. In their place rose farmhouse after farmhouse, most of them set amid their own fields, one house much like another, one farm much like the next.[8]

A determination to escape the wage relation characterises these social landscapes. Harris quoted Winthrop's acknowledgment of the need to re-impose control: labourers 'would either remove to other places where they might have more, or else, being able to live by planting and other employments of their own, they would not be hired at all'.[9] Displacement was enabling a rejection of the wage relation – and of other intrusions too, including primitive accumulation. These were societies 'with almost no institutional control over the nuclear family', Harris noted.[10] Dispersion, as we have seen, had enormous political consequences. Simplification, too, pre-empted revolution.

Of course, this was not the end of the story. Harris also emphasises that, in North America, 'cleared land brought a price, its value reflecting the labour cost of clearing'; that this was also true of the South African *leeningsplaatsen* of the interior – 'virtually freeholds', where holders 'could sell buildings and improvements'; and that even New England, which was better integrated into international markets than Canada or South Africa, displayed similar conditions.[11] There were markets after the escape, even if the hope was that contradictions would not emerge in the new places. Harris also quoted Francis Higginson, 'an important figure in early Salem', who argued that poverty would not reappear in the new land, where even 'little children by setting of Corn may earn more than their own maintenance'.[12] The proletarians, of course, are by

8 Ibid., p. 474.
9 Cited in ibid., p. 473.
10 Ibid., p. 477.
11 Ibid., p. 475.
12 Cited in ibid., p. 475.

definition those who can only afford to maintain themselves and their children. If there are no reproductive costs, there can be no proletariat!

Contradictions, however, did emerge – and one market eventually begets all others. As Humphrey McQueen has insightfully noted in an Australian context, once settlers had 'concentrated on commodities for sale', they had 'taken the first step towards becoming commodities themselves.'[13] It was only a temporary escape, even if it had permanent consequences.

Why is there no socialism in the world turned inside out?

Not only had the 'Sombart question' been asked before – it had been taken seriously by generations of scholarly debate.[14] Sombart had concluded that

> the American worker was deterred from a specifically anti-capitalist policy by the fact that he was not forced into the position of a proletarian. There was so much land to be had that he was able to become an independent farmer. Whenever a period of depression set in, the 'reserve army of industry' moved to the West, where there was room for them and to spare. This departure eased the labor market and kept wages high.[15]

Sombart's explanation insisted on material wealth, a lack of deferential relationships, and mobility – or displacement.[16] His conclusion was that

13 Humphrey McQueen, 'Improvising Nomads', *Journal of Australian Colonial History* 10: 2 (2008), p. 245.

14 See Robin Archer, *Why Is There No Labor Party in the United States?* (Princeton, NJ: Princeton University Press, 2007); Mike Davis, *Prisoners of the American Dream: Politics and Economy in the History of the US Working Class* (London: Verso, 1986). See also Leon Fink, *Workingmen's Democracy: The Knights of Labor and American Politics* (Urbana: University of Illinois Press, 1983); Eric Foner, 'Class, Ethnicity and Radicalism in the Gilded Age: The Land League and Irish America', *Marxist Perspectives* 1 (Summer 1978). The Sombart question is also raised in Bhaskar Sunkara, *The Socialist Manifesto: The Case for Radical Politics in an Era of Extreme Inequality* (New York: Basic, 2019), esp. Chapter 7.

15 Werner Sombart, *Socialism and the Social Movement* (London: Dent, 1909), p. 277.

16 Excerpts of his 1906 book were published in Werner Sombart, 'American Capitalism's Economic Rewards', in John H. M. Laslett and Seymour Martin Lipset, eds, *Failure of a Dream? Essays in the History of American Socialism* (Berkeley, CA: University of California Press, 1984).

'the explanation for the peculiarly peaceful mood of the American worker lies above all in this fact, that practically any number of people of sound body could make themselves into independent farmers without – or almost without – any capital, by settling on free land'.[17]

The possibility of moving to the frontier (as opposed to the 'Old World' practice of migrating internally towards the cities and industrial employment) stunted the growth of an 'industrial reserve army'. Moreover, 'the mere awareness that at any time he could become an independent farmer must have given the American worker a feeling of security and ease which is foreign to the European worker'.[18] A latent possibility was thus enough to defuse social conflict; Sombart remarked that settlers who had made themselves into independent farmers had ceased to be 'servants of capitalism' (many indebted farmers in the North American prairies would have begged to differ).[19]

Sombart would be criticised, his critics noting that the settlers were engaging in capitalist relations, and had not dropped out of capitalist production – but the promise of escaping the wage relation through displacement remained powerful. Besides, this 'Americanism' was not the end of Sombart's political evolution. If his simultaneous rejection of revolution (a dismissal based on his analysis of social movements) and interest in America had made him in an early phase of his career a supporter of displaced change, he later embraced the 'German war' (World War I), transitioning decisively towards explicitly reactionary positions.

He had realised that the prospect of volitional displacement was also a dead end, and that the 'bourgeois' and 'commercial' spirits would catch up. Sombart had tried revolution and displacement before finally approaching reaction, and ultimately fascism. And yet, even though his explanation was unsatisfactory and his question somewhat badly posed, the issue remained: the United States was not a revolutionary society (the other settler societies also were not).

Of course, a convincing answer to the Sombart question – an answer that only requires the adoption of a flexible definition of socialism – is that in fact there is socialism in the United States. The late-2010s political successes of Alexandria Ocasio-Cortez and Bernie Sanders may have

17 Ibid., p. 464.
18 Ibid., p. 467.
19 Ibid.

rendered the question even less relevant.[20] Besides, European socialists have historically failed to understand American socialism, as much as American socialists have failed to engage with European ones.[21] Defining socialism as an American tradition, John Nichols invoked Lincoln: 'Our idea is that Labor needs not to combat but to command capital'.[22] Lincoln, however, emphasised the 'error' of 'assuming that the whole labor of the world exists within that relation' (the relation between labour and capital).[23] Finally, Lincoln imagined that labour could exist permanently outside the wage relation, and that this outside, by merely existing, would pre-empt conflict – a point also made by Lawrence Gronlund's enormously successful *The Co-operative Commonwealth* (1884).[24] But if this is socialism, it is a displacing kind of socialism – a socialism of the world turned inside out rather than upside down type.[25]

20 John Nichols, *The 'S' Word: A Short History of an American Tradition . . . Socialism* (London: Verso, 2011); James R. Green, *The Devil Is Here in These Hills: West Virginia's Coal Miners and Their Battle for Freedom* (New York: Grove Atlantic, 2015); David R. Berman, *Radicalism in the Mountain West, 1890–1920: Socialists, Populists, Miners, and Wobblies* (Boulder, CO: University Press of Colorado, 2007); Garin Burbank, *When Farmers Voted Red: The Gospel of Socialism in the Oklahoma Countryside, 1910–1924* (Westport, CT: Greenwood, 1976); James R. Green, *Grassroots Socialism: Radical Movements in the Southwest, 1895–1943* (Baton Rouge, LA: Louisiana State University Press, 1978); Jim Bissett, *Agrarian Socialism in America: Marx, Jefferson, and Jesus in the Oklahoma Countryside, 1904–1920* (Norman, OK: University of Oklahoma Press, 2002).

21 For a classic statement outlining how European socialists have historically failed to grasp the reality of US socialism, see R. Laurence Moore, *European Socialists and the American Promised Land* (New York: Oxford University Press, 1970).

22 Cited in Nichols, *The 'S' Word*, p. 65.

23 Cited in ibid., p. 92.

24 In 1884, Gronlund emphasised evolution over revolution, stressing the particularities of American democratic and religious traditions, which, he argued, rendered class struggle and revolution unnecessary. Gronlund was a critic of George's proposals, which he deemed insufficient. Gronlund was a socialist, but a socialist without revolution. See Laurence Gronlund, *The Co-Operative Commonwealth: An Exposition of Socialism* (Boston: Lee & Shepard, 1903).

25 William Alfred Hinds's extraordinarily influential *American Communities* distinguished between European communism (which Hinds discounts for its revolutionary character) and American communism (which he surveys and praises). See W. A. Hinds, *American Communities and Co-operative Colonies* (Chicago: C. H. Kerr, 1908), esp. 158–60. On communal and socialist experiences in the United States, see also Mark Holloway, *Heavens on Earth: Utopian Communities in America, 1680–1880* (New York: Dover, 1965); Robert P. Sutton, *Communal Utopias and the American Experience: Religious Communities, 1732–2000* (Westport, CT: Praeger, 2003); Robert P. Sutton, *Communal Utopias and the American Experience: Secular Communities, 1824–2000* (Westport, CT: Praeger, 2004).

Others have answered the question differently. Eric Foner concluded in 1984 that the question itself was wrongly put, that agreement on what 'socialism' means is a necessary prerequisite for any proper analysis, and that the question therefore should not be: Why is there no socialism in the US? (as opposed to Europe, whatever that may mean – and Foner points out that a similar question has been asked of Britain too), but: What does socialism mean?[26] Foner was especially critical of Hartz's 'consensus school' insight about America as a non-revolutionary 'fragment' society.[27] Hartz had insisted on the inevitable failure of socialism in America. For him, it was the absence of feudalism that had made its emergence impossible.[28] Foner argued that the empirical evidence disproved the Hartzean interpretation, that there was both socialism and community in America, that intellectual history disproved it too, and that Locke and his individualism had not been that important after all.[29] Foner also noted that Australia was a fragment that, unlike the United States, had produced a strong Labor Party and socialist tradition.[30]

But when a space-centred analysis takes precedence over a focus on ideology – when political geometry is taken into consideration – the Hartzean perspective acquires new cogency. Foner also pointed in this direction:

> Perhaps we ought to stand Hartz on his head. Not the *absence* of non-liberal ideas, but the *persistence* of a radical vision resting on small property inhibited the rise of socialist ideologies. Recent studies of American socialism itself, indeed, stress the contrast between native-born socialists, whose outlook relied heavily on the older republican tradition, and more class-conscious immigrant socialists.

26 See Foner, 'Why Is There No Socialism in the United States?', p. 74. Then again, now it is not the early 1980s; now there is no socialism in Europe either.

27 See Louis Hartz, *The Liberal Tradition in America* (New York: Harcourt, Brace & World, 1955); Richard Hofstadter, *The American Political Tradition and the Men Who Made It* (New York: Penguin Random House, 1989).

28 Louis Hartz, 'The Liberal Tradition', in John H. M. Laslett and Seymour Martin Lipset, eds, *Failure of a Dream? Essays in the History of American Socialism* (Berkeley, CA: University of California Press, 1984), pp. 333–44.

29 See Foner, 'Why Is There No Socialism in the United States?', pp. 62–3.

30 Ibid., pp. 77, 9. Yet again, the Australian Labor Party, despite what the conservatives and then the Liberals would say, was never a revolutionary outfit.

> According to Nick Salvatore, American socialists like Eugene V. Debs viewed corporate capitalism, not socialism, as the revolutionary force in American life, disrupting local communities, undermining the ideal of the independent citizen, and introducing class divisions into a previously homogenous social order.[31]

If space is added to the analysis, the real issue becomes revolution as emplaced change, not socialism. Socialism in the United States supported the ongoing possibility of displacement against and as an alternative to revolution.

In a similar way, radical socialist Leon Samson had referred in the 1930s to 'surrogate Socialism'.[32] Samson argued that socialism was not needed in America, because a surrogate form was already substituting for it. Samson averred that, in the United States, socialism was 'privatised', that the 'emancipation of the proletariat here breaks up into so many [success stories of] emancipation from the proletariat', and that class struggle is 'with the American a private affair'.[33] For Samson, 'Individualism is in America a social style'. It was 'collective individualism', even though 'the aim of this rugged individualist is not empire – which is capitalism, but security – which is socialism'.[34] Samson concluded that, to the American individual, socialism was a Freudian wish. According to this logic, America itself was an alternative to socialism: 'So far as the disinherited of the earth are concerned, there have been up to now but two ways open to them out of their misery: to go to socialism or to go to America. America as a substitute for socialism – the one new world which proletarians do not have to rise to, but run to'.[35]

Escaping from class enabled representations of America as a classless society. In America,

31 Ibid., p. 63.

32 Leon Samson, 'Americanism as Surrogate Socialism', in John H. M. Laslett and Seymour Martin Lipset, eds, *Failure of a Dream? Essays in the History of American Socialism* (Garden City, NJ: Anchor, 1974). This essay disappeared from the second edition of the book. It was initially titled 'Substitutive Socialism'. See also Leon Samson, *Toward a United Front: A Philosophy for American Workers* (New York: Farrar & Rinehart, 1933).

33 Samson, 'Americanism as Surrogate Socialism', p. 431.

34 Ibid., p. 428.

35 Ibid., p. 427.

> the products are divided into classes instead of their producers. In this way there is achieved a dressing or rather an undressing of the social categories. As when a shop girl is said to be wearing a classy gown, that is to say, a gown that does not really belong to her class. The misconception is consummated, and everybody is happy. So far as the American mind is concerned 'social' democracy acts as a substitute for democratic socialism.[36]

And it was classless because classes were pre-emptively abolished: 'The abolition of classes – the ultimate aim of socialism, and one that involves class war and revolution, painful political overturns and economic transitions – is here taken for granted as an already established fact'.[37]

Samson insightfully described a world turned inside out (even though he does not use the term): 'The very act of coming to America is an act of escaping classes. It was those elements in European society that have refused to participate in the class struggle that have, and during periods of the sharpest class struggles, fled hot-haste away from it all in order to enter, and without struggle, into the classless state'.[38] Like socialism, which mused about the 'withering away of the state' at the end of conflict, Americanism also wishes the state away, because conflict allegedly never even begins.[39]

But there were other 'Sombart questions' – a point Foner also highlighted. Britain's protracted engagement with the politics of volitional displacement and with 'Greater Britain', as we have seen, may contribute to explaining the idiosyncrasies of British socialist traditions. Debates pertaining to urban poverty, emigration, revolution and manhood, unlike elsewhere in Europe, were framed in Britain in the language of 'colonial reform'. James Froude, who was especially influential in the 1870s and 1880s, looked at the overcrowded slums and settler colonies, and concluded that, in the latter, there was soil, sunshine and opportunities for renewed invigoration.[40] He saw 'boundless territory in which

36 Ibid., p. 430.

37 Ibid., p. 433.

38 Ibid., p. 434.

39 Ibid., p. 432.

40 See Bernard Porter, *The Lion's Share: A Short History of British Imperialism, 1850–2004* (London: Pearson, 2004), pp. 86, 87.

millions could mature into wholesome manhood'.[41] Facing the absence of revolutionary traditions in nineteenth-century Britain, despite increasing proletarianisation, 1960s and 1970s debates among labour historians centred on a seminal essay by Hobsbawm entitled 'The Labour Aristocracy in Nineteenth Century Britain'.[42] Hobsbawm's explanation relied on the 'proximity' of the aristocracy of labour to the bourgeoisie; but the ongoing possibility of displacing to the colonies of settlement had fundamentally informed British discourse. 'Greater Britain' eventually came to nothing, but images about many 'merry Englands abroad' had tremendous appeal (and still retain some; Brexit can also be seen as the expression of a desire to reconnect with imagined Anglo-worlds on the outside).[43]

If the 'Old' Britannia had an eccentric socialist tradition, the 'New' one had plenty of socialism (but still no revolution). Humphrey McQueen wrote his seminal *New Britannia* (1970) precisely to answer why the Australian Labor Party was irredeemably petit-bourgeois.[44] It was the Sombart question in antipodean garb. But if the implicit counterpoint to the British and US versions of the Sombart question had been continental 'Europe', the subordinate Australian Sombart question took the United States as a point of reference, too. In this case, the comparative approach was to explain why there was socialism in Australia but none in the United States.[45] Several further 'subordinate'

41 Cited in ibid., p. 87.

42 Eric J. Hobsbawm, 'The Labour Aristocracy in Nineteenth Century Britain', in Eric J. Hobsbawm, *Labouring Men: Studies in the History of Labour* (London: Weidenfeld & Nicholson, 1964).

43 A. G. Hopkins, 'Rethinking Decolonization', *Past & Present* 200 (2008). Hopkins emphasised Greater Britain's longevity. He saw a renewed and 'revitalized brand' of Greater Britain in the decade following the conclusion World War II (p. 227), and reminded his readers that between 1948 and 1957 over one million migrants went to the Dominions (p. 221) – a most remarkable displacement.

44 Humphrey McQueen, *New Britannia: An Argument Concerning the Social Origins of Australian Radicalism and Nationalism* (St Lucia: University of Queensland Press, 2004).

45 See, for example, Carter Goodrich, 'The Australian and American Labor Movements', *Economic Record* IV (1928); Gary Cross, 'Labour in Settler State Democracies: Comparative Perspectives on Australia and the US, 1860–1920', *Labour History* 70 (1996). For a more recent instance of this interpretative tradition, see Greg Patmore and Shelton Stromquist, eds, *Frontiers of Labor: Comparative Histories of the United States and Australia* (Urbana, IL: University of Illinois Press, 2018).

questions have been asked in a profoundly comparative mode of many 'new' societies.[46] It is significant that in his early period in Palestine Zionist leader David Ben-Gurion translated Sombart's book on socialism into Hebrew. Ben-Gurion argued that, if there was no socialism in the United States because revolution had been left behind, on the contrary, there could only be 'socialism' in Palestine because *failed* revolution in Europe demanded that socialism itself should find a refuge in Palestine.[47]

Bryan D. Palmer's Canada-centred comparative insight confirmed that the absence of revolution was a phenomenon characteristic of all settler colonies and then societies:

> Class formation's paradoxical history in 19th-century Canada and Australia was that as a class was made through struggle and solidarity, gaining much from capital and that state [i.e., the settler colonial state], it was also made against struggle and solidarity, giving much to capital and the state. The legacy of this historical making of white settler society

46 The many Anglophone settler societies, of course, but other ones as well, including Pakistan. See Faisal Devji, *Muslim Zion: Pakistan as a Political Idea* (Cambridge, MA: Harvard University Press, 2014). Western Punjab had seen intensive canal construction, reclamation, and internal immigration beginning in the mid-1880s. The 'canal colonies' were populated by Punjabi smallholders peasant producers who had moved from the densely populated parts of the state. Wealthy landlords had also been allocated significant land grants. The newly reclaimed districts had been developed with British capital, under British supervision, and had been previously appropriated as 'Crown (or State) Waste lands' (the region had been arid and sparsely populated and the claims of the local populations had been dismissed). The colonial state had engaged in significant social engineering by controlling development, water allocations, and land grants. After a new Colonization Lands Act was enacted in 1912, and after significant settler agitation, the settler tenants acquired proprietary rights. It was the spectre of anticolonial agitation and the legacy of the insurrection of 1857 that had prompted this immense reclamation and social engineering project. Punjab recruits would man the Indian British Imperial army, and 'militarization' became widespread and entrenched. These were the troops that would prevent revolution from occurring in the whole British Empire. Nationalist anticolonial organising was notably underdeveloped in Punjab during the struggle for independence, a type of revolution. Pakistan, a state born in displacement, inherited the canal colonies and their military traditions after independence. See Imran Ali, 'Malign Growth? Agricultural Colonization and the Roots of Backwardness in the Punjab', *Past & Present*, 114 (1987), pp. 117, 128.

47 See Anita Shapira, *Ben-Gurion: Father of Modern Israel* (New Haven, CT: Yale University Press, 2014).

> working classes, mobile and unusual in their dependent independence, confined by the wage, but freed by its seeming boundlessness and the access to property that this conveyed, adept at bargaining terms within their own domestic markets, has perhaps gone unrecognized by most historians, who have opted out of examinations of the peculiarities of the Australians and the Canadians.[48]

Australian labour was stronger than Canada's, which was in turn stronger than labour in the United States. The Anglophone–Francophone divide, conservative influences emanating from the United States and a variety of regionalisms all combined to explain a peculiar class formation.[49] 'Socialism', however, was always somewhere else.

Revolution and its counterparts

This book has argued that revolution is dialectically related to displacement. The politics of displacement are born in what Hobsbawm called a 'general crisis' and 'the last phase of the general transition from a feudal to a capitalistic economy', and what Christopher Hill referred to as 'the first stage in a sort of general strike against wage labour.'[50] The period Hobsbawm influentially identified as the 'Age of Revolution' was also the golden age of the political traditions aiming to turn the world inside out rather than upside down, the age of the global 'settler revolution.'[51] Yet again, this was also the golden age of reaction, but also of many more hybrid forms: German Chancellor Otto von Bismarck, who was not a revolutionary, promoted the notion of a 'revolution from above' – a pre-emptive move, likely a response to the prospect of revolution from below.

48 Bryan D. Palmer, 'Nineteenth-Century Canada and Australia: The Paradoxes of Class Formation', *Labour/Le Travail* and *Labour History*, 71 (Fall 1996), p. 34.

49 See David Camfield, 'Settler Colonialism and Labour Studies in Canada: A Preliminary Exploration', *Labour/Le Travail* 83 (2019); Barry Eidlin, *Labor and the Class Idea in The United States and Canada* (Cambridge: Cambridge University Press, 2018).

50 Eric J. Hobsbawm, 'The Crisis of the Seventeenth Century', in Trevor Aston, ed., *Crisis in Europe, 1560–1660* (London: Routledge, 1965), p. 5; Christopher Hill, *Change and Continuity in Seventeenth-Century England* (Cambridge, MA: Harvard University Press, 1975), p. 233.

51 Eric J. Hobsbawm, *The Age of Revolution, 1789–1846* (New York: New American Library, 1962).

Settler colonialism, as we have seen, also a pre-emptive move, could be seen as a 'revolution from beside'. Revolution spawned its counterparts.

'Revolution' initially referred to the movement of astral bodies. But revolution as a political concept is predicated on another revolution: the Copernican revolution. To think of revolution, in the first place one has to have a heliocentric understanding of the world, in which the astral bodies revolve around a centre. In this context, the metaphorical pivot is the state – the territorial state. Revolution and reaction share the same geography as they confront each other. By contrast, the political traditions that aim to turn the world inside out reject reaction and revolution's centralisations, and assert a sovereignty that escapes both. Settlers travel with their sovereignty, and refuse to participate in the opposition pitting reaction against revolution. To achieve this, they need space. The 'transport revolution' enables their escape.[52]

In an insightful intervention, Thomas Nail recently focused on the Aristotelian meaning of 'Revolution' (upper-case), which frames politics as revolving around the state, as 'returning to state'. For Nail, 'Revolution' acts on a specific space. It is emplaced. The contradiction between 'Revolution' and 'revolution' (lower case) is thus about space:

52 James Belich linked the 'transport' and 'settler' revolutions; the former, in his reconstruction, is a precursor to the latter. See James Belich, *Replenishing the Earth: The Settler Revolution and the Rise of the Anglo-World, 1783–1939* (Oxford: Oxford University Press, 2009). But it was actually a double movement: the transport revolution enabled distantiation, even if it was when space was annihilated by further technological advances that the settler revolution emerged triumphant, and the settlers no longer dwelled in numbing isolation. Duncan Bell likewise noted that the telegraph and the railway 'precipitated a fundamental restructuring of imperial political thought'. Nineteenth-century historian E. A. Freeman had thought that modern communication technologies would revive the very possibility of authentic citizenship that characterised ancient Greece across vast global spaces. H. G. Wells was also impressed by the collapse of space brought about by 'new transport and communications systems' – a veritable 'reconfiguration of space and time' that was 'abolishing locality'. See Duncan Bell, 'Dissolving Distance: Technology, Space, and Empire in British Political Thought, 1770–1900', *Journal of Modern History* 77 (2005), p. 526; Duncan Bell, 'Alter Orbis: E. A. Freeman on Empire and Racial Destiny', in Jonathan Conlin and Alex Bremner, eds, *Making History: Edward Augustus Freeman and Victorian Cultural Politics* (Oxford: Oxford University Press, 2015); cited in Duncan Bell, 'Founding the World State: H. G. Wells on Empire and the English-Speaking Peoples', *International Studies Quarterly* 62: 4 (2018), p. 873. Then again, as we have seen, the annihilation of space brings the world turned inside out to an end. As new and old locations are reconnected, displacement is undone and contradictions catch up.

> Thus, the difference between the cyclical, upper case definition of revolution and the lower case one illuminates two important strategic and kinetic interpretations of the word 'revolution' still in tension today. On the one hand, the upper case definition is based on the motion of a static center and a cyclical transformation of its state-constitution. It is essentially a rotational and centrifugal theory of political motion. What returns in upper case revolution is the *identity* of the state form – even if the constitution has changed. Revolution thus marks a difference internal to the identity of the state-form.[53]

On the contrary, Nail continued, 'revolutionary' (lower case) practices do not understand space as a given:

> On the other hand, the lower case definition of revolution is based on the motion of decentralized vectors assembled together in waves. Given their non-statist tendencies, these revolutionary movements have something more like trajectories or directions but without static end points – culminating in a state or constitution. They pursue their aims without a central command, vanguard, or program. Instead, their local movements are inspired or influenced by each other like the common force of a wave that moves *through* them. What returns in revolution in this case is not the identity of the circle, but the differential *process of the returning itself*. Revolution is not a difference internal to the identity of the state-form but a differential process *external* to the state and thus capable of many other social forms. In this case, revolution returns not to its starting point (the state) but elsewhere further along a decentralized and intersectional trajectory.[54]

Nail's distinction between 'Revolution' and 'revolution' summarises the distinction between world turned upside down and world turned inside out: only the latter is portable.

Most political doctrines are predicated on a foundational exchange between security and freedom ('exchange', of course, is a euphemism

53 Thomas Nail, 'Revolution', in Kelly Fritsch, Clare O'Connor and A. K. Thompson, eds, *Keywords for Radicals: The Contested Vocabulary of Late-Capitalist Struggle* (Chico, CA: AK), p. 379.

54 Ibid., p. 379.

– there was always an enormous amount of coercion involved). In an essay entitled 'Every Great Revolution Is a Civil War', and citing historian Keith Michael Baker, David Armitage proposed a reading that emphasises continuity:

> Originality and novelty define the modern script of revolution. That script was original in the sense that it had identifiable beginnings that have been precisely located in France in 1789. And it was novel because in that year 'the French imagined a radical break with the past achieved by the conscious will of human actors, an inaugural moment for a drama of change and transformation projected indefinitely into the future'. After 1789, revolution in the singular replaced revolutions in the plural. What had been understood before 1789 as unavoidable features of nature, as predetermined astronomical cycles, or as eternal recurrences in human affairs became instead voluntary, transformative, and repeatable: revolution as fact gave way to revolution as act.[55]

Then again, Armitage added, 'the modern revolutionary script was not entirely original or novel . . . [The] palimpsest over which self-conscious revolutionaries wrote their script was a conception of history not as a sequence of revolutions but as a series of civil wars'.[56] In this sense, the revolutionary traditions are much older than generally thought.[57] When 'tracing the genealogy of the modern script of revolution', Armitage concluded, 'we should seriously consider the hypothesis that civil war was the original genus of which revolution was only a late-evolving species'.[58]

Revolution and reaction may be more ancient than originally thought, but they have a neglected sister: the world turned inside out. Revolution and reaction did not shy away from contradictions, and squared off

55 David Armitage, 'Every Great Revolution Is a Civil War', in Keith Michael Baker, Dan Edelstein, eds, *Scripting Revolution* (Stanford, CA: Stanford University Press, 2013), p. 57.

56 Ibid., p. 58.

57 Reinhart Koselleck argued that it was during the eighteenth century that revolution emerged 'as a concept in contrast to that of civil war'. The latter emphasised senseless destruction, the former progress. See ibid., p. 59.

58 Ibid., p. 68.

against each other in civil war. Meanwhile, their sister consistently aimed to opt out of the founding exchange between security and freedom. Envisaging the constitution of political regimes somewhere else, she aimed to achieve both simultaneously, by way of fragmentation: the reproduction of a fragment somewhere else.

But if, for Hartz, the 'fragments' had reconnected with the Old World and as a result of World War II, it was war that had precipitated Hannah Arendt's move to America. The move resulted in a profound political transformation, and her development of the notion of 'politics' itself could be interpreted as part of a quest to turn the world inside out after her world had been turned upside down. Her search for new political beginnings, for a public space of politics, and for a political republic based on common interest had a crucial spatial dimension.[59] A number of scholars have noted Arendt's Eurocentrism and her embrace of settler colonialism; but her embrace of displacement as a political option should be noted too.[60] Her remark that the nations of the western hemisphere had solved the problem of poverty 'not by revolution but by science and technology', her blindness to the foundational dispossession of indigenous peoples, and her simultaneous rejection of revolution fitted in with the political traditions appraised in this book.[61] Others in similar circumstances – Arendt's fellow émigré Bertolt Brecht, for example – responded differently. Brecht did encounter a world turned inside out during his exile in the United States between July 1941 and October 1947, but remained

59 See Elizabeth Strakosch, 'Beyond Colonial Completion: Arendt, Settler Colonialism and the End of Politics', in Sarah Maddison, Tom Clark and Ravi de Costa, eds, *The Limits of Settler Colonial Reconciliation: Non-Indigenous People and the Responsibility to Engage* (Singapore: Springer, 2017).

60 For exceptions to this neglect, see Onur Ulas Ince, 'Bringing the Economy Back In: Hannah Arendt, Karl Marx, and the Politics of Capitalism', *Journal of Politics* 78 (2016), pp. 31, 11; David Myer Temin, '"Nothing Much Had Happened": Settler Colonialism in Hannah Arendt', *European Journal of Political Theory*, 19 December 2019. See also Manu Samnotra, '"Poor in World": Hannah Arendt's Critique of Imperialism', *Contemporary Political Theory*, 18:4 (2019). Samnotra responds to recent critiques of Arendt's 'Eurocentrism' by emphasising how she actually believed that the Jewish settlers in Palestine, like the Boers in South Africa, had been unable to genuinely leave the European world behind and move beyond their superfluity. For her, they should have been better settlers, hardly a critique of settler colonialism.

61 Cited in Ince, 'Bringing the Economy Back In', p. 15.

hostile to it; for him, Southern California was 'Tahiti in metropolitan form', with its 'cheap prettiness'.[62]

Following her displacement, Arendt reflected systematically on revolution. Her *On Revolution* (1961) compared the American and French revolutions, and argued that France's revolution was ultimately a disaster, while the American revolution was comparatively safer (even if she did acknowledge that, by the time she was writing, that revolutionary tradition had been corrupted, too). Arendt also identified how exactly these experiences had fatefully diverged: in France, the revolutionary leadership neglected to focus on freedom, while, in America, the Founding Fathers had stuck by it. More generally, Arendt developed a declensionist interpretation of modernity: modernity had impaired the possibility of civic engagement and common deliberation, just as revolution in its negative iteration had done. 'Modernity', she insisted, was characterised by the loss of the world. Totalitarianism (like revolution) introduced a profound discontinuity. As moral and political categories and standards of moral judgement had become progressively more meaningless, politics for Arendt was thus necessarily about a *return*.

Her analysis, however, was based in particular on a spatial logic. Arendt's *polis* could be located anywhere – it was a mobile institution: 'The *polis*, properly speaking, is not the city-state in its physical location; it is the organization of the people as it arises out of acting and speaking together, and its true space lies between people living together for this

62 Brecht hated its architecture, its bread, even its air (there was nothing to smell). 'America', Brecht complained, was all 'marketplace'. The drugstore 'sells' you a sandwich and the vitamins that supplement its insufficient nutritional value, he noted, adding: 'The intellectual isolation here is enormous. In comparison to Hollywood, Svendborg [the small town in the Danish island of Fyn where he had begun his exile] was a world center'. He would eventually move to East Germany. James Lyon reports that Brecht told a German-language newspaper in 1943 that he did not think his plays would be performed or be successful in America because, 'their revolutionary innovations, arose in the soil of a tradition that simply [did] not exist' there. Ernst Bloch, who knew about 'other places', described in 1939 two categories of German intellectual refugees: those who had severed connections with German life and culture and become 'Americanized', and those who wanted to create a German cultural island in America. Thomas Mann, for example, belonged to the former group, and despised Brecht. See James K. Lyon, *Bertolt Brecht in America* (Princeton, NJ: Princeton University Press, 1980), pp. 30, 33, 38, 46, 56, 99, 251.

purpose, no matter where they happen to be'.[63] Hence her embrace of settler colonialism: 'Wherever you go, you will be a *polis*' (irrespective of whether you encounter indigenous worlds and dispossess them in order to become a *polis*). She noted: 'these famous words became not merely the watchword of Greek colonization, they expressed the conviction that action and speech create a space between the participants which can find its proper location almost anytime and anywhere'.[64] Yet again, the 'sharing of words and deeds' in itself constituted a displacement (it created a 'space'), and was in turn founded on a displacement, since the sharing of words and deeds required that land be shared. But land, of course, had to be conquered first. It is not that Arendt neglected to consider the exclusionary implications of her proposition (the outer limits of this deliberative community are implicitly exclusive); she did. Empire and displacement, however, remained necessary to her politics.

As this sharing of conquered land was non-revolutionary (though Arendt appreciated the deliberation in common that revolutionary moments might enable), and as it was predicated on a displacement, she was articulating a world turned inside out rather than upside down (even though she did not use these terms). It is crucial that, for Arendt, citizenship was spatial and volitional – that the *polis* was an intentional community. Individuals decide to move there, even if they might decide to do so only metaphorically, by creating 'space' for common deliberation. The political community she had in mind emerges through the experience of displacement and the sharing of a common space of appearance. Individuals must be able to see and talk to one another in public, and to share a political space. Sharing a public space is essential to political community, but this can happen only when everyone has a location they can speak from. Space is crucial. Revolution and reaction share the same geography, and elide each other by denying their opponents' control over space – only through displacement can diverse opinions coexist in the public sphere. But what Arendt implied is more important than what she said: for her, only those who had relocated, literally or metaphorically, could be genuine political agents. For her, displacement was the necessary prerequisite for common deliberation.

---

63 Hannah Arendt, *The Human Condition* (Chicago: University of Chicago Press, 1958), p. 198.

64 Ibid., p. 198.

Dirk Moses's reconstruction of Arendt's developing ideas about conquest insightfully outlined her exploration of the necessity of imperial expansion – her theorisation, in other words, of a commonwealth of increase. Moses's intervention highlighted a dimension of Arendt's thought that had remained symptomatically underanalysed. Departing Europe, Arendt had rejected revolution and embraced the North American 'traditional instruments for facing the future': the 'Mayflower compact' and other 'voluntary associations'. She was hoping that they could be revitalised in the face of 'the great turmoil of change and of failure through which it is going at the present'.[65] Moses has analysed her method: foundation, but not just any foundation – foundation anew, foundation somewhere else. For Arendt, this specific foundation was the antidote to revolution and crisis:

> To save the West in its emergency meant reconstructing the Roman political experience that, Arendt maintained, had never been satisfactorily registered in Western political thought. She was to perform this task. Several features of the Roman republic and empire needed highlighting to remedy the defects of the Western tradition's Greek, Jewish, and Christian dimensions. The 'political genius of Rome', she wrote in *The Human Condition*, was 'legislation and foundation'. Elsewhere she added 'the preservation of a *civitas*'. State foundations, their worship in sacred memory, and the rule of law constituted this Roman political experience.[66]

But the Roman experience of foundation was not autochthonous; Rome was itself established through displacement! Rome itself had once been someone's world turned inside out rather than upside down:

> The first element [of this political legacy], then, was the myth of Rome's foundation, expressed by Virgil in his epic poem, *Aeneid*, which Arendt regarded as 'among the most remarkable and amazing events in Western history'. The poem about the foundation of Rome

65 Cited in A. Dirk Moses, '*Das Römische Gespräch* in a New Key: Hannah Arendt, Genocide, and the Defense of Republican Civilization', *Journal of Modern History* 85: 4 (2013), p. 880.

66 Ibid., pp. 881–2.

> by the survivors of Troy's destruction was, for her, a lesson in human freedom – beginning a new polity 'without the help of a transcendent God' – which is why it exerted such a fascination for the men of the American revolution. By sourcing Rome's origins in Troy rather than the fratricidal violence of Romulus, Virgil obviated the problem associated with an 'absolute new beginning', namely that its 'complete arbitrariness' and 'abyss of pure spontaneity' contained the potential for virtually limitless violence [which Arendt saw as revolutionary violence]. The utopianism and search for a 'new absolute' of a Robespierre, which she associated with Plato, threatened terror unless safely institutionalized by inserting revolutionary moments into a historical continuum. Successful revolutionary foundations were establishments not of 'a new Rome' but of 'Rome anew'.[67]

A 'new Rome' is what follows revolution – a re-foundation; 'Rome anew' is a world turned inside out, a new foundation. Arendt did not embrace revolution or civil war, Moses contends:

> Arendt was aware that the arrival of the Trojans and establishment of a new Troy entailed bloodshed, namely war with 'the native Italians'. Victory was justified, she implied, following Virgil, because the indigenous Italian farmers were pre-political, inhabiting a 'utopian fairy-tale land outside of history', bereft of laws, closer to nature than human society, 'whose circling years produce no tales worth telling'. [T]hese are the terms in which Arendt elsewhere described indigenous victims of settler colonialism who 'live and die without leaving any trace, without having contributed anything to the common world'. In contemporary parlance, they represented 'bare life' or, as Arendt presciently expressed the condition of refugees, 'the abstract nakedness of being nothing but human'. Her sympathies lay with the Trojans who were civilizing the natives by founding a political community with a temporal sense of origins: 'Action, in so far as it engages in founding and preserving political bodies, creates the condition for remembrance, that is, for history', and thereby 'a measure of permanence and durability upon the futility of mortal life and the fleeting character of human time'. What is more, they introduced settled

67 Ibid., p. 882.

> agricultural communities and inaugurated the Roman ideal of the self-sufficient and patriotic farmer praised by Cato, one of Arendt's favorite Roman authors, and by Victorian writers millennia later.[68]

She dreamt of conquest, but of settler-colonial conquest specifically, not of other types of conquest. Arendt approved of an expansion that would be followed by assimilation; conversely, and coherently, she did not endorse the permanent subjugation of conquered alterities: 'Of course, Arendt knew that the colonizing tradition originated in the Greek polis', Moses affirms, but the '*polis* was a transplantable proposition in time and space', and this 'ancient colonization was of a piece for Arendt with the spread of the Anglophone settler colonies and Zionist colonization of Palestine in the first half of the twentieth century'.[69]

And yet, even all this was not enough and replicating ancient settler colonising needed something new. Scattered worlds turned inside out can fall. What was needed was a *league* of worlds turned inside out:

> For all that, she thought the Greek example was insufficient because the polis' ethnocentric self-absorption and radical independence made empire-building all but impossible. The scattered poleis did not cohere into a greater whole, constituting mini-worlds rather than expanding the frontiers of civilization. The genius of Rome . . . was the incorporation of the colonization impulse into a once-and-for-all foundation of a polity. The memory of this foundation then congealed into a religious cult of tradition that Arendt prized as the glue that held together the *civitas* . . . This idealized view of Roman expansion as a federation that avoided outright military conquest, or at least genocide, may have been taken from James Harrington's *The Commonwealth of Oceana* (1656) and his notion of 'unequal leagues,' itself derived from Cicero, upon which Arendt drew in *On Revolution*.[70]

Oceana was indeed foundational to her thinking because, like Harrington, Arendt realised that only a commonwealth of increase – that is, only an expanding system of federated *poleis* – could permanently sustain the

68 Ibid., pp. 882–3.
69 Ibid., pp. 885–6.
70 Ibid., p. 886.

prerequisites for common deliberation against external challenges. The establishment of a new and permanent political structure without revolution was her ideal political form; but her realisation that, in a system of nation-states, rights were non-portable led her to think about politics that were permanently constituted on the outside. Only on the outside could they be portable without engendering political rupture or revolution.

The political traditions that aim to turn the world inside out constitute an anti-revolutionary sensibility that relies on three fantasies: perpetual household production, where capitalism never begins; perpetual primitive accumulation, where capitalism permanently remains in its initial stage, and where social contradictions are always deferred; and the promise of political community somewhere else – the promise of a political community that is born without the need of violence or revolution. The first two fantasies are bound to remain unfulfilled – contradictions are displaced, too, sometimes quite rapidly. The spatial fix is at best a temporary solution.[71] The third fantasy rests on a fundamental exclusion – a move that is inevitably and often spectacularly violent. Setting up a polity *against* someone – in the case of settler colonialism, against indigenous peoples – is not like setting up a polity *without* them: the settler colonial polity cannot be amended by inclusion, because it is foundationally violent and dispossessory. If this exclusion is to be addressed, the settler colonial polity must be dissolved, which is a . . . revolution. The world turned inside out cannot keep its promises.

71 See David Harvey, 'The Spatial Fix – Hegel, Von Thunen and Marx', *Antipode*, 13:3 (1981).

Index